SPORT FINANCE

WHERE THE MONEY COMES FROM, AND WHERE THE MONEY GOES

KAREN WEAVER, Ed.D

Kendall Hunt
publishing company

Cover image © Shutterstock, Inc.

Kendall Hunt
publishing company

www.kendallhunt.com
Send all inquiries to:
4050 Westmark Drive
Dubuque, IA 52004-1840

CONTENTS

Foreword   v
List of Contributors   vii
Glossary of Sport Business Financial Terms   xv

CHAPTER 1:   Introduction to Sports Finance   1

CHAPTER 2:   Business of Sports Media   13

CHAPTER 3:   Business of College Sports   37

CHAPTER 4:   Business of Mega Recreational Complexes   67

CHAPTER 5:   Business of Stadium Financing   91

CHAPTER 6:   Financing a Youth Sports Enterprise–A Case Study   115

CHAPTER 7:   Business of Esports   135

CHAPTER 8:   Business of Major League Baseball   159

CHAPTER 9:   Business of Professional Soccer   195

CHAPTER 10:   Business of Women's Sports and Pay Equity   217

CHAPTER 11:   Business of the NBA and WNBA   239

CHAPTER 12:   Business of the National Football League   277

CHAPTER 13:   Business of the National Hockey League   309

CHAPTER 14:   Business of the Olympics   331

CHAPTER 15:   Future Trends in Sports Finance   355

INDEX   377

FOREWORD

I am delighted to write this foreword to Professor Karen Weaver's book *Sports Finance*. Here is why I think sports finance teachers should read and adopt the book.

Most sports finance books do two things. First, they apply "finance" topics where they seem applicable to the sports business, for example, the fundamental value of the firm and assessing team valuations. Second, they cover "financing sports," that is, characterizing the elements of operations and balance sheets. And in the mix might be government and sports business relations, especially taxes and antitrust.

In my experience, the problem with such well-intended books, having taught from them, is they force professors and students to jump around in order to piece together a potential primary objective, namely, understanding the finances and financing of a particular sport organization of interest. Weaver's *Sports Finance* fixes that problem by providing a "finance profile" of major sports organizations.

Finance profiles allow the reader to go straight to the specifics of a particular sport organization without piecing together elements spread out across different chapters. The approach also facilitates comparisons across organizations because each chapter profile follows the same outline.

A brief history and coverage of the structure of the organization is followed by observed team valuations in a novel way, via owner buy-in amounts. Revenue sources (including media and partnerships, and subsidies), revenue distribution (including any centralized sharing), and postseason revenue structure are followed by a similar treatment of costs (taxes, liabilities, and salaries, including collectively bargained pay structure). Each of the organization-oriented chapters ends with an assessment for potential growth, informed by the profile.

Mega facilities, media, and facility financing—important, overriding elements of high interest to students—also receive the separate treatment they deserve. Weaver and Michael Cummings also address another student fascination, namely, what the future holds for sports finance.

Professor Weaver is one among the group of sports business academics best suited to produce such a volume. Her interests in the topic are both long-standing and very broad, and so are her professional contacts. The book is comprehensive, with many voices—important *academic* voices in the sports business. Sports finance teachers can expect coverage of the highest competence.

I found Karen Weaver's *Sports Finance* a compelling read, and I think sports finance teachers should read it and they will be the better for having done so.

Rodney Fort
Professor of Sport Management
University of Michigan
Copyright © Rod Fort. Reprinted by permission.

LIST OF CONTRIBUTORS

Karen Weaver is an expert on college sports as they intersect with higher education management, media, finance, and policy. A former Division I and Division III head coach and athletics administrator, Dr. Weaver examines college athletics from the perspectives of university presidents and trustees, athletic conference organization, higher education scholars, and sports finance oversight. Her research includes mid-majors and FBS Division I institutions, public finance and facility debt policies, and the role that college senior leaders can and should play in managing athletics.

Dr. Weaver has been a part of Penn GSE since 2007, when she began her doctoral studies in higher education management. After graduation, she left a 30+ year career in college athletics to join the faculty at Drexel University. Dr. Weaver began teaching at Penn GSE in 2012 and joined as an adjunct assistant professor in 2020.

In addition to teaching in Penn GSE's higher education programs, Dr. Weaver contributes to the Center for Professional Learning, developing content for senior leaders in higher education covering oversight of college athletics. She has taught undergraduate and graduate courses in leadership, sports and digital media, marketing, and promotions. While at Drexel, Dr. Weaver was recognized by the Drexel Center for Academic Excellence for her work with undergraduate student media projects.

Dr. Weaver is a regular contributor to Forbes.com and an executive producer and host of the podcast "Trustees and Presidents." She has led a research team on behalf of the Knight Commission on Intercollegiate Athletics on athletics governance, and has published over 50 articles.

A long-time athletics administrator in NCAA Divisions I and III, Dr. Weaver has received numerous honors and appointments during her years in college athletics. She has worked in several Big Ten universities, and built an athletics program from club status into full NCAA Division III membership.

As a college athlete, she was an All-American and one of the first women ever to earn an athletics scholarship under Title IX. She was part of the U.S. National Training Squad in field hockey that qualified, but did not compete, in the 1980 Moscow Olympic Games. Her USA Field Hockey playing and coaching experiences include U.S. National Training Squad, U.S. Olympic Training Center camps, and U.S. Olympic Development Camps. She currently serves on the NCAA Committee on Athlete Biometric Data. She was named in Sportico's Top 50 Sports Business Twitter Follows for 2021. She tweets at @drkarenweaver.

Wayne G. McDonnell, Jr., MBA, has been involved in education, media, coaching, and finance for two decades. He achieved the rank of clinical professor of sport management and served as academic chair at New York University's Preston Robert Tisch Institute for Global Sport. A former financial analyst and accountant at Madison Square Garden, McDonnell is a "Business of Baseball" contributor for Forbes SportsMoney.

McDonnell is an adjunct full professor at St. John's University, teaching an online course on the economics of sport in the Collins College of Professional Studies Division of Sport Management. In his spare time, McDonnell lends his expertise to inCourage, a not-for-profit that helps young athletes and adults redefine success in youth sports. He represents the company as vice president of content and curriculum on panel discussions, conferences, and events.

A winner of academic awards for teaching excellence and outstanding service, McDonnell has taught a wide variety of sport management courses which focus on finance, accounting, economics, and management. He is a regular media contributor on the game of baseball and has created a course that examines the sport's business model in great detail. He tweets at @wmcdonn25.

Morganne Flores is currently working to earn her master's degree from the University of Washington in leadership in higher education and has a bachelor's degree in environmental studies. She is also a 6th year student-athlete on the University of Washington softball team. She has played softball for the past 16 years and when her playing career is over she aims to work in an athletic department one day, specifically advising student-athlete academics. Morganne's first gaming experience was playing Super Mario Bros. on the Nintendo DS back in the day, and ever since then gaming has always been part of her life.

Meghan Gescher, MEd, holds a master's degree from the University of Washington's Leadership in Higher Education graduate program. Her background is in journalism and has spent time covering Division III football and basketball. She is also a former teaching assistant for the University of Washington undergraduate course "The Place of Sports in the University." Meghan Gescher currently works in the University of Washington Office of Undergraduate Academic Affairs supporting grants for student undergraduate programs. Meghan's peak video game experience was playing her pink Game Boy Advance in her family's Honda Odyssey during road trips along the west coast.

Ted Hayduk is an assistant professor at NYU's Preston Robert Tisch Institute for Global Sport. He is a former consultant to Major League Baseball. His current research focuses on innovation and entrepreneurship, particularly in the context of business analytics. His work has been published in high quality academic journals including *International Entrepreneurship and Management Journal*, *The Journal of International Trade and Economic Development*, *Organizational Dynamics*, and the *International Journal of Entrepreneurship and Small Business*. He is also the coeditor of *Statistical Modelling and Sports Business Analytics* (Routledge, 2020). He tweets at @TMHayduk.

Dr. Jennifer Lee Hoffman is an associate professor in the College of Education and the Center for Leadership in Athletics at the University of Washington. Her research focuses on the role of sports within higher education, including research and teaching in the areas of intercollegiate athletics and esports, women in leadership, and values-based and data-informed decision making. Her new book, *College Sports and Institutional Values in Competition: Leadership Challenges*, interrogates the relationship between athletics and higher education. Her work also appears in *College Athletes' Rights and Well-Being*, *Scandals in College Sports: Legal, Ethical and Policy Case Studies*, *Empowering Women in Higher Education and Student Affairs: Theory, Research, Narratives, and Practice from Feminist Perspectives*, and *Reconstructing Policy in Higher Education: Feminist Poststructural Perspectives*.

From playing Pong on Atari in a friend's basement to Ms. Pac-Man at the arcade and Tetris on her Game Boy, she is now exploring esports in campus life, teaching Esports and Sports in Competition and The Place of Sport in Colleges and Universities courses. She tweets at @jlhoffman.

David Hoffman is an iGen esports enthusiast, as part of the gaming generation who grew up on consoles, mobile, and PCs. He contributes his perspective on esports from the point of view of the next wave of gamers who build their own gaming computers, monetize their play over Twitch and YouTube, and use gaming technology for accessing sports and entertainment. He is currently playing Destiny 2.

David Berri is a professor of economics at Southern Utah University who has spent the last two decades researching sports and economics. He is the lead author of *The Wages of Wins* (Stanford Press, 2006) and *Stumbling on Wins* (Financial Times Press, 2010), the sole author of *Sports Economics* (a textbook published in 2018 with Macmillan Publishers), and a coauthor of *The Economics of the Super Bowl* (Palgrave, 2020). He has also been part of more than 70 academic papers published on the subject of sports economics. In the past, he wrote on the subject of sports economics for a number of popular media outlets, including *The New York Times*, the Atlantic.com, Time.com, Vice Sports, and *Forbes*. In recent years, his work has increasingly focused on gender issues, focusing on such topics as the gender-wage gap in the WNBA, how the sports media treats women's sports, women and coaching sports, attendance and revenue in women's sports, exploitation in women's sports, and Title IX issues. He tweets at @wagesofwins.

Carol Schram is a journalist with a focus on ice hockey. She has been writing about the business side of the game ever since she dissected how the introduction of salary disclosure would impact the economics of the NHL for her MBA graduating essay. Based in Vancouver, Canada, Carol is a regular contributor for Forbes SportsMoney, covering pro hockey, international hockey, and the women's game. She covered the 2020 NHL Stanley Cup playoffs from Edmonton, Alberta for *The New York Times* and has also contributed to outlets including The Canadian Press, *The Hockey News*, NHL.com and Sportsnet. Book contributions include *Fast Ice: Superstars of the New NHL*, *The Year of the Chicago Blackhawks: 2013 Stanley Cup Champions*, *Kings of the North: Kawhi, Kyle and the Toronto Raptors' Championship 2018-19 Season*, and *Canada's Team: Celebrating the Toronto Blue Jays' Incredible 2015 Season*.

Carol's background also includes time spent as an entrepreneur, a marketing consultant, and a statistician. She tweets at @pool88.

Bri Newland is an associate professor and academic director for undergraduate programs in the Preston Robert Tisch Institute for Global Sport at New York University. Dr. Newland's research interest explores active sport event tourism, with a specific focus on leveraging opportunities for the event and destination. She also conducts research in the area of sport development, examining the effects of sport delivery on sport participation across the life span. Newland has published her research in *Sport Management Review*, *Journal of Sport Management*, *Sport Marketing Quarterly*, *Journal of Sport & Tourism*, *Journal of Vacation Marketing*, and *Event Management*, among others. She has worked in conjunction with industry partners such as FOX Sports, Vacation Races, Monumental Marathon, Triathlon Australia, USA Triathlon, and more. Her research and consultancy work has offered marketing, management, and leveraging solutions to sport events and organizations, NGBs, and other government agencies, helping them improve and enhance business outcomes. She tweets at @brinewland.

Jill Harris is an associate professor and deputy head of the Department of Economics and Geoscience at the United States Air Force Academy. Her sports research includes examinations of bias and exploitation in the WNBA, noncompliance behavior in the NCAA, and recruiting tactics in college football. She edited and cowrote six chapters in *The Economics of Aquatic Sports* (Springer 2020) ranging from predicting wins produced in water polo to the analysis of doping in elite swim. Her research is published in *International Journal of Sport Finance*, Marquette Sports Law Review, *Review of Industrial Organization*, and *Journal of Political and Military Sociology*. She teaches courses in microeconomic theory, law and economics, the economics of sport, and financial markets at USAFA. She tweets at @jillharris.

Jim Reese is the program director of the undergraduate and graduate Sports Management programs at American Public University System (APUS). Dr. Reese has a long history of involvement in the sport industry, including professional, intercollegiate, and interscholastic sports. Before beginning his academic career more than two decades ago, he served as a ticketing administrator for the Denver Broncos. In addition, he served as vice president of IFSA/USA (International Federation of Strength Athletes), the governing body for the sport of professional strongman in the United States. He also worked as an athletic facility and event management assistant at Georgia Southern University and the University of Northern Colorado. He works as an industry consultant in ticket operations and ticket sales, and also currently works as an assistant high school athletic director. In addition to courses in ticket sales, Dr. Reese teaches courses in finance, high school administration, sport marketing, and sponsorship, and sport law. Dr. Reese conducts research in the areas of ticket operations, ticket sales, and legal issues related to the ticket industry. He has authored or coauthored four books, published more than 30 peer-reviewed articles and book chapters, and given more than 50 peer-reviewed and invited presentations around the world.

Spiro G Doukas is an associate professor of sport management at American Public University System (APUS). Dr. Doukas also has nearly twenty years of leadership and experience in the sport industry, marketing, and transportation/logistics as well as working with leading organizations in sports, including the Trinidad and Tobago Olympic Committee, the 2004 Athens Olympics, and the NBA (National Basketball Association) and UCFB Wembley (Wembley Stadium of London). Dr. Doukas has developed and fostered natural cultural flexibility and sensitivity by having taught at universities in the United States, Greece, the UK, South Korea, and Trinidad and Tobago.

Professor Doukas has had the opportunity to travel extensively and to participate and present in academic conference opportunities throughout the world and holds a global view of business, resulting in international initiatives and creating and participating in academic programs and societies such as ATINER (Athens Institute for Education and Research) and the China Sport Venue Association Research Center of South China Normal University.

His research areas involve sport logistics, mega events, and Olympic city residents' perceptions toward their city's hosting of the Games. He has published in both sport management–related journals and transportation journals and magazines around the world.

Stephen Engst is currently a lecturer in finance at Southern Utah University. He teaches courses that focus primarily on investments. Previously, he was a software engineer at Trimble MAPS, a senior portfolio manager at Goldman Sachs, and a commodity trading advisor for ClaraVista Capital Management. He earned his BS in agricultural economics from Rutgers University in 1984, and a certificate in applied science (software engineering) from Harvard in 1991.

Regena Pauketat is a doctoral student in "educational policy, leadership, and organizations" at the University of Washington's College of Education, and a research assistant at the Center for Leadership in Athletics.

Her research interests include teacher retention, diversity, and alternative certification programs. Her research interests centered on esports involve the role of gender and gendered environments in esports and video gaming. Her first video game memories are of Dark Castle, Lemmings, and Tetris for Macintosh and a pixelated Little Mermaid video game for Nintendo. Since then, she has become an avid Call of Duty player and Katamari aficionado.

Derek Helling is a freelance copywriter and journalist out of Chicago. He primarily covers the intersections of entertainment and sports with business and the law. His bylines have appeared in places like OZY, FOX Sports, various Catena Media properties, and Heavy. Helling is a 2013 graduate of the University of Iowa where he studied mass communications and sociology in sports. Currently, he focuses on advocating for athletes' labor rights and gender equity in the sport-entertainment industry with his podcast and newsletter, The Ninth Circle of Helling. When Helling isn't working, he enjoys his Munchkin cats and traveling to discover the best baked goods the world has to offer. He tweets at @dhellingsports.

Scott Hirko is an assistant professor, and director, of the Sport Management Program at Defiance College (Ohio), and has taught and led sport management programs since 2011. In the classroom, he focuses on the areas of sport finance, sport communication, sport marketing, and sport law. Hirko also serves as an associate of communication and research for the Knight Commission on Intercollegiate Athletics, including investigation of financial decisions in college sports. This role includes serving as the project manager for the Knight Commission's interactive, online financial tool, the College Athletics Financial Information (CAFI) Database, originally released in 2013. Hirko led the Commission's efforts to determine the impact of football on the NCAA's revenue distribution formula, as well as identify the amount of funding awarded to Division I NCAA men's basketball tournament teams not on track to graduate half of its players from 2006 to 2010. Hirko is a frequent presenter about college sports financial decision making at academic and professional conferences. He earned a PhD in higher, adult, and lifelong education from Michigan State University, a master of arts in sport administration from Central Michigan University, and a bachelor of science from Michigan State University. He tweets at @hirko_scott.

Eric Munson was a High School USA Today first team All-American at Mt. Carmel in San Diego and was selected in the second round of the Major League Baseball draft by the Atlanta Braves in 1996. Eric elected to go to college at USC, where he earned honors as a first team All-American catcher, two time Team USA member, and 1998 College World Series Champion. Eric was the third overall pick in the 1999 MLB draft by the Detroit Tigers and made his major league debut on July 18, 2000. Eric played multiple positions during his career. After parts of nine years in the major leagues, and twelve total seasons of professional baseball, Eric retired and began coaching at USC (2011-2012) and at the University of Dubuque in 2013. In the summer of 2013, Eric served as the assistant coach of the USA Baseball 18U National Team. They won the 2013 IBAF World Cup and gold medal in Taiwan. Eric opened Gold Standard Athletics by Eric Munson, a premiere indoor training facility for baseball and softball players in the Midwest in November 2013. For the past seven years, he has worked one-on-one with youth, high school, college, and professional athletes. He tweets at @EricMunsonGSA.

Shanda Munson was born and raised in Dubuque, Iowa, where her and her husband Eric's training facility is located. She is the director of operations and the director of marketing at Gold Standard Athletics by Eric Munson, as well as an adjunct professor in the Fine and Performing Arts Department at The University of Dubuque, a film producer and actress, an event planner, and a business consultant. Most recently, the Munsons signed on to consult for a large facility built in Alabama for a well-known Major League Baseball All-Star MVP. Their years of experience running a successful training facility would help guide their clients, current and future, on everything from facility design to needed technology, to marketing, to program creation, employee hiring and training, and many more. She tweets at @ShandaLeeMunson.

Robert Boland joined Penn State University as athletics integrity officer in July 2017. In this role, he works to ensure that Athletics Department meet all University standards related to integrity, ethics, and staff and student conduct and welfare, as well as NCAA and Big Ten standards.

The position, the first of its kind, was created in August 2012 in an agreement with the NCAA, Big Ten, and Penn State. It was charged with oversight and reporting of internal and external investigations into athletics. With that agreement having expired in August 2017, the University has maintained the position as part of its own broader Athletic Integrity Program. Boland chairs the University's Athletics Integrity Council, a group that brings together senior administrators and faculty to review matters related to athletics and reports to the chief ethics and compliance officer and the board of trustees.

Boland joined Penn State from Ohio University, where he was a faculty member and directed the MBA/master's in sports administration program. The program was ranked as "the #1 Graduate Sports Business Program in the World" by SportsBusiness, in each of Boland's two years there. He spent the prior 14 years at New York University: first, as founding faculty in its master's in sports business program; later as academic chair of NYU's Tisch Center for Hospitality, Tourism, and Sports Management, a division serving more than 700 students and offering five degree programs. He also taught sports law at NYU Law School. He tweets at @RobertBolandESQ.

Michael Cummings is a former entertainment executive. He attended the UCLA Anderson School of Management, where he graduated top of his class while studying the business of entertainment. He then entered the streaming world as senior product manager at Amazon Studios, helping leadership with strategic planning, project management, and internal consulting. Michael supported all major content decisions including pilot orders, series reorders, annual planning, and optimizing release calendar. He is currently a freelance consultant on entertainment strategy.

Follow Our Sports Finance Authors on Twitter

Karen Weaver: @drkarenweaver
Robert Boland: @RobertBolandESQ
Wayne G. McDonnell, Jr.: @wmcdonn25
Ted Hayduk: @TMHayduk
Dr. Jennifer Lee Hoffman: @jlhoffman
David Berri @wagesofwins
Carol Schram: @pool88
Dr. Bri Newland: @brinewland
Jill Harris: @jillharris
Derek Helling: @dhellingsports
Scott Hirko @hirko_scott
Eric Munson: @EricMunsonGSA
Shanda Munson: @ShandaLeeMunson

GLOSSARY OF TERMS

Actual Club Payroll: determined by the current collective bargaining agreement (CBA); generally defined by 40-man roster's contract plus medical benefits and performance bonuses

Base competitive balance tax acts as a penalty for ball clubs who exceed the Base Tax Thresholds. The tax rate will be applied to the difference between actual club payroll and the base tax threshold.

Base tax threshold—the amount all ball clubs are taxed each year

Bond is guaranteed by a specified tax, often on the facility or some other revenue stream connected to the facility

Churn rate—the number of people who cancel their memberships each year

Core competency—a process or procedure that a firm does exceptionally well

Competitive advantage—a process, system, or routine, typically formed by combining individual resources, that a firm can execute significantly better than its competitors

Capital improvements—any addition or alteration to real property that meets all three of the following conditions: it substantially adds to the value of the real property, or appreciably prolongs the useful life of the real property; it becomes part of the real property or is permanently affixed to the real property so that removal would cause material damage to the property or article itself; and it is intended to become a permanent installation.

Credit facility—a type of loan made in a business or corporate finance context

Conduit issuer is an organization, usually a government agency, that issues municipal securities to raise capital for revenue-generating projects where the funds generated are used by a third-party (known as the "conduit borrower") to invest in some project or activity that has a public benefit.

Debt service coverage ratio—a measurement of a firm's available cash flow to pay current debt obligations

Equity market value—Market value of equity is the total dollar value of a company's equity and is also known as market capitalization. This measure of a company's value is calculated by multiplying the current stock price by the total number of outstanding shares.

Firm resources—tangible or intangible assets that are available to a company. Examples include property, land, equipment, capital, labor, brand awareness, consumer confidence and loyalty, and professional networks

Fixed costs—A fixed cost is a cost that does not change with an increase or decrease in the amount of goods or services produced or sold. Fixed costs are expenses that have to be paid by a company, independent of any specific business activities.

Flow-on tourism—activities that the traveler partakes in beyond the sport event, such as group tours, visiting natural environments, restaurants and nightlife, and shopping

Forecasting—to calculate or predict (some future event or condition) usually as a result of study and analysis of available pertinent data

Franchise valuation. Although most sports franchises are privately held (versus publicly traded) concerns, they can be valued using generally accepted valuation methods. The valuation process entails an analysis of the relationship between the price paid for a franchise and a relevant measure of team performance, typically revenue.

Interest rates. The interest rate is the amount a lender charges for the use of assets expressed as a percentage of the principal. The interest rate is typically noted on an annual basis known as the annual percentage rate (APR).

LLC—limited liability company

Luxury tax—an excise levied on the purchase of items that are not essential for support or maintenance

Mega recreational sport complex—a multidimensional athletic facility covering expansive acreage and extending across fields and buildings supporting a variety of indoor and outdoor sports and events

Municipal bonds—bonds guaranteed by the government

Net transfer value—the difference between a ball club's contribution of local revenues and what they have received in return

Property tax—a tax levied on real or personal property

Public–private partnership—Public–private partnerships involve collaboration between a government agency and a private-sector company that can be used to finance, build, and operate projects, such as public transportation networks, parks, and convention centers. Financing a project through a public–private partnership can allow a project to be completed sooner or make it a possibility in the first place. Public–private partnerships often involve concessions of tax or other operating revenue, protection from liability, or partial ownership rights over nominally public services and property to private sector, for-profit entities.

Revenue offer sheet—An offer sheet is a contract offered to a restricted free agent by a team other than the one for which they played during the prior season.

Salary cap—The NFL salary cap is primarily designed to enable the league to control team spending on players' salaries in order to limit financial risks and underpin the financial integrity of the league.

Software as a service (SaaS)—a method of software delivery and licensing in which software is accessed online via a subscription, rather than bought and installed on individual computers

Trade association—an association of tradesmen, businessmen, or manufacturers in a particular trade or industry for the protection and advancement of their common interests

Variable costs—A variable cost is a corporate expense that changes in proportion to production output. Variable costs increase or decrease depending on a company's production volume; they rise as production increases and fall as production decreases.

501c6—Section 501(c)(6) of the Internal Revenue Code provides for the exemption of the following types of organizations.
- Business leagues
- Chambers of commerce
- Real estate boards
- Boards of trade
- Professional football leagues

CHAPTER 1

Introduction to Sports Finance

Karen Weaver

We all love to talk about numbers in the world of sports—who's in first place, what's a team's win–loss record, who scored the most points in a season, and so on. Many fans are interested in the money behind the teams, leagues, and sports—who gets paid how much, what a franchise is worth, and how much a particular stadium costs to build are some of the questions sports fans and students often ask sports finance experts.

Sports finance encompasses a huge part of our understanding of the sports world. It allows us to understand, compare, and contrast who's up and who's down, and, to some extent, what the future holds for a team or organization. Signing the next free agent who is sure to turn the team's fortunes around or trading a top draft pick for another couple of players involves financial calculations that involve the team's overall financial strength at that moment in time.

In a normal sports season, the cycle of that calendar year is predictable—in the professional sports world, it usually begins with league meetings, a player draft, out-of-season practices, year-round scouting for new talent, training camp, regular season, postseason, and the All-Star and awards games. The schedule gets published at least 6 months in advance (except for game times, as flexibility is built in for media coverage) so that fans can purchase ticket packages and other stadium and game experiences. Media companies decide which games will be shown on which "platform"— broadcast, cable, streaming, and so on. Travel arrangements are made for teams, other members of the travel party, while fans arrange their travel so that they can follow their favorite teams.

In the front office, annual budgets are built around core expenses: salaries and benefits for full time personnel; stadium fixed costs like mortgage payments, utilities, improvements, and maintenance; marketing and sponsorship expected revenues and expenses, planned media revenues and expenses; auxiliary part-time personnel, taxes, and so on. For a typical chief financial officer, these are anticipated line items.

But then, once in a hundred years, a pandemic like the COVID-19 pandemic emerges and stops the train cold. Overnight, the NBA stopped playing the rest of their season for the next several months, not knowing whether they could even complete the regular season, let alone the playoffs. Arenas were closed, workers were sent home, and the world stopped.

March 2020 should have been one of the busiest months in the entire year. Alongside the NBA, March would contain the NCAA Men's and Women's Basketball tournaments (also known as March Madness), baseball's spring training and start of the regular season; the NHL completes their season and heads to the playoffs in April. With the pandemic set in, media companies and sponsors had no games to broadcast. Across the globe, thousands of other events, from snowboarding to squash were suddenly canceled with no plans to resume for the immediate future (The Sports.org, 2020).

Suddenly, there was no revenue at all. Unless teams and leagues had financial reserves (and we learned over the course of the summer that many didn't), the entire financial fate of the sports organizational structure rested on cutting expenses, arranging for short-term financing/loans to cover costs, and renegotiating existing contracts with sponsors, apparel manufacturers, media partners, and other fixed costs. Worse still, there was no end in sight as to if or when they could predict the cash would start coming in again.

Even more complicated for organizations was the shifting guidance from the Federal Government about safe activities for individuals and teams. The Centers for Disease Control and Prevention and other health organizations drew varying conclusions as to what was safe to do: Can players practice in small groups? Indoors? Outdoors? Do they have to wear masks all the time or some of the time? (Weaver, 2020a).

The real financial challenge came when teams were trying to figure out the cost of testing for COVID-19. Teams and facilities at all levels were working overtime, trying to create a safe and clean environment that would not transmit the airborne virus. From locker rooms and showers, to athletic training rooms and buses, no one was sure how to resume "normal" practice activities, let alone the emerging expenses of COVID-19. Tests quickly evolved from costing up to $150 a piece per athlete down to $10 or less for certain kinds of testing.

But the cost wasn't the only issue—the turnaround time for the results emerged as an equally high hurdle. If you could get the testing materials, teams had wait a week or more for the results, which was hardly an answer to a coach who wanted to know which athletes he would have for practice that afternoon. The search was on for faster tests that could be done every 48 to 72 hours; inevitably, they were harder to find and more expensive.

The NBA and WNBA discussed resuming their season in June in a "bubble" in Florida, although without families and fans. All teams would be tested, quarantined, and housed, and would compete for almost 3 months at the Disney Wide World of Sports Complex in Orlando. It worked, very few players got sick, and the environment was deemed to be safe. Soon, other leagues debated and discussed whether to host their own single-site bubble. The National Women's Soccer League played in a bubble in Salt Lake City and completed their shortened season, along with naming a champion. Major League Baseball and the NFL decided against it; college football also considered the possibility, but ultimately said no (Weaver, 2020b).

Throughout the early fall, college football was one of the only NCAA sports to play games; even then, it was virtually limited to the Division I programs called the Power 5 and Group of 5 conferences. Other fall sports (except for ACC's field hockey programs) were postponed until Spring 2021, creating another logjam for facilities, sports medicine staffs, and practice access for fall and spring sports.

As predictable as financial forecasting was in the past, the disruption in sports for 2020 and beyond cannot be overstated. The NFL took on $3 billion in debt to subsidize stadium construction and maintenance, as well as plugging cash flow issues for teams. As Sportico wrote, "The new debt includes $350 million for the NFL's stadium finance program, plus $2.7 billion for clubs to use for repaying older debt or as immediate capital, according to Fitch Ratings. That $2.7 billion was issued in two different structures—$1.7 billion in bonds for longer-term borrowing, and $1 billion as a more short-term loan" (Novy-Williams, 2020).

Another fixed cost that will change in the post-COVID environment is insurance. Some of the largest insurance companies in the world are predicting 50% to 100% increases in premiums for teams and facilities at all levels. Event cancellation insurance, once considered a luxury for so many tournaments, seasons and single events, seems like a great safety net for organizations that availed themselves of the relatively inexpensive costs prior to the pandemic. The Big East Conference, an NCAA Division I basketball centric conference, recouped $10.5 million from their insurance company due to the loss of revenues from the 2020 Big East men's basketball tournament. The conference also has event cancellation insurance for the 2021 and 2022 tournaments, leaving them in much better financial shape than many other Division I conferences (Caron, 2020). Regardless of this insurance, sport organizations of all kinds are facing staggering changes in the costs of mandatory insurance coverage in 2021 and beyond, as well as litigation from pandemic related illnesses from employees, vendors and even fans (Coffey, 2020). "Insurers, teams and leagues are litigating a number of cases over pandemic coverage. As a result of the payouts and court disputes, some insurers simply aren't writing policies for sports in 2021," wrote Caron.

The impact of the pandemic can be seen in collective bargaining agreements (CBAs). Major League Soccer announced in late 2020 that they were invoking a "Force Majeure" clause with their players' association. Declaring force majeure is a staggering financial declaration; any organization only makes the declaration when they cannot see their way out of the situation; many times, the assertion frees organizations up to void contracts that normally would be legally binding.

The MLS has stated they have lost nearly $1 billion in 2020. Professional soccer in the United States is heavily dependent on gate receipts; without fans in the stands, they would lose almost 50% of their revenues. The two sides were in the middle of new CBA negotiations, with the declaration allowing for 30 days of discussions, before potentially terminating the agreement and starting over. With no resolution in sight, the MLS could be looking at a player "lockout" in 2021 (McCann, 2020).

For those who enjoy sports as an escape from mundane, everyday life, sports in this era looked nothing like how we had known sports to operate in the past—there were few or no fans in the stands, most leagues played far fewer games, and games were canceled and/or rescheduled so often that we couldn't keep up.

The financial impact of a pandemic on the sports ecosystem will be discussed for years to come. What sports would look like coming out of it will vary—would we have an efficient vaccine, would fans feel safe sitting in an arena with folks they don't know, would fans and teams at all levels feel comfortable staying in hotels, traveling on public transportation, or flying commercial? It's hard to know.

Accepting those realities, this textbook will look at two basic questions as applied to a variety of sports industries—Where does the money come from, and where does the money go? Around those questions, each chapter will start with a basic framework of ideas about how sports have traditionally thought about finance.

The book is broken down into subcategories.
- Professional sports
- International sports
- Women's sports and pay equity
- Intercollegiate athletics
- Youth sports
- Auxiliary enterprises, including facilities, stadia, and the media

Where appropriate, each chapter will consider the following concepts in order to provide each reader not only an opportunity to learn about a particular sports organization but also to compare concepts across sport structures to deepen your understanding of the application of relevant ideas. For example, in many chapters you will gain an understanding of the following.
- Brief history
- League structure
- Ownership buy-in amount

- Revenue distribution
    - Individual teams
    - From league office
- Facility revenue, subsidies, and construction
- Financial forecasting
- Tax status and liabilities
- Revenue sources and partnerships
- Media revenues
    - Individual teams
    - From league office
- Salary structures
    - Coaching staff
    - Players
    - Salary caps
- Postseason financial structures
- Final assessment of growth potential for sport/entity

In other chapters, you will learn about how the sports business structures work, which then drives the financial decisions. For example, in the chapter on sports media (Chapter 2), you will learn about the measurement and analytics behind how ESPN and other sports networks make their money, and, in turn, how they grow their revenue streams with ancillary programming while maximizing social media and technology.

In each chapter, there are learning objectives that point you to key questions that sports studies majors often ask. For example, in the NFL chapter, you will understand the structures of the 32 NFL franchises; how one becomes an owner of a team; the various revenue streams teams use to maximize their home stadium opportunities (and the expenses that offset the various tax liabilities and salary structures embedded in players' and coaches' contracts; and how the salary cap works, as well as the postseason financial structures.

One chapter (Chapter 4) considers the explosion of the mega recreational complexes being built across the country. Perhaps you played in one or more as a part of the youth sports travel industry (also known as sports tourism). Often containing 30 to 50 outdoor fields; multiple indoor courts and training areas; restaurants and hotels; and game facilities for hosting regional, national, and even international tournaments, these attractions can host from 3,000 to 10,000 or more athletes playing sports like baseball, softball, lacrosse, field hockey, tennis, and soccer.

In Louisiana, a $30 million sports complex hopes to attract tourism dollars to a local community (Calder, 2020). Called an "economic development engine," it will feature, "[t]he 94-acre complex, financed by the state and to be operated by Jefferson Parish when completed in 2022, will include batting cages, a playground, a shaded pavilion, two baseball fields and five multi-purpose fields for baseball, softball, flag football and soccer."

Another chapter (Chapter 14) will study the Olympic Games, a once-every-four-year event held both in the summer and winter in various cities around the world. You'll know about the moving parts of each country's Olympic governing body, as well as the sport federations that organize sports in each nation. The reader will learn where the Summer and Winter Olympic revenues come from, how broadcast rights are managed, and the unique relationship the International Olympic Committee has with every host city, sponsors, and organizing committee, and in particular, the exclusive relationship the corporate "Olympic Partners Program" has with venues, athletes, and sponsors.

Another chapter (Chapter 5) takes a deep look at the financing and construction of sports stadiums, both as privately owned entities and as public–private partnerships. One of the more complex topics in the text, it is a key component of the success of the team/organization because of the importance of home ticket sales, multimedia rights in and around the venue, lucrative rental fees, and, more recently, its role as a center for advancing social movements, such as becoming polling places for voters in the 2020 U.S. Presidential Election. Stadiums are community gathering spots in which the home team takes centerstage, embracing the culture of the city, state, and the team. One only has to look at the fanatical fan bases of the St. Louis Cardinals in Major League Baseball, or the venerable home of the Chicago Bears, Soldier Field, to understand the history and tradition of sports in America.

In particular, the chapter will focus on how stadiums have dramatically evolved since 1990 in the United States, as the concept of where a stadium could be located was reenvisioned by the Baltimore Orioles and Camden Yards. The project revitalized downtown Baltimore and launched the idea of an arena district across America. As a result, the in-stadium amenities provided dramatically shifted, creating newer and more lucrative revenue streams for teams.

The chapter will also examine how stadiums are financed, and how the league owners assist in a particular city acquiring and building a stadium, including the role that favorable interest rates play in determining stadium financing, despite rising construction costs. And you'll learn why a new stadium drives up a franchise's valuation, and grows the pie for all of the owners in the league.

By the time you complete reading this text, you will have understood the nuances of sports finance across multiple sports and organizations. With case studies, review questions, access to web resources for further data research, and contributions from some of the top sports journalists, academics, and practitioners in the industry, you will leave this course with a deeper understanding of the sport you love, and a host of other sports and auxiliary businesses that feed into the industry.

One other note about this text—in addition to being organized differently than other sports finance texts on the market, the book features several unique innovations not found in other volumes. First, there are eight women authors spread out over 10 chapters, the largest assembly of women in a sports finance book ever. They bring a unique writing style and perspective to this topic, while addressing topics from a variety of perspectives. Secondly, this book places significant emphasis on the issues facing women's sports and pay equity, almost unheard of in a sports finance textbook. As future sports industry professionals, it is important to see all the possibilities and inequities that inhabit our industry.

What Does a Sports Finance Professional's Job Description Look Like?

While much of this textbook will concentrate on the macro financials of teams and leagues, students may wonder, *What kind of skills do I need to work on the finance side of one of these organizations?* Here are three examples of the wide-ranging finance-focused jobs available inside and outside of the industry ecosystem. All require a range of finance and accounting skills, but understanding how the league generates revenues (and manages its expenses) in a unique environment will strengthen your candidacy.

Job Examples from Indeed.com

For a sponsor of a team or league, the job description could look like this.

#1 *Accounting Manager, Playfly Sports, Access Portfolio Company*

Company Background:
We are a full-service collegiate sports marketing company providing top tier management of multimedia rights for athletics departments, campuses and eSports, which includes the world's largest collegiate gaming league. Our company has partnered with some of the most prestigious collegiate teams, high school state associations, and sports venues across the country. Our team designs programs that deliver the revenue and exposure needed to maximize the value of sports multi-media rights, enable capital projects, and increase fan engagement on campuses. We implement community based programs, in-venue and on-campus digital displays, influence media, marketing affiliation, eSports events, experiential entertainment, and game day implementations benefiting universities, alumni, students, and passionate fan bases. Our sports solutions maximize the true value of each school by capitalizing on partnership opportunities and prioritizing the mission, goals and objectives of the institution. Our client-centered, passionate team of sports marketing professionals has decades of experience incorporating both national and local brands' messages within these innovative media assets.

Essential Duties and Responsibilities:
The accounting manager is responsible for the day to day operations within our Business Operations department for the Sports Properties division as well as specific responsibility for the LSU property. The candidate will have a strategic contribution to the efficiency of the department while supporting current processes and promoting

change to advance our initiatives and increase efficiency. This position will also work directly with Senior Management and the Accounting/Finance team in Philadelphia. This self-starter will have the ability to organize, prioritize, and manage multiple tasks concurrently and to maintain effective working relationships with internal and external contacts. The ideal candidate will have successful leadership experience, strong organizational and time management skills, be a self-starter with excellent communication and interpersonal skills.

Financial management of LSU property, including all business operations functions, budgets, forecasting, and financial reporting

- Oversee and direct the activities of the Business Operations staff, including processing sponsor agreements, invoicing, revenue recognition, receivables, and vendor payments for 20 properties
- Oversee and Liaise with Accounts Payable for set up and maintenance of employees in our Expense Reimbursement system
- Ensure company policies are communicated and followed
- Provide support to the monthly, quarterly and year-end close processes, including reconciliations and journal entries
- Ensure financial reporting for our partner agreements is timely and accurate
- Maintain accounting controls by following policies and procedures
- Assist Director with annual budgets and quarterly forecast updates
- Assist the office with administrative duties, other duties and special projects as assigned by Senior Management

Education, Work Experience Requirements and/or Competencies:
- A Bachelor's Degree in Accounting or related field
- Minimum 5 years of progressively complex positions
- Experience supervising the work of others, including workload management, reviewing, coaching and managing total skill set
- Minimum 3 years supervisory experience
- Ability to promote change by communicating to and involving others
- Demonstrated ability to manage multiple competing priorities simultaneously and drive projects to completion
- Strong analytical, communication, and interpersonal skills
- Proven track record of effectively interacting with Senior Management
- Ability to work independently and take initiative, as well as working well with a team with a high level of energy and enthusiasm
- Attention to detail
- Advanced knowledge of Excel and ability to master new systems quickly
- Strong organizational and document management skills, ability to organize and manage electronic documents
- Fundamental knowledge of US GAAP and standard business practices
- Ability to travel as needed

#2 Regional Finance Director–Sports & Entertainment

Overview

Aramark (NYSE: ARMK) proudly serves the world's leading educational institutions, Fortune 500 companies, world champion sports teams, prominent healthcare providers, iconic destinations and cultural attractions, and numerous municipalities in 19 countries around the world. Our 280,000 team members deliver innovative experiences and services in food, facilities management and uniforms to millions of people every day. We strive to create a better world by making a positive impact on people and the planet, including commitments to engage our employees; empower healthy consumers; build local communities; source ethically, inclusively and responsibly; operate efficiently; and reduce waste. Aramark is recognized as a Best Place to Work by the Human Rights Campaign (LGBTQ), DiversityInc, Black Enterprise and the Disability Equality Index. Learn more at www. aramark.com or connect with us on Facebook and Twitter.

Description
Aramark Sports And Entertainment:

The Sports and Entertainment division within Aramark Corporation serves more than 200 premier stadiums, arenas, convention centers and concert venues. Since 1975 we've created culinary memories throughout the United States. The secret to our success is that we start with great food and a well-managed facility. We understand that ensuring a memorable experience for our customers goes far beyond the food we serve.

Responsibilities:

As the Regional Finance Director, responsibilities include:

- *Management and professional development of the regional finance staff*
- *Administration of policies and programs, while working with the District Mangers, Regional Staff and Front Line Manager to achieve the Region's financial and operating objectives*
- *Oversees the budget, projection and closing processes and fosters creative solutions and collaboration with the regional field organization and headquarter support teams to achieve financial objectives.*
- *Validation of financial data, as compiled by the operational teams for renewal, rebid and new business efforts.*
- *Identification and ongoing monitoring of under-performing accounts, including leading improvement team to turnaround performance at such accounts*
- *Assists the Regional Vice President and headquarters staff in administering compliance with Aramark's Business Conduct Policy and related directives (e.g., internal controls at field locations, contract compliance and completion of audits)*
- *Conducts ongoing training sessions for regional staff regarding new accounting procedures and other relevant financial programs and initiatives*
- *Assists in the opening of new accounts to ensure sound systems and procedures are in place*
- *Manages the control of regional assets, including the capital expenditure process, change funds, inventory and equipment*
- *Monitors working capital requirements, with a particular focus on the administration of accounts receivable and their collection*
- *Evaluation of potential investments, acquisitions and/or divestitures*
- *Engages with other regional directors to identify and promote sharing of best practices*

Position is responsible for ensuring data integrity, best practices and ongoing compliance with internal and external controls. Work situations vary and require development, analysis, interpretation and implementation of policies, practices and procedures. Position works closely with senior managers across all functions to strengthen internal controls, optimize company growth and profitability.

Qualifications

Ideal candidates will possess:
- *This position requires a Bachelor's degree in Finance or Accounting, along with a minimum of 8 to 10 years finance and/or accounting experience.*
- *Master's degree and/or CPA are preferable, but not required.*
- *Proficiency in using a personal computer and prior experience with sophisticated financial computer applications, including Oracle, is preferred.*
- *It will be essential that the regional finance director have strong analytical and communication skills, as well as experience leading/championing projects.*
- *This position will require 50% travel, inc.*

#3 If you are interested in a league office finance position, here is an example.

Manager of Foundation Programs and Community Outreach

Chicago Fire FC
Chicago, IL

Chicago Fire Football Club
Chicago Fire FC is Chicago's ambassador to the global sport of football. Founded in 1997, and competing in Major League Soccer, Chicago Fire won its first championship in its debut season and was foundational in the careers of several current MLS coaches and players, as well as International and UEFA Champions League coaches.

Under new ownership, the Club recently returned to Soldier Field for the 2020 season, as well as opening new 50,000 sq ft offices in the heart of the city. With numerous new hires throughout the technical and front office staff, the Club is laying the foundation for an audacious and ambitious vision that will transform the brand and the company in the coming years.

Chicago Fire FC is committed to fostering, cultivating, and preserving a culture of diversity, equity, accessibility, and inclusion. Our diversity initiatives start with the recruitment and selection process; therefore, we'd like to welcome all diverse candidates to apply to opportunities within our Club.

Job Description

Chicago Fire Football Club is seeking a dedicated Manager of Foundation Programs and Community Outreach to join our team! This individual will be reporting to our Director of Development, CFF.

Job Responsibilities:

- *Manage day to day operations and logistics of P.L.A.Y.S. Program*
- *Order equipment and uniforms, development of training materials, scheduling of game days, track coach hours, etc.*
- *Collaborate with department staff to achieve strategic goals to ensure progress towards organization's objectives*
- *Assist with oversight of department finances and fundraising including invoices, donation receipts, budget tracking, grant calendar, reports, etc.*
- *Oversee game day initiatives including Volunteer Program, 50/50 Raffle, Auctions, Kicks for Kids, etc.*
- *Implement and oversee The Beacon Program including Best XI, staff volunteer program, and other community initiatives that prioritize Chicago's 77 Neighborhoods*
- *Manage cross functional relationships with other internal departments*
- *Serve as liaison to corporate donors*
- *Oversee all marketing and communication elements for the department*
- *Work with BI to create assessment tools for monitor and evaluation of outreach initiatives*
- *Maintain Foundation database and Donation Request Platform*
- *Oversee the engagement of players, coaches, alumni and staff for all club wide appearances and execute monthly autograph sessions*
- *Supervise and develop interns and mentor through their experience*
- *Guide the Associate Board and attend all organization activities and events as requested*
- *Administrative tasks and other duties as needed*

Qualifications:

- *Bachelor's degree or higher in related field*
- *Three to 5 years of non-profit administrative, events and/or program management experience*
- *Exceptional communication (verbal & written), interpersonal skills and ability to understand and speak Spanish a plus*
- *Strong proficiency in Microsoft Office Suite, as well as knowledge of fundraising platforms*
- *Highly organized and detail oriented with proven time management skills, and experience creating efficient systems to juggle multiple projects simultaneously*
- *Possesses a spirit of flexibility, a positive outlook and the ability to work independently and move projects forward with urgency and cooperation*
- *Must demonstrate the mission, vision and values of the organization*
- *Strong knowledge of the Chicago market and community*
- *This role requires work hours outside of normal office hours (evenings and weekends) to execute programming in community and during Fire matches*

References

Calder, C. (2020, December 25). *Will $30M youth sports complex attract businesses to Westwego? Jefferson Parish officials hope so.* www.nola.com/news/article_aea1ff4c-43d3-11eb-abd7-c3d7c-f14e1ef.html

Caron, E. (2020, December). *Big east recoups $10.5 million from men's basketball tournament insurance policy.* www.sportico.com/leagues/college-sports/2020/big-east-tournament-insurance-pay-out-1234617508/

Coffey, B. (2020, December). *Sports insurance rates poised to jump in 2021 after pandemic losses.* www.sportico.com/business/finance/2020/sports-insurance-rates-double-1234618990/

McCann, M. (2020, December). *MLS's force majeure draws eyes to CBA and antitrust exemption.* www.sportico.com/law/analysis/2020/mls-lockout-force-majeure-1234619307/

Novy-Williams, E. (2020, August). *NFL takes on $3 billion more in debt for stadium financing, cash for clubs.* www.sportico.com/leagues/football/2020/nfl-billion-debt-1234612386/

TheSports.org. (2020). *Calendar of the major sporting events of the year 2020.* www.the-sports.org/sport-calendar-2020-p0-62020.html

Weaver, K. (2020a, May). *Return to play guidance emerges for college sports.* www.forbes.com/sites/karenweaver/2020/05/09/return-to-play-guidance-emerges-for-college-sports-colleges/?sh=-c8e97191e9a3

Weaver, K. (2020b, July). *No, you cannot put college football in a bubble.* www.forbes.com/sites/karen-weaver/2020/07/25/no-you-cannot-put-college-football-in-a-bubble/?sh=246057f5b9f6

CHAPTER 2

Business of Sports Media

Karen Weaver

LEARNING OBJECTIVES

- To learn how the media system generates revenues.
- To understand the symbiotic relationship that sports, media, technology, and oversight have had for over 100 years.
- To study the shifting audience and consumption patterns that sports teams and leagues are chasing.
- To understand why second and even third screens matter more today than ever.
- To consider the impact that legalized sports betting is having on media content and creation.
- To understand how the concept of aggregating viewers drove the creation of regional sports networks and college conference networks.
- To learn why media companies will pay more for some games and not others.

Evolution and Revolution

Without question, media exposure and media revenues are increasingly driving the sports ecosystem. Some leagues and teams depend on 50% or more of their annual revenues from their media arrangements. There are many other components that comprise a team's annual budget, but the growing emphasis on maximizing media dollars has transformed sports in the last two decades.

The top of the heap continues to be the amount of media ascribed to the National Football League. Year over year, the NFL's weekly slate of games consistently rank in the top 10 of the Nielsen ratings, the primary indicator for determining who is watching and how much advertisers will spend to reach that audience. In 2020, a year with no parallel for the attention of the American public, the NFL continues its reign, despite the traditional viewership downturn of about 7% during a

Presidential election year (Murphy, 2020). The Super Bowl, year in and year out, has become a touchpoint in American culture. Even in this day of fractured audiences, the Game still manages to attract over 100 million viewers, making it one of the only "must see" events left on the calendar (see www.sportico.com/business/media/2020/2020-tv-ratings-nfl-1234619216/).

How did we get to this point? Certainly, it's the innovation of the communication devices. Since the late 1800s, with the advent of capturing radio waves on a transmitter, to the telegraph and telephone, a key method of getting Americans to adopt a new technology was to put sports on it. Just as it is today, fans will go to any lengths to access their favorite teams, whether it's via a digital or print newspaper, radio broadcast, or television program. One of the best early examples of the power of communications technology was Notre Dame's use of radio broadcasts around the country in the 1920s and 1930s. Stringing together different radio stations from the Midwest to the East Coast, the Fighting Irish became "America's College Team" because more fans were able to listen to the games (Gullifor, 2001).

When television emerged in the late 1940s and early 1950s, Saturdays were for college football with the Game of the Week. By the early 1960s, the NFL took over Sundays, and football cemented its relationship with communications technology, rarely ceding the playing field to other professional sports. Quickly, the NCAA took over control of selecting who would appear in the prime broadcasting spots on Saturdays, setting the stage for the riches of many of the premier programs in NCAA Division I college football today (Smith, 2001).

In 1978, ESPN was born. Imagined by Bill Rasmussen, a former employee of the now defunct Hartford (CT) Whalers NHL franchise, ESPN was originally only going to be a Connecticut-focused channel. Rasmussen told *Forbes* in 2012 about his idea:

> It was originally going to be a cable channel focused on Connecticut college sports—we had a lot of college sports that weren't going to get on NBC, CBS, or ABC. Someone suggested we could put it on a satellite—I didn't know anything about satellites, and as it turned out, neither did anyone else in the room. They suggested I call someone at RCA about getting on their satellite. That would be like someone suggesting today you should call Apple for more information—remember, this was the summer of 1978. I found the one RCA sales rep who must have been sitting by the phone waiting for my call, and the next day, in a conference room I rented from the local cable company for $20, I met with the man from RCA along with my son, Scott. He told us all about what satellite packages were available, including a 24-hour package that no one had ever bought. When Scott went over the pricing structure, he realized the 24-hour package was the best option. Of course, we didn't have any money, but I called the man from RCA the next day and said, 'We'll take one of those things.' 'One of what things,' he asked. 'One of those 24 hour things.' (We didn't even know they were called transponders at that point). He was surprised and said, 'you will?!!' We were extremely fortunate because they had a clause in the contract that said we didn't have to make the first payment until 90 days after our first use of the satellite! (Schwabel, 2012).

As cable became more popular, more sports teams and games appeared. New networks, needing to jump start their channels and drive subscribers to demand their cable companies place the network on the guide, often used sports as a way to quickly generate revenues. Specialty channels emerged, including MLB Network, The Golf Channel, The Tennis Channel, and the Olympic Channel, which capitalized on fans' growing demands to follow specific sports. This also allowed the league rights holders to capture incremental value in addition to the rights fees collected from media companies (Murphy, 2020).

Over time, regional networks were developed to attract sports fans across multiple demographics. In Philadelphia, Comcast created the Comcast Sports Network (CSN), which was the exclusive broadcaster for the Philadelphia Phillies, Philadelphia Sixers, and the Philadelphia Flyers. If you were a fan of Philadelphia sports, you had to subscribe to the channel on cable or satellite, but only Dish Network; Comcast would not allow the games to be shown on Direct TV. That synergy attracted local college basketball and football games to demand to have their games shown on CSN as well.

When NBC began broadcasting the Olympic Games in Berlin in 1936 (via radio), followed in 1996 by the Atlanta Olympic Games, NBC has maintained its role as the broadcasting and media partner of the American feed for the International Olympic Games, including the Winter and Summer Games. As of the Tokyo Games in 2021, NBC will have been the exclusive media partner for 11 consecutive quadrenniums.

General Electric owned NBC for a time in the 1990s; NBC and Comcast joined together to form NBCUniversal, one of the largest media and entertainment companies in the world. That partnership allowed for growth in the regional sports network categories across the country, creating even more bundled demand for cable and satellite companies (Comcast, n.d.).

In the mid-1990s, the broadcast landscape changed dramatically when Congress passed the Telecommunications Act of 1996. Hailed as the first major overhaul of telecommunications law in 62 years, the act created competition for television networks via high-speed Internet. Dial-up Internet access was gradually replaced with higher transmission speeds (ranging from 25 mbps to 100 to 200 mbps per household) available today. Those speeds have permitted more and more video content to be delivered via the Internet, rather than cable, satellite, or over the air (FCC, n.d.; Smith, 2001).

The Hill.com wrote in 2016,

> Technology has … changed substantially since the law was signed in 1996. Internet speeds have risen, with Americans making the switch from dial-up to broadband, which in turn has disrupted the old order in other industries, like broadcasting. And more recently, the rise of smartphones has forced regulators to confront challenges posed by mobile networks (McCabe, 2016)

Today's technology revolution in the media business creates multiple revenue streams for sports leagues and teams at all levels. Today, it's likely if you are a youth sports travel team, your team has likely had its game "streamed" via your high school, travel ball, or community organization. The remarkable changes in the ability to deliver high quality video content on less expensive equipment and a WiFi or cellular connection has transformed our ability to livestream almost anything. Want to show your son at the local batting cage hitting line drives to your grandparents in another location? You can do that on your mobile phone. Want to livestream a state championship field hockey game? You can do that on an iPad (Krings, 2020).

The challenge for sports finance professionals is now how to best engage and monetize fans, sponsors, and investors to take full advantage of these advances. The emergence of platforms like YouTube, Instagram, TikTok, Twitter, Facebook, Amazon Prime, and many others have allowed individuals and organizations to create their own channels, targeting specific content limited only to a creator's imagination. With the advent of podcasting, another channel has opened up for teams to share their culture and strategy (Feldman, 2020).

The growth of 5G technology will greatly accelerate wireless signals and the data being sent across them in the very near future. Requiring more antennas and additional coverage both inside and outside of structures, it will create even more bandwidth for streaming.

Take a look at the graphic here that demonstrates the generational divide in consuming media.

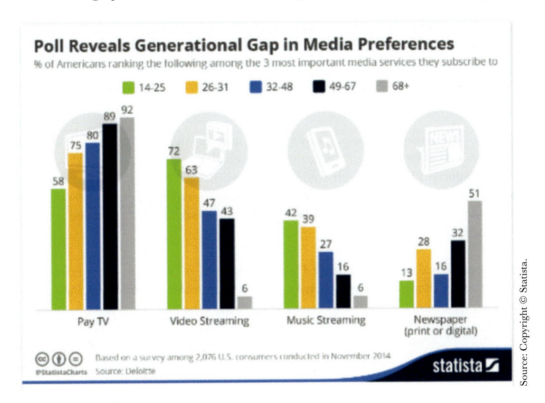

Poll Reveals Generational Gap in Media Preferences
% of Americans ranking the following among the 3 most important media services they subscribe to

Legend: 14-25 | 26-31 | 32-48 | 49-67 | 68+

Pay TV: 58, 75, 80, 89, 92
Video Streaming: 72, 63, 47, 43, 6
Music Streaming: 42, 39, 27, 16, 6
Newspaper (print or digital): 13, 28, 16, 32, 51

Based on a survey among 2,076 U.S. consumers conducted in November 2014
@StatistaCharts   Source: Deloitte

statista

Revenue Basics—Advertising

How is revenue generated in the media business? For decades, it was a unit of time that was purchased on an over-the-air device, that is, a 30-second advertising spot on a morning radio show. Radio stations attract different demographics, so if your service or product was appealing to a certain demographic (18-49-year-old males, as an example), your company would purchase "ad time" on that radio station in 30 second increments.

The same strategy worked for years with television. Ad rates rose as the television audience grew bigger for a particular event. As shown earlier in the chapter, companies like Nielsen and others specialize in tracking who is watching that event and for how long. Measurement by third party companies like Nielsen is the currency that determines what ESPN, Fox, and others can charge. For example, if a network like ESPN has 25 million viewers for the College Football Playoff, their ad rates are higher for a product or service to buy time during that game. Conversely, if it's a regular season major league baseball game of 5 million viewers, the ad rates are generally much lower (Murphy, 2020).

How many ads one can sell in any particular game drives the majority of the broadcast revenues. Each sport or event has different available blocks of time in a game. For example, basketball has quarters or halves, with breaks between each, and timeouts called by coaches during play. Conversely, soccer is a much freer flowing game of two halves; there is rarely time for typical 30-second ad spot during play.

As the desire for revenue has grown, sports channels have expanded the revenue pie by adding in "quick pitches" in between breaks in the action. In baseball, specific innings are sold as promotions for certain products. The announcers could tell the audience, "if the home team hits a home run in this half of the inning, XYZ product will donate $1,000 to a local animal shelter." There are countless other examples of in-game product placement, all adding to the revenue generated for that particular event.

If a game is on a local network (as defined by the geography of that area), ad rates are measured in CPMs (cost per thousand). Simply, it means if you want to reach a thousand viewers, we will charge you a specific rate. If the local evening news attracts the most viewers to the nightly news, the television station will charge more than a local afternoon talk show. If the CPM is $200 and the evening news attracts 500,000 viewers, the cost for that 30-second spot is $100,000 (Thorp, 2019). It is in the station's best interest to drive viewers to the most expensive property in their inventory, and typically those are local news and local sports. How much more? Whatever the market will bear. Networks do offer ad packages sold to higher rated programs the opportunity to advertise for minimal costs on lower rated programs to increase sales.

A newer trend in local advertising involves geofencing. Because so many households and devices are connected to cable or Internet, it is easy to identify the location of the viewer. Geofencing places a virtual fence around a zip code area, a county, or some other geographical area targeted (and coveted) by the advertiser. If a local sporting goods store wants to advertise in their local market, they could employ this technique. It can be a win-win for the media company and the advertiser, as generally it costs less than a typical ad, while delivering a higher ROI (return on investment) for the sporting goods reseller. And geofencing allows for multiple ads to be run at the same time, targeting many specific locales.

Affiliate revenues are more lucrative than advertising rates and subscriptions. In the 1980s and early 1990s, networks like ESPN used to pay the cable or satellite company to carry their programming; in the mid-1990s, that model flipped when ESPN bought the NFL (Murphy, 2020). This is where the real economic battles are being waged, via streaming services, apps, satellite radio, and on-demand events. A company like ESPN had a massive advantage to buy sports content for decades because they had two sources of income to use—subscribers (or subs), who paid a monthly fee to their cable or satellite provider to get the channel (or channels, as ESPN has multiple outlets, including ESPN2, ESPNU, and ESPNews), and demand higher ad rates because of the size and demographics of their audience.

In order to compete for sports content, traditional OTA (over the air) broadcasters began charging in 2013 a new fee, related to "retransmission consent agreements," was imposed (Bode, 2013). This fee was paid for the right to carry the "over the air" channel on the distributed networks (cable and satellite). Collected from every cable subscriber whether they watched sports or not, it suddenly gave national broadcasters like CBS, ABC, NBC, and FOX a chance to remain competitive while bidding for sports content. It also has driven the price of sports content higher and higher.

For years, cable and satellite companies charged customers more for video content than Internet streaming, assuming that viewers were coming to them primarily for video content. Today, that no longer applies. In fact, cable companies have upended their business model to try to hold on to customers on the Internet side, as the great unbundling of cable channels accelerated in 2020. Today, these same companies know their future lies in holding on to market share via Internet usage, higher and faster speeds, and the massive amounts of data they collect on the viewing and streaming habits of their customers.

The biggest question for rights holders going forward is this: Will sports support a "Direct to Consumer" model? Will fans (aka subscribers) be willing to pay $20 to $40 to watch baseball every season? And what happens to the baseball fan after the season is over—will they pay another $20 to $40 to watch basketball?

Traditionally, sports networks charge higher sub fees because live sports production has been so expensive. Post-COVID-19, many efficiencies have been discovered and implementer. But sports may still end up tied to the "bundle" of a cable or streaming service simply because these companies need to spread the costs among a larger group of consumers.

Another significant worry is the "cord-cutting" or "cord-shaving" consumers have been doing. Once well over 100 million subscribers paid monthly for cable or satellite access; some analysts predict that these platforms may dwindle down to 50 to 60 million subscribers. The sports networks have survived quite nicely inside a pay TV ecosystem. What happens when enough consumers have left that world completely behind? How will sports rights be subsidized?

Expenses of Executing a Media Rights Deal

Once the Grant of Media Rights is agreed to and the contract is signed, sports media companies like ESPN, FOX, and CBS have to spend money to get the games on. The production of live events has traditionally been expensive, if you consider bringing all of the technology and crew to the site of the game. Since COVID-19, the emphasis has shifted to doing more and more work remotely, meaning trucks, crew, and remote satellite uplinks don't have to be moved around.

Networks like the ACC Network have gone so far as to build out their own production studios on campus, investing up to $10 million of their own monies to bring their onsite work up to 4K standards. Viewers expect to see high-definition content, so the games must be produced on HD or 4K quality equipment.

Production managers build out budgets that include:
• The actual costs of buying the media rights;
• The estimated production costs of fulfilling the contract;

- What technology needs to be installed on site versus what can be brought in (includes the fiber connection to the home studios);
- SG&A: Selling, General, and Administrative Expenses assigned to the contract; and
- Marketing expenses.

Sometimes, if a media company really wants to bid for a property coming on the market, they may have to decide to forgo renewing another contract. ESPN did this when the NFL contract was up for renegotiation; they decided not to renew their NASCAR agreement (Murphy, 2020).

Generally, the pecking order for securing rights goes like this.
1. National Football League
2. College Football
3. National Basketball Association
4. Major League Baseball

Building a Media Network

If you want to start your own media empire today, there are a thousand things to consider as the marketplace keeps shifting. We'll review a few of them here, as they are important in understanding the synergies of the industry.

- **Technology.** As you construct the physical and satellite locations for your company, the ability to transmit content in real time is crucial. Access to gigabyte Internet speeds is challenging, and may require your company to build infrastructure as well as partner with companies who companies that already built what you need. Inside, you'll need to "future proof" your technology so that you don't need to upgrade it every year. Finally, you'll need to build in redundancies so that if one part of your network distribution crashes, another part can immediately pick up where the disruption occurred. What happens if you don't build in redundancies? Your networks crash in the middle of the Super Bowl, as happened to both the Comcast and Fox Sports live streams in 2017 (Liptak, 2017).
- **Second Screening.** If 2020 taught the sports industry anything, it is that viewers under 35 are consuming more content on their phones and iPads during a game than are actually watching the game on a big screen television. Nielsen reported that more than 90% of Americans watching sports were holding a second screen. The website e-marketer found that the number of hours per day individuals were consuming content on their phones exceeded the number of hours watching television for the first time in history. Some described the shift as a move toward "ambient" TV, meaning it was noise in the background, akin to elevator music (Feldman, 2020). This shift requires analysis from teams, leagues and media companies to think about

the platform's viewers are on during a game. Viewers are immersed in the second (and third) screens; the business model requires that you create "sticky" content (content that makes them stay with it) in order to drive revenues.

- **Data, Data, Data.** Media companies know more about their viewer's habits, consumption patterns, social networks and other personal data today than ever before. Data aggregation will only accelerate in the coming years. How will you monetize that data? Will there be any newly imposed government restrictions that limit the amount and kinds of data you collect? How does the unlimited ability to collect your viewer's habits compare to other countries rules? As an example, Germany and other countries in the European Union have much tighter standards for data privacy (International Trade Administration, n.d.).

Regional Sports Networks

As mentioned earlier in the chapter, the rise of regionally focused sports networks (hence the name regional sports networks or RSNs) in the early 2000s sparked the rise of acquiring and gating local sports teams on to cable or satellite sport "tiers." Previously, each professional or college team would negotiate their regular season games individually with multiple local stations, typically "over the air" stations that had the widest reach. In fact, many local stations were loath to lose their connections to local professional teams, as it gave them regular content for many months in a season.

As mentioned earlier, the Telecommunications Act of 1996 and the creation of more than 500 channels on a cable or satellite system created opportunities for specialized sports networks. Over the next decade, Fox Sports Networks became the de facto model for how local sports could be packaged. These networks included Fox Sports Arizona, Fox Sports Carolinas, Fox Sports Detroit, Fox Sports Florida, Fox Sports Indiana, Fox Sports Indiana, Fox Sports Midwest, Fox Sports New Orleans, Fox Sports North, Fox Sports Ohio, Fox Sports Oklahoma, Fox Sports San Diego, Fox Sports San Diego, Fox Sports Southeast, Fox Sports Southwest, Fox Sports Sun, Fox Sports Tennessee, Fox Sports West Prime Ticket, and Fox Sports Wisconsin. Other channels like the YES Network and SportsTime Ohio also emerged (Harris, 1997).

NBC launched their own sports networks in that same time period. NBC Sports Bay Area, NBC Sports California, NBC Sports Chicago, NBC Sports Washington, NBC Sports Boston, NBC Sports Northwest, and NBC Sports Philadelphia, along with SportsNet New York. AT&T and Spectrum also launched sports channels during that time period, along with Altitude Sports, Buckeye Sports Network, Comcast, Cox Sports Madison Square Garden (MSG), New England Sports Network (NESN), and Mid-Atlantic Sports Network (Steinberg, 2017).

How many of these networks do you recognize today? For some readers, you may have heard of very few. This industry has been ripe for mergers and acquisitions as media companies have worked to consolidate their empires to include not only sports but movies, entertainment, theme parks, and streaming services. There are dozens of defunct networks today that lost out on the bidding wars for sports content. It stands to reason that the larger companies are able

© Jonathan Weiss/Shutterstock.com

to make stronger bids for that content when the contracts are up. It is a key reason as to why sports media rights are so valuable; they are truly "must see TV" (to coin an old phrase)—people rarely want to "time shift" a live game.

In many of the professional sports chapters in this textbook, you will read more about their negotiated arrangements with television networks and streaming platforms.

College Conference Channels

An equally notable pattern emerged in 2007 when the Big Ten Conference, arguably the most powerful athletic conference in college sports at that time, struck a partnership with Fox, and decided to launch their own cable channel. Originally called the Big Ten Channel, the network followed a pattern familiar to those who were part of the early development of RSNs—acquire media rights to a host of content that could fill 24 hours a day, 7 days a week of airtime for Big Ten fans around the country. Coming on the heels of the Mountain West Conference network's 2006 launch, the Big Ten Network (BTN) faced multiple early hurdles in getting distribution both regionally and nationally, as Comcast refused to negotiate carrying the network on their cable system, thinking it would compete with their sports networks. More details about BTN's arrival on the sports media scene can be found in the case study (Weaver, 2009).

A few years later, the Pac-12 became the next Division I athletic conference to launch their network. Done in an entirely different economic environment, the rush to create a profitable network led to the most recent conference realignment for the Pac-12 in 2010 and 2011. Called the Pac-10 in 2010, the conference presidents hired a new commissioner, Larry Scott, to not only assume the duties of an athletic league but to act as the head of a sprawling media empire that would generate billions for the universities—or at least they hoped.

One key metric both conferences needed in gaining revenues was to acquire households in dense regions of the country. Large metropolitan areas (and the high-profile Division I football programs located became targets for adding additional schools. At one point, Commissioner Scott was seen landing his private plane in Austin, Texas (home of the University of Texas); Norman, Oklahoma (University of Oklahoma); Boulder, Colorado (University of Colorado); and Salt Lake City, Utah (University of Utah). By 2011, Colorado and Utah joined the Pac-10 to create the Pac-12, and Texas and Oklahoma kept the Big 12 alive and negotiated a more favorable revenue distribution for themselves with the newly formed Big 12 Network and the Longhorn Network (Gall, 2012). The Pac-12 Network, by most accounts, has underwhelmed everyone—fans, coaches, athletic directors, and presidents.

Not far behind, the Southeastern Conference (SEC) announced their new 24-hour cable partnership with ESPN after another frenetic round of rumors in schools abandoning their old conferences to join the SEC. After the dust settled, three more schools joined the SEC. Saturdays Down South told the story this way:

> Rumors began to pick up steam after Texas A&M officials met to discuss the impact of Texas, a fellow Big 12 member, launching its own television network. After two decades of interest, Texas A&M was given a 72-hour deadline in August 2011 to decide between the Pac-10 and the SEC, choosing the latter in the end and leaving the Longhorns and the Big 12 behind. With Texas A&M's addition, rumors continued to swirl that the SEC would take another team. West Virginia, then in the Big East, and several ACC schools were among the teams mentioned; however, the ACC raising its exit fee to $20 million amidst all the realignment thwarted the idea of adding FSU or Virginia Tech.

> Late in 2011, the Big 12 indicated that Missouri was on its way out, not including the school among its expected members for 2012-13. It became obvious why when, in November 2011, the SEC announced it would be bringing Mizzou into the fold.

> Texas A&M's decision to ditch the Longhorns and their television network turned out to be a good call. A year after the Aggies and Tigers officially joined the conference, SEC commissioner Mike Slive and ESPN president John Skipper announced a 20-year partnership between the two entities to launch the SEC Network, which would make its debut in August 2014. In its first fiscal year, the channel helped generate a record-setting $455 million in total revenue for the conference (Weisband, 2014).

In 2019, well behind its peer group, the Power 5 Conferences, the Atlantic Coast Conference (ACC) announced the start date of their long-awaited sports network, a partnership with ESPN. Unlike the

Big Ten Network, which provided $3 million upfront to each Big Ten school in 2007, the ACC told schools they would have to build out their own on-campus television studios and produce the games themselves. Also a participant in the conference realignment merry-go-round, the ACC picked up Syracuse, the University of Pittsburgh, and the University of Notre Dame (for nonfootball competition only), while losing the University of Maryland to the Big Ten Conference in their second round of adding members. After that upheaval, the ACC required all members to sign a grant of media rights that lasts until 2027, effectively ending any further poaching of ACC teams to other conferences for the foreseeable future. The GOR requires if a school leaves for another Conference before 2027, all of their media rights are retained by the ACC, a powerful incentive to stay together (McMurphy, 2013).

The ACC Network is currently owned by ESPN, and the ACC receives an annual payment for the media content provided on the linear and streaming platforms. Their financial relationship is entirely based on the network's successful carriage on cable and satellite systems and digital channel providers, also known as vMVPDs (Murphy, 2020). As of October 2020, the ACC Network had yet to be picked up by Comcast, who serves 20 million homes in the ACC footprint (Hite, 2020). Justin Connolly, the ESPN's executive in charge of distribution, told The New York Times, "We don't really view it as 'Hey this is just a linear television channel.' Hundreds of events produced by the network will be presented digitally, and ESPN's distribution strategy has included streaming providers" (Draper, 2019).

The Explosion in College Sports Media Revenues

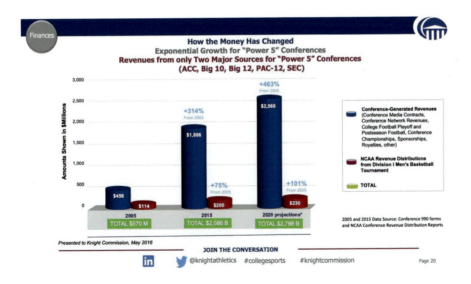

Source: Knight Commission on Intercollegiate Athletics

Tier One, Two, and Three Revenues Matter in College Sports

Beyond Conference networks, the Power 5 Conferences and powerful independents like the University of Notre Dame also have access to additional revenues from networks with larger audiences. A mid-season football game between Michigan and Ohio State would be elevated to ABC or Fox's national platform. Auburn and Alabama would be elevated to CBS's national platform (at least until the contract transfers to ESPN). Those networks are offered "first rights of refusal" for the premium games (often moving them to "primetime window"). These games are called Tier 1 events, and attract the most hype, the most advertising dollars and are generally available to the widest possible audience. They also pay the conferences more money (see chart "College Football Rights Deals by Media Network"). In recent years, conference championship games have added more revenue to the mix, and because of their significance to the College Football Playoff, often times are treated as Tier 1 properties (Colombo, 2020).

Tier 2 events are the remaining football (and, sometimes, men's basketball) inventory that will remain on a conference's own channel. Tier 3 events are all the other regular season inventory (soccer, lacrosse, softball, volleyball, ice hockey, etc.). These events are used to aggregate smaller amounts of viewers together to create attractive audiences for advertisers (Cotroneo, 2019).

Another revenue stream is the "sub rate" (subscribers) to a conference channel. The monthly cost of the subscription varies inside and outside of the conference footprint. The footprint is defined as the states that each university in the conference resides in. The channel costs more inside the footprint than outside the footprint.

This concept resides only in a cable system model; for satellite and streaming, one size and one price fits all (unless it is part of a bundle with other content). A good example is a streaming bundle of Disney+, Hulu, and ESPN+—separately, they would cost a subscriber $18 or more a month; bundled together, they are advertised at $13 a month.

Streaming services like ESPN+ aggregate a wider range of content; things like the Ivy League Network, Conference USA Network, and MMA sports are all available on streaming platforms. It provides access for a number of disparate sports properties who want their content delivered on the sports network and are willing to produce most of the content at their own expense.

College Football Rights Deals by Media Network ($mm)
*Indicates which conference is being broadcast
Data compiled from ESPN, Sports Business Journal and other sources

COLLEGE FOOTBALL TV RIGHTS	2017	2018	2019	2020	2021	2022	2023	2024	2025
ESPN/ABC									
*SEC	144	151	158	166	174	183	192	292	307
*Big Ten	160	168	176	185	194	204	205	216	226
*ACC	139	146	153	160	168	177	186	195	205
*Big 12	88	92	96	121	127	134	140	147	155
*Pac-12	96	101	106	111	116	122	128	137	144
*AAC	18	19	20	21	63	66	69	72	76
*Mid American	20	21	22	23	24	25	27	28	30
ESPN/ACC Totals	663	696	731	788	868	911	947	1087	1142
FOX									
*Big Ten	200	210	221	232	243	255	256	269	283
*Pac-12	96	101	106	111	116	122	128	137	144
*Big 12	79	83	87	91	96	101	106	111	117
*Big East	36	38	40	42	44	47	49	51	55
*Mountain West	-	-	-	20	21	22	23	24	26
FOX Totals	411	432	453	496	521	547	563	593	624
CBS									
*SEC	62	65	67	70	74	77	81	-	-
*Mountain West	17	18	19	20	21	22	23	24	26
CBS Totals	79	83	86	90	95	99	104	24	26

Streaming

This chapter has briefly touched on the importance of streaming as an extension of the technology shifts in media consumption. However, it is critical to understand how important streaming has become to emerging sports, niche sports, smaller college conference sports, and even high school and youth sports. The ability to attract a wider audience to your event or program is an obvious advantage for sport organizers; the challenge becomes in breaking even revenue wise, and ultimately using it as a revenue tool for your financial portfolios.

There are two forms of revenues for streaming events: a pay-per-view model and a subscription model. Both are widely accepted by fans, and due to technological advances, they make the payment and access processes nearly seamless. Live sports streaming can attract new fans, for sure; it can also attract new product partners and placement, new sponsors, and even new participants.

There are financial and logistical considerations involved in launching a live stream event. Cost of the equipment, selecting a video hosting platform, promotion of your event, monetization, test runs (and redundancies should the live stream crash!), and, most importantly, considering your viewer and the devices they will be using (phone, tablet, big screen TV, etc.; Krings, 2020).

League	Network	Skinny Bundle	Pure Play	Tech and E-Sports
MLB.tv	B/R Live	DirectTV NOW	DAZN	Amazon Prime Video
NBA	CBS Sports HQ	fuboTV	Flo Sports	Facebook
League Pass	ESPN+	hulu with Live TV	HotStar	Twitch
NFL Game Pass	Fox Soccer Match Pass	Sling TV	Stadium	Twitter
NHL.tv	NBC Sports Gold	SONY Playstation Vue		
UFC Fight Pass		YouTube TV		
WWE Network				

Adapted from Harry Stevens/Axios

Emergence of Legalized Betting and Media Consumption

One of the most dramatic changes in the media space has been the acceleration of legalized sports betting in the United States. More states have granted permits to open physical casinos, thus allowing for the explosion of online betting in a particular state. If you are physically located in a state that permits online gaming, all you need is your mobile device.

In the Commonwealth of Massachusetts alone, illegal sports betting is a $680 million business, primarily in offshore casinos, while U.S. gamblers made $196.2 billion in illegal bets nationwide, 47 times the size of the legal sports betting market (Glaun, 2019).

It couldn't come at a better time for the sports media industry as a whole, as generational shifts in viewers (skewing older fans—55+ in many cases, while younger fans aren't inclined to want to watch an entire 3 ½ football or baseball game [and some are even less inclined to pay the higher ticket prices]). Gambling on the final score (or who scores first) gins up the interest in the game, and knowing how "the line" is moving becomes important to winning money.

According to *The New York Times*, "Sports bettors watch about twice as much sports coverage as non-bettors do." Almost $5 billion was wagered in Las Vegas in 2017, before states began to legalize betting. Sports broadcasters, always looking to appeal to their audience, are investing in gambling graphics, pregame and postgame shows, and in game chyrons. Knowing that their audience is also watching a second screen, media companies are delivering content that dives behind the scenes, providing injury reports, weather analysis, and loads and loads of analytics to allow fans access to more information (Draper, 2018).

Late in 2020, William Hill Bookmakers announced a partnership with Monumental Sports in Washington, D.C. to build a sports book inside the Capitol One Arena Bix Office. The arena is home to the Washington Wizard NBA franchise, and the Washington Capitals NHL franchise. William Hill also announced that they were the exclusive sports betting partner of the Washington Mystics WNBA franchise and all of Monumental Sports properties (Rangappa, 2020).

© Koshiro K/Shutterstock.com

New Competitors Entering the Sports Inventory Space

Sports inventory will continue to be one of the hottest properties in the world, as fans cannot get enough sports. Sports finance professionals are keeping a very close eye on the FAANG+M (Facebook, Amazon, Apple, Google, Netflix, and Microsoft) companies for their emergence into this space. They have the largest amount of cash on hand, and all have proven to be disruptors in whatever space they enter.

Sportico reported in 2020, "Despite the nattering of digital futurists and other Wall Street nay-sayers, the legacy broadcasters have reason to believe that they will maintain a stranglehold over football's most prestigious time slots." The "legacy" broadcasters are CBS, NBC, and Fox, with ESPN holding down the Monday night slot as part of the ABC legacy. Each of these networks counts on the large audiences NFL games deliver to drive announcements and promos to their own programming. It is simply the biggest lead-in for any nonsports show on their network. NFL chief media and business officer Brian Rolapp threw some cold water on the FAANG fire. "Our entire model is about reaching as many people for as long as we can. We can reach 25 million people [on broadcast TV], and I have not seen a live event on the Internet that can serve 25 million concurrent users at a high quality" (Crupi, December 2020).

While the NFL model may continue broadcasting on traditional over the air networks for the foreseeable future, emerging and niche sports are thriving on some of the FAANG platforms (Facebook, Apple, Amazon, Netflix, and Google). One has to look no further than YouTube (a Google company) to see the success in sports. Microsoft has made its entry into the tech side by its prominent relationship with tablet technology on the football and soccer sidelines. Instagram (a part of Facebook) has become the platform of choice for many new sports looking to broaden their appeal. And Amazon has paid $200 million at the NFL to stream Thursday night football for Prime users through 2022 (and an occasional Saturday game on Twitch), hardly very much for a company that has a $1.6 trillion valuation (Crupi, August 2020).

Financial officers need to be aware of the speed in which media and technology are shifting the underpinnings of the industry. While Netflix and Amazon have yet to do more than put their big toe in the water, the "digital futurists" alluded to earlier are pretty convinced it will happen at some point.

CASE STUDY

The creation of the Big Ten Network, a television and broadband endeavor devoted to the 11 Universities that comprise the Big Ten Conference launched in August of 2007, immediately sent a ripple throughout higher education. Instead of receiving broadcast rights fees for the televising of selected football and basketball games, the presidents in the Conference decided to start their own broadcast venture. While conference television networks seem "normal" today, the vision of former Big Ten Conference Commissioner Jim Delany back in 2004–05 was prescient. This content was originally published in Forbes.com.

How Jim Delany's Media Intuition Changed the College Sports Ecosystem

Think back to the television landscape in 2004—regional sports networks were all the rage, most owned by Fox, Comcast, AT&T, while independent distributors like Raycom were buying and redistributing games. ABC, CBS, and NBC were all lopping off the best Big Ten games in football and men's basketball, leaving the remaining games for ESPN to pick up. There was a ton of inventory left on the table that Delany knew could be "monetized," if the right set of circumstances arose.

The Big Ten's agreement with ABC/ESPN was scheduled to expire in 2006, and network executives were already signaling that a future deal would not include an increase in revenues. Frustrated, he began to think about whether the Big Ten Conference could create its own "Channel"—sort of like its own regional sports network. The idea itself was not that far out of the box, but other factors were, especially the timing of other media rights deals expiring (including professional deals like the NFL, NBA, and the Olympics), which greatly impacts the amount of cash media companies can bring to the table at any given point.

Another major hurdle was distribution. The eight-state footprint that encompassed the Big Ten Conference in 2004 was a hodgepodge of cable and satellite systems—each would require negotiations that would place the channel on their systems. Add to that the "sub rate" (the rate subscribers would pay to access the channel), on a basic tier, it might cost only 10 cents, but be available to every household; on a sports tier, it might cost $4, but be purchased by fewer homes. Streaming technology was nowhere in the lexicon—every game needed to come to a fan's TV via a cable or satellite feed.

Delany had to solve another massive problem—who was going to pay for all of the startup costs? There were three models available that Delany asked the university presidents and chancellors to consider: a wholly owned conference entity (like the Pac 12 is today), a branded channel owned and subsidized by a media entity (SEC on CBS), or a partnership with a media company (preferably at 51% or greater so that the conference could control content and value-based decisions around advertising, adding new conference members, etc.).

By far, these were some (but not all) of the major decisions Delany and the council of presidents/chancellors had to make in the run-up to the creation of the Big Ten Network.

Leadership requires out-of-the-box thinking; take a look at some of the ways Delany creatively led the Big Ten Conference through a three-year evolution of building a network from scratch. I noticed the following in reviewing archival e-mails, memos, and directives from that time period.

- Delany was cognizant of the quarterly financial goals of each competitor in the media space—he knew when they need inventory, and when they needed to preserve cash by studying their financial reports.
- He was astute at playing the networks against each other—whether ABC/ESPN really believed he would pull off an owned conference network was one thing, but he was able to convince them he had the ability to do it.
- He knew exactly when the NFL, NBA, MLB, Olympics, and FIFA rights would expire and anticipated who might be bidding for them.
- He articulated clearly the value proposition that the Big Ten Conference brought to the table compared to the aforementioned entities. He made no mention or comparison to other collegiate properties; instead, he presented the conference to presidents and network executives as if the Big Ten Conference *deserved* to be in the mix with those properties.
- Building on this, he emphasized that the Big Ten Conference was simply *better*—better financials, larger alumni associations, more All-Americans, more National championships, better traditions, and broader-based sports programs.

He also presented the values of the Big Ten in a compelling way.

- The conference had a long and deep tradition of revenue sharing and an "all for one, and one for all" mentality. Delany often said "We'll compete like hell on Saturday against each other, and cheer each other on every other day of the week." There was little history of outward infighting, unlike many now defunct conferences. The Big Ten Conference was viewed as a stable enterprise.
- He kept in mind throughout the process what a valuable public relations tool a 24-hour-a-day/365-day-a-year channel could be—he called it "shopping the conference's identity across 8 (now more) states." The network was *designed* to be a public relations vehicle, not a media or journalistic effort. That belief was never more obvious than when the Sandusky scandal broke at Penn State—the network adequately covered the breaking news on head coach Joe Paterno's and former President Graham Spanier's dismissals (as well as the 2012 NCAA sanctions and fines) , but compared to ESPN and other outlets, it was low key and straight forward. Interestingly enough, Spanier was one of the few Big Ten presidents to take advantage of the platform, hosting his own show called "Expert Opinion" on current college sports issues. Delany never wanted the conference to lose control of the advertising and the editorial oversight—a point embraced by the presidents.

Certainly, the conference during Delany's tenure has not been without controversy; journalists have documented that 11 of the 14 institutions have been mired in scandals since 2010. Still, BTN never shied away from covering the scandals, with Dave Revsine leading the reporting nearly every time.

Finally, and from the earliest stages, Delany and the presidents/chancellors all agreed they wanted a 50/50 split on coverage of men's and women's sports. Any partner would have to agree to that, and if you think about it, that could have been a major sticking point. Women's sports (beyond basketball) have had no track record on linear television beyond small audiences. The same could be said about many men's sports. The trick was to find a partner who could aggregate those fans into demographic groups that could pool viewers. The early answer was to market to each fan base—Iowa fans to all Iowa sports, Minnesota fans to all Minnesota sports, and so on. Today, with the BTN+ app, more of the women's sports content appears on the digital side, and the linear channel on your cable or satellite system is stacked with football and men's basketball-based content.

Delany reflected on this in an interview with CBS Sports' Dennis Dodds, saying, "As much as anything, Fox [network partner] has allowed us to brand it in a way that is comfortable to us. It's the only network that I know of that made a commitment to men's and women's sports across the platform."

In July 2006, after the signing of all the contracts with Fox, and in the one-year run-up to the Big Ten Network's launch, Ohio State athletic director Gene Smith sent an e-mail to Karen Holbrook, then president of OSU, with this comment: "On another topic, the Big Ten ADs are aware you are on a small team dealing with Jim Delany's compensation. We hope he is recognized for this unbelievable deal that he ushered in that will benefit our institutions. What he has accomplished is truly amazing. He has no peer in our industry and is light years ahead of other commissioners. He is simply the best. I hope our conference can be generous and think beyond our normal restrictions."

Two weeks later, the presidents awarded Delany a $1.5 million recognition bonus and newly renegotiated contract that included a 16.7% increase in base salary, a $1 million annuity, and graduated retention incentives. Fast-forward to 2019, USA Today and others report that Delany's compensation has reached over $5.5 million and $20 million in bonuses.

When Jim Delany retired at the end of June 2020, the Big Ten Conference had had four commissioners prior to his arrival in 1989. One could argue persuasively that his impact will be felt for years to come—all you have to do is open the nearest video screen and watch (Weaver, 2020).

Sports Media References

Bode, K. (2013, February 15). *AT&T hits U-verse with new fees, rate hikes.* www.dslreports.com/shownews/ATT-Hits-UVerse-Users-With-New-Fees-Rate-Hikes-123160

Colombo, H. (2020, December 14). *How Ohio state playing in the big ten championship benefits the whole conference.* Columbus Business First. www.bizjournals.com/columbus/news/2020/12/14/big-ten-championship-game-ohio-state-revenue.html

Comcast. (n.d.). *Comcast timeline.* https://corporate.comcast.com/press/timeline

Cotroneo, N. (2019, August). *In depth: A journey from the creation of conference networks until now.* The Osceola. https://theosceola.com/in-depth-a-journey-from-the-creation-of-conference-networks-to-now/

Crupi, A. (2020a, August 3). *FAANG NFL offensive is toothless as legacy partners rally for one last big score.* Sportico.com. www.sportico.com/business/media/2020/faang-wont-sink-its-teeth-into-nfl-1234610664/#!

Crupi, A. (2020b, December 18). *NFL retains its TV crown as sports prevail over politics and entertainment.* www.sportico.com/business/media/2020/2020-tv-ratings-nfl-1234619216/

Draper, K. (2018, May 15). *How betting will change the sports media business.* Nytimes.com. www.nytimes.com/2018/05/15/sports/sports-betting.html

Draper, K. (2019, August 22). New cable network for ACC heightens arms race in College Sports. Nytimes.com. www.nytimes.com/2019/08/22/sports/ncaafootball/acc-network-espn.html

FCC. (n.d.). *Telecommunications Act of 1996.* www.fcc.gov/general/telecommunications-act-1996

Feldman, J. (2020, December 31). *In 2020, TV became the second screen (and other tech and media trends that aren't going away.* www.sportico.com/business/media/2020/televised-sports-changed-2020-tech-media-trends-1234619330/

Gall, B. (2012, July 2). *The history of Pac-12 conference realignment. Athlon Sports.* https://athlonsports.com/college-football/history-pac-12-conference-realignment

Glaun, D. (2019, January 30). *Illegal sports betting is already big business in Massachusetts, where residents spent estimated $680 million on offshore gambling.* Masslive.com. www.masslive.com/news/2018/05/illegal_sports_betting_already.html

Gullifor, P. F. (2001). *The fighting Irish on the air: The history of Notre Dame football broadcasting.* Taylor Trade Publishing.

Harris, E. (1997, June 24). Fox putting together national sports net-changes ahead for sports channel. *Chicago Sun-Times.* https://web.archive.org/web/20150924194306/http://www.highbeam.com/doc/1P2-4383098.html

Hite, P. (2020, October 29). *More than a year after its debut, the ACC Network still not in Comcast's lineup.* NewsLeader.com. www.newsleader.com/story/sports/2020/10/29/acc-network-comcast-virginia-virginia-tech/3742878001/

International Trade Administration. (n.d.). *Germany-country commercial guide; data privacy and protection.* www.trade.gov/knowledge-product/germany-data-privacy-and-protection

Krings, E. (2020, September 10). How to live stream sports: Making your virtual sports event a success. www.dacast.com/blog/live-sports-streaming/

Liptak, A. (2017, February 5). *The super owl live-streams crashed for both comcast and fox sports*. www.theverge.com/2017/2/5/14518386/super-bowl-2017-live-stream-down-crash-comcast-fox-sports

McCabe, D. (2016, February 7). *Bill Clinton's telecom law: Twenty years later*. The Hill. https://thehill.com/policy/technology/268459-bill-clintons-telecom-law-twenty-years-later

McMurphy, B. (2013, April 22). *Media Deal OK'd to Solidify Acc*. ESPN.com. www.espn.com/college-football/story/_/id/9200081/acc-media-rights-deal-lock-schools-okd-presidents

Murphy, T. (2020). Personal conversations about media rights at ESPN. *Tom Murphy is the former Senior Vice President for Finance at ESPN.*

Ozanian, M. (2020, June 8). *Here's the college football TV money at stake for each conference and network*. Forbes.com. www.forbes.com/sites/mikeozanian/2020/06/08/heres-the-college-football-tv-money-at-stake-for-each-conference-and-network/?sh=554c09b77dc9

Rangappa, A. (2020, August 3). *William Hill officially opens first-ever sports book within a U.S. Sports complex at capital one arena in Washington, D.C.* https://monumentalsports.com/news/

Schwabel, D. (2012, September 13). *How Bill Rasmussen started ESPN and his entrepreneurship advice*. www.forbes.com/sites/danschawbel/2012/09/13/how-bill-rasmussen-started-espn-and-his-entrepreneurship-advice/?sh=386b66b5714e

Smith, R. A. (2001). *Play-by-play: Radio, television and college sports*. The Johns Hopkins University Press.

Steinberg, D. (2017, August 23). CSN mid-Atlantic re-branding as NBC Sports Washington. *Washington Post*. www.washingtonpost.com/news/dc-sports-bog/wp/2017/08/23/csn-mid-atlantic-is-rebranding-as-nbc-sports-washington/

Thorp, E. (2019, November 25). *How much does local TV advertising cost?* https://liftintent.com/blog/how-much-does-local-tv-advertising-cost/#:~:text=Local%20TV%20commercial%20advertising%20costs,time%2C%20day%2C%20and%20location

Weaver, K. (2009). *The launch of the Big Ten Network: How 11 universities created their own television network and changed the landscape of college sports*. Unpublished dissertation. https://repository.upenn.edu/dissertations/AAI3354331/

Weaver, K. (2020, January 2). *How Jim Delany's media intuition changed the college sports ecosystem*. Forbes.com. www.forbes.com/sites/karenweaver/2020/01/06/how-jim-delanys-media-intuition--changed-the-college-sports-ecosystem/?sh=5a3d1fb26b59

Weisband, B. (2014). *A brief history of the Southeastern Conference*. www.saturdaydownsouth.com/sec-football/brief-history-southeastern-conference/

Web Links

Sportico.com

sportingnews.com

skysports.com

sbnation.com

secsports.com

news.22bet.com/news

Espn.com

Bloomberg.com

SI.com

USAToday.com/sports

Sports.Yahoo.com

CBSSports.com

www.forbes.com/sportsmoney

FoxSports.com

BTN.com

Fansided.com

TheACC.com

Pac-12.com

Big12sports.com

TheAthletic.com

Yesnetwork.com

MLB.com./network

NHL.com/info/network

NBA.tv

NBCOlympics.com

CHAPTER 3

Business of College Sports

Scott Hirko and Karen Weaver

LEARNING OBJECTIVES

- To learn about the basic structures of college sports, including how the NCAA breaks different institutions into divisions.
- To learn about NCAA Division I Football Bowl Subdivision Conference (FBS), by far the most athletically prestigious subdivision in America.
- To understand the basic myths of how revenues are earned and spent in Division I.
- To take a deeper dive into the revenue streams of FBS football and March Madness, the NCAA Division I Men's Basketball Tournament, and how important they are to the Autonomous 5 conferences and the rest of college sports.
- To discover how conference revenues are received and distributed inside the conference structure.
- To learn more about the impact of rising coaches' salaries as compared to other higher education professionals.

College athletic competition began in 1852 in New Hampshire, when Harvard College and Yale College were invited to row against one another to determine who was the "best." As *The New York Times* wrote, "In order to encourage rail travel to the resort area of Lake Winnipesaukee, New Hampshire, the Boston, Concord, and Montreal Railroad provided the college crews with an all-expense-paid, two-week vacation in return for participating in the resort's regatta. The company promoted the event with bright red fliers and advertisements of excursion train schedules" (Kennedy, 2001).

There was money flowing into college sports in 1852, and there is even more money in college sports today. In the last 170 years, college sports at the highest levels has found itself to be entre-

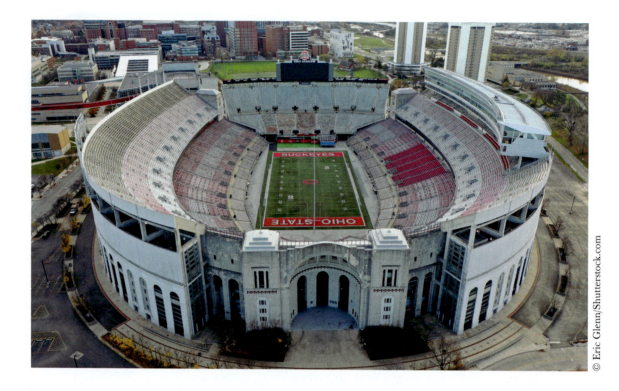

preneurial and market smart, able to leverage fan passion and alumni pride into millions of dollars that (partially) offer financial support to the rest of the athletics department.

Colleges have created numerous revenue streams to support the increasingly large department budgets (some now over $200 million). A partial list of revenue streams include:

- Media revenues;
- Ticket sales;
- Sponsorships (for nearly every event and activity);
- Fundraising (annual and capital); and
- Multimedia rights (digital and social, advertising partnerships).

This chapter will help students understand the enormously complex financial systems of inter-collegiate athletics. There is no system like it in the world, as it operates primarily as a part of a nonprofit, tax-exempt entity (higher education). Colleges do not pay business taxes like professional leagues do (sometimes up to 40% of gross revenues). This is a huge advantage for college athletics.

A second significant advantage in college sports has been its historical unwillingness to pay their labor force, the athletes. While athletes in some sports receive full tuition, fees, room, board, books, and "cost of attendance" dollars (which includes other costs such as transportation, computers, and supplies), they are not permitted under "amateurism" rules to receive a paycheck, or compete for salaries in the open market place, as their coaches do.

These two factors shape how athletics spends its money and the priorities each institution sets for itself. Without question, the biggest "bang for your buck" comes from two places—either a magical run through the NCAA Division I men's basketball tournament or, if you have a football program, making massive investments in coaches, facilities, and recruiting to try to knock off the established powerhouses like Alabama, Ohio State, or Clemson, and compete in the College Football Playoff.

If you choose to swim in this lane, the demand for revenues is daunting. Most schools in Division I can't keep up and come to rely on their university's budget to bail them out. All have minimum sport offerings required (in Division I, it's 16 sports), Title IX requirements for equity for both men and women, and debt service on facilities.

All that is changing. In the Summer of 2021, two major events happened. First, the Supreme Court heard the case NCAA v Alston, and ruled 9-0 against the NCAA. They ruled that the NCAA's by-laws were in violation of antitrust laws in restraining schools' ability to provide additional educational benefits to Division I FBS athletes in football, men's and women's basketball. Effective immediately, schools and conferences can determine the extent of educational benefits they want to provide, including paying for graduate and professional school (medical, law) educations (McCann, 2021).

Secondly, athletes are now permitted across all Divisions to monetize their publicity rights (names, images and likenesses) with third parties. They are permitted to strike deals with any vendor; the issue is whether there will be restrictions placed on athletes by their own institutions. It is an area fraught with both possibility and chaos (Bender, 2021).

One of the challenges in learning about Division I finances is the stark divide between finding and accessing department spending data. If a university is public, it is generally easier to get current data. But if a university is a private school, it does not have to comply with FOIA (Freedom of Information Act) requests. The data presented in this chapter are from public universities. Other than the Federal Government's Equity in Athletics Database, this is the only insight we have into how college athletics departments make and spend their money.

First principle—everything in major, Division I college sports revolves around football. Conference affiliation, what division you are in, even how your alumni and potential students view whether you are a "real" school, all depend on the investment and success you have in football. Knowing that, let's take a look at how the NCAA organization works.

Financial decisions in college athletics programs involve "fixed costs" and "variable costs." For instance, scholarships are a *fixed* cost, because athletics departments do not set the price of tuition and fees (which is the cost of a scholarship determined by the university each year)—so, if offering a scholarship at any athletics department, athletics must pay it but in turn require conditions of each athlete (such as practice, eligibility, travel, and following rules) to receive that scholarship. Alternatively, coaches' and administrators' salaries are *variable* costs, because administrators in charge of hiring can make decisions on hiring a staff member based on their belief of the value of that staff member relative to other expenses.

For example, if a student is on a full scholarship, an athletics department would be required to pay a $40,000 scholarship for a student to participate in volleyball because that is the cost to attend the school (*fixed cost*). However, an athletics department is not required to pay a head football coach $3 million to coach the football team (*variable cost*).

Governance Structures—An Overview

College sports are considered "amateur," meaning they are different than professional sports because the student participants are not paid directly for their athletic performance (NCAA Amateurism principle). In college sports, sports leagues include higher education institutions who join a membership organization (association) that align with their values, aspirations, and finances. The membership organization

© Jonathan Weiss/Shutterstock.com

includes institutional members, as well as subunits called conferences, which have institutional members whose teams compete against each other in regular season competition; this could be an all-sports conference (such as the Big Ten conference), or a single-sport conference (such as the Western Water Polo Conference for Women). The conference champion receives an automatic qualification to the NCAA tournament for all sports except Division I FBS football.

The characteristics of each division are unique to the institutions that are part of each division (Table 1). Much of this chapter will focus on the NCAA because of its dominant stature to sports in American higher education.

TABLE 1: Significant different characteristics of NCAA Divisions I, II, and III

National Collegiate Athletic Association (NCAA) membership		
Division I	**Division II**	**Division III**
Separated into three subdivisions based on football competitiveness: FBS, FCS, and NF	All institutional member teams compete equally	All institutional member teams compete equally
354 institutional members 29 NF, 10 FBS, and 13 FCS	319 institutional members; 23 conferences	449 institutional members; 70 conferences
*Athletes: 182,681	*Athletes: 122,722	*Athletes: 193,814
Annual fees: $1,800 institutional fee; $900 conference fee	Fees: $900 institutional fee; $450 conference fee	Fees: $2,000 institutional fee; $1,000 conference fee
To be a member: must have at least same number of sport teams than male: 16 FBS, 14 FCS, and 13 NF	To be a member: sponsored by another member; elected by two-thirds of Division 2 Membership Committee	To be a member: elected by vote of Division 3 Membership Committee
Meet full/partial scholarship requirements	Meet less/partial scholarship requirements	No athletic scholarships

Sources: NCAA 2019–2020 Division I Manual, NCAA 2019–2020 Division II Manual, NCAA 2019–2020 Division III Manual; *NCAA Sports Sponsorship and Participation Rates Report 1981–1982 to 2018–2019.

Other college athletics associations in the United States include the National Association for Intercollegiate Athletics (NAIA), the National Junior College Athletics Association (NJCAA), the California Community College Athletic Association (CCCAA), the United States College Athletics Association (USCAA), and the Northwest Athletic Conference (NWAC). In 2019, the NAIA governed 21 athletics conferences, and over 77,000 college athletes in the same level of competition across the association, and provided minimal athletics scholarships; the National Junior College Athletics Association (NJCAA) oversaw three divisions and limited scholarship levels helping more than 59,000 students in 510 schools; and the CCCAA provided sport leadership for 26,000 students in 108 schools (NCAA, 2018a).

To be an institutional member of a national sport organization, each institution pays an annual fee to the organization. The member school may also pay a fee to join a conference organization, unless it decides to participate independently, outside a conference. In return, each institutional member receives the opportunity to discuss and impact rules and regulations of each sport, the finances (revenues and expenses), and how the organization operates.

College students who play sports are often recruited by colleges from high schools to play a sport (or sports) for their college. In the most competitive divisions of college sports (NCAA Divisions I and

II), as well as in the NAIA, students may receive compensation from an institution in the form of a "scholarship" to play sports in exchange for their athletic participation representing an institution. Any student receiving an athletic scholarship must follow certain rules and fulfil expectations from the institution, its athletic conference, and the national association to maintain their commitment to education, and to ensure that one institution does not have an athletic advantage over another.

Membership organizations operate with their institutional members, and in many cases, with sub-organizations, also known as athletic conferences, which pool members together for competition based on many principles, including public or private status, academic expectations, religious affiliation, institutional size, geography, finances, and competitive considerations. Several institutions decide not to be a member in a certain sport, and prefer to play independently: these "independents" in the sport of Division I FBS football include Notre Dame University, Brigham Young University, and the U.S. Naval Academy (Navy), among others.

Revenue Distribution

This chapter focuses its discussion on the NCAA Division I FBS because it is by far the most significant financially as well as the most athletically prestigious. Within FBS, this chapter investigates two groups of institutions based on their conference affiliations because of the significant differences in business models, differences primarily based on football, and the structural allowances given to certain schools to make decisions within the NCAA's operating structure (Knight Commission, 2020a). Those given special allowances to decide on areas of finances and recruiting that other NCAA members do not have are the Autonomous 5 conferences or, "Power 5" (Table 2). The other group is referred to as the "Group of 5" conferences.

TABLE 2: 2020 Membership in NCAA Division I FBS Power 5 and Group of 5 Conferences

Autonomous 5 (aka "Power 5") Conferences	Group of 5 Conferences
Atlantic Coast (ACC)	American Athletic (AAC)
Big Twelve (Big 12)	Conference USA (C-USA)
Big Ten (Big 10)	Mid-American (MAC)
Pacific 12 (Pac 12)	Mountain West (MWC)
Southeastern (SEC)	Sun Belt Conference
Notre Dame University	Other football independents: U.S. Military Academy (Army), Brigham Young University, Liberty University, New Mexico State University, University of Connecticut, University of Massachusetts—Amherst

1. NCAA Revenue Distribution

With more than 1,100 member organizations, it is common to think the NCAA generates multiple billions of dollars of revenue through the many championships it hosts. But that is only partially true. The NCAA, as a membership organization, creates rules and regulations to try to create a level playing field among the different institutions. However, the institutions, and their affiliations with athletics conferences, create vastly more revenue than the NCAA. One of the NCAA's primary duties is to hire staff to enforce rules so that one institution does not have an unfair advantage over another (such as paying an athlete to attend one school instead of another).

© Al Sermeno Photography/Shutterstock.com

Here are some common myths.

Myth #1: The NCAA controls all the revenue from college sports.

Except for championship competition, revenue from all athletics teams is controlled by individual schools, and not the NCAA. For instance, in 2018, the Michigan State University (MSU) women's volleyball team generated $75,274 in ticket sales. Similarly, the University of California-Davis (UCD) women's volleyball team generated $7,525 in ticket sales. That same year, the MSU football team generated $28,213,375 in ticket sales. And the UCD football team generated $278,341 in ticket sales. In each case, ticket sale revenue from volleyball and football went directly to their athletics department (MSU, 2019; UC Davis, 2019), and not the NCAA.

Myth #2: The NCAA receives money from the College Football Playoff.

The College Football Playoff (CFP) is a private, nonprofit organization. The NCAA is also a private nonprofit. But neither share money with each other: they are two separate organizations. The CFP directs a football national championship, earns and distributes revenue, and spends money for several championship football games in major NCAA Division I FBS college football. The NCAA directs national championships in every sport agreed upon by its members for every Division, including the NCAA Division I "March Madness" Men's Basketball Tournament, with one exception: the championship of Division I FBS football (directed by the CFP). Thus, the $462,433,107 distributed by the CFP in the 2018–2019 football season was shared directly with schools or their athletics conferences, and not shared with the NCAA (NCAA, 2018c).

Myth #3: The money from "March Madness" Division I Men's Basketball Tournament is greater than college football revenue.

As was stated earlier, football is king in the United States, no matter the financial consideration. College athletics generated $20.1 billion in revenue in 2019 from the NCAA, NAIA, NCJAA, and others (EADA, 2019). And of the more than 2,750 colleges offering sports in the United States, an astonishing $3.9 billion of that revenue (19.5%) came from the sport of football at just 52 public institutions in Division I FBS. These 52 institutions are members of the most prestigiously competitive conferences, the Power 5 (Berkowitz, 2020). For instance, the Michigan State versus Michigan or Alabama versus Auburn weekend football rivalries top the financial mountain of college sports, and each contest at 75,000+ seat stadiums earns millions of dollars in profit for each school from ticket sales, conference TV agreements, and donations. College basketball in the regular season has smaller arenas (ergo less ticket sales) and earn less revenue from the media: while the money is significant, it is far less than football. Regardless, for the regular season games of football, basketball, wrestling, soccer, and all other sports: none of that money is shared with the NCAA. The NCAA only earns money from its championships (not the CFP), membership fees, and some sponsorships.

Financially, the 52 public FBS schools earned $3.9 billion in revenues in 2019. This is more than four times as much compared to the $868 million earned from the Division I men's basketball tournament (NCAA, 202). Basketball revenue was shared among 354 member Division I schools; the remaining amount was shared with NCAA's Divisions II and III.

In other words, on average, the following revenues were distributed in 2019.
- $75 million from football revenues was distributed to each of the 52 public Power Five members,
- $2.54 million from the March Madness basketball tournament was distributed to each of the 354 Division I public and private members (including the 52 Power Five members) (with some leftover funds toward championships for Divisions II and III).

2. Conference Revenue Distribution: Robin Hood or Sheriff of Nottingham?

The foregoing demonstrates the staggering differences between schools that are successful in football, and the schools that do not have football, but offer basketball as their primary sport (known as "basketball centric" schools). The vast amounts of revenue earned by the NCAA in Division I are not shared equally. Conferences earn revenue and distribute it to their members based on conference agreements. For instance, revenues earned by the Big Ten Network are shared equally among 14 members. Other conferences may have agreements with their member schools to reward individual institutions for postseason competition revenues differently than those who do not compete in postseason. For instance, the Big Twelve conference allows the University of Texas at Austin to keep its revenue from its own television network (the Longhorn Network), and not share with the rest of the Big 12. Conferences make the final determination as to how revenues are distributed from March Madness, football bowl game revenue (including the CFP), conference championships, and other types of media agreements.

NCAA revenue provided to conferences includes postseason ticket sales, sponsorships, and media coverage from all national championship competitions except football: this includes the men's and women's Division I basketball tournaments, the College World Series, the men's ice hockey Frozen Four championship, and all other championships.

$642 million was earned and shared by postseason football among all Division I football schools (some Division I schools do not have football, also known as "NF"), while $591 million was earned and shared by all Division I basketball schools (all Division I schools have men's and women's basketball; Figure 1).

FIGURE 1: Revenue Distribution to NCAA Division I from Postseason Football and Men's Basketball, 2019.

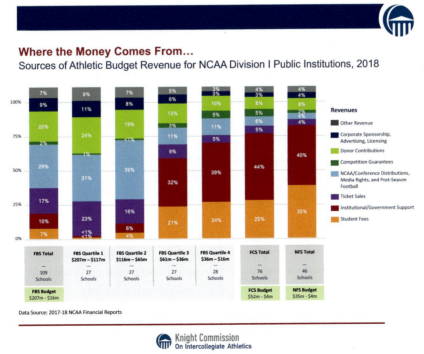

Source: Knight Commission on Intercollegiate Athletics

CHAPTER 3: Business of College Sports

45

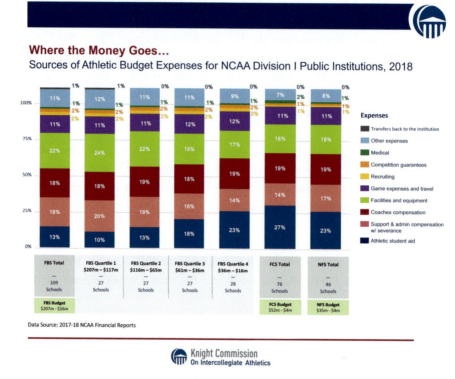

Where the Money Goes...
Sources of Athletic Budget Expenses for NCAA Division I Public Institutions, 2018

Data Source: 2017-18 NCAA Financial Reports

Knight Commission
On Intercollegiate Athletics

Source: Knight Commission on Intercollegiate Athletics

3. Other Institutional Revenue Sources

Ticket sales are an important part of the revenue stream, but under increasing pressures. Arenas built to seat 19,000 fans place pressure on the athletic department to sell out every home game. Athletic departments have responded by either growing their internal teams (adding more costs with salary and benefits), or outsourcing their ticketing (and multimedia deals) to a third-party company (such as Learfield IMG College) or secondary market (such as StubHub) that will guarantee them an annual revenue stream (Lawrence, 2019).

In many markets, the ticket prices have risen close to their maximum price point, limiting the options for department budgets to expand this category. Premium seating and seat licenses have helped get departments over the hump by requiring an additional commitment to secure the best seats in a preferred location. Suites are also added into existing facilities to try to drive more revenues, but incurring additional construction and staffing costs.

A substantial number of Division I institutions are dependent upon student fees to support their programming. Some mid to low major schools charge every student as much as $2,000 per semester for athletics, money that goes directly to the department (Figure 2). Recently, students, sensitive to the rising costs of their education, have started asking questions and trying to opt out of this mandatory fee, claiming they get little to no benefit from the activity (Weaver, 2020).

FIGURE 2: NCAA Division I FBS Power 5 and Group of 5 Revenue Sources for Public Institutions, 2018

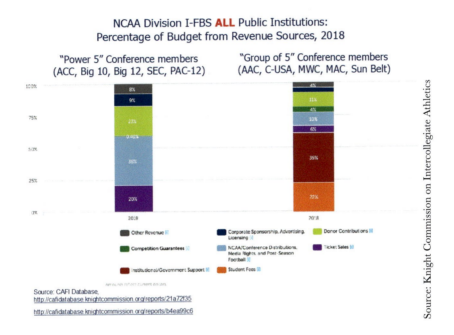

Competition guarantees and donor support are additional forms of revenue that is crucial to funding a non–Power 5 athletics program. One institution will pay another to compete in athletics, typically in football or men's basketball. Institutions from the Power 5 are willing to pay millions of dollars to have their athletics team compete against lesser competition (from the Group of 5 or Division I FCS). In fall 2018, Michigan State University paid Utah State University (USU) $1.4 million for the USU football team to travel to East Lansing, Michigan, with MSU winning, 38-31.

A famous case of a "guarantee game" gone awry occurred when then-FCS member Appalachian State University was paid $400,000 to play FBS's University of Michigan in football in 2007, with Michigan losing at home, 34-32; it was supposed to be an easy win (Fox Sports, 2012).

Competition guarantees totaled:
- $139.97 million in FBS,
- $78.4 million earned by Group of 5 institutions,
- $61.5 million earned by Power 5 institutions,
- $63.18 million earned by FCS institutions,
- $16.0 million for Division I schools without football (CAFI Database, 2020).

The NCAA's main revenue source is its Division I Men's Basketball Tournament, also known as "March Madness," which generated nearly $900 million in revenue as of 2018. For the most part, the NCAA distributes this revenue to conferences, and not directly to each institution. What each conference earns is based upon a variety of factors that have historically emphasized athletics participation and athletics success in men's basketball (https://ncaaorg.s3.amazonaws.com/ncaa/finance/d1/2019D1Fin_RevenueDistributionPlan.pdf).

Where Does the NCAA Money Go?

Athletic departments are consistent with one thing—they spend everything they take in, and frequently, they spend more. When COVID-19 pandemic led to cancellation of athletics contests and tournaments, it highlighted how few athletic departments had emergency or rainy day funds available. In a $150 million budget, it seems irresponsible to not have 5% or more set aside for emergencies. Financial officers are learning a valuable lesson coming out of the pandemic—expect the best, but plan for the worst. One must understand the finances to determine how to consistently drive success for an athletics program.

Revenue is given back to athletics conferences based on criteria that include money sent to schools based on:
- Opportunities provided to students through athletic scholarships and number of teams;
- Additional revenue to disadvantaged students (receiving Pell Grants);
- Special assistance for other benefits—such as limited catastrophic injury insurance (for instance, a neck injury paralyzing a volleyball player); or
- Travel home (for holidays, or death of a family member; NCAA, 2019e).

One area of significant distribution is based on success in the March Madness tournament, with institutions winning increasingly amounts of money based on their success in the tourney, called "units" (shown in Figure 4 as the "Basketball Fund"). As of 2020, this amount was worth roughly $300,000 per game played in the tournament, for six successive years. It is also a rolling average, which eliminates the pressure on one athlete to win one game in one tournament. This incentive was known as the "Million Dollar Free Throw," describing a player who made a last-second basket in a conference tournament to advance its basketball team into the national tournament. Simply put, it is not a good look for a team to ask a college basketball player to assume this kind of pressure (Figure 3).

Source: Knight Commission on Intercollegiate Athletics

FIGURE 3: Financial Overview to Explain Impact of CFP Revenue Growth

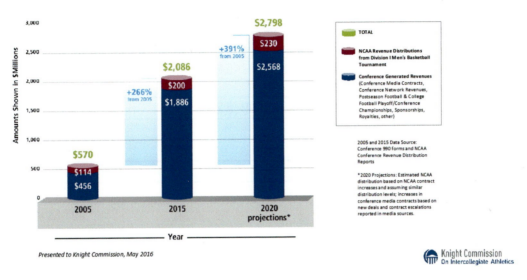

In 2020, Division I institutions will receive NEW revenues based on the academic success of all athletics teams (including nonbasketball teams such as football, baseball, swimming, or field hockey). Any new monies shared are based on academic success. The new revenue is projected to be an additional $55,000 per institution in 2020, and rising to $460,000 by 2025 (NCAA, 2018b).

Finances in NCAA Divisions II and III

In NCAA Divisions II and III, and other smaller athletics associations, the revenues are less dependent on external dollars generated by athletics departments, and are more dependent on financial support from the institution and its students. For instance, in Division II, Grand Valley State University (Michigan) reported in 2014–2015 a total of $15.6 million in expenses, and $15.9 million in revenues (Table 3). It could be assumed that GVSU earned more money than it spent. Upon review of the budget, it shows the athletics department's revenue was subsidized by 76.8% (or $12.2 million) by institutional fees (from the general fund, including student tuition dollars), as well as other institutional support to help pay for debt service, utilities, security, and facilities management.

TABLE 3: Grand Valley State University Athletics Revenue and Expense Totals in Academic Year 2014–2015

Category	Revenue (% of total)	Expense (% of total)
Ticket Sales	$343,779 (2.2%)	
Institutional Support	$9,835,407 (61.9%)	
Indirect Institutional Support	$2,363,400 (14.9%)	$1,783,092 (11.2%)
NCAA Distributions	$373,273 (2.3%)	
Fundraising: Royalties, Licensing, Sponsorships	$891,241 (5.6%)	$883,992 (5.6%)
Sports Camp Revenues/Expenses	$827,190 (5.2%)	$409,589 (2.6%)
Scholarships (athletics student aid)		$3,848,772 (24.2%)
Coaching salaries and bonuses		$2,934,085 (18.5%)
Athletics staff salaries and bonuses		$1,414,921 (8.9%)
Team travel		$1,117,977 (7.0%)
Sports Equipment/supplies		$580,597 (3.7%)
Game Expenses		$606,572 (3.8%)
Debt Service		$580,308 (3.6%)
TOTALS	$15,899,541	$15,639,460

* NOTE: There were no student fees for athletics charged to GVSU students in 2014–2015. Instead, much of this funding was taken from the general fund of institutional support, which includes tuition.

Source: MLive.com (2015). Grand Valley State University (2019)

NAIA, NJCAA Revenue Distribution

The NAIA, which includes roughly 50,000 college athlete participants at 250 institutions, reports a net return on athletics spending of $3.9 million per institution. The median total expense budget of an NAIA institutions is $3.2 million, with roughly 45% ($1.4 million) devoted to scholarship costs; however, its data do not present net revenues generated by athletics (NAIA, 2020).

Facility Costs

Many sports fans think the university exclusively pays to build and maintain athletic facilities. For decades, though, institutions have turned to state legislatures, debt markets, alumni, students, and corporations to fund increasingly expensive facilities.

© Gian Lorenzo Ferretti/Shutterstock.com

There are three things to consider when looking at building an athletic facility.
1. Who will use the facility?
2. What is the life expectancy of the facility?
3. How will you pay for the facility?

Athletic directors' contract with architects to design and provide cost estimates for a new facility, while construction companies are hired to repair and renovate facilities. Both must provide accurate cost estimates so that financial officers can figure out the debt service plan. Nearly every facility on campus is either a) university owned, operated, maintained or b) a public–private partnership (more and more campus recreational facilities are being built as P3 entities or c) a privately owned facility leased to the university.

Because athletic departments expect their facilities to be available to coaches and players 24 hours a day 7 days a week, athletic departments typically elect to build and finance these projects with their own resources. Debt service on each project is annualized into one or two payments in a fiscal year. If necessary, universities will offer short-term loans (with interest) to the athletic department to allow the project to begin.

Here is how the construction manager approached building and upgrading the University of Minnesota's football stadium, built in 2009, the first one in the Big Ten Conference since 1960:

> "Home to the Golden Gopher Football team, the open-air stadium features a horse-shoe-shaped bowl, 50,000 seats, 36 private suites, 750 loge seats, 300 indoor club seats, 1,250 outdoor club seats, and a 30,000 square foot indoor club. Located in the heart of the University's bustling athletics campus, Mortenson worked safely amidst pedestrians, bicycles and bus traffic. Completed six weeks ahead of schedule, this Big 10 Conference

stadium earned the first LEED Silver Certification by the US Green Building Council for a collegiate or professional football facility.

With a drive to maximize fan experience, Mortenson also installed the stadium's technology infrastructure. This included a distributed antenna system (DAS), broadcast cabling, satellite master antenna television (SMATV), and surveillance and security systems. Specialized electrical power distribution, lightning protection, and low voltage scopes were self-performed as well.

In 2013, the University selected Mortenson upgrade TCF Bank Stadium to meet NFL regulations, which allowed the Minnesota Vikings to play two seasons here during construction U.S. Bank Stadium." (Mortenson, n.d.)

The Minnesota Stadium project anticipated revenues to pay for the construction of the stadium from multiple sources:
- Private contributions
- Legal claims and settlements from environment remediation
- Stadium-drive revenues (including a ticket surcharge)
- Student fees
- Parking and transportation services (University of Minnesota, 2003)
- Rental fees for outside groups

In the last 20 years, Minnesota has gone on a building spree, adding a new football stadium, outdoor track complex, a second ice hockey arena/indoor tennis complex, a new baseball stadium, upgraded parking and traffic flow, and an Athlete Village complex. Each of these facilities required debt financing, leading to some of the severe financial problems of an estimated $75 million deficit the athletic department faced during 2020 and beyond from the COVID-19 pandemic (Greder, 2020; Weaver & Tegtmeyer, 2018).

Other Division I programs are faced with same choices as Minnesota—repair or replace aging facilities, along with making them ready for both 21st century recruiting and technology. Fan engagement is a huge factor in attracting a crowd to the game; upgraded amenities are crucial, especially in a city competing with professional football fans (i.e., Minnesota Vikings).

Financial Forecasting in Division I Athletics

You may hear the term the "athletics arms race" in describing college sports. Everything from facilities (mentioned earlier) to coaches' salaries, to athlete-only villages, to 24 hour nutrition stations are part of creating separation between your program and your competitors. What's unique about college sports is that your competition is often members of your conference. So, how do you compare yourself financially?

Until 2016, it was hard for conference members to compare financial data with others, especially if their peers were private institutions. The NCAA created the Institutional Performance Program (IPP), a dashboard that allows key members of a campus' senior leadership teams, boards of trustees and selected athletic department personnel, to study key metrics in how their peers are spending money in various sports (Knight Commission on Intercollegiate Athletics 2020b). For more insights on the revenue and expenses of NCAA schools, visit https://www.ncaa.org/about/resources/research/finances-intercollegiate-athletics-database.

Media Contracts and Other Revenue Partnerships

Looking at the aforementioned link, you can see where the vast majority of revenues come from in college sports. Clearly, the overwhelming growth of media rights values, and consequently the amounts paid, has continued to be the foundation for many Power 5 athletics programs. This area is examined more deeply in the chapter on the business of sports media. Additional revenue streams come from post season opportunities (primarily in men's basketball, but occasionally from Bowl Games and the College Football Playoff), licensing agreements, investment income, ticket sales (single game and season packages, suite sales, etc.) and donations (annual and ongoing). The vast majority of these revenues are counted upon to fund the department from year to year.

Another revenue partnership lies in facility naming rights. Looking back at the University of Minnesota football stadium (mentioned earlier), the University worked diligently to identify a "naming rights partnership" for their new stadium. In the last 20+ years, this has become standard in both professional and college sports. The University signed a $35 million naming rights agreement for 26 years with TCF Bank supporting the construction of the new stadium. In 2020, TCF Bank's merged with Huntington Bank for $22 billion, leaving the future of the naming agreement in flux (Navera, 2020).

Tax Status and Liabilities

Intercollegiate athletics programs in the United States are exactly that: one program (like the biology department, or the power station, or residence hall administration) at any school of higher education. As such the vast majority of the 2,700+ higher education programs with athletics programs are public or private, and do not exist to earn a profit (very few are commercial, for-profit companies with athletics programs).

As non-profit organizations, higher education institutions (and athletics conferences) in the United States are required by law to submit a "990 form" with the Internal Revenue Service (IRS) (from Section 990 of the IRS tax code) to affirm their status and report basic revenue and expenses. Many not-for-profit institutions are considered public, such as Michigan State University or the University of California. Others, like Notre Dame University or the University of Indianapolis, are private institutions, and do not exist to earn a profit. The reasons for each to be public or private relate to their mission (for publics, as part of a government entity to improve public welfare through agriculture, research, etc., or for privates, to support religious or other important belief systems).

Salary Structures

The rise of college coaching salaries is of significant concern in the dialogue about big-time college athletics. Focusing on Division 1 athletics, and more particularly, Autonomous-5 FBS schools, the concern becomes more pronounced.

Coaches' salaries can't be capped. In 1999, assistant coaches in college football in Division I won a lawsuit against the NCAA's rule limiting the maximum compensation for coaches' salaries (*Law v. NCAA*, 1999), claiming it anticompetitive according to the Sherman Anti-Trust Act of 1896. The reason stated by the court was that coaches should have the opportunity to make more money on the open market. In other words, associations (e.g., the NCAA) cannot set coaches' salaries. An institution can decide on the amount for a coach to be paid, but not an association. It is illegal for an association to cap a maximum amount of salary for college coaches.

Because of the growth in media revenues (see Figure 4), it has led to the rise in salaries for football and basketball coaching staffs (and their support staffs). This is challenging in college sports because colleges want to pay for the best talent to coach athletes to win, similar to paying the best professor to educate future engineers or biologists. Coaching contracts are developed in a commercial marketplace environment to entice the most desired coaches to become employed at specific universities. The University of Michigan in 2017 offered Jim Harbaugh a $52.1 million contract over 7 years to include $7 million in annual salary, $4,000 for an "apparel allowance," two cars, a $150,000 bonus based on the academic performance of the football team, and a bonus of $125,000 for appearing in the Big Ten championship game (NewsDay, 2018).

COVID-19 led to greater scrutiny of the impact of coaches' salaries at the NCAA Division I level. Salaries for all coaches in all sports at public institutions in the FBS division make up $1.6 billion (18%) of athletics budgets. From 2009 to 2018, coaching salaries at public schools in FBS nearly doubled. Within that amount, over the same 10-year period, football coaches (head coaches and assistants) at public schools within the Power 5 conferences were recipients of a 122.3% increase in salaries and benefits up to $509.9 million in 2018 (CAFI Database, 2020).

Students should also note the escalation in athletic student aid in the FBS conferences. This is directly related to the relaxation of NCAA restrictions on "cost of attendance" monies, paid to the athlete above and beyond tuition, fees, room, board, and books. More change to the monies coming to college athletes begins in 2021, as the NCAA v Alston ruling from the Supreme Court will permit nearly $6,000 per athlete for academic awards, plus additional educational benefits.

FIGURE 4: Growth rates in coaching compensation and athletics student aid in NCAA Division I, 2009–2018.

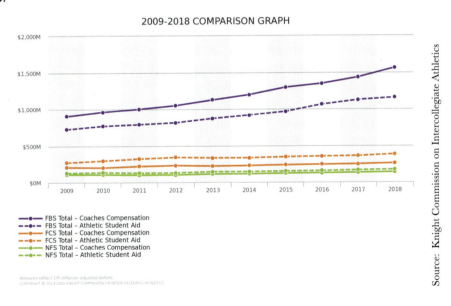

Other Expense Categories in College Sports

Many other expenses go into building an annual athletics budget. Expenses can include the following.
1. Insurance costs: There are several kinds of insurance that are required:

a. Athletic departments are required to pay 20% of the athlete's medical insurance claims if/ when they get injured.

b. Cancellation insurance: if a major event occurs in the future similar to COVID-19, athletic departments are seriously considering event cancellation insurance, which will allow them to recoup losses if tournaments are unable to be held.

2. Certain medical professionals are required to have malpractice and other kinds of legal protections in case they are sued.

3. Facility maintenance costs: Every week, facilities have work that needs to be done to keep the facility safe. A budget needs to be utilized to plan for normal wear and tear on facilities.

4. Professional certifications, development, and training: Many athletic department personnel are required to maintain certifications or participate in annual continuing education programs.

© Debby Wong/Shutterstock.com

5. Technology infrastructure and enhancement: This is one of the most challenging areas for budget officers. Every area and sport are inundated with technological opportunities and advancements; how to manage these costs is critical.

6. There is increasing pressures to add more mental health and social justice opportunities to all athletes, not just football and men's basketball, as well as training for coaches and staff in those areas as well.

7. The looming name, image, and likeness legislation will eventually require oversight, either by the NCAA, the states or the Federal government, potentially adding more spending on oversight and compliance.

In the Post–COVID-19 era, where is college athletics headed financially?

In late 2020, the Knight Commission on Intercollegiate Athletics recommended three major changes to allow for a reset in the incentives and motivations for big time college sports. They outlined what they believe will prioritize the education, health, safety and success of college athletes. They wrote,

- Create a new entity, completely independent of the NCAA and funded by the College Football Playoff revenues, to govern the sport of football in the Football Bowl Subdivision (FBS). The new governing entity would oversee all FBS football operations, including its national championship, and manage all issues related to FBS football athlete education, health, safety, revenue distribution, litigation, eligibility, and enforcement.
- The NCAA should govern and conduct national operations and championships under a reorganized governance system for all Division I sports, including football at the Football Championship Subdivision (FCS) level, but excluding what is now FBS football. This new system should establish equal voting representation for all Division I conferences. The NCAA Division I Men's Basketball Tournament should retain its current structure, open to all Division I schools. NCAA Division I should retain its current membership of institutions and conferences with athletics programs classified in the FBS for all sports except football, FCS programs including football, and Division I schools that do not offer football. Governance and oversight of football in NCAA Divisions II and III should remain unchanged.
- The NCAA and the new FBS football entity should adopt governing principles, such as those articulated by the Commission in this report, to maintain college athletics as a public trust, rooted in the mission of higher education. Those principles must prioritize college athletes' education, health, safety, and success in the operation of intercollegiate athletics. Regardless of the sport or governance entity, college presidents and chancellors should be responsible and accountable for the conduct of all intercollegiate athletics programs at their institutions.

Knight (2020c)

Others have made more radical proposals over the past 10 years, including pulling funding for all colleges from the Federal Government via the Higher Education Act of 1965, until athlete health and safety issues are standardized and addressed across all of Division I. The Knight Commission provided a summary of all of the recommendations for change offered by journalists, academics, practitioners, state legislators, and Congress over the past decade.

In 2020, Karen Weaver et al. provided to the Knight Commission on Intercollegiate Athletics a *Literature Review of Division I Athletics Reform*. The following is the summary of the issues and recommendations for Division I to address, drawn from over 100 scholars and journalists, primarily with a finance and governance focus.

> All agree the College Football Playoff monies should come under the NCAA umbrella; most agree that those monies should *not* be redirected to coaches' salary increases, or financing debt on athletic villages. Instead, they should be redirected to some of the *Duty of Care* ideas discussed below, including educational, financial, insurance, and health resources.

> Many bemoaned the lack of financial transparency (and cheered the KCIA financial database that allows for more transparency in the public universities) and argue that,

as part of a new governance model, clearly demonstrating how money is spent on athletics at a university should be more easily available to all. However, a few noted that the new NCAA portal called the Division I Institutional Performance Program (IPP), a dashboard metric presented to the KCIA a few years ago as a benchmarking tool, may in fact, be encouraging spending to *keep up with your conference peers*.

Over the past decade, there have been several proposals about restructuring (or federation) of sports within NCAA Division I programs as a viable alternative to the spending arms race. Many commentators also have spoken out about the impacts of conference realignment, and the unintended consequence it has had on increasing travel time and costs. Originally, decisions were made primarily by TV/football concerns, these changes have left all FBS conferences, especially those outside of the Autonomous Five, with conference footprints stretched over multiple states (and time zones), frequently requiring mid-week air travel and ground transportation costs.

Other voices have advocated for a stricter classification standard to join Division I in order to curb the intentions of schools to become Division I programs *in name only*. These schools are spending far more institutional funds and student fees on their athletic programs than the top tier programs with whom they are trying to keep up.

Almost all who addressed the financial issues mentioned the explosion of coaching salaries, additional staffing, and lavish facilities as targets of their displeasure. And a side effect of that spending is the disproportionate impact on non-revenue sports, sometimes leading to cuts and program discontinuations, not in the salaries and staffing of football and men's basketball, but in the sports that *cost money*. The reality is that all sports cost money: it's the *inability* to say no to football and men's basketball that is the central thesis in their arguments.

The emergence of the Names, Images and Likenesses (NIL) legislation, as well as the continued advocacy by some writers that athletes share in the revenues generated by them, has brought clear discord. Some scholars advocate that in addition to NIL rights, athletes also share in the institutional revenues their programs produce, whether via an Olympic-style trust fund or some other indirect mechanism, or as a straight deposit to their student accounts. Others, while in agreement with the NIL discussions, see the need for reinvestment in the *non-revenue* sports referenced above. While there is much discussion, pro and con, about *paying athletes*, there is no clear-cut opinion as to what constitutes doing that.

While all commentators seem to agree on the need to have some uniform national resolution of this issue, rather than many conflicting state laws, it's not clear this can happen quickly, and there are multiple opinions as to the right form of any Congressional intervention and/or independent oversight. There is, however, consensus that there must be political will from the Congress to take on this decision if it is to happen. There are many political battles being waged at the national level in 2020: whether there is the desire to expend political capital in *bailing out* intercollegiate athletics, thus allowing institutions and conferences to avoid addressing these issues *at home*, is up for debate.

A number of writers have noted that a conditional antitrust exemption might be the best path to follow to strengthen integrity guardrails, operate in an efficient and cost-effective manner, while prioritizing the athlete's collegiate experience. There is some precedent in higher education for advocating for this type of oversight, but few scholars have linked such an exemption to what institutions would have to provide, in return, to serve the *public interest*; i.e., promising specific benefits for college athletes which would serve their interests, while also serving the general public's understanding of a distinction between amateur and professional athletics. Such dedicated funding for athletes could include enhanced athlete health and safety measures and educational benefits, allowing for institutions to more effectively allocate resources in other areas, instead of in spiraling salaries and unnecessary facility enhancements.

While embracing *spending restraints* is widely popular among scholars to combat the never-ending arms race, a few also describe the impact it has on the revenue race, as Division I programs try to make up the spending gaps created by the current landscape. This trade-off is mostly bad for athletes, teams and fans: rather than addressing the spending problem, the athletics modus operandi has been to try to find ways to make more money, which adds more stress to the athlete experience—as by receiving more television revenues for "time shifting" games (and travel) to weekday nights.

A conditional antitrust exemption would almost assuredly require some sort of oversight or reporting mechanism to ensure the promised trade-offs/benefits are met. Scholars are not in agreement when it comes to this area—some feel there is a need for Congressional oversight and annual reporting, some believe there is a need for an agency approach (like the Federal Trade Commission), and some believe the entire supervisory board should be comprised of people currently outside of higher education, but with deep knowledge of the infrastructure.

All agree as to the need for regular reporting and/or oversight: some feel tying in a "hammer" type of approach (like removing Federal funding for non-compliance) would best achieve the goals, articulating the need for robust penalties for non-compliance (or even non-cooperation) if higher education is to move effectively towards organizational integrity in Division I athletics.

There are also issues around whether both athletic scholarships and "UBIT Income (Unrelated Business Income Tax)" could be treated as taxable income to athletes and institutions, respectively, with current holes in the Internal Revenue Code (that could be modified at any time). Any movement towards an antitrust exemption would be wise to settle these issues definitively.

Similarly, there has been much discussion of how Title IX would be applied under various "antitrust" and/or NIL approaches, and any federal legislation in either area should provide a clear answer in this regard.

And especially recently, there have been several scholars and commentators who have recommended or speculated on the separation of the Autonomous 5 conferences from the rest of Division I, thereby potentially creating educational (as to the definition of a student-athlete), and commercial separations. All who wrote of this concept advocated for it to apply to all of Division I sports, not just to particular sports. Beyond that, there was not much discussion of what this would mean or how it would work.

Weaver et al. (2020)

Summary

There is no doubt that Division I college sports is a big business. It is faced with existential issues regarding names, images, and likenesses for athletes; a loss of focus on athlete health, welfare, and safety; the emergence of social justice issues; and the ever-looming crisis around debt. COVID-19 has exposed for all to see the fissures that existed in the athletics business model.

Financial analysts in the future will need to build cooperative working relationships internally and externally, while understanding that the enterprise is undergoing tremendous change. Building in contingency plans, reserve funds and seeing the longer view are all critical skills for the next generation of financial specialists.

Review Questions

1. NCAA Division I is under tremendous pressure and is in danger of splintering into different segments. If that happens, most of the total college football revenues and some of the NCAA Men's Basketball revenues would remain with one organization. What can college sports do to prevent this rift from occurring?
2. What happens to college sports if the media revenues begin to fall off due to technology shifts? How can athletic departments manage that shift?
3. Are there other sports in athletic department's portfolios that could be on the verge of becoming either revenue neutral or even revenue positive? State which ones and why you think that's a possibility.

Case Study: Conversation with Kevin Blue, PhD, Athletics Director at the University of California at Davis and Bill Beekman, Athletics Director at Michigan State University

An example of how college athletics departments make decisions on their finances can be learned through the following conversation and by reviewing the different ways they report financial information. Members of the NCAA, such as the University of California at Davis and Michigan State University, report their information based on a federal legal requirement to the U.S. Department of Education (EADA) to comply with Title IX. However, as a member, these institutions also must comply with the requirements to be an NCAA member, and that includes reporting information through the NCAA's financial reporting system. Yet both of these are reported *after* most of the revenues and expenses are accumulated in any year; this is different from a working budget, which is a road map to project potential financial impact in any year.

Below is a discussion of Michigan State and UC Davis budget, EADA, and NCAA report forms to better understand how money is reported and to better understand the outcome of decisions. In addition, there is a conversation with athletics directors at both UC Davis and Michigan State to learn about each's decision-making process.

How do you create a budget?

Blue: We consider previous year's revenues and expenses as benchmarks for our budgeting. Modeling projects generated revenues from fundraising and ticket sales, as well as allocated revenues from student fees. For instance, enrollment trends help to project student fees. Expenses don't necessarily consider competitors, but rather cost of living and payroll costs based on regional differences. For instance, minimum wage is higher in California than Montana for game day operations.

Beekman: Historically, the budget process is to look at the previous year and adjust the next year's for inflation. However, with COVID-19, the process feels closer to a zero-based line-item budget because we are not sure about the virus' impact in the academic year.

How is this done?

Blue: Budgets are created from the athletic director, chief financial officer (CFO), and other senior administrators with formulas for revenue generation. We send budget request to administrative

Interview contributed by Kevin Blue. © Kendall Hunt Publishing Company.
Interview contributed by Bill Beekman. © Kendall Hunt Publishing Company.

units and sport teams. Budgets are projected based on previous year expenses and expected costs from team travel schedules and other team needs.

Beekman: The athletics budget is independent of the university budget, and we float on our own resources. In the first half of the academic year, Amy CFO and I discuss revenue and expense projections. Amy works with individual units and each sport to determine their needs and rolls them into one budget. Then, that budget is presented to the board of trustees in a working session first; then, it is revised after discussion for formal approval by the trustees.

Can you explain the different sources used in reporting your financial information to the NCAA, the federal government (EADA), or in a budget to your board of trustees?

Blue: There are different areas required within each reporting requirement. A budget is a plan, while the NCAA and EADA require providing actual expenses. One big difference is debt and debt service, which are not included in the reporting requirements for EADA, but are required to be shared with the NCAA because we are a member of the NCAA. Another example would be difference in coaching compensation: Some of our coaches receive funds as instructors in Physical Education and Exercise Science programs, and those are educational and not athletics expenses.

Beekman: The revenues and expenses are different for different reports because there are different philosophies and perspectives that require different information be sent, or information be sent in different ways. Our goal is to be efficient, wise, and effective, with a reasonable reserve. We may consider budgets by area, such as event management; however, the NCAA requires reporting by sport. In addition, the university has a new accounting system which provides greater efficiency for budgeting than in the past. This allows for us to look at things in a certain area different from what EADA or the NCAA requires.

What are examples of a financial challenge?

Blue: Field hockey and lacrosse costs more to travel to the Midwest and Northeast for a higher level of competitiveness than the cost to stay closer at home to compete in soccer. And … the cancellation of the 2020 NCAA Men's Basketball Tournament will cost UC Davis at least $1 million from its $38 million revenue.

Beekman: The hiring of a new football coach. Considering the knowledge of Big Ten and Power Five as key drivers, we created a package to hire the coach and his assistants. There are competitive market forces which are beyond our control. Because it was an early spring hire outside of the normal hiring cycle (late fall), we decided to pay a premium for that hire. For football, we track carefully relative to peers, knowing we don't have the resources to be as competitive in some non-revenue sports (such as softball).

When challenged with the COVID-19 virus, financially what were your decisions to make up the differences?

Blue: In the Spring, we saved travel and recruiting expenses of $300k to $400k from the virus; in addition, we expected an additional $100k less in donations from revenue. From 'back of the envelope math' it totals about $500k total, and the end of the fiscal year is in June. We will request this additional sum from the institution, but do not expect a cash flow problem if we pay it back over a number of years (CAFI Database, 2020).

Beekman: When we think of football, premium seating, suites, ancillary revenue, licensing, concessions, and parking is about 80% of what we make from our television revenue of football. Football is an absolutely massive component in our budget. Do we take out a $50 million loan to balance books minimalistic, do we consider possibly laying off two-thirds of athletics staff? Need to have ideas in backs of our heads. If we don't find a way to play football, we are in an existential moment in the Power 5.

Beekman: We have a blended approach in budgeting at MSU in our dialogue with head coaches: If students want to return, we will figure it out, but each sport must fall within current budget for existing scholarship limits. If there is not money within the scholarship limit, each sport must raise it. If not, they can appeal to the bank of the athletics director for 'worst case' scenario.

References

Bender, B. (2021, June 25) Name, Image and Likeness (NIL) and July 1: How much change is coming to college football? SportingNews.com https://www.sportingnews.com/us/ncaa-football/news/name-image-and-likeness-nil-and-july-1-how/2jie2fdxbk331c1nvbnp33lf5

Berkowitz, S. (2019). Power five conferences had over $2.9 billion in revenue in fiscal 2019, new tax records show. *USA Today*. www.usatoday.com/story/sports/college/2020/07/10/power-five-conference-revenue-fiscal-year-2019/5414405002/

Berkowitz, S. (2020). Major public college football programs could lose billions in revenue if no season is played. *USA Today*. www.usatoday.com/story/sports/ncaaf/2020/04/14/college-football-major-programs-could-see-billions-revenue-go-away/2989466001/

CAFI Database. (2020). *Knight commission on intercollegiate athletics*. http://cafidatabase.knightcommission.org/

Equity in Athletics Disclosure Act. United States Department of Education, Washington, D.C. https://ope.ed.gov/athletics/#/

Fox Sports. (2012). *Money makes FCS-FBS mismatches go round*. www.foxsports.com/wisconsin/story/money-makes-fcs-fbs-mismatches-go-round-083012

Grand Valley State University. (2019). *General fund budget 2019-2020*. www.gvsu.edu/cms4/asset/8D86E681-E631-FDD9-C965A207536EA137/2019-20_general_fund_budget.pdf

Greder, A. (2020, April 7). *Gopher athletics revenues could see $75 million hit from coronavirus*. Twincities.com. www.twincities.com/2020/04/07/gophers-athletics-revenue-could-see-75-million-hit-from-coronavirus/

Kennedy, Robert C. (2001, July 27) On This Day. *New York Times* archives. https://archive.nytimes.com/www.nytimes.com/learning/general/onthisday/harp/0727.html

Knight Commission on Intercollegiate Athletics. (2016). *Financial overview to explain impact of CFP revenue growth*. www.knightcommission.org/wp-content/uploads/2020/08/Media_Power5_wide.pdf

Knight Commission on Intercollegiate Athletics. (2020a). *Finances of college sports*. www.knightcommission.org/finances-college-sports/

Knight Commission on Intercollegiate Athletics. (2020b). *NCAA division I-FBS ALL public institutions: Percentage of budget from revenue sources, 2018*. Presented September 16, 2020 as slide 11 within "Session 1: Follow the Money: Breaking Down D-I Finances." www.knightcommission.org/wp-content/uploads/kcia-transforming-the-ncaa-d-i-model-session-1-slide-deck-091620-01.pdf

Knight Commission on Intercollegiate Athletics. (2020c). *Transforming the NCAA division I model: Recommendations for change*. www.knightcommission.org/wp-content/uploads/2020/12/transforming-the-ncaa-d-i-model-recommendations-for-change-1220-01.pdf

Lawrence, S. (2019, September 8). *As college football attendance slumps, new ways to ticket may hold an answer*. Tech Crunch. https://techcrunch.com/2019/09/08/as-college-football-attendance-slumps-new-ways-to-ticket-may-hold-an-answer/

LAW v. NATIONAL COLLEGIATE ATHLETIC ASSOCIATION (1998, January 23) United States Court of Appeals,Tenth Circuit. Nos. 96-3150, 96-3186 and 96-3200.

McCann, Michael (2021, June 21) Supreme Court Rules Unanimously Against NCAA In Alston Case. *Yahoo Sports.* https://sports.yahoo.com/supreme-court-rules-unanimous-ly-against-142956893.html?guccounter=1&guce_referrer=aHR0cHM6Ly9kdWNrZHV-ja2dvLmNvbS8&guce_referrer_sig=AQAAAAQqtX56xTOBIwrL1YpyY-3dN_ZLQ6G-GCKEmxTDTKSwrl2cUzpbVdhT9doTZNj_G4lzxXlCnXPjojrYFmcg0clV4SDYqhX-r1mINDGjtwe9Qjzxk5wMV158b-dpXUqWlMk5VX0C1cNPz0jQgmAyXdorJMET-Loo4Hx2MmfKAdv4hEB

MLive.com. (2015). *Grand Valley State University NCAA Financial Report Form*. http://media.mlive.com/news_impact/other/GVSU.PDF

Mortenson. (n.d.). *How do you build the first Big Ten stadium since 1960 while preserving a legacy?* www.mortenson.com/sports/projects/tcf-bank-stadium

NAIA. (2020). www.naia.org/why-naia/pdf/NAIA_Membership_Profile.pdf

Navera, T. (2020, December 16). *Huntington Center, Huntington Tower, Huntington Stadium: Naming rights go with TCF merger*. Columbus Business First. www-bizjournals-com.proxy.library.upenn.edu/columbus/news/2020/12/16/naming-rights-go-with-huntington-tcf-merger.html

NCAA. (2018a). *Academic based revenue distribution*. http://www.ncaa.org/academic-based-revenue-distribution#:~:text=Home-,Academic%20Based%20Revenue%20Distribution,to%20qualify%20for%20more%20funds

NCAA. (2018b). *Major rule changes division ii track and field*. http://www.ncaapublications.com/productdownloads/TF20.pdf

NCAA. (2018c). *NCAA post season football (CFP) revenue distribution by conference*. https://collegefootballplayoff.com/sports/2017/9/20/revenue-distribution.aspx

NCAA. (2019e). *NCAA Division I revenue distribution plan*. https://ncaaorg.s3.amazonaws.com/ncaa/finance/d1/2019D1Fin_RevenueDistributionPlan.pdf

NewsDay. (2018). *Jim Harbaugh Contract at Michigan*. https://projects.newsday.com/college-football-coaches-salaries-contracts/jim-harbaugh/

University of Minnesota. (2003). Stadium Feasibility Study. www.leg.mn.gov/docs/2004/other/040634/Stadium/www.stadium.state.mn.us/meetings/040106/university.pdf

Weaver, K. (2020, March 8). *In the chase for winning athletics programs, women are paying more than men*. Forbes.com. www.forbes.com/sites/karenweaver/2020/03/08/in-the-chase-for-winning-athletics-programs-women-are-paying-more-than-men/?sh=3533c15588b9

Weaver, K., & Tegtmeyer, J. (2018, May 22). Big time athletic villages—Gated communities emerging on campus. *Change: The Magazine of Higher Learning, 50*, 1, 54–62. https://doi.org/10.1080/00091383.2018.1413908

Weaver, K., Osborne, B., Haagen, P., Weight, E. A., Broome, L. L., Schmalbeck, R., Bates, B., & Shropshire, K. (2020). *Literature review of division I athletics reform.* Prepared for the Knight Commission on Intercollegiate Athletics, Miami, Florida. https://www.knightcommission.org/wp-content/uploads/2020/11/literature-review-division-i-athletics-reform-1020-01.pdf

CHAPTER 4
Business of Mega Recreational Complexes

Ted Hayduk and Bri Newland

LEARNING OBJECTIVES

- To learn about the explosion in building mega recreational facilities and why they are becoming increasingly popular places to host large tournaments and showcases.
- To understand why one complex may look completely different than another due to weather, local interests and funding, and whether there is an academic component tied to the complex.
- To learn about Disney's Wide World of Sports, which became the center of the NBA's COVID-19 return-to-play strategy in the summer of 2020.
- To understand why flexibility in facility setups can speed turnaround and drive profits.
- To understand how sports tourism has driven cities and counties to partner in building mega complexes, further aiding the growth of youth and adult sports industry.
- To study the other revenue streams in a complex that can make or break profitability.
- To understand how facility owners are maximizing revenues with technology investments like apps and tailored software.

Key Terms

- Churn rate—the number of people who cancel their memberships each year
- Core competency—a process or procedure that a firm does exceptionally well
- Competitive advantage—a process, system, or routine, typically formed by combining individual resources, that a firm can execute significantly better than its competitors
- Firm resources——tangible or intangible assets that are available to a company. Examples include property, land, equipment, capital, labor, brand awareness, consumer confidence and loyalty, and professional networks.

- Flow-on tourism——activities that the traveler partakes in beyond the sport event, such as— group tours, visiting natural environments, restaurants and nightlife, and shopping
- Mega recreational sport complex——a multidimensional athletic facility covering expansive acreage and extending across fields and buildings supporting a variety of indoor and outdoor sports and events
- Public–private partnership (P3)—the combination of public and private resources (typically financial in nature) toward the construction, operation, and/or maintenance of a sport complex
- Software as a service (SaaS)—a method of software delivery and licensing in which software is accessed online via a subscription, rather than bought and installed on individual computers

History of Mega Recreational Sport Complexes

In recent years, there has been tremendous growth in youth and recreational sport. With youth sport expanding into select and travel teams, this sector of the industry has grown to a value of $24.9 billion globally, and $19.2 billion in the United States (Research & Markets, 2019). Likewise, the global recreational sport market is valued at about $109.7 billion, and the participatory sport market has reached ~$277 billion (Business Wire, 2019b). With this growth, the participatory, recreational, and youth sport markets have seen a push to build mega recreational sport complexes across the United States.

© Eugene Onischenko/Shutterstock.com

Of primary importance for this chapter is the need to define what exactly is meant by the term *mega recreational sport complex*, as the term is certainly multidimensional. Mega recreational sport complexes may incorporate elements of health and fitness clubs, indoor and outdoor sport facilities, recreation and entertainment centers, and outdoor public parks. Many of these complexes include multiple natural and turf fields that can support soccer, football, lacrosse, field hockey, and more. Many include baseball and softball fields and full track-and-field facilities. The indoor facilities include basketball and volleyball courts, rock climbing walls, and swimming pools. Many have even begun to include agility courses, like those seen in the popular TV show "American Ninja Warrior." Moreover, some of these complexes have even been intertwined with the business model and capital investment strategy of private boarding schools. As the industry will likely see continued evolution in this sector, it is difficult—and perhaps imprudent—to employ too narrow of a working definition. For the purposes of this chapter, the definition of *mega recreational sport complex* is "a multidimensional athletic facility covering expansive acreage and extending across fields and buildings supporting a variety of indoor and outdoor sports and events." Ultimately, mega recreational sport complexes are located all throughout the United States, but any given facility's final form is dictated by local and regional market conditions, such as land costs and availability, weather patterns, and culture. Examples of such complexes include the expansive IMG Academy in Bradenton, FL; ESPN Wide World of Sports at Walt Disney World in Orlando, FL; the Apex Sports & Events complex in Hillsborough, NJ; and the Spooky Nook Sports complex in Lancaster, PA. Also important for this discussion is the stipulation that while mega sport recreational complexes exhibit similarities to mixed and multipurpose real estate development (a dominant trend in recent years), the former are regarded as conceptually and operationally distinct.

CHAPTER 4: Business of Mega Recreational Complexes

Each of the foregoing complexes shares important characteristics, but is distinct in its own way. The IMG Academy is a 450-acre, $200 million facility that functions primarily as a college preparatory boarding school for students who also aspire to play competitive sports at the collegiate level and beyond. The school combines specialized academic instruction with world-class training for a range of sports, including football, soccer, basketball, golf, tennis, and lacrosse to help their students have a wholesome journey of learning. The facility also offers year-round sport camps for adults and nonenrolled children, professional and collegiate sports performance training, team training, corporate retreats, and tournament hosting. The Apex Sports & Events complex, set to open in March 2020, is a $23 million sports complex that will include three outdoor turf fields. Inside the 160,000 square-foot complex, Apex features a fourth artificial turf field, basketball and volleyball courts, rock climbing, and a kids adventure area modeled after "American Ninja Warrior," an arcade, virtual reality space, and a ropes course. Last, Spooky Nook Sports complex located outside Lancaster, Pennsylvania is the largest indoor sports complex in the United States, costing $35.5 million to build. The 700,000 square foot indoor facility is capable of hosting over a dozen indoor sports simultaneously, and an adjacent field can accommodate a range of outdoor sports, too. The complex is also home to the Warehouse Hotel, which houses tournament guests and large groups who wish to stay on-site while competing. Additionally, the complex features a climbing center and rock wall, gym and fitness center, food court, arcade, and a conference center.

As these examples show, there are a number of manifestations a mega recreation sport complex can adopt. They frequently share many characteristics and business objectives, but the processes and products they employ to realize those objectives can be very different. To be certain, the emergence of the truly "mega" recreational sport complex is a relatively recent phenomenon. The formalization and standardization of the youth sport industry has been the predominant driving factor, with youth sport shifting from primarily a public-provision model in the 1970s, 1980s, and 1990s to a privately procured, for-profit model executed at the enterprise (i.e., "big business") level. As public schools in the United States began to deemphasize the provision of physical education and school sports, and as city governments found their budgets unable to fund low-cost recreational leagues, businesses began to sprout up, offering youth the opportunity to play organized sport—for a significant fee, in many cases (Bowers, Chalip, & Green, 2010). Thus, the fields, courts, and diamonds essential to providing youth sporting opportunities also shifted toward private ownership, operation, and maintenance (Fielding, Pitts, & Pederson, 2014). Furthermore, American families have been spending more on recreation every year: this figure grew from approximately $334 billion in 1999 to ~$512 billion in 2020 (Ibis World, 2020). The confluence of these two macro drivers has produced a culture of recreational sport centered on the pay-for-play model. Learn more at this link: www.espnwwos.com/complex/venues/.

Industry Structure

The prior section proposed a general definition of mega recreational sport complex, provided three similar yet distinct examples of what these types of complexes "look" like, and suggested two important drivers that have shaped the development of this industry. From that discussion, it should be clear that mega recreational sport complexes operate at the nexus of multiple related industries rather than constituting a unique industry or segment in and of itself. While all provide various opportunities to participate in organized sport, no two mega facilities are alike in the services they offer, the revenue sources they leverage, or the clientele they service. Recall, for example, that the IMG Academy operates as both a private boarding school *and* an elite sport training facility, while the other two facilities do not. Therefore, the goal of the current section is to provide a more nuanced investigation of the industrial sectors and subsectors that most directly affect (and have been affected by) the mega recreational sport complex trend.

Gyms, Health, and Fitness Clubs

The Gyms, Health, and Fitness Clubs industry in the United States is a ~$38 billion industry (Le, 2020). This industry is pertinent to mega recreational sport complexes in that many mega facilities offer some type of physical fitness training and/or gym equipment to their membership. Membership fees make up almost 70% of the revenue for gyms, health, and fitness clubs, with personal training services (12%) accounting for the next largest revenue slice. Many gyms offer introductory, lower-cost membership tiers that include access to free weights and cardiovascular machines, but invoke additional fees for bespoke classes like yoga. In addition, many of these facilities include rock climbing walls and agility courses as part of the design, which can often be used for additional fees. Several important drivers most directly affect the demand for gyms, health, and fitness clubs. Namely, increases in disposable income, consumer confidence, and leisure time all contribute to the growth of this sector, while decreases in any of them contributes to demand contractions. This sector is also sensitive to seasonal effects and cyclical trends. Younger consumer segments are most overtly targeted by gyms, health, and fitness clubs—consumers under the age of 35 produce almost half (48.8%) of the segment's revenue.

This segment has benefitted from increasing amounts of leisure time in the United States, increases in disposable income per capita, the lack of public support for youth recreational sport, and cultural trends that prioritize health and wellness. However, the industry also faces a number of challenges. First, it is estimated that roughly one-third (29/100) of gym members will cancel their memberships each year (i.e., "churn rate"). And the cost of obtaining and registering a new member is almost two times the cost of retaining an old member. This will require gyms, health, and fitness clubs to devote increasing volumes of capital toward relationship building, customer service, addition of amenities, and lowering ancillary costs for members. The sector is also relatively capital intensive, as the provision of bespoke fitness equipment requires large financial outlays plus routine maintenance and support from manufacturers. Additional allocations related to human resources (~34% of revenue), insurance and administrative costs (~22%), and rent (~13%) make this industry a lower-margin business. Estimated profit margins for firms competing in this industry range from 11% to 13%.

Construction and Installation of Athletic and Sports Fields

The construction of sport and athletic fields is a $5.3 billion industry in the United States (Roth, 2019a). It is another key industry that both affects and is affected by the trend toward mega sport recreation complexes because these firms are the ones most frequently contracted to build them. Firms in this industry construct and install artificial and natural grass fields, track-and-field surfaces, fixed equipment, bleachers, and lighting systems. Firms that design, invest in, and/or build sport stadiums and arenas are *excluded* from this segment because the product–market considerations related to large venues intended for sport consumption are radically different than those for sport complexes directed at participatory sport. The construction and installation of athletic and sport fields is situated within the larger "specialist engineering,

infrastructure, and contractors" segment, which insinuates that this sector requires unique considerations, resources, and capabilities. Firms in this segment typically do business with a range of buyers, such as private sport complexes and municipal recreational areas (69% of revenue), and universities and school systems (31%).

As with gyms, health, and fitness clubs, firms that construct and install sports and athletic fields have benefitted from a general upswell of support for health and wellness trends in North America. Furthermore, a healthy economy over the 5 years to 2019 means that the demand for nonresidential and commercial construction has increased steadily. Both cities and entrepreneurs alike have been in favorable financial positions to invest in the construction and renovation of property, plant, land, and equipment (PPLE) resources—a notable contingency of which has been related to athletic fields and facilities. Moreover, scientific and technological advancements in artificial surfaces have increased the demand for this particular product category. Artificial turf was invented in the 1960s by the agrochemical firm Monsanto. However, early versions were notably inferior to natural grass, and significant improvements were only made beginning in the latter portion of the 1990s. Modern versions more accurately recreate the look, feel, and safety of natural surfaces while also drastically reducing maintenance costs, which explains the dramatic increase in demand for this product category.

Being that this industry is rooted in construction, the largest single cost for this industry relates to nondepreciable purchases of materials, componentry, and subcontracting (45.5% of revenue). The negotiating ability of a firm's leadership and their personal networks often affects a project's cost structure, and thus profit potential. The second largest cost for firms that construct and install such facilities fall under legal, regulatory, and administrative spending (23.2%). It should be noted that together, these two cost categories are frequently unpredictable, and in the case of nondepreciable purchases, nondeferrable. Competition in this sector is high due to significant entry barriers related to personal networking and relationships, capital and equipment costs, and skilled project management labor. Overall, firms in this sector report margins of ˜7%.

Management of Indoor Sports Facilities

The management of indoor sport facilities is a $1.3B industry in the United States (Roth, 2019b). Because mega recreational sport facilities are complex, evolving, ever-growing in physical size, and increasingly diversified, they require special considerations when it comes to their day-to-day management, maintenance, and operations. This sector relates to both for-profit and nonprofit sport facilities that charge membership fees much in the same manner as gyms, health, and fitness clubs. But, importantly, this sector excludes gyms and fitness clubs using the logic that the provision of team sports is fundamentally different from providing access to physical fitness. It also excludes other indoor recreational activities such as bowling alleys, dance halls, collegiate facilities, and large sport venues because these types of venues do not utilize similar business models. This sector *does* include indoor facilities that cater to soccer, basketball, ice hockey, tennis, swimming and diving, "futsal," volleyball, and so on. While this sector is treated as orthogonal to gyms, health, and fitness clubs for analysis purposes, from the three examples in the "History of Mega Recreational Sport Complexes" section, it should be clear that mega recreational sport complexes often incorporate components of both, and do not fit neatly into either of these two sectors.

© Branislav Nenin/Shutterstock.com

Generally, indoor sport facilities of the type referenced here can transition quickly between setups to accommodate a range of sports, or can accommodate multiple setups simultaneously in order to host concurrent tournaments of various sports. Like the gyms, health, and fitness clubs, the management and operations of indoor sports facilities have benefitted from increasing amounts of leisure time in the United States, increases in disposable income per capita, the lack of public support for youth recreational sport, and cultural trends that prioritize health and wellness. These trends have contributed to the construction and renovation of such facilities, complicating and enhancing the need for specialized management and operations. Moreover, low capital requirements mean that the management and maintenance of indoor sport facilities require large initial outlays, but very little or nonexistent inventory. However, this segment has even tighter margins as the result of high labor costs (34% of revenue), administrative, insurance, repair, and maintenance costs (27%), and rent (16%). Together, this environment produces an average gross margin of 6% for firms in the management of indoor sport facilities.

Sport Tourism

Sport tourism represents 10% of the global tourism industry, with a total addressable market of $800 billion (World Sport Tourism, 2020). In the United States in 2019, leisure and recreation-based travel accounted for 11% of all domestic travel, generating an estimated $106 billion in revenue (U.S. Travel Association, 2019). Due to mega sport complexes'

© Rnoid/Shutterstock.com

ability to host tournaments and other events, the degree of tourism generated could be quite significant. In fact, it is predicted that the total addressable market for sports tourism market will grow at a compound annual growth rate (CAGR) of about 32.3% between 2019 and 2023 (Business Wire, 2019a). For this sector, the sport tourist is defined as athletes and their accompanying friends and family who travel specifically to participate in competitions, training, tournaments, or other activities related to sport. Athletes who travel for sport as well as their travel companions can produce greater "flow-on tourism" (Aicher & Newland, 2018; Aicher, Buning, & Newland, 2020). Flow-on tourism are activities that the traveler partakes in beyond the sport event—group tours, visiting natural environments, restaurants and nightlife, shopping, and so on. Athletes who travel with family, friends, and/or spouses are more likely to engage in the tourism assets available in the destination (Buning & Gibson, 2016).

Mega sport complexes have the opportunity to make a significant economic impact on the destination in which they operate if they strategically leverage the tourism assets by bundling entertainment activities that align with tourists' interests (Aicher & Newland, 2018). Certainly, restaurants and hotels will benefit from sport tourists, but strategic planning with key tourism operators is necessary to generate an economic benefit from flow-on tourism (Aicher & Newland, 2018; Buning & Gibson, 2016).

Business Model Considerations

Thus far, the chapter has provided an overview of the history of mega recreational sport complexes and discussed three industry segments that are most related to the provision of these mega recreation complexes. As noted in the "Industry Structure" section, there is no single "best" financial model for mega sport recreational complexes, as each one employs a unique revenue strategy and possesses unique sets of resources. Thus, the natural question to ask is, How do these complexes find success? Because no "recipe" for success exists for this segment of the sport industry, the balance of this chapter leverages the information from prior sections to identify and outline the strategic and financial considerations most important for mega recreational sport complexes. These considerations include the versatility of revenue sources, the importance of determining core competencies, and analyzing cost and revenue structures associated with various revenue sources. The section aims to provide a set of prescriptive insights managers can use when making decisions that impact the financial state of mega sport recreational complexes.

Importance of Memberships to Revenue Strategy

The first consideration one must make with respect to owning or operating a mega sport recreational complex relates to establishing a revenue strategy. Indeed, the singular commonality amongst the mega complexes discussed earlier was the provision of physical resources for participatory sport. For that reason, this section makes the natural deduction that the provision of sport and athletic space generates the plurality or even the majority of revenue for these complexes. There are multiple ways complexes can provide field time, with one-off purchases of field access on one end of the spectrum, and yearly, monthly, or seasonal membership dues on the other end of the spectrum.

While one-off purchases can be a significant portion of overall field bookings, recurring revenue sources are regarded as particularly favorable, regardless of industry. This is because the firm has secured sources of capital that are contractually guaranteed well into the future. As discussed in the "Gyms, Health, and Fitness Clubs" section, some gym membership pricing strategies employ tiers, with various levels of access to different product categories implied by each tier of membership. Basic memberships constitute access to introductory and general services, while "add-ons" or upgrades can provide access to specialized services and exclusive products. There is certainly reason to assume that recurring revenue sources and structures can be transferred directly into the context of a mega complex, as well.

© Tyler Olson/Shutterstock.com

There are two favorable aspects of offering a tiered membership. The first is that the recurring nature of a membership means there is less worry on the behalf of investors and managers that a mega complex will experience dramatic fluctuations in revenue (Mehta et al., 2016). Additionally, a multitiered approach allows for customizability of memberships across various consumer segments. For example, younger and more novice teams may simply require field access, while older and more experienced teams may also desire physical fitness and athletic cross training, nutritional advice, or even physical rehabilitation—which are services that can be added onto a basic field access membership. Customizability is important because it may help reduce the high churn rate exhibited in the gyms, health, and fitness sector (Mehta et al., 2016). When consumers feel as though their unique needs are being met in a thoughtful way, they are less likely to change providers. If structured properly, tiered membership pricing can act as a reliable, central pillar for most—if not all—mega recreational sport complexes.

Determining Core

© Kheng Guan Toh/Shutterstock.com

Competencies and Revenue Strategy

Beyond the use of tiered memberships, managers of mega sport recreational complexes have many other options for revenue generation. As evidenced in prior sections, the sources of revenue for mega sport recreational complexes are numerous, and in principle they are limited only by one's imagination. Examples include memberships, sponsorships and advertising, personal training, strength coaching, multiday conferences, events and tournaments, and hospitality and entertainment. As discussed in the "History of Mega Recreational Sport Complexes" section, the IMG Academy has even produced significant revenue streams via offering specialized academic instruction. Implementing any combination of these ancillary revenue streams is technically feasible based on the evidence documented so far. However, just because a proprietor *can* leverage a broad range of revenue sources does not necessarily mean they *should*. This is the central idea behind building a reliable, focused revenue strategy.

For a given mega complex in a certain locale, there are a range of considerations that will dictate how managers in this space should approach revenue management practices. First, it is important for managers to take stock of the resources that are at their disposal. Resources are discussed most often in terms of dependency (Barney, 1991; Wernerfelt, 1984), but it is critical that managers have the ability to identify the resources that are most associated with performance outcomes (Hayduk, 2017). Intuitively, a mega complex's resources can be tangible or intangible—examples include property, land, equipment, capital, labor, brand awareness, consumer confidence and loyalty, and professional networks. Resource(s) that are plentiful for a given mega complex should be the predominant driver(s) of revenue. Resources that are the most valuable, rare, inimitable, and nonsubstitutable pose the greatest potential for generating competitive advantage (Barney, 1991). Furthermore, the more a resource can be combined with other resources and adapted over time, the greater the likelihood it can lead to competitive advantage (Hayduk & Walker, 2017). The header image for this section of the chapter provides a solid working model for understanding how resources can become competitive advantages.

For example, consider Grand Park Sports Campus in Westfield, Indiana. Grand Park is one of the most expansive youth sports complexes in the world and was constructed at a cost of $145 million (Scott, 2017). It was built on over 400 acres, and includes 31 outdoor soccer fields, 3 indoor soccer fields, and 26 baseball and softball diamonds. The property can accommodate 400 teams and 7,000 athletes *per week* during peak season. The city of Westfield, in coordination with private developers and investors, successfully transformed an expanse of underutilized soybean farms into its current form. The city and its partners realized the opportunity to leverage their vast tract of physical space for meaningful revenue. Thus, an expanse of outdoor fields offered the perfect repurposing effort, and it allowed them to do so at a scale unequaled in the region. While Westfield's resource abundance and leveraging effort are straightforward, there are less overt applications of the same approach. While many other mega sport recreation complexes do not enjoy the same abundance of physical space on which to build fields, others may have an abundance of social capital built up, which may be deployed in order to reduce churn rates and enhance consumer loyalty. Alternatively, personal and professional networks are commonly regarded as a valuable intangible resource. Managers of a particular mega sport recreational complex could deploy that resource in order to acquire advantageous partnerships, sponsorships, and contracts to host large events. For managers operating a mega complex, it is primarily important to establish an honest consensus with respect to their facility's resource portfolio and tailor its specific resource endowments to a corresponding revenue strategy.

Relevant Costs for Mega Recreational Sport Complexes

Managing a business model for a mega sport complex can be a very unique challenge in that there are a number of specialized costs associated with their construction, maintenance, and daily operation. Mega sport complexes typically face a number of risks related to initial capital investment and ongoing capital-intensive projects.

© kitzcorner/Shutterstock.com

First, because these facilities are so specialized and expansive, they are nearly impossible to repurpose if the facility is not successful. For example, the company TriHabitat proposed a self-contained triathlon venue with a 14-mile bike course, 6.5-mile run course, 25-acre lake, five stadiums, 20-room lodge, 50-site recreational vehicle park, 25 economy cabins, a campsite and bath house facilities for race participants, a race village for vendors, and an amphitheater. However, despite gaining approval from the country commissioners, TriHabitat was unable to secure investor support. What often happens in situations like TriHabitat's example is that the company would struggle to demonstrate to its investors an ability to attract events, teams and athletes, and partners to ensure viability and future success. In the event that TriHabitat's business model became unfeasible, the range of exit strategies (i.e., liquidation prospects) was low because there were few entities that could step in to repurpose what TriHabitat had built. Instead, the company turned its sight away from North Carolina and toward Florida, where investment opportunities were more promising. From the very beginning, then, it is necessary for owners and managers of mega sport complexes to consider their risk preferences with respect to the physical infrastructure they plan to build and the exit strategies they wish to leave on the table.

Additionally, individual capital investments can be cumbersome, both financially and strategically. Depending on the complexity of the design and structure of the building, many mega sport complexes offer an increasingly wide range of specialized equipment. Rock walls typically cost between $30 and $40 per square foot and considering that these tend to occupy 3,000 to 12,000 square feet, the total cost can range from $90,000 to $480,000 (*Climbing Business Journal*, 2020). Other unique costs include football goal posts, which range from $4,500 to $8,900 or agility courses that require rigging and other specialized equipment to create the structure. Adding aquatics facilities to a mega sport complex is also costly. Installing a 50-meter pool can cost up to $500,000 (Home Advisor, 2020), and maintaining it will cost another $250,000 a year (Brown, 2008). These types of specialized equipment are so expensive because they are not mass produced, meaning economies of scale cannot help reducing costs on a per-unit basis. Thus, when mega sport complex operators are developing revenue strategies, the costs to implement these unique sport offerings must be considered closely. If the local area does not have significant interest in swimming, diving, and aquatics activities, from individuals or teams, there will likely not be enough revenue to rent the facility to offset aquatic costs in a reasonable amount of time. Thus, it is unlikely to be a wise decision for the complex to provide aquatics offerings. In sum, considering a full range of the demand-side revenue drivers is essential for mega sport complex operators if they want to establish a reliable stream of income.

Human resources are another area where hidden costs might affect a mega sport complex's likelihood of success. Certainly, hiring the appropriate full-time, part-time, and seasonal staff is part of any business operator's calculus. However, knowledge is a resource that comes at a premium in all industries, and sport is no exception. As the sport industry has become more specialized and formalized, effective transference of knowledge has become a main priority. To maintain high-quality knowledge transfer, personnel require more advanced certifications—and those can be costly. Moreover, because the costs of these certifications are ballooning rapidly, and in order to remain competitive in a crowded marketplace, mega sport complexes are increasingly offering to cover all or part of their employees' certification costs.

Consider, for example, that if a mega sport complex offers personal training or strength coaching to athletes and teams, then certifications will be necessary. The National Strength and Conditioning Association (NSCA) Certified Personal Trainer or Certified Strength and Conditioning Specialist certifications range from $300 to $475 (NSCA, 2020), while CrossFit Level 1 and Level 2 certifications cost $1,000 each (CrossFit, 2020). Other certifications like CPR and First Aid are less capital intensive (these typically cost about $40 each), but can add up when proprietors must obtain certifications for a staff of 25, 50, or more.

Ancillary Considerations

Availability of Public Funding and Subsidies

Because spectator and participatory sport can be seen as producing both economic value for various stakeholders *and* social value for those in their host communities, there are often debates around which entities should pay for the construction, operation, and maintenance of sport facilities. On the one hand, there are those who believe that only those who stand to profit economically should be responsible for making the significant capital investments required to build and maintain facilities. On the other hand, there are those who believe that a sport facility can generate meaningful social value for an entire community or region, and therefore residents and governments are responsible for bearing some of the costs, as well. This debate is frequently a philosophical one, and is influenced by local culture, the sports being serviced, and the participatory or spectating elements of the facility. In sum, there is no definitive "optimal" way to fund a sport facility.

The debate described earlier is primarily relevant to large professional and intercollegiate teams and leagues because these entities typically require the most elaborate and expensive facilities. However, the same concepts apply to mega sport complexes, as well, because while mega recreational complexes are still smaller and less public-facing than professional stadia, there are often questions as to their total value to a community or region. Moreover, that they require significant land and real estate investments means that prior ownership of these assets is often a bridge to be crossed during the early planning stages.

If a private entity needs to buy a large swath of publicly owned land to build athletic fields, for example, there will likely be significant negotiations that need to take place relating to which entities are able and willing to invest which types of resources into the project. When this happens, it is referred to as a public–private partnership (P3). The number of forms a P3 can take is almost infinite, and will depend on the specifics of each project, developer, and municipality. The structure of any given P3 is strategized via a series of multifaceted bargaining processes. If the mega recreational complex in the prior example shows potential as an economic driver and job creator for the region, the city may be inclined to provide incentives to the potential mega recreational complex, which can take a number of forms. Among other options, a municipality hoping to lure a mega recreational complex into its jurisdiction can:

- Sell the land to the mega recreational complex at a discount.
- Provide tax credits and easements to the developer, owner, and/or operator.
- Commit public funding to the construction of the mega complex.
- Commit public resources to the operation and/or maintenance of the mega complex.

In the past, cities and municipalities were eager to provide various forms of funding and support to athletic facilities and sport complexes. However, as the economic literature has coalesced around the notion that cities generally never reap financial rewards from those investments, they have become much more reticent to contribute. That empirical work, coupled with cities' need to focus on essential functions like public safety and transportation, means that there is often little to no public support to be found for mega recreational sport complexes.

Maximizing Revenues and Optimizing Cost Efficiencies: Impact of Technology

As is the case for many modern sport and service industries, the availability of new technology is continuing to revolutionize how these entities operate. Broadband and (eventually) 5G internet connectivity make the digitization process more democratized and fluid for small and medium sized businesses the world over. Software as a service (SaaS) companies continue to provide small businesses technology solutions with a combination of convenience, affordability, and customer service. For gyms, fitness, and health clubs that employ a membership revenue model, there exists an entire suite of SaaS products tailor-made for this sector—such as ClubExpress, MindBody, and GymMaster. For sport teams, LeagueApps helps sport organizations manage registrations, payments, and communications. These products help reduce the time, energy, and costs related to "back of house" functions like membership renewals, e-mail communication, staffing and recruiting, booking of resources, and inventory management. The use of these products can significantly aid in the reduction of expenses.

© Alexey Boldin/Shutterstock.com

Other SaaS products and mobile applications focus on managing the "front of house" operations like marketing, brand development, and community building. Examples include Hivebrite, Vanilla, and Khoros, which are all designed with the intent of helping groups of people develop a sense of community, buy-in, and shared meaning. Relatedly, mobile devices and applications provide highly specialized capabilities that were previously cost-prohibitive for small business operators. Products like JOGO Smart Football Training, Skills & Drills App, Zepp Play, TrackMan, and Volt provide features like sport-specialized training regimens, mechanisms for recording and tracking skills progress, and personalized recommendations. Other offerings such as CoachCam, myDartfish, Coach's Eye, and Hudl use computer vision and analytics to aid coaches in the analysis of team video content. These "front of house" technologies can help owners and operators of mega recreational sport complexes provide robust, differentiated products and experiences to consumers and in so doing produce and extract additional value.

Growth Potential

The growth potential for this budding sector of the sport industry is positive. Each of the sectors discussed in the "Industry Structure" section has a positive growth potential through 2025. Gyms, health, and fitness clubs are expected to grow at an annualized rate of 2.6%, and the construction and installation of athletic and sports fields is expected to experience 6.2% growth annually. The management of indoor facilities is expected to grow at a more modest rate of 1.2% while the sport tourism sector is expected to grow 5%. Overall, these trends point to a general acceptance of mega sport complexes as the de facto replacement for school-offered or publicly funded sport in the United States.

© Nattapol_Sritongcom/Shutterstock.com

Due to macrotrends related to health and wellness, mega sport complexes have the opportunity to provide value for a larger number of consumer segments beyond youth sport participants. One untapped market segment is adult participation sport. Research indicates that while sport participation does decline with age, much of that is due to access and opportunity (Jacobs et al., 2016; Newland & Aicher, 2018). These mega sport complexes should therefore consider providing sports that are attractive to adults. Offering sport leagues at varied experience levels and age categories could help mitigate declines in sport participation (Haycock & Smith, 2018). Knowing that adults have a desire to maintain an active participatory sport lifestyle is important, but analyzing how those trends fluctuate over time could also be helpful. Many adults shift from team sports to activities like running, triathlon, cycling, CrossFit, swimming, and other individual sports because it's easier to train alone on their own timetable. It is expected that the most successful mega sport complexes of the near future will provide both youth and adult programming at similar times, in order to make it easier for the entire family to participate in sports.

Impact of COVID-19 on Mega Sport Recreation Complexes

Mega sport recreational complexes promote close-quarter interaction between athletes on the field or court as well as spectators on the sidelines. Thus, throughout and in the wake of the Coronavirus pandemic, it is expected that mega sport recreational complexes will experience sets of unique challenges. First, the temporary decline of participatory sport and sport spectatorship means that complexes will see a drastic decline in use and, with that, a decline in revenue. Certainly, private and public sources of finance for new the development of these centers will wilt, too. Fewer teams and athletes will be likely to patronize these facilities due to health concerns. Spectatorship may be limited due to social distancing regulations, and the revenue that comes from the provision of food, beverages, and merchandise may be correspondingly affected. Facilities will also likely incur additional costs related to janitorial services and hygienic products.

While these restrictions are in place, complexes will be forced to innovate in order to survive. Some will adopt the use of technologies that they previously did not employ—for example virtual personal training via Zoom—in order to stay afloat. The complexes that are most open to new technology and innovative delivery methods will be the ones to survive.

Case Study

United States Tennis Association (USTA) Billie Jean King National Tennis Center

Author: David S. Abrams, clinical assistant professor, NYU Preston Robert Tisch Institute for Global Sport

© Leonard Zhukovsky/Shutterstock.com

Mega sports complexes have emerged across our nation in significant numbers with the intent of filling the needs of amateur and professional athletes for both training and event exhibition. One of the most recognizable sports complexes in the United States, and perhaps the world, is the USTA's National Tennis Center (NTC). USTA made the move from Forest Hills, New York to Flushing Meadows in 1978, and this initiated a legacy of expansion and world notoriety as a premier professional tennis center. What is far less known outside of New York City is that not only the NTC serves as the venue for the USTA's U.S. Open, but this world-recognized complex is also a public facility that plays host to a variety of events and is open to the public for use.

Host to Big League and Local Events

The NTC serves as host to the 4th Tennis Major each year in September—the United States Open. This facility also hosts a variety of other events including an event for the WNBA Liberty (2008) and more recently (2019) hosted the Fortnite World Cup Finals, with a prize purse equivalent to the U.S. Open itself. The USTA Get Out and Play agenda uses the NTC as a cornerstone to host state tennis championships, youth tennis programs, college tennis program, and USTA adult leagues, tournaments, social play, and wheelchair tennis programs. This facility is truly a mega sports facility with a local mission to promote athletics and not just tennis. The NTC is the local response to making tennis accessible to everyone through the creation of playing opportunities, grants and assistance, support of local programs, and partnering with numerous organizations that support the mission of the USTA.

The NTC has been on a trajectory of growth from its opening in the late 1970s. With the meteoric growth in popularity of its stars like Chris Evert, Billie Jean King, Martina Navratilova, Steffi Graf, Serena and Venus Williams, John McEnroe, Pete Sampras, and Andre Agassi, tennis in Flushing Meadows became a see and be seen event. In the early 1990s, it was determined that the NTC needed a face-lift to improve its stadium court to both attract more sponsorship and to provide the type of premium seating that is similar to most stadia around the United States.

The list of major improvements would be costly, and the once-a-year event was unlikely to feasibly support the cost of capital and maintenance necessary to fund these improvements. After a long debate, USTA was finally prepared to sell debt to fund the balance of its capital improvement program. In addition to the USTA's own contribution of $112 million, in 1994 the New York City Industrial Development Agency sold $150 million of debt on behalf of the NTC to make considerable improvements over the next 4 years. In 1994, the NTC owned over $28 million of U.S. Open ticket revenues. The new and renovated facilities would accommodate a significant increase in attendance at the U.S. Open beginning in 1997 and would allow the Center to become the focal point of the community, offering facilities for various public events throughout the year.

To ensure the transformation would become reality, the USTA staff and its advisors applied unique public–private partnership techniques to leverage both the city's access to the debt markets and the ability to use tax-exempt debt in a structure that provided for low cost capital with a strong ability for repayment from U.S. Open ticket receipts and the pledge of the substantial broadcast revenues derived from each year's U.S. Open tournament. Of significance, the publicly owned "park" would receive no public or governmental support for its debt repayment. Of even more significance, Fitch Ratings and S&P Global Ratings provided underlying investment grade ratings of BBB+ and BBB respectively, which represented the first stand-alone revenue bond ratings for a "recreational facility." This financing set the stage for several financings on behalf of the NTC and preserved its place in sports as both a recreational facility and a marquee venue in professional sports.

Growth of the NTC

In 1994, the U.S. Open experienced paid attendance of over 500,000 with gross ticket and broadcast revenues in excess of $53 million. The NTC's commitment did not end here and among other financial investments, the USTA borrowed additional $24 million in 2007 to complete a state-of-the-art indoor tennis building. This facility would include various teaching and fitness facilities as well as a museum and bookstore. The total investment was well over $60 million. By this time, paid attendance at the U.S. Open was attracting 700,000 attendees with gross revenues from tickets and broadcasting exceeding $138 million. It was the vision of the USTA that expansion of their facilities would not only serve their professional tournament, but also pave the way to build and maintain a premier community venue.

Paid attendance for the next several years leveled off at around 700,000 attendees. Ticket Sales and Broadcast Revenues exceeded $163 million in 2013, showing remarkable resilience after the 2008 to 2009 financial crisis that hit New York so severely. Not only had the USTA succeeded on using its financial leverage wisely to expand its New York footprint, but the USTA's ability to repay the debt on the NTC was stronger than ever.

Current Day
Based on the success of its multifaceted expansion programs from the early 1990s through the mid-part of the first decade of this millennium, the NTC set itself on a course to radically improve its facilities again. In 2014 and beyond, the USTA borrowed over $450 million to make vast improvements to this community asset including placing a roof over the main stage—Arthur Ashe Stadium. The U.S. Open was commanding revenue close to $300 million for the two-week event and expectations were that once the improvements were completed, this figure would rise significantly.

In the 1990s when the USTA borrowed $150 million to fund the construction of Arthur Ashe Stadium, it used a structure that provided low cost capital for the time period and at tax-free rates. Interest rates have been on a downward direction since that time period; and as such, the USTA has accessed the less restrictive taxable bond markets in recent years. To the credit of the USTA and its management, this was a bold move to allow its expansive facilities to host events that are not core to its mission of tennis—that is, the Fortnite World Cup Finals EPIC Games.

Review Questions

1. Recreational complex owners are always looking for additional sources of revenue. Make a list of some ideas that could leverage the adult population's interest in lifetime fitness and activities.
2. Disney's Wide World of Sports Complex attracts thousands of youth teams and their families every year. Could this idea be franchised around the country? Why or why not?
3. Compile a list of emerging technologies that could help owner/operators of recreational complexes emerge from the COVID-19 pandemic and return to normal usage.

References

Aicher, Thomas J., Buning, Richard J., and Newland, Brianna L. (2020) Running Through Travel Career Progression: Social Worlds and Active Sport Tourism. *Journal of Sport Management. Volume 34*; Issue 6; pp 542-553.

Aicher, T. J., & Newland, B. L. (2018). To explore or race? Examining endurance athletes' destination event choices. *Journal of Vacation Marketing, 24*(4), 340–354.

Barney, J. (1991). Firm resources and sustained competitive advantage. *Journal of management, 17*(1), 99–120.

Bowers, M. T., Chalip, L., & Green, B. C. (2010). Youth sport development in the United States and the illusion of synergy. In B., Houlihan, & M. Green (Eds.), *Participation in Sport: An International Perspective* (pp.173–183). Routledge.

Brown, N. (2008). *Municipal aquatics providers seek right mix of competition and leisure.* www.athletic-business.com/aquatics/municipal-aquatics-providers-seek-right-mix-of-competition-and-leisure.html

Buning, R. J., & Gibson, H. J. (2016). The role of travel conditions in cycling tourism: Implications for destination and event management. *Journal of Sport & Tourism, 20*(3–4), 175–193.

Business Wire. (2019a, October). *Key trends in sport tourism 2019 Report.* www.businesswire.com/news/home/20191015005836/en/Key-Trends-Sports-Tourism-2019-Report

Business Wire. (2019b, May). *Sports–$614 billion global market opportunities & strategies to 2022.* www.businesswire.com/news/home/20190514005472/en/Sports---614-Billion-Global-Market-Opportunities

Climbing Business Journal. (2020). Construction costs are on the rise. www.climbingbusinessjournal.com/construction-costs-are-on-the-rise/

CrossFit. (2020). *Certificate courses.* www.crossfit.com/certificate-courses

Fielding, F. W., Pitts, B. G., & Pederson, P. M. (2014). Historical aspects of the sport business industry. In P.M. Pederson & L. Thibault (Eds.). *Contemporary sport management* (5th ed., pp. 56–81). Human Kinetics.

Haycock, D., & Smith, A. (2018). Adult sport participation and life transitions: The significance of childhood and inequality. In R. A. Dionigi & M. Gard (Eds.). *Sport and Physical Activity across the Lifespan* (pp. 195–210). Palgrave Macmillan.

Hayduk, T. M., III. (2017). The case for a complete model of strategic resource utility in sport and entertainment management. *Journal of Applied Sport Management, 9*(3). https://doi.org/10.18666/JASM-2017-V9-I3-8310

Hayduk, Ted and Walker, Matthew (2018) Mapping the Strategic factor for sport Entrepreneurship. *International Entrepreneurship and Management Journal. Volume 14*, Issue 3. Pp. 705-724.

HomeGuide. (2021) *How much does it cost to own and maintain a swimming pool?* https://homeguide.com/costs/pool-maintenance-cost

Ibis World. (2020, April). *Total recreation revenue.* www.ibisworld.com

Jacobs, B., Newland, B. L., & Green, B. C. (2016, November). *Sustained sport participation: Exploring the role of sport in the lives of adults.* Presentation at the conference of the North American Society for the Sociology of Sport (NASSS) Conference. Tampa, Florida.

Le, T. (2020, May). *Gym, health, & fitness clubs in the US.* www.ibisworld.com

Mehta, N., Steinman, D., & Murphy, L. (2016). *Customer success: How innovative companies are reducing churn and growing recurring revenue.* John Wiley & Sons.

National Strength and Conditioning Association. (2020). *Certification overview.* www.nsca.com/certification/certification-overview/

Newland, B. L, & Aicher, T. J. (2018, June). *Aging and sport participation: Exploring the influence of addition to sport.* Presentation at the conference of the North American Society for Sport Management (NASSM) Conference. Halifax, Canada.

Research and Markets. (2019, December). *Youth sports market projected to reach $77.6 billion by 2026–comprehensive industry analysis & insights.* www.globenewswire.com/news-release/2019/12/26/1964575/0/en/Youth-Sports-Market-Projected-to-Reach-77-6-Billion-by-2026-Comprehensive-Industry-Analysis-Insights.html

Roth, R. (2019a, June). *Sports & athletic field construction.* www.ibisworld.com

Roth, R. (2019b, April). *Indoor sports facilities management.* www.ibisworld.com

Scott, D. (2017). *Youth sports, Inc* [film]. HBO. www.youtube.com/watch?v=9ATwFkYpVys

U.S. Travel Association. (2019). *Domestic travel fact sheet.* www.ustravel.org/system/files/media_root/document/Research_Fact-Sheet_Domestic-Travel.pdf

Wernerfelt, B. (1984). A resource based view of the firm. *Strategic management journal, 5*(2), 171–180.

World Sport Tourism. (2020). *Sport tourism.* www.wst-show.com/en/sport-tourism

Examples of Mega Sport Recreational Facilities

1. www.espnwwos.com/
   Address: 700 S Victory Way, Reunion, FL 34747
2. www.imgacademy.com/
   Address: 5650 Bollettieri Blvd, Bradenton, FL 34210
3. https://apexsportsevents.com/
   Address: 137 Mountain View Rd, Hillsborough Township, NJ 08844
4. www.spookynooksports.com/
   Address: 75 Champ Blvd, Manheim, PA 17545
5. www.dallassports.org/venue/view/17882/Advantage-Sports-Complex.html
   Address: 2800 N Interstate 35E, Carrollton, TX 75007
6. https://silverlakespark.com/
   Address:5555 Hamner Ave, Corona, CA 92880
7. https://grandpark.org/
   Address: 9000 Grand Park Blvd, Westfield, IN 46074

CHAPTER 5
Business of Stadium Financing

Robert Boland

LEARNING OBJECTIVES

- To understand why 1992 became a pivotal year for stadiums in the United States, as the concept of where a stadium could be located and the amenities it provides dramatically shifted.
- To learn what elements do stadiums contain today that maximize revenues for stadium owners.
- To study how stadiums are financed and how league ownerships assist in a particular city acquiring and building a stadium;
- To understand how local and state agencies assist in driving and funding a stadium project as a form of economic development.
- To understand the role that loan interest rates play in determining the financing of a stadium, despite rising construction costs.
- To learn the strategies behind building a stadium for owners—increasing franchise appreciation and value.
- To understand why public–private partnerships can both complicate and simplify a desire for a new stadium or arena.

This chapter focuses on how new revenue streams generated by new or significantly renovated stadiums and arenas have driven a period of extraordinary development of new facilities in professional sports; this began as a North American trend but has spread across the world. In turn, the development of these new revenue streams and new facilities has also led to an increase in the value of professional franchises.

With the addition of an NHL expansion franchise in Seattle slated to begin play during the 2021-22 season, the five major North American Sports Leagues (MLB, MLS, NBA, NFL, and NHL)

comprise a total of 150 individual clubs and franchises. All but 13 of these clubs play in facilities that have been built or substantially renovated since 1990. This means that 137 (91%) of North American major professional teams play in new facilities. This is a marked contrast to a time, not so long ago, when many professional teams played in municipally owned facilities that they rented or leased and over which had limited control (Simard, 2020).

The year 1992 is an important line of demarcation due to the opening of Baltimore's Orioles Park at Camden Yards. This new yet retro-designed ballpark brought several structural innovations: seating closer to the field-of-play because of the ballpark's asymmetric design; expanded lower-bowl seating; and wide concourses adjacent to the field for expanded dining, vending, and entertainment options for before, during, and after games ("Oriole Park at Camden," n.d.). Each of these innovations became transformative, not just in terms of design, but also in terms of revenue generation across all professional sports; this transformation helped spark a building and renovating boom that has not slowed for the past 30 years.

Camden Yards is not alone in being a revolutionary facility, and this chapter will look at significant moments in stadium development and their correlation to franchise value at a variety of key moments, up to the 2020 opening of Los Angeles' SoFi Stadium. The development of SoFi Stadium, the new home of the Los Angeles Rams and Los Angeles Chargers of the NFL, opened with a total cost of $5 billion and has increased the value of the Rams from 31st out of the 32 NFL franchises in 2012, when they were still in St. Louis, to fourth overall ($3.8 billion) in the NFL, as noted in *Forbes Magazine*'s most recent valuation of all NFL Franchises (Stuter, 2020).

This chapter attempts to answer why these changes occurred and explores the driving forces behind the remaking of the sports facility landscape that, by extension, has led to explosion in franchises value, the overall value of the team or club. This chapter also helps identify and define the primary elements of modern sports facilities that have the potential to produce the most revenue. These elements produce not only more game-day revenue but also contractually obligated income (COI) that is owed on multiyear bases; this contractually obligated income correlates to increased topline club and league revenue, the amount generated by the team and all teams in the league and, ultimately, increased franchise valuation.

This chapter also explores the financing mechanisms used by professional leagues and teams to fund new, more revenue-friendly facilities. The chapter includes the perspective of league officials as to the benefits of using leaguewide revenue sources to secure novel credit facilities that help team owners improve their facilities. Further, this chapter will look in-depth at how a modern facility is funded, examining secured, mezzanine, and public-financing structures used in modern facility development, discussing exemplars from across major sports, and including a basic balance sheet from a recent facility.

Also included in this chapter is an examination of the trends in stadium and arena design and the technology that has supported and driven this building boom. The chapter includes the municipal perspective, profiling the reasoning of those elected officials who have made the decision to support private–public partnerships related to the development of sports facilities. Additionally, the chapter examines how this trend is expanding globally, both in terms of professional sports clubs and major sporting events, building or updating facilities to enhance revenue generation, and thus supporting club success through player spending.

Finally, the chapter introduces relevant economic and financing terminology and supports a student user's development and familiarity with these terms.

The Story of the House That Ruth Built: How the Old and the New Yankee Stadium Illustrate the History of Stadium Development

The original Yankee Stadium, which opened in 1923, played host to a long list of historic athletic contests—from the games of the powerhouse New York Yankee teams of the 1920s, 1940s, and 1950s to significant college football games, including the game during which Notre Dame's Knute

Rockne gave the famed halftime speech imploring his team to "win one for the Gipper," referencing deceased star player George Gipp. Rockne inspired his team to a 12-6 victory over Army in 1928; the 1958 National Football League Championship Game between the Baltimore Colts and New York Giants went into overtime and has been hailed as "the greatest game ever played;" famous boxing matches have been contested; and the stadium even held visits from religious leaders (Sullivan, 2008).

The stadium was built on land acquired in 1921 at a cost of $675,000, and the stadium was erected at a cost of $2.5 million; when adjusted for inflation, this works out to a price tag of approximately $350 million, a remarkable bargain considering that the 2008 incarnation of the stadium, built adjacent to the old stadium's footprint, checked in at a cost estimated between $1.6 and $2.3 billion, between 500% and 700% more than the original cost of construction in constant dollars (Sullivan, 2008).

The old Yankee Stadium, in its original layout, was closed and was significantly renovated starting in the fall of 1973, thus giving the stadium a 50-year useful life span during its first incarnation. The stadium was renovated by its then owner, the City of New York, at a cost of $48 million, although high interest rates during the 1970s and insolvency issues by New York City that required refinancing put estimates for the cost of debt service on this $48 million renovation as high as $150 million (Reisler, 1999). Even so, the stadium reopened and remained in service from 1976 to 2006, a total of 80 years, not including time for renovations ("Yankee Stadium," n.d.). Despite the New York Giants NFL club's departure for a single-use stadium in nearby New Jersey in 1976 and the range of major events the stadium accommodated decreasing slightly, the renovated stadium still played host to several papal visits, a classic heavyweight championship title defense between champion Muhammad Ali and challenger Ken Norton, and the North American Soccer League debut of Pelé as a member of the New York Cosmos (Dame, 1999).

The old Yankee Stadium had two principal owners during its total 80-year life, the New York Yankees baseball club and its owner, beer brewer Jacob Ruppert who led the effort for the 1923 project to build the original stadium. Then, in 1972, when significant structural renovations were needed to maintain the aging facility, the Yankees, then owned by broadcasting giant CBS, conveyed the stadium to the City of New York and signed a 40-year lease to serve as tenants in exchange for the city to undertake significant renovations (Rotondi, 2020).

How a historically successful team went from developing and building a stadium in the 1920s to conveying that facility after nearly 50 years to the municipality to ultimately deciding in 2006 to build a new stadium, owned and operated again by the team but with significant municipal support, to opening as the most expensive sports stadium ever built is perhaps the main point of this chapter. The change from 1972 to make owning and operating a new stadium or arena go from being a liability for the Yankees to leading the teams' owners to build the most expensive stadium built in the first decade of the 2000s and having that decision make business sense both in terms of the revenue produced and increase in the value of the Yankees' franchise is nothing short of revolutionary.

The story of the original Yankee Stadium, "the House that Ruth Built," that was built cheaper, lasted longer, and was ultimately replaced at far higher cost, is an illustration of the broad modern trend wherein 137 major league sports teams, 91% of all the teams in the United States, replaced their stadiums more often, more quickly, and at significantly higher cost than their prior facilities. The reason for this trend is explained in greater detail in the upcoming sections of this chapter. Looking back and seeing professional teams play in facilities that had 50-year or more useful life spans that were either municipally owned or maintained was commonplace, but it is now exceptionally rare.

© eddtoro/Shutterstock.com

Interest Rates

Prior chapters have introduced the importance of interest rates. Simply put, interest rates, the costs paid upon repayment of borrowed money, also called principal, based on a percentage of the total principal borrowed, can favor or deter new development.

If interest rates are high, the cost of borrowing money for a capital project, a project of significant size that is undertaken to create more revenue or support or improve a major asset, is also going to be higher.

The City of Portland, Oregon's City Budget Office defines a capital project in a succinct and understandable way as any project that helps maintain or improve a city asset (often called infrastructure); these projects must be more than $10,000 in cost, purchases in excess of $50,000, and have a 10-year expected life span (*Definition*, n.d.).

By contrast, if interest rates are low, the cost of borrowing money for a capital project is lower because the amount of interest to be repaid with the principal is less.

In calculating the total costs of a large-scale capital project like a sports stadium or arena, interest will represent a large portion of the cost for building a new facility, especially when recognizing that this interest will be paid for many years. If interest rates are low, the cost of building a new stadium will be lower than when interest rates are high. Interest rates are typically benchmarked to the rates of United States Treasury Bills.

The following chart indicates that U.S. interest rates remained fairly stable throughout the founding years of the nation up to the middle portion of the 20th Century when the Great Depression, the New Deal recovery of the administration of President Franklin D. Roosevelt, and victory in World War II saw interest rates drop to previously unseen lows. However, from 1946 to 1981, interest rates spiked, reaching historical highs. Since then, they have dropped precipitously, if not evenly, in the nearly 40 years since 1981, reaching historic lows in recent years.

Interest rates alone fail to tell the whole story of capital finance generally, or stadium finance specifically, but they do broadly influence whether new facilities are being developed, whether teams are staying in ones already built, or whether teams are seeking to play in municipally owned or publicly funded facilities.

The Yankees ownership's decision in 1972, discussed earlier, to essentially give Yankee Stadium to the City of New York, took place while the team faced both significant costs for capital improvements to renovate the stadium and occurred at a time during which interest rates were quite high. By contrast, the stadium and arena building boom of the last 30 years has occurred during a time of rising construction costs but sharply declining interest rates. How significant is this?

Using a very simplistic example of just $1 million—recognizing that stadium costs are hundreds, if not thousands of times greater than this; financing a stadium or arena is significantly more complex than a simple fixed-rate mortgage or loan. If one were to raise that interest rate to the 10% interest rate that predominated the early 1980s, the interest amount paid on that same $1 million loan adds $1,316,051 in interest to the $1 million principal.

Decrease the interest down to 3%, and the amount of interest to be repaid over 20 years goes down to $331,034; every increase or decrease in interest rates makes a significant difference to the ultimate cost of money spent and the total project cost.

Interest rates have not absolutely barred new stadium and facility development projects from being undertaken, but they have a significant effect on such projects and have forced team owners and leagues to find alternative strategies to support stadium and facility development during periods of higher interest rates. Not surprisingly, teams and team owners now employ every method they can to access lower interest rates on their projects. These methods will be discussed in the upcoming sections of this chapter.

Capital Assets and Capital Budgets

Stadia are typically considered and financed as capital assets, and developing a new stadium or arena is done through the creation of a capital budget. It would be ideal if an extraordinarily wealthy individual could go to a bank and get a loan for a billion or more dollars to develop a new stadium; however, it is almost never nearly so simple. As extremely costly capital assets, new stadium and facility development usually involve the purchase or acquisition of land, the improvement of public infrastructure leading to and from and adjacent to the facility, the construction of a complicated and technologically advanced building, and the payment of the costs of construction and the debt service on all of these debts (e.g., land purchase, infrastructure, and facility loans), along with the operation and maintenance that such a building requires.

Why would an owner adopt such a massive undertaking? Sports franchises are generally fairly small organizations, with most having fewer than several hundred full-time employees, counting players. Undertaking a stadium or facility development will force any organization to take on numerous more employees or consultants with roles ranging from frontline facility operations staff to senior and specialized leaders who manage the complex construction and transactional processes that go into the creation of a stadium or arena.

What is the benefit to an owner to take on a billion dollars of debt, add staff, and hire consultants? The answer is far more complex than just having a shiny, new facility or upgraded locker rooms. The benefit to the detriment analysis is almost always focused on two specific outcomes: to increase the value of the franchise (asset appreciation) through the addition of a real property asset, the arena or stadium, and to increase top line revenue (overall income before expenses). Over the last 30 years, there has been a positive correlation between new or improved stadium development and increases in franchise revenue, as well as appreciation in franchise values. If an owner can, by building a new facility or significantly improving an existing one, increase the value of their team, the owner's asset, and generate increased revenue that might be near or close to the debt service on the new facility, then what may be a calculated risk becomes a much more sound business decision.

Appreciation, Revenue, and History

In February 1991, after winning the Super Bowl the prior month, the New York Football Giants sold a 50% interest in the team. This example has been chosen because the time period around 1990 or 1991 becomes a key time period for the study of stadium and facility finance. The foregoing historic interest rate chart indicates that the sale occurred in the middle of a period during which interest rates began dropping precipitously. From a two-century high, in excess of 10%, reached in 1981, interest rates retreated throughout the 1980s, so much so that, by 1990, the financing climate for all borrowing, especially private borrowing, was much more favorable.

The 50% ownership interest in the Giants had been in the Mara family since 1925. It had been previously been held by Tim Mara, the grandson of the Giants' founder, also named Tim Mara. The elder Tim Mara paid $500, around $8,000 in today's dollars, for the rights to a franchise, as the fledgling NFL searching for a New York outlet to showcase its product. When Giants' founder Tim Mara died, the team passed in equal shares to his two sons John "Jack" Mara and Wellington Mara. Jack Mara died in 1965 and passed his interest in the team to his son Timothy Mara, II. It was Tim's interest that was sold to Preston Robert Tisch, a New York investor who had, at various times, owned a variety of business interest through the Loews Corporation. That 50% share was sold by the Mara family to help offset anticipated inheritance taxes on the team's appreciation. Timothy Mara, II's uncle, Wellington Mara, maintained the other 50% interest, and the price tag on the sale is reported to have been $80 million, making the 1991 snapshot value of the team $160 million (Graziano, 2015).

In 1991, the Giants played in a facility, Giants Stadium, that had been built less than two decades earlier; the facility was state owned. The Giants paid rent to the State of New Jersey and had primary use of the stadium and adjoining practice fields as part of its lease. The Giants moved to New Jersey from the old Yankee Stadium in 1976, incentivized by the lure of being the primary tenant of a football-specific facility with improved sightlines. The New York Cosmos of the then-called North American Soccer League (NASL) ultimately joined the Giants in New Jersey's "Meadowlands" ("Giants Stadium," n.d.).

This project was a large one for the time (total value), but it was undertaken by the State of New Jersey for several reasons in the early 1970s: the project brought land that previously been unused and without tax value onto the tax rolls; the Meadowlands project paired private development with a stadium and a horse racing track and then ultimately an indoor arena about 12 miles from downtown New York City; and it was designed to help build a corridor of economic activity from wealthy suburban bedroom communities in Bergen County to New York City. It was emblematic of the kinds of projects that were built in the 1960s and 1970s, publicly financed and surrounded by parking lots that produced revenue to offset the costs of development and enhanced concessions and in hopes of becoming hubs for future economic growth. Several economists who research the economic impact of sports facilities have been highly critical of this generation of facilities (Noll & Zimbalist, 1997; Baade & Matheson, 2011).

Economists' criticisms have generally focused on how the public money used could have been better spent and that the hopes and objectives of the communities have been seldom achieved. The fact that most of these suburbanized facilities are no longer in use in 2020 and were ultimately replaced in much a shorter period of time than their predecessor facilities at least lends fact-based anecdotal support for these criticisms (Baade & Matheson, 2005).

Looking at each of "old" funding sources and stadium revenue streams makes it easier to understand why the Giants crossed the Hudson River to play in "the swamps of New Jersey." Northern New Jersey, especially near the stadium complex in the early 1970s, was comprised of urban communities that most closely ringed the Hudson River that separated New Jersey from New York. It also consisted of a few more-developed outlying, densely populated community centers and an expanding and increasingly populous (and prosperous) suburban communities, mostly made up of largely single-family homes surrounded by lawns and greenspace (Mallach et al., 2006).

Older, more urbanized communities like New York City and those nearby communities of New Jersey, just described, were beset by social problems and public budget challenges based on stagnant or slow-growing tax bases and increasing public needs in the late 1960s and early 1970s. Relocation of more affluent residents from these communities contributed this downward cycle and the growth of more outlying suburban areas (Mallach et al., 2006).

These suburban areas were increasing their tax revenue annually, primarily through new home development and new residents moving to them, sparking additions to the property tax rolls of these suburban communities. Additionally, increased population produced greater local sales and other use tax revenues. These newer communities typically had budget surpluses and the ability to deliver large tracts of land for development and supportive infrastructure. This was true not only for the Meadowlands project but for the move of the Detroit Lions and Pistons to Pontiac, Michigan and the Pistons onto Auburn Hills; the Los Angeles Rams to Anaheim, California; the Dallas Cowboys to Irving, Texas; and so on ("A Look at the History," 2017).

The chief asset these communities offered to professional franchises was the continuing tax revenue surplus to support public financing of gleaming new facilities that were far nicer, more modern, and more revenue friendly than their aging early 1900s-built, Yankee Stadium–era predecessors. They could also be said to have brought teams closer to their preferred fans' front doors.

The New York Giants followed many in their fan base to the suburbs in 1976 and were playing in a publicly built, publicly financed stadium, when, in 1991, as the reigning World Champions, the snapshot of their total team value was placed at $160 million; a low-end valuation was placed around $120 million (Eskenazi, 1991).

Flash forward to 2020 and the *Forbes* valuation, a common standard for sports franchise valuation, showed the Giants' value now at $4.3 billion, a 28-fold increase over 30 years. This also computes to just short of doubling year over year (Traina & Watkins, n.d.).

As a means of comparison, the Dow Jones Industrial Average, one of the key measures of New York Stock Exchange equity market values, saw an increase of approximately 5 to 5 1/2-fold over the same period; this is generally thought of as an historically favorable period of equity investment appreciation. The Dow Jones Industrial Average grew from an index average of approximately 5,000 in 1991, when the Giants were valued via sale, to the high 20,000s by 2020. This is an illustration of the extraordinary power of franchise appreciation far outpacing even other high-powered appreciation friendly investment opportunities ("Dow Jones," n.d.).

It is fair to consider that a portion of this appreciation is also fueled by increases in leaguewide broadcast revenues, which are generally publicly announced and accounted for. Professional sports have maintained their power as one of the few consistently watched sources of live television content, and league broadcast rights fees have continued to rise, especially as new distribution services have come onto the scene. Some of the growth of appreciation for the Giants may also be attributed to the size and wealth of the New York metropolitan area as a home market. However, it is impossible to ignore the exceptional appreciation of this franchise and of the hundred or so more that have taken on the cost and challenge of building a new state-of-the-art facility.

In 2006, the Giants undertook the task of building a substantially privately financed new stadium at cost of $1.6 billion, arguably the most expensive open-air stadium ever built. This new stadium would increase seating capacity from 76,000 at its opening to 80,000 at its closing to 82,000 in the new stadium but increased space in the stadium's seating bowl only by a small amount. Compare this to the new Met Life Stadium, which opened in 2010 and expanded over the prior Giants Stadium, which opened in 1976, and showed an increase in every area of the stadium behind the main seating bowl. This allowed for accommodation for revenue-friendly amenities, including lounges, club seats and luxury boxes, promenades for luxury amenity customers, and digital screens for advertising ("About us," n.d.).

The appreciation of the Giants allowed the team to build a more revenue-friendly facility that included a naming rights sponsor and four pillar sponsors that produce annual revenue to pay the debt service on the stadium and reward the team owners with multiple annualized revenue streams that did not exist in the prior publicly built and run stadium, which, in turn, increased the value of the Giants franchise. Simply put, by building a new facility, even a largely family-run, an old-school franchise like the Giants has been able to identify new revenue streams that would provide annualized revenue and reap the extraordinary benefit of appreciation of the franchise.

This positive correlation of having a modern stadium that generates high levels of revenue has reshaped the last 30 years of North American sports business. Teams and leagues have adjusted

© NYCStock/Shutterstock.com

to this by setting up credit facilities, organized borrowing structures secured by leaguewide appreciation in franchise value and by leaguewide broadcast media rights, to help teams continue to develop newer and more revenue-friendly facilities.

These new facilities typically contain a series of attributes or amenities, discussed in greater detail later in this chapter, but a simple list will include naming rights; sponsorship or influence zones; personal seat licenses; increased digital advertising capability such as exterior digital screens, interior ribbon board, and larger video boards; and luxury amenities such as like club seats, luxury boxes, or other specialized seating, entertaining, and dining areas that generate multiple times more than regular ticket revenue. These physical attributes have combined with the ability to use the facility regularly on non-game days for meetings and special events, since they are owned and controlled by the team, to generate even more revenue; this additional revenue stream has launched the rush on facility building or renovation. The building or redesigning of facilities to capture more of this enhanced annualized revenue and the wave of franchise appreciation that has gone hand in hand with these revenue increases has become a significant portion of the business of major professional sports leagues in the United States, North America, and around the world.

The Boland Box: Examining Revenue Streams in modern North American Sports

The Boland diagram, developed by the author as professor of sports business at New York University in the early 2000s who taught courses in sports economics, sports finance, and professional franchises, helps conceptualize the importance of and the basis for the correlation between facility-based revenue and having a modern, state-of-the-art facility to franchise value (R. Boland, personal communication, 2007)[1].

The column on the left of the diagram approximately ranks sources of revenue in North American professional sports teams. These rankings may vary slightly between different sports and different markets or franchises. Nonetheless, the items ranked from #2 to #6 as sources of revenue into the team sports are each facility-related, and most also represent forms of contractually obligated income (COI).

Contractually obligated income is usually found in revenue streams that are supported by multiyear contracts. These are legally enforceable obligations on the part of the sponsor, consumer, or renter to pay the team, usually for multiple years and are obligations that may be more easily collateralized, used to secure additional lending, building, or improving facilities.

---

1. This information included in this table was compiled through a series of personal interviews and a review of various other data sources including *Forbes* and *Sports Business Journal* published data ranking franchise revenue streams and personal experience doing due diligence on several professional franchise acquisitions.

Several types of contractual obligations related to a new stadium or arena are likely to include the following.

1. **Personal seat licenses** (PSLs). A PSL is a multiyear payment for the right of the PSL holder to purchase game tickets; this mechanism has allowed team owners to use contractual revenue stream as collateral to borrow against for stadium development.

2. **Facility naming rights**. Teams have played in facilities named for corporate interests for the better part of a century. Wrigley Field was intended to serve as an advertisement for Wrigley products when the chewing gum manufacturing family owned the Chicago Cubs, but as the need to find additional revenue streams has dramatically expanded, the use of contractual naming rights agreements between corporations and teams and facilities has increased. In 2020, only 4 of 32 NFL Teams did not play in stadia with a corporate naming rights sponsor, meaning that 28 of 32 do play in stadiums with corporate naming rights sponsors ("SPORTS-BUSINESS," n.d.). Looking back to 1990, only one NFL team played in a facility with a naming rights sponsor: the Buffalo Bills played in Rich Stadium, named after a Buffalo-based dairy and food company, and signed a 25-year deal in 1973 ("Bills Stadium, Buffalo Bills," n.d.). New stadia dramatically increase both the value of naming rights and the desire of a company to be associated with a facility. Recent naming rights relationships have topped $20 million annually, most commonly over 20, 25, or 30 year terms, with the Las Vegas Raiders' new stadium, Allegiant Stadium, crossing the $20 million threshold (Ozanian, 2019).

3. **Luxury boxes**. Enhanced luxury sections of a stadium are typically rented or leased under a multiyear contract and offer significantly upgraded amenities when compared to a traditional stadium seat. The Houston Astrodome, built in 1965, was the first facility to feature luxury seating. Texas Stadium in Irving, Texas, home of the Dallas Cowboys, had a significant number of luxury boxes that offered enclosed, indoor seat-

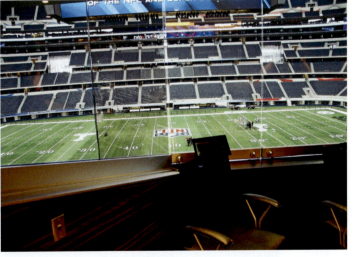

© Ken Durden/Shutterstock.com

ing. There were multiple appeals for luxury boxes. First, they offered the ultimate in a weather-controlled corporate entertainment experience. Second, they were rented on multiyear contracts. Third, luxury suites could generate as much as two times the revenue of all other seats in the stadium. Madison Square Garden in New York City, built in 1968, added 80 luxury suites at the top of the arena, a less than ideal position, in the early 1990s during a major renovation of the then 20-year-old facility. Kevin Wynne, who served as vice president for sports and consumer sales for Madison Square Garden from 1998 to 2004, described these 80 suites as producing gross revenue of nearly $40 million annually and producing net revenue between $35-39 million annually (K. Wynne, personal communication, October 2005). Wynne indicated that when the Knicks (NBA) and Rangers (NHL), the two primary tenants of Madison Square Garden, were competing for titles in the mid-1990s, Madison Square Garden had full occupancy, and every suite was rented on a multiyear basis. When the teams fell off competitively, Wynne and his staff could manage vacancies and special events to keep revenue nearly as high. The suites produced more attributable revenue than did either the Knicks or Rangers. Madison Square Garden's very extensive reimagination of its now 50-year-old building, undertaken over three years in the early part of the 2010s, relocated many of these suites to the top of the lower seating section, making them even more desirable (Zim, 2012).

4. **Club seats**. Club seats are typically open entertainment areas that provide semiprivate enhanced space to professional customers. These spaces often offer separate entrances and are separated from the rest of the stadium or arena bowl. Most club seat areas include enhanced dining and drinking options, many permitting liquor sales. Club seats commonly compile 10,000–15,000 total seats in a large outdoor stadium and 2,000–3,000 seats in an indoor arena and generally produce revenue equal to all regular seats in the arena; this occurs on a COI basis with multiyear, enforceable agreements. These enhanced options are available to most small businesses and have historically offered tax advantages (prior to 2018 federal tax reform, which minimized the deductibility of a number of corporate entertainment options).

Looking at the Boland box, one can see the comparatively modest impact normal fans can have on overall franchise revenue as ticket sales are lower than other revenue sources; however, ticket sales remain approximately the 8th largest source of revenue in American professional sports.

Technology Breakthroughs

Naming and seating innovations were not the only breakthroughs that drove new facility development; digital innovations have also produced COI streams in the form of sponsorship and advertising capacity to reach arena audiences. In arenas, audiences tend to be affluent, certainly more so than the public at large, and sponsors and advertisers reaching this audience have shown an eagerness to enter into complex, often guaranteed, sponsorship deals made possible by enhanced video and digital technology, thus turning the modern arena into much more than not only a facility to watch a game but a place to consume highly targeted advertising content.

Debt Service Coverage Ratios Become the Key Aspect of Stadium Development

What emerges as the singular key aspect of the rush to build new stadia and arenas is whether these new revenue streams can yield enough income to pay the annual debt service for the new facility. If a stadium produces enough new cash flow to exceed what the former facility produced and exceed the annual debt service required by its construction, this makes the rush to build a new facility and add value to the franchise almost an affirmative obligation for the owner.

Debt Service Coverage Ratio (DSCR) is defined as a measurement of a firm's available cash flow to pay current debt obligations. The DSCR shows investors whether a company has enough income to pay its debts and is used as an evaluative tool by lenders and investors. The minimum DSCR a lender requires is something that varies from business to business, industry to industry, and is determined by broader economic trends. The cost of borrowing in terms of interest rates can logically be assumed to rise when DSCR ratios are lower. (The formula for calculating DSCR is **DSCR=Net Operating Income/Total Debt Service Cost**)

While new stadia do not immediately affect net operating revenue for teams, they certainly offer projected or anticipated revenues based on a variety of factors related to market size, size of a team's fan base, market position, which has stratified already intense market competition in cities with two or more teams in the same sport such as Los Angeles and New York, and comparable revenues produced by new facilities in similar market sized peers. This has allowed teams to speculate on the effect new stadia will have on revenue.

A market downturn or a dip in franchise competitiveness can often have a substantial impact when a team has undertaken to build a new facility with a DSCR of less than 2, meaning available operating income is only two times larger than total debt service cost (Hayes, 2020).

When cash flow produced by the new stadium exceed only the amount of debt service and not the prior amount generated by the old stadium, this makes financing a new stadium a more difficult. Most commercial lenders seek annual cash flow that exceeds debt by a factor of 4, 5, or 6 times, creating DSCRs of 4, 5, or 6 (Hayes, 2020).

When an owner recognizes that new facility construction costs are rising dramatically, the new facility race becomes a challenging one, so lenders and leagues have entered the fray to either help increase DSCR or provided alternative sources of zero or low interest lending to allow more teams to build more cheaply. This is done by securing either lower interest rates by providing strategies to increase DSCR, by finding more favorable and secure forms of lending, or by reducing the amount a team must borrow to enjoy the revenue and appreciation that comes from having the multiple revenue streams arising from a new build or substantial renovation. At least one major stadium lender in the peak of this building boom was forecasting just 2 to 1 DSCR in financing new stadia (Selting, 2014).

Modern League Credit Structures

Leagues and lenders have aligned to this new reality of teams wanting to develop new more revenue-friendly facilities and increase their overall valuation. Each has recognized that traditional financing structures and DSCR standards are not ideally suited to financing modern arenas and stadia. Traditional methods are poorly suited for this purpose because individual sports franchises do not produce revenue that is comparable to their overall valuation as ordinary businesses do. In many businesses, overall revenue is a key valuation factor, in addition to market capitalization of stock for publicly traded companies.

For North American sports franchises, the nature of the franchise represents an exclusive and protected right to operate within a league structure that limits competitors and designates exclusive territory (Buzzacchi et al., 2003). This shows great contrast to open-league formats common in Europe and elsewhere where teams can be promoted or relegated based on performance.

The same closed-league structure that North American sports leagues use to create value and exclusivity in franchise ownership has also enabled leagues to use two primary assets: the value of leaguewide media rights and the broad and consistently upward trend of appreciation of franchises' values to establish credit facilities to support the development of new facilities. A credit facility is a type of loan made in a business or corporate finance context. It allows the borrowing business to take out money over an extended period of time rather than reapplying for a loan each time it needs money. In effect, a credit facility lets a company take out an umbrella loan for generating capital over an extended period of time, and the assets or cash flow supporting the loan or facility may, in some cases, be changed (Hayes, 2020).

Leagues, notably the NFL, have sought to build a source of zero-interest lending to their teams; this has paid off handsomely in terms of both new revenue streams and appreciation in franchises values. Consider the prior example of the New York Giants, discussed earlier in the chapter; revenue has grown in a new privately funded stadium while, at the same time, the value of the franchise has increased exponentially due to that revenue growth. The NFL established the G-3 and G-4 credit facilities[2] to help teams build new stadia with zero-interest loans of up to $125 and $150 million, respectively, to lower the cost of teams borrowing ("Fitch Rates National Football," 2020).

Municipal Financing Options

Just as leagues have become lenders or used their respective assets to help individual owners, so too have municipalities reentered stadium financing, but in very different ways than the examples seen earlier in this chapter. Whereas municipalities in the 1960s and 1970s either built stadia like the old Giants Stadium in the Meadowlands or took over the upkeep of the old Yankee Stadium using the power of public entities to raise revenues for such facilities,

© Faizal Ramli/Shutterstock.com

the trend has shift to municipalities, local and state governments issuing municipal bonds guaranteed by the government; as such, bonds are considered low-risk investments, usually offer low interest rates (lower than traditional lending sources), and having the franchise pay the interest on these bonds.

This is a model that has become increasingly common—governments support private businesses by offering borrowing to a conduit issuer. A conduit issuer is an organization, usually a government

2. G-3 and G-4 were the respective credit facilities/programs started by Tagliabue that provided funding for stadia to keep teams in cities in the NFL by Tagliabue after the Oilers moved to Tennessee and the Rams and Raiders both left Los Angeles.

agency, that issues municipal securities to raise capital for revenue-generating projects where the funds generated are used by a third party (known as the "conduit borrower") to invest in some project or activity that has a public benefit. Here, the franchise, secured or collateralized by the wealth of the owner or owners or the assets of the franchise, and the league become the conduit borrower and pays the interest and principal payments, usually at much lower cost than through private borrowing. The benefit to the municipality is that it increases tax revenue in and around the new stadium and is paid back by the conduit borrower ("Conduit Issuer Definition," 2020).

There are generally two types of municipal bonds issued to fund stadia. General obligation bonds (GO bonds) are guaranteed by tax revenues broadly and ideally by the increased tax revenue produced by the facility itself. However, if a facility does not generate sufficient tax revenue to pay the interest on the bonds, which has not been uncommon, the government must find income from other tax revenues. Therefore, rather than choosing between new arenas or hospitals or road improvements, many municipalities now issue revenue bonds to fund arena development. A revenue bond is guaranteed by a specified tax, often on the facility or some other revenue stream connected to the facility. It is not uncommon to guarantee stadium bonds with taxes on visitors—specifically hotel room taxes, rental car taxes, and airport landing taxes; these taxes not borne by residents, but by visitors.

Review Questions

1. There have been a variety of trends in stadium development and ownership across the last 120 years in the major North American professional sports; what are the major trends in stadium development?
2. During the last 30 years, professional teams have built or renovated their stadia and arenas more often than at any time in history; what are all the factors that have caused this trend?
3. Funding professional stadia and arenas is a complex process; how do government bonds and league credit facilities play a key role in reducing borrowing costs and why are they used by team owners?

Case Study

Financing the Stadium

There are several major league cities in North America that have lost professional franchises or are at risk of possibly losing franchises because of outdated or retrograde stadia or arenas. The names of Atlanta, Winnipeg, Minneapolis–St. Paul, Seattle, St. Louis, Quebec, Oakland, San Diego, and Kansas City come to mind as all having lost a Big Four professional team in either the recent or at least not so distant past.

There are risks for a municipality that takes place when it loses a big four team. That risk is enlarged when that franchise represents the single or perhaps one of just two Big Four pro teams located in that market because it usually indicates that the market (the municipality or adjoining municipalities that a team or teams may reasonably draw fans from) is smaller in terms of population, wealth, or is geographically dispersed to such a degree to make it difficult to select a single location to develop a revenue positive arena or facility. Having franchises in all Big Four North American sports is an indicator of a city being a major city that carries with it certain advantages in attracting more tourism, investment and business, maintaining its population and the overall social and economic health of that city or market. While having multiple professional sports teams and facilities is not absolutely indicative of a city being a first-tier business city, it is generally supportive of a conclusion that that market has sufficient wealth, population and development to support its teams and their facilities. Carrying through this line of thought to its logical conclusion, a market with only a single team in a single sport (Buffalo, Ottawa, Winnipeg, Calgary, Green Bay, Orlando, St. Louis, Jacksonville, Oakland, San Diego, Sacramento, as just some examples) faces greater risk if it were to lose its franchise and may have limitations in relocating a current or expansion franchise. Simultaneously some, perhaps not all of these cities have limitations in generating the revenue that would support a modern, revenue friendly stadium and successfully meet debt service obligations. New York with nine Big Four franchises in its core or suburbs, Los Angeles with eight franchises in its core and suburbs, followed by Chicago, Dallas, Denver, Detroit, Miami, Minneapolis–St. Paul, Philadelphia, Phoenix, and Washington, D.C., with four franchises each are the only markets that have all four Big Four teams. The San Francisco Bay area has five Big Four Franchises, but the Bay Area is made up of three significant cities, San Francisco, Oakland, and San Jose, and the franchises are spread throughout all of this area and recently Oakland has lost two teams in recent years—the NBA's Golden State Warriors moving to much wealthier and more densely populated downtown San Francisco and the NFL's Raiders, which decamped to Las Vegas in 2020 after failing to get a stadium deal in Oakland or be included in the NFL's sweepstakes to move to Los Angeles (Wickersham & Van Natta, 2019).

This case sets up as its challenge to ask users to serve as consultants in one of these critical smaller market teams or cities and explore the questions posed generally by this chapter.

Market and City Factors

To answer these questions, it will helpful to refer to and base your answers on data obtained from a listing of city populations, metropolitan area populations, cross-referenced to the respective wealth of these cities and areas. It may also be helpful to identify several peer cities that have built a new stadium or arena to help support your forecasting. Finally, it is also helpful for you to refer to the *Forbes* listing of franchise valuations. The *Forbes* listings aren't always exact, but if the revenue of an identified peer city that has recently built a stadium or arena has increased or the valuation of that franchise has been positively affected by that new facility, there is a stronger argument for anticipating such growth. Be wary of cross-sport comparisons unless they are in the same market because the revenue structures of each of the leagues can at times be like comparing apples and oranges.

- What is the risk if the city were to lose the franchise?
- What are the advantages of keeping the franchise in the market through the renovation our existing stadium or construction of a new stadium?
- Is the franchise functionally relocatable to another city or market where it could be significantly more valuable? (See the Rams or Raiders *Forbes* valuations after relocating from St. Louis to Los Angeles and Oakland to Las Vegas respectively.)
- If a facility is to be built with stadium-based revenue streams, as described in this chapter, can it be anticipated to be strong based on market size, wealth, and population?

Wickersham and Van Natta's analysis of the NFL's decision on deciding on competing proposals to relocate teams into the Los Angeles market is illustrative of how the ability to locate a facility may have a favorable relationship to potential revenue streams that the facility can generate and how it will be financed.

Building a Capital Structure

When trying to define the kind and type of facility a team can build, it is appropriate to consider both the ability for the market to generate and support the anticipated revenue streams but also consider the ability of the franchise and its owner to finance the facility. The former represents anticipated revenue. The latter represents anticipated debt service. The difference between the two is the debt service cover ratio (DSCR). While naming rights, luxury, and club seating have been proven revenue generators along with in-arena advertising and upgraded concessions, tapping into these revenue streams add cost to a facility. Building a capital structure including DSCR and anticipated amounts to be financed.

Questions for Assessing a Capital Structure

- How much and at what interest rate can this market and franchise reasonably spend on a new facility?
- The interest rate is governed by anticipated revenue, anticipated cost of construction, and anticipated costs of borrowing; exploring these using the peer facilities identified in the first portion of this process—what aspects of the peer facilities have performed well, and what aspects of the same have performed poorly?
- What was the overall cost of the peer facility?
- Are infrastructure improvements necessary to optimize facility revenue?
- If infrastructure improvements are necessary, is there a strong case for the municipality bearing the cost of these?
- If the municipality is undertaking infrastructure improvements, does this impair the municipality's ability to provide conduit issued bonds?
- Lenders are generally unlikely to provide funding or lending up to the full cost of a private facility. Does your proposed facility require land acquisition, or can it be built on land already in control of the franchise or municipality? If no land acquisition is required, that could lower facility costs by several hundred million dollars.
- In putting together a credit structure for the proposed new facility, is funding available from the league, municipality, state, or other source? All of these have lower interest rates than commercially sought credit structures.
- What percentage of the credit structure for the proposed facility will require the team's owners to use their own money? Remember the advantages that go with borrowing money for capital projects.
- Realistically, what will the credit structure and prevailing repayment rates look like including calculating DSCR?

The author would like to acknowledge the work of research assistant- Meagan McNeary, J.D.

References

A look at the history of expansion and relocation in the NFL. (2017, March 27). *Las Vegas Review-Journal.* www.reviewjournal.com/sports/raiders-nfl/a-look-at-the-history-of-expansion-and-relocation-in-the-nfl/

About us. (n.d.). *MetLife stadium.* Retrieved December 5, 2020, from www.metlifestadium.com/stadium/about-us

Baade, R., & Matheson, V. (2005, July). *Have public finance principles been shut out in financing new sports stadiums for the NFL in the United States?* Economics Department Working Papers. https://crossworks.holycross.edu/cgi/viewcontent.cgi?article=1081&context=econ_working_papers

Baade, R., & Matheson, V. (2011, January). *Financing professional sports facilities.* Economics Department Working Papers. https://web.holycross.edu/RePEc/hcx/HC1102-Matheson-Baade_FinancingSports.pdf

Bills Stadium, Buffalo Bills football stadium—Stadiums of Pro Football. (n.d.). Stadiums of Pro Football. Retrieved January 6, 2021, from www.stadiumsofprofootball.com/stadiums/bills-stadium/

Buzzacchi, L., Szymanski, S., & Valletti, T. M. (2003, September 1). Equality of opportunity and equality of outcome: Open leagues, closed leagues and competitive balance. *Journal of Industry, Competition and Trade.* https://link.springer.com/article/10.1023/A:1027464421241?error=cookies_not_supported&code=b674adf6-80d4-4ef8-bab8-e8697f3d56fb

Conduit issuer definition. (2020, November 4). Investopedia. www.investopedia.com/terms/c/conduit-issuer.asp

Dame, K. T. (1999). *Yankee Stadium in your pocket: The Yankee fan's guide to Yankee Stadium.* Baseball Direct.

Definition—What is a capital project? (n.d.). The City of Portland Oregon. Retrieved December 5, 2020, from www.portlandoregon.gov/cbo/article/50495

Dow Jones—DJIA—100 year historical chart. (n.d.). *MacroTrends.* Retrieved January 6, 2021, from www.macrotrends.net/1319/dow-jones-100-year-historical-chart

Eskenazi, G. (1991, February 21). PRO FOOTBALL; Robert Tisch agrees to buy 50% of the champion Giants. *The New York Times.* www.nytimes.com/1991/02/21/sports/pro-football-robert-tisch-agrees-to-buy-50-of-the-champion-giants.html

Fitch Rates National Football League's G-4, league-wide notes and bank revolver; outlook stable. (2020, August 27). Fitch Ratings. www.fitchratings.com/research/infrastructure-project-finance/fitch-rates-national-football-league-g-4-league-wide-notes-bank-revolver-outlook-stable-27-08-2020

Giants Stadium—History, photos & more of the former NFL stadium of the New York Giants & Jets. (n.d.). Stadiums of Pro Football—Your Ticket to Every NFL Football Stadium. Retrieved January 6, 2021, from www.stadiumsofprofootball.com/stadiums/giants-stadium/

Graziano, D. (2015, March 18). *New York Giants ownership at a glance–NFL Nation–ESPN*. ESPN. com. www.espn.com/blog/nflnation/post/_/id/164371/new-york-giants-ownership-at-a-glance

Hayes, A. (2020, December 27). *Understanding the debt-service coverage ratio (DSCR)*. Investopedia. www.investopedia.com/terms/d/dscr.asp

Mallach, A., Frazier, A., & Sterner, D. (2006, September). *Cities in transition: New Jersey's urban paradox*. Housing & Community Development Network of New Jersey. https://hcdnnj.memberclicks.net/assets/documents/Cities%20In%20Transition%20NJ%20Urban%20Paradox%20Final.pdf

Noll, R. G., & Zimbalist, A. (1997). *Sports, jobs, and taxes: The economic impact of sports teams and stadiums*. Brookings Institution Press.

Oriole Park at Camden Yards history. (n.d.). MLB.Com. Retrieved January 6, 2021, from https://www.mlb.com/orioles/ballpark/information/history

Ozanian, M. (2019). *Oakland Raiders reportedly nab NFL's most valuable stadium rights deal*. Forbes. www.forbes.com/sites/mikeozanian/2019/08/06/oakland-raiders-reportedly-nab-nfls-most-valuable-stadium-rights-deal/?sh=7c20555c1a9a

Reisler, J. (1999). *Babe Ruth slept here: The baseball landmarks of New York City*. Diamond Communications.

Rotondi, A. (2020, June 19). *A brief history: Yankee Stadium*. Bronx Pinstripes | BronxPinstripes. Com. http://bronxpinstripes.com/yankees-history/a-brief-history-yankee-stadium/

Selting, A. (2014, September 16). *Project finance framework methodology*. S&P Global Ratings. www.maalot.co.il/Publications/MT20171116151537.pdf

Simard, N. (2020, November 10). *List of arenas & stadiums United States*. Digital & Traditional Outdoor Advertising—New York, Los Angeles & All Major Domestic Markets. https://outdoormediabuyers.com/list-of-stadiums-in-united-states/

SPORTSBUSINESS–Stadium naming rights. (n.d.). ESPN. Retrieved January 6, 2021, from www.espn.com/sportsbusiness/s/stadiumnames.html

Stuter, B. (2020, September 11). *LA Rams news: Team 4th most valuable NFL franchise per Forbes*. Ramblin' Fan. https://ramblinfan.com/2020/09/11/la-rams-4th-most-valuable-nfl-franchise-per-forbes/

Sullivan, N. J. (2008). *The diamond in the Bronx: Yankee Stadium and the politics of New York* (Illustrated ed.). Oxford University Press.

Traina, P., & Watkins, J. (n.d.). *New York Giants on the Forbes NFL team valuations list*. Forbes. Retrieved January 6, 2021, from www.forbes.com/teams/new-york-giants/?sh=30c78e71b78c

Wickersham, S., & Van Natta, D. (2016, February 11). *The wow factor*. ESPN. Retrieved January 6, 2021, from http://www.espn.com/espn/feature/story/_/id/14752649/the-real-story-nfl-owners-battle-bring-football-back-los-angeles

Yankee Stadium—history, photos and more of the New York Yankees ballpark from 1923-2008. (n.d.). Ballparks of Baseball—Your Guide to Major League Baseball Stadiums. Retrieved January 6, 2021, from www.ballparksofbaseball.com/ballparks/old-yankee-stadium/

Zim, R. (2012, March 31). *Then and now–Madison Square Garden | NYC then/now: Great Depression & Great Recession*. Macaulay Honors College. https://eportfolios.macaulay.cuny.edu/brooks12/2012/03/31/then-and-now-madison-square-garden/

CHAPTER 6
Financing a Youth Sports Enterprise–A Case Study

Eric Munson and Shanda Munson

LEARNING OBJECTIVES

- To provide students with an insight into how a youth sports facility got off the ground financially.
- To understand the concept of due diligence to compare an idea to the needs of the market-place.
- To learn about facility renovation costs and multiple income streams needed to keep the enterprise profitable.
- To help students calculate how much to pay an instructor based on attendance and income from fees.

BEGINNING OF GOLD STANDARD ATHLETICS

Eric Munson, former Major League Baseball player, retired in 2011 after twelve years of playing professionally. Eric was drafted once after high school in the second round by the Atlanta Braves, but elected to go to the University of Southern California instead, and a second time in the first round, third overall pick, by the Detroit Tigers in 1999 during his junior year at USC.

Since he was unable to finish his college degree, once he was drafted and subsequently signed, he made a promise to his parents and himself that he would complete his degree once he retired. Thus, when his playing career officially ended, he joined the coaching staff of his alma mater, USC, as an undergrad assistant. He coached just one season at USC before moving with his wife Shanda, and their two children Solen and Soraya, to her hometown of Dubuque, Iowa. Eric immediately

joined the coaching staff at the University of Dubuque, once again as an undergrad assistant, until opening his own training facility in the fall of 2013. Eric did complete his liberal arts degree at the University of Dubuque.

We, Eric Munson and Shanda Munson, were given an opportunity to take over an existing indoor training facility that was located at a local sports complex. The owner was no longer interested in trying to run both the indoor facility and the five outdoor fields that hosted tournaments and leagues. The two-story building was approximately 10,000 square feet (roughly 8,000 square feet of useable space) and was located in-between the two largest fields of the complex. The location was ideal in our opinion, and with thousands of area families and athletes visiting the complex throughout the year, the visibility couldn't be better matched for a new business.

It's not uncommon for former professional athletes to branch out into coaching or to become facility owners once their playing careers wind down. They are often quite young by standards of other industries because of typically shorter careers. For Eric personally, the decision to open a facility was an easy one; he knew he wanted to coach and share his experiences and knowledge with the next generation of athletes. He also wanted to help area athletes get exposure on a national level, which was often difficult because of their locale and unusual summer baseball and softball seasons in Iowa.

We did our due diligence by talking with other former professional athletes and Eric's teammates to find out whether this would be a wise investment. To our surprise, most of them warned them against it. We learned from others that statistically, the majority of these types of training facilities close within a few years. Because the business is very seasonal, with peak and very slow times too, one must have the business experience to sustain throughout the year. With very few consistent revenue stream options, again success would come down to the owners' ability to manage their finances through the ebbs and flows. It would also require them to adapt to an ever changing youth sports climate.

We took the risk, and 7 years later, have had enough success to demand that we expand our business, moving to a newly renovated, much larger space, thankfully with even better visibility and expanded revenue opportunities. Our 16,000 plus square foot facility is located at the local shopping mall.

MARKETPLACE AND COMPETITORS

One serious consideration was the market in Dubuque, Iowa. At the time we opened, there was only one other baseball and softball sports training facility in operation, run by a former Minor League player, unlike larger markets where you can often find one within minutes of another one. This was ideal. For a population of just over 58,000 at the time, it was small certainly, but still large enough to warrant more than one training option. And Eric would be able to offer something that no one in the area could, the highest possible level of expertise.

Research showed early on that the majority of potential clients were going to be ages 8 to 18. The majority of training for students in baseball and softball programs in three area colleges were dictated by their own programs. Thus, the focus had to be initially on what could be offered to young area athletes, and any training with college age athletes would be a bonus. While opening a new business with zero clients can be a challenge, we strongly felt we were filling a niche that had been largely untapped up until then.

One crucial component of opening any new business is market research. And besides considering similar businesses, talking with area residents about what it was they want or need in regard to their children's training was vital. Having moved recently from the Los Angeles area to Dubuque, we found the area to be behind the larger markets. Many of these places, due to better weather throughout the year, allow for athletes to play year-round, which can contribute to them being more advanced athletically. Because of this, many seemed to be more heavily involved in personalized training. Many better understood the importance of training outside of team practices. Private instruction was the norm and finding any opportunities to get ahead skillwise in talented markets was a necessity. So the success of our new facility would depend on buy-in from parents in the area. We had to show them why spending the extra money was worth it. And in a market where people tended to be more conservative financially than perhaps somewhere like Los Angeles, the value of such a venture had to be evident immediately. The business had one chance to make a first impression and we planned to make the most of it.

In addition to the training opportunities, this market was behind in youth travel baseball and softball teams as well in 2013. While our competitor had a handful of teams, it wasn't a large organization in comparison to others in bigger markets. But this wasn't something Eric wanted to explore in his first year of business. Instead, we had one team during the first year, our son's 9U team, and waited to expand further until year two when we had a better handle on the overall costs, what it would take administratively to run the facility, learning more about tournament expenses and opportunities, and when we could anticipate the true training needs for teams versus individuals. In year two, our organization expanded from one team to eleven. Never could we have imagined how this would propel the business, but also lead to unanticipated challenges that often lead us to question whether to keep going or abandon the program.

Finally, we put together an in-depth business plan that explored several possible areas of revenue and a plan to effectively utilize the entire space as often as possible. Looking back on it 7 years later, very little of the original business plan came to fruition. Thankfully, our ability to adapt made our initial inexperience forgivable.

Within several years, the market changed significantly in regard to comparable competition. Our original competitor closed his business up the street from ours, to later open up a new, smaller facility several months later in a nearby community. Eventually, he opened up another facility in a neighboring state, Wisconsin, only to fold both eventually.

And by 2020, there were three facilities, including theirs, operating within the city limits. And while one might assume that it would have negatively impacted our business financially, it hasn't. In fact, our business has grown consistently year after year since the beginning—partially due to the increased demand for training, and also due to our reputation for consistently offering quality service.

START-UP COSTS

We were given the opportunity to lease our first building that saved them some upfront costs. We felt strongly about not buying or building something new until we had a better handle on the business and whether it would thrive financially.

We had to first make minor cosmetic renovations to the building, including painting the entire space, which cost a couple thousand dollars. There were no labor expenses, since we and our family painted the whole space ourselves. We also had to purchase outdoor and indoor signage costing approximately $2,500, and add training equipment like batting tees, L screens, batting mats, baseballs, and softballs, all of which cost roughly $3,000. Thankfully, the prior tenant (who still owned the complex where the building was located) left several batting cages and other equipment, like Iron Mike pitching machines and pitching mounds, adding to our upfront cost savings.

Through the years, other improvements have been made to the facility. We purchased a used turf for $5,000, completely redid the batting cage system for $3,000, added fencing for $800, and purchased new office furniture and facility seating for $1,500. Our biggest investment equipmentwise was a HitTrax machine (baseball and softball simulator), which cost $25,000 plus an annual subscription of approximately $800. One should always keep in mind that equipment, like baseballs and L screens, need to be replaced or replenished yearly due to repetitive use.

For several years, the owner of the building had made it known that he wanted to sell the entire complex. We had the option to buy the building, but the investment was too large for a building that we had truthfully outgrown through the years. Thus, it became clear in 2018, in anticipation of a pending deal, that it was time for us to look for other alternative spaces.

Years earlier, we had traveled to visit other sports training facilities throughout the country. It was during those visits to nine facilities of different sizes that we determined exactly what we liked and didn't like should we ever decide to build our own or renovate an existing space. We spoke with an area general contractor who assisted us in getting quotes for a brand-new building between 15,000 and 20,000 square feet. But with a potential price tag of $800,000 to a million dollars, that option was quickly eliminated.

Marketwise, it was nearly impossible to find a space to lease that was large enough, with high enough ceilings, and that was also reasonably priced. After several months of searching, only one

Source: Shanda Munson

space checked the first two boxes, but was so high priced that we had to walk away from that option too.

As luck would have it, with shopping malls across the country struggling to keep tenants, as many people preferred shopping online, the local mall had been creatively adding tenants who fell within recreational and training areas. On one end of the mall, in the downstairs of a former departmental store, a fitness chain and trampoline park took over the majority of the space, leaving just over 16,000 square feet available for a third tenant between the two. But the mall had difficulty leasing the space, due to its odd L shape. We were contacted by

Source: Shanda Munson

the mall's leasing agent with an offer to lease the space, and upon our initial inspection, we became very interested. While the space would need a complete overhaul, it was certainly big enough, and the visibility our facility would get by being in the mall was also very appealing.

While the complex had consistent traffic due to leagues and tournaments being hosted there, we found that most players weren't actually utilizing their facility during those times. Their clients consisted mostly of players with appointments, or teams will scheduled practice times. In addition, the parking at the complex wasn't ideal and the location, hidden at the bottom of a hill, kept potential clients from just stopping in without being scheduled. We felt strongly that a move to the mall could increase our revenue streams from walk-ins, as long as we had new options to offer.

Once the decision was made to relocate, we began working with a general contractor to once again get construction quotes. From the point of signing our lease, we would have just 5 weeks to finish construction before our grand reopening in the spring of 2019. Our general contractor enlisted the help of only subcontractors that were willing to work efficiently, with a lightning fast turnaround.

We had to invest significantly to renovate our expanded facility. The space would have to be completely gutted and transformed to operate as a training facility. With construction costs, equipment, and miscellaneous items, we needed north of $200,000.

After considering all financing options, we decided to take out a line of credit (for up to $175,000) with a low interest rate, and open two credit cards at introductory interest rates of 0% for 18 months to cover the rest of the expenses. The plan was to simultaneously pay down the line of credit and credit cards over the required amounts monthly, as quickly as possible.

BREAKDOWN OF COSTS (rounded)

Construction—$41,000

Plumbing—$17,000

Flooring—$11,000

Turf—$26,000

Batting cages—$10,000

Poles—$7,500

Paint—$8,100

Sprinklers—$2,300

Plaster—$2,300

Signage—$9,500

Pitching machines—$19,000

Utilities—$27,000

Countertops—$1,100

Fencing—$13,000

Concrete—$1,600

Lawyer—$600

Misc.—$10,000 (equipment, TVs, router, membership cards, alcohol and vending, apparel, furniture, etc.)

REVENUE STREAMS

BATTING CAGES—OLD FACILITY

For the first 4 years in the old facility, there were five 55 foot cages available to rent out to individuals and teams. These cages were individual, in that they couldn't be opened up to one another to make a larger training space. Thus, it was difficult to host a team that wanted a larger space to run a defensive practice, for example, simultaneously with players who just wanted to hit.

COST TO RENT CAGES

30 minutes—$15

45 minutes—$30

60 minutes—$45

In the initial business plan we thought a majority of our revenue would come from cage rentals. We considered weekly hours from August-June between 3:00 p.m. and 9:00 p.m. (the majority of clients were children, so hours would begin after school), and weekend hours of 8:00 a.m. to 5:00

p.m. on Saturdays and 8:00 a.m. to 8:00 p.m. on Sundays. If all cages were rented out for the fifty-one possible hours weekly, that would bring in a weekly revenue of $1,530, or $6,120 monthly.

That wasn't the case. While cage rentals happened, they averaged several hundreds of dollars monthly, not thousands monthly. So we needed to find a way to boost that revenue stream.

So in year four, Eric completely retooled the caging system. This meant creating a boxlike cage system that covered the majority of the main floor in the facility. It was separated into five areas. Tunnel 1 and Tunnel 2 were approximately 5,000 square feet combined. They had a single divider in between them, that could be rolled up to the ceiling to create a larger, more open training space if needed. Directly behind those two tunnels were two additional 55 foot cages. While those couldn't open up to one another, they could be pulled back to the fence line to add to the 5,000 square foot space.

Eric liked this setup much better, because it allowed for clients to still rent cages to hit, and also for teams to be working in there at the same time in the tunnels. This led to the facility being rented out more often. And a full capacity meant more revenue.

We further separated the main floor with fencing, and on the other side of the "box" was a wide, long pitching tunnel and strength and conditioning area—two more areas that could be rented out or used for lessons or programming. Finally upstairs, which was primarily an open area used for pitching, we added another cage for clients to use for rentals or lessons.

This increased the revenue significantly, in the four figure range monthly, in the final 2 years at the old facility.

BATTING CAGES—NEW FACILITY

Source: Shanda Munson

Layout, and space maximization, was the biggest consideration when finding a new facility location. And based on the inflow in the previous years, we needed more cages to continue to boost our revenue. More cages means more people inside the facility at one time.

We did this by having nine traditional cages (of different sizes) to rent and use for lessons and programming. Six of the cages in the main floor had dividers, which meant they could be opened up easily to create larger training spaces.

We purchased two new pitching machines (for baseball and softball players) for two more additional cages that could be used with tokens. These two pitching machines/cages brought us a new walk-in clientele we didn't have previously.

Price for renting cages (excluding token cages) (for individuals or teams)
Discounted pricing when clients rent multiple cages.

1 cage
30 minutes—$15
60 minutes—$30
90 minutes—$45

2 cages
30 minutes—$25
60 minutes—$40
90 minutes—$55

3 cages
30 minutes—$35
60 minutes—$50
90 minutes—$65

4 cages
30 minutes—$45
60 minutes—$60
90 minutes—$75

5 cages
30 minutes—$55
60 minutes—$70
90 minutes—$85

6 cages
30 minutes—$65
60 minutes—$80
90 minutes—$95

Price for renting token cages
$2 per token
special pricing (offered periodically)—that is, buy 8, get 2 free

Block rentals
30 minutes—$30 (for individuals or teams)
45 minutes—$45 (for individuals or teams)
60 minutes—$60 (for individuals or teams)

PRIVATE LESSONS

The largest revenue comes from private lessons. In our case, this is especially lessons offered by Eric because we get to keep 100%. In the beginning years, we only had one other instructor working with us. We were very particular about the level of experience of the instructors, and a little bit wary about the mixed messaging that can happen if you allow just anyone to instruct. Over the years, we have started to hire more instructors as we have become more familiar with them and their experience and knowledge. We are fortunate to work with them, and our clients benefit from having more choices for training when Eric is booked. Eric also recommends other instructors who specialize in an area, like pitching. From a revenue standpoint, and also a time standpoint in regard to Eric, the more the number of instructors who are booked, the more the money the facility makes, besides freeing up Eric's time to focus on management.

MEMBERSHIPS

Our memberships are created in order to give an opportunity for players to get in extra work outside of team practices. We need to create different memberships, at different price points, and different needs. For example, we may have a player who just needs access to our pitching tunnel and not our hitting cages or token cages. We also have memberships for players who want access to the whole facility, when cages are available. These memberships come in monthly durations.

TRAVEL TEAMS

Next to private lessons, the largest revenue stream for us is travel baseball teams. However, this also requires the most work. Each season our hope is that this at the very least covers our fixed expenses for the year. How much we bring in does change by the number of teams we have.

Youth teams, ages 8U-14U, practice with us from November to July. Those players pay us a set fee of $500 for those months of practices and team expenses (like coaches fees, team equipment, team insurance, and registration). In the early years, we charged more. But, even though our competitors are significantly more expensive, our objective is to not let price get in the way of someone playing. So we do it to cover our costs, but realize it isn't going to contribute much beyond that.

Our high school teams are handled differently. Instead of player fees like our youth teams, players pay for the number of practices they attend during a nine-week period of time. They pay approximately $40 per two-hour practice. If they don't attend at least three practices, they have to pay a buyout fee of $150. This urges players to make practice a priority. There is a huge value in practicing with their teammates too. We do, however, have many players who live hours away. So if they have the option to practice elsewhere instead, they can do that too.

Additionally, players have other expenses (uniforms, league fees, and tournaments), but those are handled separately from our team expenses and do not positively impact our bottom line.

CAMPS

Camps are a great revenue stream. A key to the success of our camps from early on has been including special guest instructors, like former World Series champions or current MLB coaches, and also by staying ahead of the current technology trends (like utilizing HitTrax) and including it. We currently offer a few different styles of camps.

HALF- TO FULL-DAY CAMPS

These camps are typically All-Skills camps and will last three to five hours. We run multiple sessions to limit group sizes. We will have hitting, pitching, fielding, and catching instructors for these camps. Players spend equal amounts of time at each skill. Pitching and catching happen at the same time, for obvious reasons. We do at least one a year, usually in April ahead of the start of the travel ball season. We have had as many as 125 players at these camps. Cost for a full-day camp averages $125. The price is always higher for this camp than that of our other services, not only because of the duration but because of the cost involved in bringing in other professional instructors. Their fees have range from $1,500 to $4,000 for the day.

MINI CAMPS

In year five, we determined that mini camps would be a great alternative. We pride ourselves on one-on-one instruction even in a camp setting, and by having smaller groups (between 12 and 16 players max) for shorter periods of time, between 1.5 and 2.5 hours, we are able to do just that. And as a bonus for our clients, these mini camps are more affordable, ranging between $35 and $40.

MULTIDAY CAMPS

Summertime is the perfect opportunity to offer multiday camps. These, like our springtime camp, often cover multiple skills. They also include fun activities that the players really enjoy, like All-Skills competitions

Source: Shanda Munson

(speed, throwing, home run derby, around the horn, etc.). Cost for a three-day camp has ranged from $125 to $225, with between 40 and 60 players attending.

Throughout the year, they will host full-day, half-day, and mini camps. Camps may focus on either one skill or several. Clients can also hire their instructors to do a camp for their team, school, or organization. The instructors do travel as well.

Eric's Camps
Instructors are paid hourly between $25 and $100 (depending on the size and duration of camp).

Other Instructors' Camps
They get paid 45% of overall revenue generated through them.

TEAM PRACTICES

In addition to our travel baseball teams, two other types of teams practice at our facility: one, area high schools that Eric provides training for during the off-season, and two, independent travel and league teams, both baseball and softball, that aren't under our travel organization. If a team just wants to practice at the facility, but doesn't require instruction, they just pay normal cage rental fees. With regard to the high schools that Eric works with, individual contracts are worked out with their schools based on the number of sessions and the number of players in each. While there is revenue made here, it is not a big revenue stream for us. It's valuable because players from these teams often come in outside of their team practices for additional training, special programming, or may have memberships, or to use the token cages.

FITNESS

We feel it is very important to partner with local businesses that could provide on-site fitness training for our athletes. In our old facility, our partner kept equipment at the facility, but only came to train our athletes for a couple of eight-week sessions during the off-season. Financially, they received a majority of the players' fees, while we received a small cut. Again, it was a revenue stream that didn't require us to do the work, so even though it was a smaller percentage, it was worth it in our opinion. And most importantly, we were providing something worthy to help our players take their game to the next level.

In our new facility, we made the decision to bring in a partner who would be willing to work on-site permanently. This partner pays us a monthly lease payment, which helps us with our own monthly fixed expenses (lease payment, utilities). We work closely with this partner to create programming for our athletes as well, and take a small percentage of the overall fees for these referrals.

APPAREL

In the old facility, we didn't have a pro shop per se, just one demo night, with equipment and apparel for sale, ahead of the start of the season. In that situation, it was often one vendor that would come in for a day or two, and we would receive a percentage of the profits. But our clients could impulse-buy nothing that was stocked that while in the facility. We decided when we opened up the new facility that we were going to stock more apparel (specifically hats and shirts) and equipment (like bats and batting gloves). We also have deals with multiple vendors that allow for us to get our clients the equipment they want, whenever they want. Like all retail, there is a small markup on these items so that facilities make some money for the work they do to sell the products.

ALCOHOL AND VENDING MACHINE SALES

We decided to add a vending machine with drink products in our new facility. We've found that it generates additional revenue, while not a lot, certainly easy money. It's also very convenient for our clients and often keeps them from bringing in outside products during training.

When designing the facility, we wanted to make sure that we had a large, comfortable, seating area for people to be if they were watching someone train. In addition to tables and chairs, we have a large couch and a bar. We sell packaged food items and canned alcoholic beverages too. We keep our beer affordable, ranging from $2 to $3 apiece, and that has kept us needing to replenish our stock often.

Source: Shanda Munson

PARTIES

In our new facility, we have a multipurpose room that has a large window that overlooks the main floor. This room can be rented for classes, meetings, camps, and get-togethers. We offer different birthday party packages that include use of this room and different areas of the facility as well. This room is also used by Eric with our teams to go over situation training.

STAFF INCOME

For the first 6 years, outside of us, the only contracted employees were the instructors who worked part-time. It's not uncommon for coaches/instructors to have other 9-to-5 jobs while doing instruction in their off-hours. Until an instructor has built up a large enough clientele, that makes the most sense financially because if they don't work, they don't make money. It is completely commission based for many instructors.

In 2019, one contracted instructor was promoted to full-time in order to assist with the day-to-day operations, both behind the scenes and inside of the facility. In addition to their commissions, they are paid a set base pay. This pay requires thirty-five hours of administrative work, twenty from home, and fifteen hours at the facility while not doing instruction.

The instructors are compensated very well. The pay structure is set up as follows.

PRIVATE LESSONS

This is one-on-one instruction.

Clients first pick a desired duration time. Instructors recommend that the client choose either 30 or 45 minutes if the client would be working on one skill (i.e., hitting), whereas they recommend that the client choose 45 or 60 minutes if the client would be working on two skills (i.e., hitting and catching). They also recommend that younger clients (i.e., eight-year-olds) do no more than 30 minutes due to their shorter attention span.

They sell packages of lessons. These are typically a minimum of six lessons. While they don't turn away a new client who wants to try one lesson, Eric recommends clients do at least six to see significant progress in their skills. He also recommends that the lessons be done closely together rather than spread out, which could negate any progress made. A couple of times a year, they will discount lessons (i.e., buy six, get one free); however, that is typically only done in the slower months to keep revenue flowing.

Eric Munson (Owner)
30 minutes—$55
45 minutes—$82.50
60 minutes—$110

Other Instructors
30 minutes—$45 (charged), $25 (commission)
45 minutes—$67.50 (charged), $35 (commission)
60 minutes—$90 (charged), $45 (commission)

SPECIAL PROGRAMMING

Special programming consists of any program that lasts multiple sessions. These sessions are usually 60 to 120 minutes each, and will focus on one skill (i.e., pitching, hitting velocity, catching, throwing velocity, etc.). Pricing varies depending on the number of sessions, but instructor compensation stays the same.

Source: Shanda Munson

Other Instructors
They get paid 45% of overall revenue generated through them.

ONLINE VIDEO ANALYSIS

Clients submit videos for one skill to be evaluated by the instructors. The instructor evaluates the video and gives their analysis, and additionally sends drill recommendations to work at from home.

Other Instructors
They get paid 45% of overall revenue generated through them.

FRONT DESK WORKERS

Typically high school or college students ($9 to $10 per hour)

COACHING FEES

Unless you are a part of a large organization, many travel teams have volunteer coaches. After the first year in business, they decided they wanted to pay at least two coaches per team something. Due to low team fees ($500 total per player to GSA), the organization was only able to provide stipends of $500 to their coaching staff.

An organization could consider payment in more than one way. If you have a coach with a child on the team, they could deduct their coaches' fee from the overall team fees. Or they could elect to get a credit for future training (lessons, camps, special programming, etc.). For coaches who don't have players on the team, they typically take a lump sum.

SPONSORSHIP OPPORTUNITIES

GOLF TOURNAMENT

Our organization hosts an annual golf tournament. Multiple levels of sponsorships are available.

- **Single sponsorship** ($50): includes signage at the tee box and social media acknowledgment.
- **Double sponsorship** ($100): includes signage displayed on tee box #1, acknowledgment in event program and social media acknowledgment.
- **Triple sponsorship** ($250): includes signage displayed on tee box #1, acknowledgment in event program, entry and dinner for two golfers, and social media acknowledgment.
- **Homerun sponsorship** ($500): includes signage at tee box #1, signage on beverage carts, acknowledgment in event program, recognition during dinner, entry and dinner for four golfers, and social media acknowledgment.
- **Grand slam sponsorship** ($1,000): includes signage at tee box #1, signage on beverage carts, acknowledgment in event program, recognition during dinner, entry and dinner for four golfers, social media acknowledgment, and a customized 2 × 3 foot sponsor banner that will be hung for a year at Gold Standard Athletics.

FACILITY ADVERTISING

In addition, customized 2 × 3 foot banners can be created for sponsors and hung in the facility for $500 annually. The facility hosts thousands of athletes each year, so it's a great advertising opportunity for local businesses looking for visibility on a budget. Larger banners, at a higher annual fee, could be offered if the facility has the space to hang them.

CASE STUDY

Objective: To calculate how much the facility makes in 1 month from one instructor, and what that instructor is paid in commissions as well.

PRIVATE LESSONS

Twelve—30 minute lessons

Nine—45 minute lessons

Seven—60 minute lessons

SPECIAL PROGRAMMING

HITTING VELOCITY

Six Sessions

Eight clients

Clients were charged $325 each.

CAMPS

1ST MINI CAMP

16 clients

Clients were charged $40 each.

2ND MINI CAMP

35 clients

Clients were charged $40 each.

CASE STUDY ANSWER KEY

GOLD STANDARD ATHLETICS = $3264.50
INSTRUCTOR = $3,018

WEBSITE RESOURCES

Gold Standard Athletics by Eric Munson Website
Our official business website that includes links to our active social media pages
www.goldstandardathletics.com

City of Dubuque Website
The city where Gold Standard Athletics by Eric Munson is located
www.cityofdubuque.org

Pax Financial Planning
Provides comprehensive wealth management for businesses and individuals
https://paxfinancialplanning.com

The Sports Facilities Companies
Resources for people or partnerships looking to build sports training facilities in their communities. Includes planning, funding, development, and start-up
https://sportadvisory.com

Field of Dreams Website
Tourist destination with original movie site and new field that will host future MLB games
www.fieldofdreamsmoviesite.com/the-field

REVIEW QUESTIONS

1. What due diligence would be most advantageous to Gold Standard Athletics by Eric Munson before opening a similar business?
2. Based on this chapter, which sources of revenue are the beneficial and why?
3. *(Think Outside The Box Question)* What are some potential tax liabilities for this business?

Sample Financial Spreadsheet

Gold Standard Athletics
Sample Financial Statement

Business Expense	Amount
Administrative	1,876
Construction/Start-Up Costs	156,681
Cleaning	1,440
Coaches	69,476
Equipment	24,922
Insurance	5,745
Meals	480
Merchant Fees	659
Miscellaneous	467
Repairs & Maintenance	821
Tournament Fees	17,208
Merchandise	1,766
Wages	15,697
Utilities	6,859
Total	**304,097**
2019 - 2020 GSA Deposits	**427,356**
Vending	**7,452**
Arrears	**6,000**
Gross Profit/(Loss)	**136,711**

*This spreadsheet is an example only and does not contain actual financials.

CHAPTER 7

Business of Esports

Jennifer Lee Hoffman, Regena Pauketat, Morganne Flores, Meghan Gerscher, and David Hoffman

LEARNING OBJECTIVES

- To understand the emerging financial structures of the world wide esports industry.
- To learn the differences between traditional competitive sports like basketball and football and the audience-driven environment of esports.
- To learn about how much it costs to start up a collegiate esports league.
- To discover the world of microtransactions, the economic engine of esports.
- To dive deeper into the world of live esports events that attract thousands of fans in larger arenas.
- To learn about the emerging partnership between esports and NASCAR.

Evolution of Esport Finance: Competition Goes Digital

Authors' Note: In all of sports and nearly every other aspect of social life, there is a divide between before and after the COVID-19 pandemic that shut down competitions, arenas, and athletes around the globe. Here we focus on esports—an area with a long history but more quickly emerging area of sports finance that skyrocketed into public consciousness as iNASCAR and iFormula esports events engaged audiences around the world in unexpected and unprecedented ways at the start of the global pandemic. While esports are more than just iNASCAR and NBA2K, the early moments of the global pandemic pushed simulated motorsports competitions to the forefront of esports. Esports, however, have a much longer story in sports finance.

© Turu23/Shutterstock.com

Electronic sports, now widely known as esports, are a significant form of competition in the global sports industry. Compared to the early years of widespread video gameplay in arcades with Ms. Pac-Man and Atari home consoles, video game competition now includes professional players competing in elite-level tournaments for prize pool awards as high as $21 million for international play (BITKRAFT Esports Ventures, 2017). Estimates for worldwide advertising and sponsorship revenue generated from competitive esports ranged from $800 million to $905 million in 2018 and $950.6 million in 2019 (BITKRAFT Esports Ventures, 2017; Newzoo, 2020). Projections for esports revenues in 2020 were $1.1 billion worldwide (Newzoo, 2020) prior to the disruption from the coronavirus. This surge in the global esports market projections was up $230 million from 2018 on growth in sponsorships, merchandise, and ticket sales (Willingham, 2018).

Global viewership estimates for esports was over 200 million people in 2018 and 300 million by 2019 (BITKRAFT Esports Ventures, 2017). Newzoo's 2020 Global Esports Market Report estimates a global esports audience of 442 million in 2019 and 495 million in 2020. Newzoo further differentiates esports audiences as enthusiasts with 222.9 million and another 272.2 million as occasional viewers (Newzoo, 2020). In North America, the audience is 57 million and in China, the largest viewing audience is 163 million (Newzoo, 2020), with established audiences in western Europe, Japan, and South Korea. The remaining audiences in Latin America, the Middle East, Africa, and Southeast Asia are growing as IT infrastructure and mobile gaming enthusiasm grows (Newzoo, 2020). While half of the esports audience come from Asia, this only accounts for about 5% of the population, signaling growth in this region (Goldman Sachs, 2018). Furthermore, 79% of the esports audience is under age 35 (Goldman Sachs, 2018). In a global survey by Eventbrite, 75% of live event attendees were age 18 to 34 and 44% were college students (Eventbrite, 2017).

Live streaming platforms such as Twitch also bring in audiences comparable to traditional sports. A 2018 Goldman Sachs report suggests that the esports audiences will be comparable to the NFL audience by 2022. Viewing audiences for esports are already on par with other North American professional leagues and their finals. Esports garnered 167 million viewers in 2017, compared to 270 million in the NFL, 231 million in the NBA, 114 million in MLB, and 65 million in NHL (Goldman Sachs, 2018). In 2017, League of Legends was second only to the Superbowl for viewership in a final event (Goldman Sachs, 2018). The second live iNASCAR event held after the COVID-19 sports shutdown of 2020 brought in 1.33 million viewers on Fox and FS1, breaking all previous esports viewing records for linear television (Dawalibi & Collis, 2020).

Today's esports enthusiasts, observers, players, leagues, and corporations, like their traditional sports predecessors, are navigating a changing sports and entertainment industry that is swiftly moving. This is due, in part, to esports reliance on the ways in which the computing industry is driven by rapid turnover in technology advances and game developer company sales strategies that rely on updates and new releases (Dawalibi & Collis, 2020). Additionally, esports are not only moving swiftly but in some respects are changing traditional sports. From streaming, to casting, to influencers, to games that may fade after only a few years of intense popularity, esports have a growing influence on global sports market trends. This chapter focuses on the key components of esports, similarities and differences with traditional sports (tsports), and financial aspects and trends likely to impact esports in the future.

A Brief History of Esports

Close observers of esports will likely trace the emergence of competitive video gaming to 1972 with the Space Invaders Championship that included 10,000 participants (Heilweil, 2019; Scholz, 2019). Esports began without a standardized governance structure, and since its early inception, it has been self-organizing for competition driven mainly by the business interests of electronic gaming companies (Scholz, 2019). Technology is the underlying medium of esports, which aggressively manages rapid change with updates, upgrades, and new computing features. The fast, aggressively managed change that the computing industry has perfected has created limits on the gaming industry's ability to develop more permanent technology and consumer trends (Dawalibi & Collis, 2020). This sociocultural history contributes to more contemporary challenges in the finance of esports, including the lack of long-standing traditions and rituals beyond the gaming community that many associate with traditional sports counterparts. Traditional sports have decades of broad cultural relevance even to those who are not close observers. For example, conventional sports have well established stadiums, such as Wrigley Field in Chicago, Madison Square Garden in New York, or Old Trafford in Manchester, England. Esports are relatively new and highly reliant on change, making them less accessible to a general audience, until very recently.

The esports gaming history has been characterized in computing software terms as esports 1.0, 2.0, and 3.0 (Higgins, 2020). Esports 1.0 emerged in the 1990s with the availability and affordability of video game consoles in which two players could compete simultaneously on a single split screen (Ward & Harmon, 2019). This brought more players together and more interest than arcades of the 1980 that were dominated by single-player play. However, stabilizing the monetizing needed to support competition remained challenging for tournament organizers. The video game industry also relies heavily on video game sales, new releases, and updates to engage players, mainly in single player on consoles. In the 2000s, esports 2.0 emerged when shifts from dial-up to broadband Internet fostered more PC-based gameplay in addition to video game consoles. PC-based play is strengthened by Internet capacity that supports LAN play, where players on PCs can compete across separate screens. Continued improvements to Internet speed and bandwidth popularize posting video uploads of gameplay to YouTube. In 2008, sophisticated broadband meant that video gaming could also be streamed simultaneously during play to larger audiences through YouTube and later Twitch and others. This innovation of player live-streaming also gave rise to casting (also known as shoutcasting), fusing streaming, and live play as part of the esports environment. Today's 3.0 esports gaming industry includes live events where esports are on par with conventional sports audiences, viewership, and revenue—surpassing some professional major leagues. Additionally, varsity-style college teams are growing quickly and esports demonstration events will be held at the 2024 Olympics.

What Are Esports?

Esports, a name that is a "portmanteau of 'electronic' and 'sports'" (Scholz, 2019, p. 2), are characterized by competitive electronic games that require specialized equipment and professionally trained coaches and support, and that garner a following by engaged fans and spectators who tune in on Twitch and YouTube, and increasingly attend live events. In short, esports are competitive, organized video gaming (Higgins, 2020). Video games, that is, "an electronic game that can be played on a computing device," are further described by their platform: console, personal computer (PC), mobile, social, and virtual (Scholz, 2019). While video games played on consoles, mobile devices, and social networks remain an important part of the financial landscape of electronic gaming, our focus here is on competitive electronic gaming with parallels to traditional sports, where players compete against an opponent for a prize or championship, now known as esports (See Figure 3: Glossary).

BITKRAFT Esports Ventures, an esports investor, further describes esports as "the transformation of gaming into a spectator sport" (BITKRAFT Esports Ventures, 2017, p. 2). Newzoo's 2020 Global Esports Market Report Factsheet defines esports as, "Competitive gaming at a professional level and in an organized format (a tournament or league) with a specific goal (i.e., winning a champion title or prize money) and a clear distinction between players and teams that are competing against each other" (Newzoo, 2020).

Esports are typically played using computerized gaming platforms that utilize specialized computers, monitors, and keyboards. Players also use microphones, headphones, a computer mouse, and ergonomic gaming chairs adapted specifically for competitive play. Accessories in tandem with gaming platforms in simulated environments, to create driving or flight simulations or virtual reality, have limited use in competitive esports, with a notable exception in motorsports during the 2020 pandemic. Traditional drivers from NASCAR and Formula 1 competed in iNASCAR and F1 using their personal training simulators, replacing their esports counterparts in iRacing, while live conventional racing was suspended. Console-based play gaming platforms are also popular in esports.

Main Platforms and Gaming Infrastructure of Esports

Esports generally are those competitive video games with multiplayer gameplay (Mir, 2019). We use the term conventional sports to refer to traditional competitive sports, such as professional, Olympic, high school, college, and nature sports. This term also includes emerging and contemporary sports such as parkour, ultimate Frisbee, and skateboarding. In the esports industry, the term traditional sports often refers to a range of common team and individual competitive sports known as stick and ball sports. We add to this list of traditional sports competitions characterized by combat and weapons, judging, motorsports, nature, strategy games, stick and ball sports, and time, collectively referred to as conventional sports (Table 1: Conventional Sports Competition Description).

TABLE 1: Conventional Sports Competition Description

Competition	Example
Combat and weapons	Fencing Wrestling
Judging	Diving Figure skating Gymnastics
Motorsports	Formula 1 NASCAR
Nature	Snow sports Surfing
Strategy games	Chess Poker Magic: the Gathering
Stick and ball sports	Baseball Football Golf
Time	Track Swimming

In esports, there are several different characterizations based on style of play. Esports competitive gameplay includes playing against other players in person or online, while playing for trophies or points (Ruvalcaba et al., 2018). Like traditional sports, esports players engage in competition in a particular game style against an opponent. Esports players specialize in a particular type of gameplay, then perfect their skills within it. For example, traditional athletes specialize within a sport such as tennis, mastering styles of play on clay courts or hard surfaces. Golfers perfect their swing with several different clubs in their bag and master putting, an altogether different type of swing.

Esports share many of these characteristics with some key differences. Competitive esports are always in direct competition against other players, where conventional sports may be based on time, judging scores, or navigating natural terrain. Esports have less off-time such as changing sides in baseball, time between downs in football, or adjudicating violations with free throws in basketball. Esports are faster paced, like soccer, than conventional sports. They are also more player-centric than coach-centric, as in hockey, with fewer breaks from time-outs by coaches to strategize. Esports are also audience-driven, with the spectator experience an integral part of competitive play through streaming and casting (BITKRAFT Esports Ventures, 2017, p. 3). While there are many variations of electronic gameplay, the most common types of esports gameplay are Battle Royale,

Fighting Games, First Person Shooter (FPS), Multiplayer Online Battle Arena (MOBA), and Traditional Sports (See Table 2).

TABLE 2: Esports by Game Type, Style of Play, Title, and Company

Game Type	Style of Play	Example Title	Company
Battle royale	Last person or team remaining wins	Fortnite Apex Legends	Epic Games Electronic Arts Inc.
Fighting games	Player versus player against another character(s)	Street Fighter Super Smash Bros.	Capcom Nintendo
First person shooter (FPS)	Played from the first person viewpoint	CS:GO Rainbow Six Siege	Valve Ubisoft
Multiplayer online battle area (MOBA)	Team versus team battle; incorporates other genre elements	League of Legends Dota 2	Riot Valve
Traditional sports	Video game play of traditional sports	FIFA NBA 2K	Electronic Arts Inc.2K Games
Other	Incorporates game play from multiple genres; or distinct game play	Rocket League	Psyonix

Case Study #1: Gender Equity and Inclusion in Esports

Among the critiques of esports are the ways in which esports follow conventional sport constructs over gender. In the gaming community, approximately 45% are women, but most face barriers and issues of toxicity and harassment (Seiner, 2019). In competitive gaming, there are few professional women gamers—only one in the Overwatch inaugural season and none

© Friends Stock/Shutterstock.com

in the LOL Championship series since 2016. And, according to data from the Esports Earnings website, which ranks the earnings of nearly 500 women players, the number-one ranked woman in earnings is ranked only 355 among total earnings in 2019 (Esports Earnings, n.d.). Women report mixed experiences in gaming as players (Ruvalcaba et al., 2018). This is especially true among the high school and college ranks with concerns over gender equity and toxic or unwelcoming gaming environments from other players or anonymous fans. "The last few years have witnessed a tremendous rise in esports in the U.S. and, with it, a growing concern about the lack of diversity and its underlying probable cause: toxicity toward women and minorities" (University of California Irvine, n.d.).

University of California (UC) Irvine addresses inclusion on their website, and even has an inclusion plan that was formed in 2017. "Our goal is to also live up to our own long standing commitment to diversity and inclusion across all aspects of campus life" (University of California Irvine, n.d.). The UC Irvine Esports Program realizes how prevalent the gap is between women's and men's participation in esports as a whole and is making steps toward fixing that situation. They have taken their platform and visibility as the first public institution to start an esports program to promote inclusion in esports and women's gaming.

Esports Structures, Organizations, and Leagues

Esports do not have the same organizing infrastructure for competitive play as conventional sport at any level—recreational, youth, college, professional, or national team competition. This lack of structure and "strict regulations enables organizers, teams, and companies to experiment freely in understanding the fans' preferences" (BITKRAFT Esports Ventures, 2017, p. 11). Game developer companies, gaming organization companies, and nonprofit organizations and federations similar to traditional sports have each had a role in building the competitive gaming infrastructure for events rules and organizing league play and championships, but game developer companies and corporate gaming organizations control all the professional teams and play (See Figure 1).

Professional Gaming Video Games: The Publishers Are the League

One of the most distinguishing features between esports and conventional sports is the role of corporatization in controlling nearly every aspect of video game competition. Video game publishers are the primary stakeholder controlling esports, whereas in conventional sports there are multiple stakeholders (Esports Explained, 2018). Furthermore, no single entity owns any single sport. Women's soccer games can be organized by anyone who wants to pair teams for competitive play. From youth and recreational leagues to professional and world-class play, no one stakeholder controls all of women's soccer or access to broadcast rights. In esports, game developers own the game title and

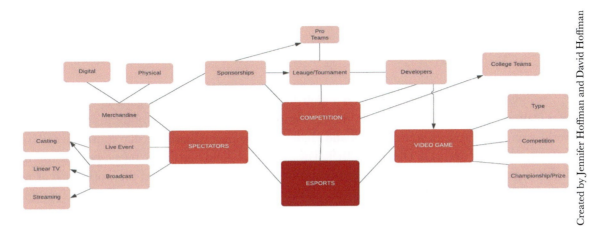

Created by Jennifer Hoffman and David Hoffman

control the league, any championship play, and much of the broadcast distribution. Riot Games owns League of Legends, the World Championship event, and how it is streamed over the Internet or linear television. Where the NBA organizes the game of basketball, but don't own ESPN or the game itself, video games, their league play, and media are all controlled by video game companies that developed the game.

The power of video game developers as the primary stakeholder comes from the video games. These are built from commercial, private-sector companies that produce games and, in turn, control most professional esports. Video games as commercial products are the platform that esports have grown from. Here the game, the structure of competition, and governance are all determined by the game developer—which is a company. This key feature is distinct from conventional competitive sports that are derived from leisure activities, where the sports themselves are not the property of any given corporation. While the Union of European Football Association (UEFA) Champions League has 37 football teams, each its own separate corporation, the UEFA of any of its franchises do not own and control the sport of soccer (Kruskic, 2019).

The game of soccer as it is known to American audiences is developed, played, and governed in a variety of corporate, private, or nonprofit infrastructures for teams to organize and govern play. Bundesliga, MLS, U.S. Soccer, and FIFA govern professional and World Cup play through a variety of corporate and nonprofit models, but none of these organizations owns the game of soccer. However, in esports, EA Sports created an electronic soccer game, titled FIFA, and EA Sports owns the FIFA video games franchise. Bundesliga later added an esports team and players to represent various teams in video gameplay, but this is governed by EA sports, rather than FIFA. The corporate control of games such as League of Legends by Riot Games or Fortnite by Epic Games is one of the key characteristics of esports and a key distinction between esports and conventional sports. This characteristic not only has implications for play but drives much of the economic and financial trends in esports.

Gaming Organizations

Professional esports team play occurs in a global competition where sport gaming organizations own teams and pay player salaries in multiple game franchises. Teams are located around the world vying for a spot in tournaments and championship play. Championship tournaments are typically 16 teams (Ward & Harmon, 2019). For example, Cloud9 or Fnatic own esports teams in multiple games such as League of Legends and have teams located around the world such as in Europe, North America, or South Asia that are vying for a spot in the LOL World Championship.

According to The Esports Observer, the top 10 gaming organizations in 2019 were ranked #10 to #1 in the following order: Cloud9, Ninjas in Pyjamas, Team Vitality, Evil Geniuses, ENCE, G2 Esports, NRG Esports, Fnatic, FaZe Clan, and Team Liquid. These organizations were ranked based on how their teams fared in competitive play at top tournaments and leagues in 11 different video games, based on viewership and prize money (Ashton, 2019). These gaming organizations are private companies and own teams based in multiple regions and that compete in multiple games. Conventional sport leagues, such as the NBA, have franchises in several cities. The LA Lakers are owned by a private group of investors and only competes in one basketball league. However, if the Lakers ownership group were an esports organization, they would have multiple teams playing in a variety of leagues such as Rocket League, Super Smash Bros, and League of Legends. In conventional sport terms, the Lakers would own teams that play in the WNBA, NBA, NFL, NASCAR, and World Series Poker leagues (Esports Explained, 2018).

Governing Organizations

However, several organizations have emerged with the aim of creating structure and support in competitive esports, independent of game developers. The International Esports Federation (IESF) and International eGames Committee (IEGC; Ntelia, 2019) focus on developing Olympic-level play. The National Association of Collegiate Esports (NACE) organizes competition among colleges and universities in the United States. Other college organizations include selected traditional sport conferences and the Electronic Sports League (McGrath, 2019). High school esports have been governed by the High School Esports League (HSEL).

Electronic Gaming Federation and the World Esports Association (WESA) promote competitive play but have tethers to the esports industry (Mir, 2019). For example, WESA consists of an executive chairman and commissioner that oversees a six-member executive committee, external auditors, and a seven-member players' council. WESA mirrors some aspects of traditional sport

governance, but also reflects the unique role of industry in esports, with its founding a collaboration between professional esports teams and esports companies that produce games. According to WESA's website, its aims are to be an "open and inclusive organization that will further professionalize esports by introducing elements of player representation, standardized regulations, and revenue shares for teams" (WESA, n.d.).

Among the challenges for esports governance is the "lack of standardization for all esports stakeholders" (Mir, 2019, p. 109). Namely, the publishers of video games control nearly every aspect of individual games, from drafting the rules, to game updates or upgrades. This fluidity of gaming also means that participants are likely to migrate from game to game as their needs and interests change. This power by publishers has posed challenges for WESA, NACE, and others to develop systems for setting common standards and adjudicating decisions over disputes to rules of play, standards for competitions, team structures, player welfare, health standards for training, and other conventional sports concerns such as illegal betting and match fixing, equipment manipulation, or doping.

College Sports

Esports are emerging on college campuses as a unique opportunity to "prepare students for 21st century careers," while strengthening campus enrollment (McGrath, 2019). A large proportion of esports fans are in college (Eventbrite, 2017) and "esports companies and investors are betting that millennials will continue to engage with video games throughout their life while quitting regular sports with age and injury" (BITKRAFT Esports Ventures, 2017, p. 7). Opportunities for casual and serious recreational gaming are increasingly playing an important part of campus strategic planning. This includes the addition of esports programs.

© Gorodenkoff/Shutterstock.com

Since the inception of NACE in 2016 with six member schools, institutions and students are quickly drawing on esports as a school-sponsored, competitive activity. Robert Morris, a university in Chicago, was the first school to offer esports scholarships in 2014 (Robert Morris University, n.d.). The University of California Irvine (UCI) was the first public institution to fully support an esports competitive program, including scholarships, training and coaching, and specialized facilities and equipment in September 2016 (University of California Irvine, n.d.). Additionally, UCI's esports program is closely affiliated with the Computer Game Science major and is administered by Student Affairs, not by the athletic department.

In 2020, the National Association of Collegiate Esports (NACE) reported 170 member institutions and 5,000 college esports athletes. Esports are likely to continue growing in colleges and universities as high school students increasingly participate and expect opportunities in college. There are an estimated 50,000 esports athletes on high school teams at 2,000 schools worldwide (Niedan, 2020).

Through 2019, $16 million was distributed in scholarships by 200 institutions to esports students (Heilweil, 2019; NACE, 2020). Like traditional athletics, esports offers a financial incentive for students as well. Those scholarships aren't just for top esports athletes, either. Esports recruits "are assessed not only on performance-based criteria (their demonstrated skill within esports as represented by rank) but also their teamwork, ability to follow instructions, coachability, interpersonal skills, and understanding of our commitments to diversity and inclusive excellence" (Amazan-Hall et al., 2018).

Like their traditional sports predecessors, esports are touted as training grounds for other skills. College esports programs are likely to have close ties to academic programs with technology skills and knowledge that are already deeply embedded in the esports industry. For example, observers of eChess suggest that "people that are into chess like forecasting and are great at pattern recognition ... chances are they will be interested in finance data and numbers in the future" (Soliev as quoted in Santana, 2020).

Case Study #2: How much does it cost to start a collegiate esports team?

Several key questions will help you think about the resources needed and costs associated with starting a collegiate esports team. NACE reports that a program serving 15 students in the first year, starting with recruitment, has an average startup cost of $41,000 (NACE, 2020). This includes repurposing existing campus space and purchasing computing hardware and accessories for a basic competitive gaming setting. Designing the space requires maximizing the floor layout to serve the greatest number of students. Costs for a new, dedicated space to support an individual esports-only program increase to $250,000 to $500,000. The first key consideration is building a core of competitive gaming computers, specialized monitors, keyboard, microphones, headphones, mouses, and ergonomic gaming chairs adapted specifically for competitive play. Other amenities for training and hosting LAN competitive play include a coaching office, analyst studio, team strategy rooms, lounges, additional computers, and an elevated platform (M. Brooks, personal communication, March 30, 2020). Coaches or team manager salaries are low by computer industry standards but are in the range of $80,000 per year (Personal Communication), and scholarships add additional costs. Questions for starting a competitive gaming program also include considerations for larger events that require staging for players and a seated gallery for spectators, partnerships with STEAM (Science, Technology, Engineering, Arts, Mathematics) academic programs, and industry partnerships for program financial support and career training.

Understanding Esports Revenues

For some organizations and observers of the sports industry, esports are an important part of a portfolio of other sports and entertainment activities. For others, financial investment in esports is just emerging. Esports, with their strong revenue streams from viewing revenues, have strong alliances with sports and other forms of entertainment. BITKRAFT Esports Ventures, an investor company, positions esports as a strong investment within entertainment broadly (BITKRAFT Esports Ventures, 2017). This is due, in part, to the financial strength of the audience, their viewership online and at live events, and spending power. Esports fans earn an average of $45,000 per year and household income ranges from $75,000 per year to over $90,000, signaling their financial strength (BITKRAFT Esports Ventures, 2017) and strong spending potential to investors. For example, spending during the coronavirus pandemic on digital games jumped 11% from the previous year to $10 billion in March 2020, in mobile, PC, and console gaming (Superdata, 2020).

From playing and in-game purchasing, to watching other gamers stream online, to ticket and merchandise sales at live events, the esports audience's enthusiasm fuels much of the esports industry

revenue. For example, Riot's League of Legends generated $1.5 billion in revenue in 2019 (Martinello, 2020). The main source of League of Legends revenues are microtransactions, "with champions, skins, and portraits available to purchase in the store with either Influence Points earned from playing games, or Riot Points purchased with real money" (Mueller, 2016).

Streaming, where gamers live stream in real time and interact with a live audience while engaging in competitive play, is integral to the popularity of today's electronic gaming. Through live streaming, fans can watch skilled players compete in whatever game they are interested in. "The two main user-generated live streaming systems are Twitch and the live service of YouTube. While YouTube ranges from 300 to 700 channels, Twitch counts with one order of magnitude more, with always more than 6,000 channels" (Burroughs & Rama, 2015). Streaming draws viewership, which, in turn, generates revenue from advertising and subscriptions. In 2019, Twitch and YouTube Gaming generated approximately $1.5 billion each (Iqbal, 2020). Tyler "Ninja" Blevins broke with Twitch in 2020, moving to Microsoft's Mixer exclusively for an estimated $20 to $30 million dollars (Leslie & Byers, 2020).

Case Study #3: Economic Engine of Microtransactions

Like streaming, a unique feature of video games is in-game microtransactions. These microtransactions are lucrative revenue engines to the esports industry. In-game economies generate revenue through in-game microtransactions. Some games have an in-game currency and a market for items such as cosmetics that can be traded between players. These games have either an in-game market such as an auction house or the community has developed an outside system (often a website) where items can be traded and then gifted between players. In this case, the money is held by a third-party site, such as Steam.

Video games use familiar economic systems to develop a realistic world play, where players can interact, progress, and complete challenges with one another. This in-game economy uses economic principles as a reward system for completing interactions, progressions, and completing challenges. For example, items can be bought within the game space and transactions—during play. Video games also have outside economic incentives that result in profits that have real monetary value.

Here's how.

Games have a purchased currency to go in tandem with the in-game currency that can also be converted. Let's say that the currency you can only earn in the game is called gold and the currency you can purchase with actual money is called gems. You can convert 100,000 gold for 100 gems. The gems can purchase in-game items for a fraction of what it would cost to get in gold. But you can only buy certain cosmetic items (items that don't affect gameplay) or power changing items with gems. This does three things: (1) It allows players with massive amounts of in-game currency to deflate the in-game market, without devaluing the purchased currency; (2) it allows the in-game currency to have an anchor value; and (3) it makes money for the developers. This allows players' cosmetics to also hold value and increase and decrease in real-world money. Once those items are no longer for sale in the shop, they can only be obtained by trading with other players. The price of those items is then determined by supply and demand.

Not Your Parent's Esports—Live Events

Spectating in conventional sports has a cultural spectator construct, where families and other collections of spectators pass on customs and practices of fanship that generate forms of sport among children, which they then carry into adulthood (Mir, 2019). The evolution of esports has always included live, in-person events. However, live events in sports today are moving toward some of the same characteristics of traditional sports with specialized venues. Unlike tsports, where the rituals and traditions of fan experiences are deeply tied to a sense of place in the stadiums and arenas themselves, live esports events draw a community of people with established online connections. The ritual and traditions of live esports events play a different role and as such will drive what organizers offer and what fans are willing to pay for.

Increasingly, teams travel around the globe to compete in arenas in front of fans, similar to other live events such as music concerts or sports. Live events in esports are wildly popular, typically lasting several days, with finals for games such as League of Legends drawing crowds of 80,000 to 90,000 (Orland, 2017). Much like traditional sports, these live competition events expand sales and merchandise revenue. These esports also draw heavily on activities and experiences with similarities to Comic-Con and other fan cultures where the experience and community built from a live event are a major draw for esports fans. Being a part of a crowd that is reacting and co-creating the experience in real time is a huge part of the draw (Orland, 2017; Taylor, 2016). To experience an esports live event is to be "immersed in a new world" (Naraine & Wear, 2019). Colorful stage lighting, jumbo screens, and bursting audio recreate an atmosphere from within the games themselves. Cosplayers express fandom through the costuming and performance of characters. Similar to traditional sports, fans show team affiliations by wearing their favorite team or player jersey. Live events offer engagement with other fans and often engagement with esports superstar players themselves. Sponsorships and advertisements, along with new technology perks from major brands and fan merchandise at live events, result in 38% of attendees being more likely to purchase products and services later (Eventbrite, 2017).

Unlike traditional sports, live esports events allow fans to get much closer to professional esports players. There may be autograph booths with players, similar to other conventions, to meet and greet favorite players. Fans are also able to access more interactivity at esports events, due to the accessibility of esports to a wide audience, allowing for engagement not only with other fans but also with new equipment and services for their own gameplay (Naraine & Wear, 2019). The drama of play is heightened when you are able not only to see the play but interact with other fans around you as well as the players.

Live esports events are held for final championships of some of the largest games, but league play events in front of a live audience in addition to streaming, as in traditional sports, are emerging. For example, in early 2020, Overwatch League (OWL) added a 20-team, city-based league with home and away matches played in live local matches in addition to the typical esports streaming on Twitch and YouTube (Sprung, 2020). This arrangement was novel in esports for its live, spectator-oriented stadium play and for its cultivation of regional rivalries often associated with traditional sports. This OWL event drew fans willing to pay $80 in ticket pricing or more for other packages and passes for VIP access such as player meet and greets and the opportunity to purchase more additional merchandise only available at the event (Sprung, 2020).

Case Study #4: Live Event Ticket Pricing

The cost of tickets can vary; a quick StubHub search shows that tickets can range from $200 for a one-day pass to over $400 for the VIP experience. League of Legends Championships tickets in 2016 were selling for $47 to $71 (Lolesports, 2016); however, scalped tickets to The International 2019 (TI9) in Shanghai were being sold for upward of $2000, while the original price was about $300 (Ye, 2019). Tickets to this event sold out in less than one minute, making this a prime opportunity for the illegal reselling of tickets for inflated prices. In a sport where games such as DOTA 2's finals have the largest prize pool (which is crowdfunded) at $34 million. For Call of Duty, another of the most popular games in esports, tickets start at $25 a day for entry to the venue and a standing spot, while they rise to $150 a day for a VIP pass, which includes a special entrance, prime seating, a themed t-shirt, and a tour of the venue (Fadilpasic, 2019).

Esports Labor Market: Prize Pools and Superstars

As in other sports and entertainment industries, superstar athletes and celebrities capture widespread attention and often garner the largest salaries. Esports with their large prize pools for tournaments and live events add to the headlines over the player compensation. In 2019, the Esports Observer reported the total tournament play prize money at $211 million in U.S. dollars from 4,000 esports tournaments, a 29% jump from $163 million in prize money in 2018. The top prize pool in 2019 was Fortnite at $64 million dollars (Hitt, 2019). The Esports Earnings website reports slightly higher tournament prize money of $228 million dollars in 5,100 total tournaments.

According to the Esports Earnings website, a "community-driven competitive gaming resource" reports player earnings from prize pools among the top 500 ranked players in 2019 to be from $66K to $3.2 million. However, only a few hundred players worldwide earn "enough to remain professional exclusively" (Ward & Harmon, 2019, p. 987). When accounting for all 26,000 active players in 2019, the average player earning from tournament play is $9K, with the median being $700 (Esports Earnings, n.d.).

Currently, these large prize pools and earnings by top players reflect a labor market characterized by superstar players. Ward and Harmon (2019) suggest that esports are a superstar labor market where "[t]he better the e-games and the larger the gap between skilled and amateur players, the bigger the winning money" (Bhardwaj, 2018). In any profession, workers with higher ability are paid more money, but it is "distinctly higher in superstar markets" where top players earn significantly more money than others (Ward & Harmon, 2019; see also Rosen, 1981). There is a gap between the most skilled professional esports players and those in the amateur ranks. "Right now, professional gamers are winning big" (Bhardwaj, 2018). Once tournament prize pools are considered outside of the esports superstars (Ward & Harmon, 2019), there are 26,000 active esports players vying for these tournament prize earnings in an average prize pool of $45K and the median of $1,500 (Esports Earnings, n.d.).

This superstar labor market means that it is more challenging to break into the professional ranks in esports than in other traditional sports (Scholz, 2019). The large prize pools and the widespread availability of online gaming create a critical mass of players. Reliance on this critical mass is the primary way that esports draw amateurs into the professional ranks (Ward & Harmon, 2019). It also means that only the superstars have the power in salary contract negotiating contracts with sponsoring teams (Scholz, 2019). This further contributes to the wide range of player salaries and shorter team contracts, and increases player reliance on prize money and other monetization.

Endorsements and sponsorships for esports players are another source of player income. However, just as streaming is integral to esports play, so too it is a key feature of player salaries. Twitch and the rise of streaming accelerated the growth of esports, but also changed the earning structures for esports players. "Suddenly professional esports players could broadcast their training and create other events. The aspect of streaming became a steady revenue stream" (Scholz, 2019, p. 32).

Streaming by players increases all aspects of income—merchandising, endorsements, and sponsorships, broadcast revenue, and salary negotiation. However, income from streaming is not limited just to the superstars or competitive players. "It used to be that you had to be one of the top 500 players in the world to get paid, but not anymore. Streamers are achieving significant fame making $100,000 in revenue" (Santana, 2020). Ninja Evans is among the most popular esports streamers, notable for pivoting from professional gaming to professional streaming. His estimated annual income from streaming and related activities is not clear, but estimates put his current streaming contract with Mixer, Microsoft's streaming service, at $20 to $30 million per year (Leslie & Byers, 2020).

Conclusion: The Future of Esports

The 2019 League of Legends World Championship Tournament boasted 100 million viewers and 21.8 million Average Minutes Audience (AMA) viewer rating (Webb, 2019). Esports are both quickly changing the traditional sports landscape and adopting practices long held by traditional sports. From the ways in which streaming over YouTube has altered the practices of the 2020 College Football Championship with ESPN's "Megacast" bringing more content to the traditional broadcast (Newsday.com, 2020), esports live events are adopting characteristics typically associated with conventional sports. The evolution in video games from console to online to LAN events has also ushered in new forms of viewership via streaming and are also influencing other games, not just traditional athletic contests. Competitive eChess is just another example where the tool of esports—computer-based gaming, paired with streaming, in professional play for prize money—is quickly influencing sports and entertainment economics. People are playing eChess not only for the enjoyment aspect but also for the financial incentive.

Despite the growth in nearly every measure of esports, there are important considerations in the future of esports finance.

© Turu23/Shutterstock.com

For example, the main gaming audience today is millennials, and they are more adept at developing control over the content that they consume and in models that are freely available (Mir, 2019). Revenues are driven by the interests of these gaming consumers, adding vulnerability to the finances of the esports market. Among the huge revenues and numbers of users in video gaming and viewership in esports, there are also disputes over the actual revenues reported in the data (Mir, 2019), and player salaries are not easily made available.

As in traditional sports, sponsorships bring financial support to esports, and streaming and casting bring event coverage to live audiences. Esports were also vulnerable to the shutdown of live events in the wake of coronavirus. Not only will there be the same losses of ticket sales, but advertisers' and sponsors' budgets will be vulnerable even for events that are still held online. Then there are the issues of LAN play events that don't migrate well to online play, due to competitive equity over Internet services and preventative cheating measures (Ashton, 2020). The cancellation of major events like the League of Legends Mid-Season Invitational (Ashton, 2020) signals that despite many bright spots in video game sales during the coronavirus pandemic, esports may also be vulnerable to declines in revenue. Additionally, despite the initial excitement of iNASCAR during the coronavirus pandemic and despite their great potential to bring in new audiences and revenue, esports are not just about moving conventional athletes into their sports' video game. Competitive gaming is a unique sport and not just about mimicking conventional sports (Infinite Esports & Entertainment, 2018). Understanding esports and the financial components that make them popular is essential for understanding the current and future financial trends of esports.

Case Study #5: Esports: A Coronavirus Remedy for Sports Fans?

The coronavirus global pandemic is changing every aspect of sports. In the early days of the U.S. outbreak, the NBA was the first to suspend their games. Other leagues and championships such as the NHL and NCAA soon followed, until nearly every stadium and arena went dark. As live traditional sport events were cancelled, so were live esports events.

Yet, at the outset, esports did not lead the way in replacing conventional sports content on mainstream sports media on ESPN and Fox Sports. In the first weeks of the pandemic, U.S. sports fans first turned to the content they knew. Esports ranked 6th, behind sports documentaries, classic games, sports countdown shows, sports talk shows, and obscure sports (Statista, 2020).

It was the established, conventional sports that were first to try and capture the attention of audiences broadly with esports play from Madden, NBA2K, and Formula 1 racing. However, it was NASCAR with its already established reliance on simulation for training that was able to quickly pivot to its companion esports league, iNASCAR, that quickly filled the early void on conventional televised sports events from canceled NBA, NHL, MLB, and the NCAA Final Four.

In the coronavirus void of conventional sports, the success of iNASCAR and Formula 1 as motorsports is attributed to several factors, including an established fan base, existing relationships and contracts with Fox1 and FS1, and the need for replacement content that already "looks the same" (Dawalibi & Collis, 2020). Digital racing is the most similar, accurate representation of its conventional peer in all of sports (Dawalibi & Collis, 2020). The racing audience already like existing racing and support replacing it with something as close to the existing thing as they can get in the digital racing domain. "Racing has been the esport that is the furthest along in terms of direct and accurate simulation of the underlying sport" (Dawalibi & Collis, 2020).

NASCAR launched the iNASCAR Pro Invitational series with drivers from conventional live racing such as Dale Earnhardt, Jr., to race in a simulated NASCAR event using their own race simulation training equipment. According to Nielson, the first event on March 22, 2020 had 903,000 viewers and was the highest-rated esports event in history. The next event, just one week later on March 29, 2020, had an audience of 1.3 million viewers airing on both FOX and FS1. The characteristics of motorsports as a proxy, combined with the little effort needed to reach an already existing fan base, launched esports into linear television that the other professional sports leagues could not replicate.

FIGURE 2: Most Popular Video Game Titles by Sales

Top Grossing Console Titles, March 2020
1. Animal Crossing: New Horizons
2. FIFA 20
3. MLB the Show 20
4. Doom Eternal
5. Call of Duty: Modern Warfare
6. NBA 2K20
7. Grand Theft Auto V
8. Fortnite
9. Tom Clancy's Rainbow Six Siege
10. Madden NFL 20

6. Coin Master
7. Roblox
8. Monster Strike
9. Clash of Clans
10. Mafia City

Top Grossing PC Titles, March 2020
1. Dungeon Fighter Online
2. League of Legends
3. Crossfire
4. Fantasy Westward Journey Online II
5. Doom Eternal
6. Counter-Strike: Global Offensive
7. Borderlands 3
8. Half-Life: Alyx
9. World of Warcraft West
10. World of Tanks

Top Grossing Mobile Titles, March 2020
1. Honor of Kings
2. Gardenscapes
3. Candy Crush Saga
4. Last Shelter: Survival
5. Pokémon GO

Source: SuperData, April 22, 2020

FIGURE 3: Glossary

Accessories: PC-centric for mouse, keyboard, monitor; also known as peripherals
Conventional sports: in addition to major traditional sports, includes motor or nature sports, emerging physical sports such as ultimate Frisbee, skateboarding, and strategy games like chess and poker
Cosmetics: a visual change to the appearance of a video game character or object. See In-game currency.
Esports: "electronic" and "sports"; where video games are played against an opponent in a competition for a prize or championship
Gaming: the action of playing video games
In-game currency: functions as in-game currency, purchased with real-world funds
Local area network (LAN): side-by-side game play, in real time, in the same location
Linear TV: Live television where programming is aired based on a schedule
Microtransactions: micropurchases in a game such as cosmetic items, bought currency, and experience and time boosters
Streaming: broadcasting in real time by video game players; allows the audience to follow along with players as they play the game
Traditional Sports (Tsports): Common esports term and abbreviation for traditional sports such as stick and ball sports and motorsports. See also Conventional sports.
Video game: an electronic game played on computer, gaming console, or mobile phone

Review Questions

1. Conventional sports have a long gender-separate history and contemporary competition remains largely gender-separate. Should esports adopt the gender-separate structures and spaces, such as women-only leagues? Why or why not?
2. As esports league play grows, where should these events be held? At existing stadiums where other professional sports and entertainment events such as concerts are held? Who should be responsible for the technology upgrades? Should publishers and other venture organizations build and maintain their own specialized esports venues instead of sharing current arenas?
3. What is the status of the gaming community on my campus? What is the campus infrastructure and oversight for esports—in an academic unit, athletics, activities, or recreation? What are the financial considerations for esports? Assess how welcoming and inclusive gaming and esports are in our campus context.

References

Amazan-Hall, K., Chiang, K., Chen, J. J., & Cullen, A. (2018). Diversity and inclusion in esports programs in higher education: Leading by example at UCI. *International Journal of Gaming and Computer-Mediated Simulations, 10*, 71-80. https://doi.org/10.4018/IJGCMS.2018040104.

Ashton, G. (2019, December 31). Top 10 esports team organizations of 2019 by competition results. Retrieved April 24, 2020, from https://esportsobserver.com/top10-esports-teams-2019/

Ashton, G. (2020, April 23). League of legends mid-season invitational canceled for 2020. Retrieved May 1, 2020, from https://esportsobserver.com/riot-cancels-lol-msi/

Bhardwaj, P. (2018). *Gaming tournaments now offer prize pools comparable to some of the most established traditional sporting events.* Business Insider. Retrieved May 5, 2020, from www.businessinsider.com/esports-prize-pools-vs-traditional-sports-2018-6

BITKRAFT Esports Ventures. (2017). *Esports 101: A deep dive into the world of competitive video games.* https://esportsobserver.com/product/bitkraft-esports-101-whitepaper/

Burroughs, B., & Rama, P. (2015). The eSports Trojan horse: Twitch and streaming futures. *Journal for Virtual Worlds Research, 8*(2). https://doi.org/10.4101/jvwr.v8i2.7176

Dawalibi, P., & Collis, W. (2020, April 3). *Episode #73: NASCAR Win, Epic Reward, OverActive Fail, Valorant Opportunity, Japan Esports 2025.* Retrieved April 21, 2020, from https://thebusinessofesports.com/2020/04/03/episode-73-nascar-win-epic-reward-overactive-fail-valorant-opportunity-japan-esports-2025/

Esporst Earnings. (n.d.) Retrieved from: https://www.esportsearnings.com/history

Esports Explained: Vol. Season 1. (2018, June 27). Netflix.

Eventbrite. (2017). *The eSports effect: Gamers and the influence of live events.* Eventbrite Blog. http://mkto.eventbrite.com/rs/269-CEG-133/images/DS01_The%20eSports%20Effect%20Gamers%20and%20the%20Influence%20of%20Live%20Events.pdf

Fadilpasic. (2019, November 13). *Call of duty league tickets cost HOW MUCH!?* He Gamer. Retrieved April 6, 2020, from www.thegamer.com/call-of-duty-league-tickets-cost/

Goldman Sachs. (2018). *Esports: From Wild West to Mainstream*. Goldman Sachs.

Heilweil, R. (2019, January 21). *Esports players are cashing in big when it comes to college*. Wired. www.wired.com/story/infoporn-college-esports-players-cashing-in-big/

Higgins, C. (2020). Esports: The athletic trainer's very new frontier. *NATA News*, (February), 16–18.

Hitt, K. (2019, December 27). The top 10 esports of 2019 by total prize pool. *The Esports Observer*. Retrieved April 25, 2020, from https://esportsobserver.com/biggest-esports-2019-prize-pool/

Infinite Esports & Entertainment. (Producer). (2018, September, 12). *Esports roundtable podcast: Past, present and future of business in esports*. [Audio podcast]. https://audioboom.com/channel/esports-roundtable-podcast

Iqbal, M. (23 July 2020). *Twitch Revenue and Usage Statistics*. Retrieved from: https://www.businessofapps.com/data/twitch-statistics/

Kruskic, H. (2019). UEFA champions league explained: How the tournament works. Retrieved April 18, 2020, from https://bleacherreport.com/articles/2819840-uefa-champions-league-explained-how-the-tournament-works

Leslie, C., & Byers, P. (2020, March 9). *How much money does Ninja make?* Retrieved April 25, 2020, from https://dotesports.com/culture/news/how-much-money-does-ninja-make-21954

Lolesports Staff (2016). *League of Legends*. Retrieved from https://nexus.leagueoflegends.com/en-us/2016/08/worlds-2016-finals-tickets/

Martinello, E. (2020, January 3). *League of Legends generated $1.5 billion revenue in 2019*. Dot Esports. Retrieved April 25, 2020, from https://dotesports.com/league-of-legends/news/league-of-legends-generated-1-5-billion-revenue-in-2019

McGrath, K. (2019). Leveraging esports in higher education. In R. Rogers (Ed.), *Understanding Esports: An Introduction to the Global Phenomenon* (pp. 201–217). Lexington Books. http://ebookcentral.proquest.com/lib/washington/detail.action?docID=5884644

Mir, R. (2019). The legal validity of e-sports as a sport. In K. Margaritis (Ed.), *Law, Ethics, and Integrity in the Sports Industry* (pp. 101–123). IGI Global. https://doi.org/10.4018/978-1-5225-5387-8

Mueller, S. (2016, January 26). *Report: League of legends made $1.6 billion in revenue last year*. Retrieved April 25, 2020, from https://dotesports.com/league-of-legends/news/league-of-legends-2015-revenue-2839

Naraine, M. L., & Wear, H. (2019). The esports consumer experience. In R. Rogers (Ed.), *Understanding esports: An introduction to the global phenomenon* (pp. 85-93). Lexington Books.

National Association of Collegiate Esports. (n.d.). *What is NACE?* Retrieved from: https://nacesports.org/about/

Newsday.com. (2020, January 9). *How to watch ESPN's MegaCast of CFP title game*. Retrieved April 24, 2020, from www.newsday.com/sports/college/college-football/lsu-clemson-espn-megacast-cfp-national-championship-game-1.12875547

Newzoo. (2020). *Global esports market report 2020*. https://newzoo.com/insights/trend-reports/newzoo-global-esports-market-report-2020-light-version/

Niedan, C. (2020, February 12). *The new power-up on campus: Video Games–the elective*. The Elective. https://elective.collegeboard.org/new-power-campus-video-games

Ntelia, R. (2019). E-Sports at the olympic games: From physicality to virtuality. In K. Margaritis (Ed.). *Law, ethics, and integrity in the sports industry* (pp. 124-143). IGI Global. https://doi.org/10.4018/978-1-5225-5387-8

Orland, K. (2017, November 19). *What I learned visiting my first live eSports tournament.* https://arstechnica.com/gaming/2017/11/the-odd-appeal-of-watching-esports-live-and-in-person/

Perez, M. (2020, April 20). *Report: Digital video game revenue hit $10 billion in March, its best month ever.* www.forbes.com/sites/mattperez/2020/04/22/report-digital-video-game-revenue-hit-10-billion-in-march-its-best-month-ever/?sh=439b10ea63d9

Robert Morris University. (n.d). *Robert Morris University Illinois is now Roosevelt University.* Retrieved May 5, 2020 from www.rmueagles.com/article/907

Rosen, S. (1981). The economics of superstars. *American Economic Review, 71*, 845.

Ruvalcaba, O., Shulze, J., Kim, A., Berzenski, S. R., & Otten, M. P. (2018). Women's experiences in eSports: Gendered differences in peer and spectator feedback during competitive video game play. *Journal of Sport and Social Issues, 42*(4), 295–311. https://doi.org/10.1177/0193723518773287

Santana, D. (2020, February 27). Esports chess league taps streaming and quick pace for growth. *Front Office Sports.* https://frntofficesport.com/esports-chess-league/

Scholz, T. M. (2019). *eSports is business: Management in the world of competitive gaming.* Springer International Publishing. https://doi.org/10.1007/978-3-030-11199-1

Seiner, J. (2019, January 3). "You're a girl, you're being targeted": Women in esports navigate toxicity, other barriers. *The Denver Post.* www.denverpost.com/2019/01/03/esports-women-navigate-toxicity-barriers/

Sprung, S. (2020). *Overwatch league homestands debut as NYXL, others experience true esports rivalries.* Forbes. Retrieved March 30, 2020, from www.forbes.com/sites/shlomosprung/2020/02/10/overwatch-league-homestands-nyxl-shock-spitfire-owl/

Statista. (2020). *Coronavirus: Impact on the sports industry worldwide* (p. 93). www.statista.com/study/71572/the-sports-industry-impact-of-the-covid-19-pandemic-2020/

Taylor, N. T. (2016). Play to the camera: Video ethnography, spectatorship, and e-sports. *Convergence: The International Journal of Research into New Media Technologies, 22*(2), 115–130.

University of California Irvine. (n.d.). *Inclusion: UC Irvine.* UCI Esports. Retrieved April 19, 2020, from https://esports.uci.edu/inclusion/

Ward, M. R., & Harmon, A. D. (2019). ESport Superstars. *Journal of Sports Economics, 20*(8), 987–1013. https://doi.org/10.1177/1527002519859417

Webb, K. (2019, December 18). *2019 League of legends world championship reaches 100 million viewers.* Retrieved April 27, 2020, from www.businessinsider.com/league-of-legends-world-championship-100-million-viewers-2019-12

Willingham, A. (2018, August 27). *What is eSports? A look at an explosive billion-dollar industry.* CNN. Retrieved April 20, 2020, from www.cnn.com/2018/08/27/us/esports-what-is-video-game-professional-league-madden-trnd/index.html

World Esports Association. (n.d.) https://www.wesa.gg/

Ye, J. (2019, August 23). *Esports tournament tickets are going for $2,000, but fans say seats are empty.* Abacus. Retrieved April 6, 2020, from www.abacusnews.com/esports/esports-tournament-tickets-are-going-2000-fans-say-seats-are-empty/article/3024111

CHAPTER 8
Business of Major League Baseball

Wayne McDonnell

LEARNING OBJECTIVES

- To discover the various revenue streams that Major League Baseball has created in the last few decades that factor into determining each ball club's revenue share.
- To understand what a ball club's EBITDA is and how it factors into potential monetary sanctions and team attendance at ownership meetings.
- To understand why local media revenues are critical to the success of the ball club, and how Spanish language radio broadcasts are unique in North American professional franchises.
- To understand how a major league ball club manages its payroll and the luxury cap.
- To consider where MLB is financially post–Covid-19, and assess its future growth potential.

A Brief History of Major League Baseball

Historians have traced aspects of baseball as far back as the 18th century. The origins of the modern game began in 1842 with the informal organization of the New York Knickerbocker Base Ball Club. Throughout the second half of the 19th century there were multiple attempts at developing amateur and professional leagues, but it was not until the American and National Leagues joined forces in January 1903 and created what we now know to be Major League Baseball.[1]

---

1. John Thorn, "October 1845: The First Recorded Baseball Games In New York," Society For American Baseball Research (https://sabr.org/gamesproj/game/october-1845-first-recorded-baseball-games-new-york), Monica Nucciarone, "Alexander Cartwright," Society For American Baseball Research, (https://sabr.org/bioproj/person/09ed3dd4), "Alexander Cartwright," National Baseball Hall Of Fame And Museum, (https://baseballhall.org/hall-of-famers/cartwright-alexander)

The 1919 Black Sox scandal, Great Depression, and two World Wars adversely affected the business of baseball and tested its resilience during the first half of the 20th century. Innovations, pioneers, and larger than life personalities were helping to grow America's National Pastime. Ticket sales dominated as the primary source of revenue, but the emergence of radio (1921) and television (1939) were beginning to shape how the sport was consumed outside of the ballpark. Most importantly, it was new streams of revenue for ball clubs to embrace after an initial reluctance.[2]

During the second half of the 20th century, there were periods of expansion and relocation to cities west of the Mississippi River. The birth of the Major League Baseball Players Association (MLBPA) led to the first collective bargaining agreement in professional sports (1968), arbitration, increases in salaries, and the abolishment of the reserve clause. After decades of animosity, the mid-1990s began a period of unprecedented labor peace that has lasted until present day.

A boom in stadium and mixed-use development projects has led to increasing franchise values and new revenue streams, especially local and national television deals. Major League Baseball Advanced Media (MLBAM) has changed the business of baseball in a profound manner. Interleague play, the wild cards, and World Baseball Classic are bringing new forms of excitement and pride to fans as attendance has been regularly eclipsing 70 million on an annual basis.

2. Joel D. Treese, "President Herbert Hoover And Baseball," The White House Historical Association (www.whitehousehistory.org/president-herbert-hoover-and-baseball), Eldon L. Ham, " Broadcast 90 Years Ago Was First To Help Listeners 'See' Series," Sports Business Journal, October 17, 2011 (www.sportsbusinessdaily.com/Journal/Issues/2011/10/17/Opinion/Eldon-Ham.aspx), Matt Monagan, "75 Years Ago Today, The First Major League Baseball Game Was Televised," MLB.com-Cut 4, August 26, 2014 (www.mlb.com/cut4/75-years-ago-the-first-baseball-game-was-televised/c-91371436)

Major League Baseball's League Structure

Major League Baseball is composed of 30 franchises which operate out of 27 cities in the United States and Canada and are split into two leagues: American and National. A joint organizational structure has been in place between the two leagues since 1903. Each league is broken down into three, five ball club divisions: East, Central, and West. A major league season is 162 games usually played over 187 days.[3]

Robert D. Manfred, Jr. is Major League Baseball's tenth commissioner. He began his tenure on January 25, 2015 after previously serving as Major League Baseball's Chief Operating Officer (2013-2014) and Executive Vice President (1998-2013). Tony Clark is the current Executive Director of the Major League Baseball Players Association (MLBPA). A veteran of 15 major league seasons, Clark is the first former ball player to become Executive Director of the MLBPA.[4]

Major League Baseball's Constitution is used to govern the sport. It has undergone several changes since its origins in 1876 when it was called the National League Constitution. The constitution outlines the role and responsibilities of the commissioner and executive council.[5]

Major League Baseball Ownership Buy-In Amount

Chart #1 Ownership Buy-In Amount

Rank	Ball Club	Current Value	Purchase Price	Year of Purchase	Owner(s)
1	New York Yankees	$4,600,000,000	$8,800,000	1973	The Steinbrenner Family
2	Los Angeles Dodgers	$3,300,000,000	$2,000,000,000	2012	Guggenheim Baseball Management
3	Boston Red Sox	$3,200,000,000	$380,000,000	2002	John Henry and Thomas Werner
4	Chicago Cubs	$3,100,000,000	$700,000,000	2009	The Ricketts Family
5	San Francisco Giants	$3,000,000,000	$100,000,000	1993	Charles Johnson
6	New York Mets	$2,300,000,000	$2,420,000,000	2020	Steve Cohen
7	St. Louis Cardinals	$2,100,000,000	$150,000,000	1996	William DeWitt, Jr.
8	Los Angeles Angels	$1,900,000,000	$183,500,000	2003	Arturo Moreno

3. "Service Time Definition," MLB.com, (http://m.mlb.com/glossary/transactions/service-time)
4. Mark Feinsand, "Manfred's Contract Extended Through 2024," MLB.com, November 15, 2018 (www.mlb.com/news/rob-manfred-contract-extended-c300765450), "Rob Manfred-Commissioner of Major League Baseball Bio," MLB.com, (www.mlb.com/official-information/executives/rob-manfred)
5. Sports Reference LLC, "Major League Baseball," Baseball-Reference.com-Baseball Statistics and History, March 5, 2020 (www.baseball-reference.com/bullpen/Major_League_Baseball), "MLB Constitution," (https://assets.documentcloud.org/documents/6784510/MLB-Constitution.pdf)

9	Philadelphia Phillies	$1,850,000,000	$30,000,000	1981	John Middleton and The Buck Family
10	Houston Astros	$1,775,000,000	$465,000,000	2011	Jim Crane
11	Washington Nationals	$1,750,000,000	$450,000,000	2006	The Lerner Family
12	Atlanta Braves	$1,700,000,000	$400,000,000	2007	Liberty Media
13	Texas Rangers	$1,650,000,000	$593,000,000	2010	Ray Davis and Bob Simpson
14	Chicago White Sox	$1,600,000,000	$20,000,000	1981	Jerry Reinsdorf
15	Seattle Mariners	$1,575,000,000	$1,200,000,000	2016	John Stanton and Chris Larson
16	Toronto Blue Jays	$1,500,000,000	$137,000,000	2000	Rogers Communications
17	San Diego Padres	$1,350,000,000	$600,000,000	2012	Ron Fowler and Peter Seidler
18	Arizona Diamondbacks	$1,290,000,000	$238,000,000	2004	Ken Kendrick
19	Baltimore Orioles	$1,280,000,000	$173,000,000	1993	Peter Angelos
20	Pittsburgh Pirates	$1,275,000,000	$92,000,000	1996	The Nutting Family
21	Detroit Tigers	$1,250,000,000	$82,000,000	1992	The Ilitch Family
22	Colorado Rockies	$1,225,000,000	$95,000,000	1992	Charles Monfort and Richard Monfort
23	Minnesota Twins	$1,200,000,000	$44,000,000	1984	James Pohlad
24	Milwaukee Brewers	$1,175,000,000	$223,000,000	2005	Mark Attanasio
25	Cleveland Indians	$1,150,000,000	$323,000,000	2000	Lawrence Dolan and Paul Dolan
26	Oakland Athletics	$1,100,000,000	$180,000,000	2005	John Fisher
27	Cincinnati Reds	$1,050,000,000	$270,000,000	2006	Robert Castellini
28	Kansas City Royals	$1,025,000,000	$1,000,000,000	2019	John Sherman
29	Tampa Bay Rays	$1,010,000,000	$200,000,000	2004	Stuart Sternberg
30	Miami Marlins	$1,000,000,000	$1,200,000,000	2017	Bruce Sherman

Sources: Kurt Badenhausen and Mike Ozanian and "Baseball Team Values 2019: Yankees Lead League At $4.6 Billion," Forbes. com, April 10, 2019 (www.forbes.com/sites/mikeozanian/2019/04/10/baseball-team-values-2019-yankees-lead-league-at-46-billion/#54d8b86369b2) and Mike Ozanian, "John Sherman Buys Kansas City Royals For $1 Billion," Forbes.com, November 22, 2019 (www.forbes.com/sites/mikeozanian/2019/11/22/john-sherman-buys-kansas-city-royals-for-1-billion/#7e71624a3851)
Mike Ozanian "Steve Cohen To Buy Mets For $2.42 Billion, Within 1% Of Forbes Valuation Of Team," Forbes.com, September 14, 2020 www.forbes.com/sites/mikeozanian/2020/09/14/steve-cohen-to-buy-mets-for-242-billion-within-one-percent-of-forbes-valuation-of-team/?sh=79decf501d21

Ownership of a major league franchise is an exclusive fraternity. The traditional model has primarily been wealthy individuals, families, and companies. Investment funds have also been given permission to purchase minority stakes in multiple ball clubs. Professional sports franchises have become entertainment, media, and real estate companies.[6]

Major League Baseball Revenue Distribution

Individual Teams

Major League Baseball is amid a successful run when it comes to generating revenues thanks to media rights, streaming, and sponsorship deals. The sport is constantly setting a record for revenues as they are regularly exceeding $10 billion beginning in 2017 and are on the verge of eclipsing $11 billion. Between the 2004 and 2017 seasons, Major League Baseball averaged an estimated 74.6 million fans per season with 2007 producing nearly 79.5 million fans, a historic achievement that has yet to be matched by any season.[7]

Forbes gives us with the closest examinations of ball clubs' financials through a detailed methodology. Even though it might not be a perfect model, Forbes provides us with an opportunity to think in a manner that aligns with the key financial aspects of the business of baseball. Forbes' valuations of Major League Baseball's franchises began in 1998 and have become a trusted and essential resource.

From League Office

Each year, a ball club completes a financial information questionnaire and submits audited financial statements to Major League Baseball. Defined gross revenue is the aggregate revenues earned and received by a ball club. This includes a ball club's local revenues as well as the central revenues allocated through Major League Baseball. Postseason revenues are excluded from this definition.[8]

Central revenues are distributed and controlled by the Commissioner's Office. These revenues are national and international broadcast agreements, Major League Baseball Properties Inc., Major League Baseball Advanced Media, MLB Network, Copyright Arbitration Royalty Panel, All-Star Game, and national marketing and licensing. Local revenues are calculated by subtracting a ball club's defined gross revenue and its share of the central revenues. A ball club's actual stadium

6. Kurt Badenhausen and Mike Ozanian and "Baseball Team Values 2019: Yankees Lead League At $4.6 Billion," Forbes.com, April 10, 2019 (www.forbes.com/sites/mikeozanian/2019/04/10/baseball-team-values-2019-yankees-lead-league-at-46-billion/#54d8b86369b2)

7. Maury Brown, "MLB Sees Record $10.7 Billion In Revenues For 2019," Forbes.com, December 21, 2019 (www.forbes.com/sites/maurybrown/2019/12/21/mlb-sees-record-107-billion-in-revenues-for-2019/#2bbc25075d78), Sports Reference LLC, "Major League Baseball Miscellaneous Year-By-Year Averages And Totals," Baseball-Reference.**com**-Baseball Statistics and History, March 15, 2020 (www.baseball-reference.com/leagues/MLB/misc.shtml).

8. 2017 MLB CBA, art. XXIV, at 130-149, William Juliano, "Looking Under The Hood Of MLB's Revenue Sharing Plan," The Captain's Blog, March 7, 2020 (http://www.captainsblog.info/2020/03/07/looking-under-the-hood-of-mlbs-revenue-sharing-plan-yankees-baseball-red-sox-mets-how-does-baseballs-revenue-sharing-work/25425/)

expenses are subtracted from the local revenues. This will present you with a ball club's net local revenue for a given year[9] (see charts 2, 3, and 4).

Chart #2

Defined Gross Revenues
-Central Revenues
Local Revenues
-Stadium Expenses
Net Local Revenue

Source: 2017 MLB CBA, art. XXIV, at 130-149.

Thirteen ball clubs have a market score of at least 100 or greater in the current collective bargaining agreement. These ball clubs are disqualified from receiving revenue sharing. One ball club in this group operates under a different set of rules: the Oakland Athletics.

Chart #3

Ball Club	Market Score
New York Yankees	235
New York Mets	235
Los Angeles Dodgers	178
Los Angeles Angels	178
Chicago Cubs	124
Chicago White Sox	124
Toronto Blue Jays	119
Washington Nationals	113
Philadelphia Phillies	111
Oakland Athletics	108
San Francisco Giants	108
Boston Red Sox	101
Texas Rangers	101

Source: 2017 MLB CBA, Attachment 26 and art. XXIV (A), (12).

---

9. 2017 MLB CBA, art. XXIV, at 130-149, William Juliano, "Looking Under The Hood Of MLB's Revenue Sharing Plan," The Captain's Blog, March 7, 2020 (http://www.captainsblog.info/2020/03/07/looking-under-the-hood-of-mlbs-revenue-sharing-plan-yankees-baseball-red-sox-mets-how-does-baseballs-revenue-sharing-work/25425/)

Chart #4

Year	Disqualification Percentage
2017	25 Percent
2018	50 Percent
2019	75 Percent
2020	Fully Disqualified
2021	Fully Disqualified

Source: 2017 MLB CBA, art. XXIV (A), (12).

The intent of revenue sharing is for 30 ball clubs to put 48 percent of their net local revenue into a straight pool plan and equally redistribute the funds. The difference between a ball club's contribution of local revenues and what they have received in return is called the net transfer value. The results could either be positive ("payees") or negative ("payors") and expressed as percentages for the "payors."[10]

A revenue pool calculation looks at three previous years of net local revenue. A blended average is based on 50 percent of a ball club's net local revenue for the prior year, 25 percent from two years prior, and 25 percent from three years prior. A ball club's total contribution to this pool is called the blended net local revenue. It is equally divided among 30 ball clubs and produces net payment or net receipt. The results are presented as percentages of the total net transfer of the blended net local revenue pool. This is also called the transfer percentage.[11]

After the net transfer value and transfer percentage, the revenue sharing process turns into a multiplication problem.

Chart #5

Net Transfer Value x Transfer Percentage
Ball Club's Payment Or Receipt For The Year

Source: 2017 Major League Baseball Collective Bargaining Agreement, art. XXIV (A), (10), (c).

---

10. 2017 MLB CBA, art. XXIV, at 130-149, William Juliano, "Looking Under The Hood Of MLB's Revenue Sharing Plan," The Captain's Blog, March 7, 2020 (http://www.captainsblog.info/2020/03/07/looking-under-the-hood-of-mlbs-revenue-sharing-plan-yankees-baseball-red-sox-mets-how-does-baseballs-revenue-sharing-work/25425/)

11. 2017 MLB CBA, art. XXIV, at 130-149, William Juliano, "Looking Under The Hood Of MLB's Revenue Sharing Plan," The Captain's Blog, March 7, 2020 (http://www.captainsblog.info/2020/03/07/looking-under-the-hood-of-mlbs-revenue-sharing-plan-yankees-baseball-red-sox-mets-how-does-baseballs-revenue-sharing-work/25425/)

Revenue sharing funds cannot be used to address a ball club's debt. They are allocated for on-field personnel or a ball club's player development. Ball clubs must submit a comprehensive report that outlines what they have done to improve performance-related issues, a strategy for improvement, and detailed financial data covering topics such as payroll costs, nonpayroll costs, operating profits, and projections.[12]

Major League Baseball's Facility Revenue, Subsidies, and Construction

Major league ballparks are a multifaceted real estate endeavor that provide additional opportunities to develop adjacent land for hospitality, entertainment, residential, and commercial purposes. Ball clubs are constantly vying for a customer's limited disposable income. It is one thing to own the ballpark, but it is a far more lucrative endeavor owning the ballpark and developing the surrounding land that directly benefits the community and overall value of the franchise.[13]

© cunaplus/Shutterstock.com

Wide open concourses, social gathering spots, and outstanding experiences with exciting food and beverage options are commonplace in ballparks. Concessionaire contracts are capturing a new spirit and energy regarding ballpark dining options. Professional sports franchises hire a concessionaire company to manage the process. The concessionaire deal will likely involve an upfront payment or capital investment to the professional sports franchise, and they will also get a percentage of the sales (gross or net). The concessionaire company handles all matters with food vendors, contractors, suppliers, and other business-related aspects.[14]

Technological advancements are being used when it comes to serving guests. There have been significant improvements regarding in-seat delivery, digital technology to streamline the purchasing

12. 2017 MLB CBA, art. XXIV, at 130-149

13. Cobb Chamber Of Commerce, "Fiscal Impact Of SunTrust Park And The Battery Atlanta On Cobb County Executive Summary," September 18, 2018 (www.cobbchamber.org/economic-development/suntrust_park_fiscal_impact.aspx), SunTrust, "The Evolution Of Stadium Financing And Development," (www.suntrust.com/resource-center/wealth-management/article/the-evolution-of-stadium-financing-and-development#.XnfcuYhKjIV)

14. Greg Swistak, "The Whys And Hows Of Restaurant/Stadium Partnerships," QSRweb, May 21, 2014 (www.qsrweb.com/blogs/the-whys-and-hows-of-restaurantstadium-partnerships/)

process, and the utilization of modern kitchen equipment that can handle massive volume. Thanks to these innovative improvements, it feels as if the dining experiences at major league ballparks are far more personal rather than the old mentality of feeding the masses with generic offerings.[15]

Major League Baseball Financial Forecasting

Financial forecasting is challenging regardless of the industry, but there are variables in the business of baseball which make it far more unpredictable. Major League Baseball has specific revenue streams that can be long-term and fixed in nature: national and local broadcast deals, sponsorships, and naming rights. The dynamics of forecasting payroll expenses thanks to free agency, trades, arbitration, and contract extensions is a difficult task to manage alone. A ball club's performance can positively or negatively affect ticket and suite sales. Winning and losing impacts the overall ballpark experience in terms of concession sales.[16]

Major league ball clubs are constantly thinking of different scenarios that are driven by performance when it comes to creating financial forecasts. It is not as easy as winning and losing. An injury to an all-star ball player, inclement weather, postseason chances, and unforeseen circumstances can alter a ball club's financial outlook. Some of the worst scenarios to plan for are work stoppages or suspensions of play in due to collective bargaining issues or widespread catastrophe.[17]

Major league ball clubs who are recipients of revenue sharing proceeds have a responsibility to use the money accordingly since salaries are a large component of a ball club's annual budget. Another interesting dynamic is the value of corporate dollars. Sometimes, it takes time for these dollars to materialize since they might come after an extended period of winning, roster improvements, and timing of the season when the sales teams push for new corporate sponsors.[18]

As Major League Baseball is enjoying annual revenues in the eleven figures, questions are being posed regarding the long-term financial health and outlook. Leaguewide attendance has been

15. Daniel P. Smith, "How Sports Stadiums Are Upping Their Foodservice Game," QSR Magazine, May 2018 (www.qsrmagazine.com/menu-innovations/how-sports-stadiums-are-upping-their-foodservice-game), Aramark Press Release, "New York Mets and Aramark Team With CLEAR and Mashgin to Deliver the First Fully-Automated Concessions Experience in Sports," Aramark Press Release, September 23, 2019 (www.aramark.com/about-us/news/aramark-general/mets-clear-mashgin-automated-concessions)
16. Craig Calcaterra, "A Warning About Major League Baseball's Record Revenues," NBC Sports, January 7, 2019 (https://mlb.nbcsports.com/2019/01/07/a-warning-about-major-league-baseballs-record-revenues/), David McCann, "Baseball CFO Looks To Win With CPM Software," CFO, April 20, 2017 (www.cfo.com/forecasting/2017/04/baseball-cfo-looks-to-win-with-cpm-software-scenario-planning/)
17. Craig Calcaterra, "A Warning About Major League Baseball's Record Revenues," NBC Sports, January 7, 2019 (https://mlb.nbcsports.com/2019/01/07/a-warning-about-major-league-baseballs-record-revenues/), David McCann, "Baseball CFO Looks To Win With CPM Software," CFO, April 20, 2017 (www.cfo.com/forecasting/2017/04/baseball-cfo-looks-to-win-with-cpm-software-scenario-planning/)
18. Craig Calcaterra, "A Warning About Major League Baseball's Record Revenues," NBC Sports, January 7, 2019 (https://mlb.nbcsports.com/2019/01/07/a-warning-about-major-league-baseballs-record-revenues/), David McCann, "Baseball CFO Looks To Win With CPM Software," CFO, April 20, 2017 (www.cfo.com/forecasting/2017/04/baseball-cfo-looks-to-win-with-cpm-software-scenario-planning/)

declining and frustrations exist between owners and ball players regarding salaries. Certain ball clubs have not tried their best to field a competitive team and new revenue streams are coming into baseball that are not related to producing a winning product. Franchise values are exploding, and owners are richly profiting but it does not necessarily mean the money is being reinvested in the ball club or correlates to winning.[19]

Financial forecasting in baseball relies on sound judgment and a solid quantitative approach. It is important to have well-organized and detailed historical information to serve as the basis for planning. Ball clubs must exhaust a wide array of scenarios and pick an appropriate time period for forecasting. A three- to five-year forecast can produce far more accurate results than a decade long plan. Forecasting puts a great emphasis on what the future will look like for management based on a multitude of variables.[20]

Major League Baseball's Tax Status and Liabilities

Major League Baseball decided to surrender its 501(c)(6) status that permitted a professional sports league to claim tax exemption in 2007. The league's central office was once considered a not-for-profit entity, but the status did not directly apply to the individual ball clubs. Professional sports franchises are mostly structured as limited liability companies and pass-through businesses.[21]

Debt is not an easy task to manage, especially for major league owners. The collective bargaining agreement addresses it with the debt service rule. Ball clubs should only carry debt that can be reasonably supported by their earnings before interest, taxes, depreciation, and amortization (EBITDA). There are certain guidelines in place to measure what it means to be "reasonably supported by EBITDA."[22]

Debt can accumulate in many ways. It can come from Major League Baseball's credit facility, basic business activities, deferred compensation on contracts, ballpark construction and improvements,

19. Craig Calcaterra, "A Warning About Major League Baseball's Record Revenues," NBC Sports, January 7, 2019 (https://mlb.nbcsports.com/2019/01/07/a-warning-about-major-league-baseballs-record-revenues/),
David McCann, "Baseball CFO Looks To Win With CPM Software," CFO, April 20, 2017 (www.cfo.com/forecasting/2017/04/baseball-cfo-looks-to-win-with-cpm-software-scenario-planning/)
20. Craig Calcaterra, "A Warning About Major League Baseball's Record Revenues," NBC Sports, January 7, 2019 (https://mlb.nbcsports.com/2019/01/07/a-warning-about-major-league-baseballs-record-revenues/),
David McCann, "Baseball CFO Looks To Win With CPM Software," CFO, April 20, 2017 (www.cfo.com/forecasting/2017/04/baseball-cfo-looks-to-win-with-cpm-software-scenario-planning/),
Matthew T. Brown, Daniel A. Rascher, Mark S. Nagel, Chad D. McEvoy, *Financial Management In The Sport Industry* (Arizona: Holcomb Hathaway, Publishers, 2010), Pages 134-136
21. Andrew Zimbalist, "The Nonprofit Status Of Sports Leagues Is Irrelevant," The New York Times, September 4, 2014 (www.nytimes.com/roomfordebate/2014/09/03/should-pro-sport-leagues-get-tax-breaks/the-nonprofit-status-of-sports-leagues-is-irrelevant),
"2019 Instructions for Form 990 Return of Organization Exempt From Income Tax," IRS.gov (www.irs.gov/pub/irs-pdf/i990.pdf)
22. 2017 MLB CBA, Attachment 22, at 226-235

advances on future revenue, general obligations on ball players' contracts, responsibilities to the benefit plan for ball players, and the industry growth fund. The debt service rule acts as a checks and balance system for ball clubs.[23]

The EBITDA Multiplier is a formula that determines the maximum amount of debt a ball club can handle in relation to its EBITDA. A ball club can carry debt eight times its EBITDA. If a ball club has incurred debt due to ballpark construction or renovations, their EBITDA is 12 for the first decade after the opening of the ballpark. There are penalties for noncompliance ranging from a ball club submitting a written plan on how they will return to compliance, denying ball clubs representation at meetings, monetary sanctions, and guaranteeing compliance for an extended period of three years.[24]

Major League Baseball's Revenue Sources and Partnerships

Major League Baseball's sponsorship revenues are approaching $1 billion on an annual basis and is set to surpass this impressive number with a decade long uniform deal with Nike beginning in 2020 that is valued at more than $1 billion. It was announced in January 2019 that Nike would become the official uniform and footwear supplier of Major League Baseball and Fanatics would also be a partner in the deal. Fanatics is a global leader in licensed sports merchandise.[25]

Sponsorship revenues from the league and ball clubs have climbed from $548 million in 2010 to $938 million in 2018. Since 2016, sponsorship revenues have exceeded $820 million on an annual basis. The creation of new postseason sponsorship opportunities and balancing long-tenured sponsors with a new and diverse group of innovative companies have led to success for Major League Baseball.[26]

23. 2017 MLB CBA, Attachment 22, at 226-235
24. 2017 MLB CBA, Attachment 22, at 226-235
25. Ryan Gaydos, "Nike's Uniform Deal With MLB Worth More Than $1B, Report Says," Fox Business, December 19, 2019 (www.foxbusiness.com/sports/nikes-uniform-deal-mlb-1-billion-report)
Nike News, "Nike Enters 10-Year Partnership With Major League Baseball," Nike Press Release, January 25, 2019 (https://news.nike.com/news/nike-major-league-baseball) Major League Baseball Press Release, "MLB, Nike And Fanatics Form 10-Year Partnership," MLB.com, January 25, 2019 (www.mlb.com/news/mlb-nike-fanatics-form-10-year-partnership-c303162762)
26. Christina Gough, "MLB League And Teams Sponsorship Revenue 2010-2018," Statista, August 30, 2019 (www.statista.com/statistics/380197/mlb-sponsorship-revenue/), IEG Sponsorship Report, " Sponsorship Spending On MLB Totals $892 Million In 2017 Season, IEG Sponsorship Report, October 23, 2017 (www.sponsorship.com/Report/2017/10/23/Sponsorship-Spending-On-MLB-Totals-$892-Million-in.aspx), Daniel Roberts, "As NFL Falters, MLB Sponsors Spent Record-High $892 Million," Yahoo Finance, November 8, 2017 (https://finance.yahoo.com/news/nfl-falters-mlb-sponsors-spent-record-high-892-million-132837545.html)

Major League Baseball's Media Revenues

Individual Teams

The ability to generate healthy revenue streams in a major league ball club's local market is an important aspect to their success. Local media revenues are an integral component to how a major league ball club functions financially but not all broadcast and radio deals are created equally. These deals are negotiated by the major league ball clubs themselves. Market size, quality of the ball club, brand, and ownership are some of the factors considered when it comes to negotiating local broadcast and radio deals.

Ball clubs have a flagship radio station and a radio network that covers the affiliates from the surrounding region as well as Spanish language stations. It is an interesting time for baseball on the radio due to Major League Baseball's business relationship with Sirius XM satellite radio and how ball clubs are managing their local radio rights. Revenues from local radio broadcasts vary from market to market.[27]

Some ball clubs have parted ways with terrestrial radio and have embraced a tech savvy approach through streaming. The Oakland Athletics set up an audio streaming station called A's Cast on TuneIn. They decided A's Cast would be the official home of the ball club's audio content: Game broadcasts, podcasts, and daily sports shows would run through this service beginning in 2020.[28]

From League Office

Major League Baseball has broadcasting agreements with ESPN, Fox, and Turner Sports. ESPN extended its rights beginning in 2014 and running through 2021 at a cost of $5.6 billion which averages to $700 million on an annual basis. The agreement includes both television and radio rights in the United States and internationally. Major League Baseball agreed to eight-year contracts with Fox and Turner Sports through the 2021 season. The Fox deal was for $4.2 billion ($525 million annually) and TBS' deal was $2.6 billion ($325 million annually).[29]

27. Barry Jackson, "The Most Important Negotiation Of Jeter Ownership Hangs In Balance For Miami Marlins," Miami Herald, January 23, 2020 (www.miamiherald.com/sports/spt-columns-blogs/barry-jackson/article239526553.html)

28. Shayna Rubin, "Oakland Athletics Off The Radio Waves In The Bya Area, Commit To A's Cast Stream," The Mercury News, February 18, 2020 (www.mercurynews.com/2020/02/18/oakland-athletics-off-the-radio-waves-in-the-bay-area-commit-to-as-cast-stream/), Oakland Athletics Press Release, "A's Cast On TuneIn Is Now The Exclusive Home Of All Oakland A's Audio Content," Oakland Athletic Press Release, February 18, 2020 (www.mlb.com/press-release/press-release-a-s-cast-on-tunein-is-now-the-exclusive-home-of-all-oakland-a-s-au)

29. Richard Sandomir, "ESPN Extends M.L.B. Deal, Doubling What It Pays Yearly," The New York Times, August 29, 2012 (www.nytimes.com/2012/08/29/sports/baseball/espn-extends-deal-with-mlb-through-2021.html), Associated Press and ESPN.com News Services, "MLB Completes New TV Deals," ESPN.com, October 2,2012 (www.espn.com/mlb/story/_/id/8453054/major-league-baseball-completes-eight-year-deal-fox-turner-sports), MLB.com, "MLB, DAZN Agree To 3-Year Live Digital Rights Deal," MLB.com, November 15, 2018 (www.mlb.com/news/mlb-dazn-agree-to-3-year-digital-rights-deal-c300774598), James Wagner, "M.L.B. Extends TV Deal With Fox Sports Through 2028," The New York Times, November 15, 2018 (www.nytimes.com/2018/11/15/sports/mlb-fox-tv-deal.html), MLB Press Release, "MLB And ESPN Reach Eight-Year Broadcasting Agreement," MLB.com, August 28, 2012 (www.mlb.com/news/mlb-and-espn-reach-new-eight-year-broadcasting-agreement/c-37475930)

Fox and Major League Baseball decided to extend their national television rights agreement for an additional seven years and $5.1 billion ($728.6 million annually). The contract with Fox will now run through the conclusion of the 2028 season. Fox will expand its digital programming and will see an increase in regular season and postseason games broadcast beginning in 2022.[30]

Major League Baseball entered a digital rights partnership with DAZN in the fall of 2018. The estimated $300 million deal covers three seasons (2019-2021) for daily highlights, on-demand content, and a live look-in show. They have also been actively experimenting with digital platforms such as Facebook and YouTube TV for streaming live ball games.[31]

The origins of Major League Baseball Advanced Media (MLBAM) are based on a simple idea: consolidate the league's digital rights while creating websites for major league ball clubs. In 2000, Commissioner Bud Selig created MLBAM with $1 million annual investments from all 30 major league ball clubs over a four-year period. The $120 million investment also gave the ball clubs an equal ownership stake. MLBAM would operate as its own company to maintain a fair and balanced playing field.[32]

MLBAM began to evolve into different businesses. One of the first was an online ticketing service thanks to an early partnership with Ticketmaster. MLBAM embarked upon streaming video with the creation of MLB.TV, a mobile website, MLB At Bat mobile app, Pitch f/x, Statcast technology,

30. Richard Sandomir, "ESPN Extends M.L.B. Deal, Doubling What It Pays Yearly," The New York Times, August 29, 2012 (www.nytimes.com/2012/08/29/sports/baseball/espn-extends-deal-with-mlb-through-2021.html), Associated Press and ESPN. com News Services, "MLB Completes New TV Deals," ESPN.com, October 2, 2012 (www.espn.com/mlb/story/_/id/8453054/ major-league-baseball-completes-eight-year-deal-fox-turner-sports), MLB.com, "MLB, DAZN Agree To 3-Year Live Digital Rights Deal," MLB.com, November 15, 2018 (www.mlb.com/news/mlb-dazn-agree-to-3-year-digital-rights-deal-c300774598), James Wagner, "M.L.B. Extends TV Deal With Fox Sports Through 2028," The New York Times, November 15, 2018 (www.nytimes. com/2018/11/15/sports/mlb-fox-tv-deal.html), John Ourand and Eric Fisher, "MLB Signs Seven-Year Extension With Fox Worth $5.1 B," Sports Business Daily, November 15, 2018 (www.sportsbusinessdaily.com/Daily/Issues/2018/11/15/Media/MLB-Fox. aspx?hl=Eric+Fisher&sc=0), Mark J. Burns, "MLB, Facebook Scale Back Streaming Deal For 2019 Season to 6 Non-Exclusive Games," Morning Consult, March 29, 2019 (https://morningconsult.com/2019/03/29/mlb-facebook-scale-back-streaming-deal-for-2019-season-to-6-non-exclusive-games/), Sam Carp, "MLB Trims Facebook Streaming Deal To Six Games For 2019," Sports Pro, April 1, 2019 (www.sportspromedia.com/news/mlb-facebook-live-streaming-rights-six-games), Maury Brown, "MLB Extends Partnership With YouTube TV; MLB Network Now available On Platform," Forbes.com, March 8, 2018 (www.forbes.com/sites/ maurybrown/2018/03/08/mlb-extends-partnership-with-youtube-tv-mlb-network-now-available-on-platform/#478330f3702a), Major League Baseball, "MLB, YouTube TV Expand Partnership," MLB.com, March 8, 2018 (www.mlb.com/news/mlb-youtube-tv-expand-partnership-c268161958)
31. Richard Sandomir, "ESPN Extends M.L.B. Deal, Doubling What It Pays Yearly," The New York Times, August 29, 2012 (www. nytimes.com/2012/08/29/sports/baseball/espn-extends-deal-with-mlb-through-2021.html), Associated Press and ESPN.com News Services, "MLB Completes New TV Deals," ESPN.com, October 2, 2012 (www.espn.com/mlb/story/_/id/8453054/major-league-baseball-completes-eight-year-deal-fox-turner-sports), MLB.com, "MLB, DAZN Agree To 3-Year Live Digital Rights Deal," MLB. com, November 15, 2018 (www.mlb.com/news/mlb-dazn-agree-to-3-year-digital-rights-deal-c300774598), James Wagner, "M.L.B. Extends TV Deal With Fox Sports Through 2028," The New York Times, November 15, 2018 (www.nytimes.com/2018/11/15/ sports/mlb-fox-tv-deal.html)
32. Ben Popper, "The Changeup: How Baseball's Tech Team Built The Future Of Television," The Verge, August 4, 2015 (www. theverge.com/2015/8/4/9090897/mlb-bam-live-streaming-internet-tv-nhl-hbo-now-espn), Shalini Ramachandran, "MLB's Streaming-Tech Unit Goes Pro," The Wall Street Journal, February 23, 2015 (www.wsj.com/articles/mlbs-streaming-tech-unit-goes-pro-1424718022), Craig Edwards, "MLBAM And the Future Of MLB's Revenues," Fangraphs.com, August 6, 2015 (https://blogs. fangraphs.com/mlbam-and-the-future-of-mlbs-revenues/)

and enhancements to MLB.com. In 2014, the technical unit of MLBAM alone achieved over $100 million in revenues. After adding the baseball specific operations, roughly $900 million of Major League Baseball's $9 billion in revenues came from MLBAM.[33]

In August 2015, approval was given to begin the spin-off of a media company from MLBAM. BAMTech would be the name of the new company as Major League Baseball's 30 owners would enjoy majority ownership. The National Hockey League would be a minority partner as the media company would focus on initiatives outside of baseball. MLBAM would still focus on digital innovations and current services for baseball.[34]

The Walt Disney Company decided to acquire majority ownership in BAMTech. They held a 33 percent stake with an option to acquire majority ownership after a $1 billion deal in 2016. By August 2017, The Walt Disney Company acquired an additional 42 percent interest in BAMTech for $1.58 billion. Major League Baseball's 30 owners would receive at least $50 million from the transaction. Major League Baseball owns roughly 15 percent in BAMTech with the National Hockey League holding just less than 10 percent.[35]

Satellite radio has been an important media partner for Major League Baseball since 2005. Major League Baseball had an 11-year, $650 million broadcasting rights agreement with XM prior to the merger with Sirius in July 2008. A six-year contract extension was announced in August 2013 that provided Sirius XM an opportunity to be the official satellite partner of Major League Baseball through the 2021 season.[36]

---

33. Ben Popper, "The Changeup: How Baseball's Tech Team Built The Future Of Television," The Verge, August 4, 2015 (www.theverge.com/2015/8/4/9090897/mlb-bam-live-streaming-internet-tv-nhl-hbo-now-espn), Shalini Ramachandran, "MLB's Streaming-Tech Unit Goes Pro," *The Wall Street Journal*, February 23, 2015 (www.wsj.com/articles/mlbs-streaming-tech-unit-goes-pro-1424718022), Craig Edwards, "MLBAM And the Future Of MLB's Revenues," Fangraphs.com, August 6, 2015 (https://blogs.fangraphs.com/mlbam-and-the-future-of-mlbs-revenues/)
34. Ben Popper, "The Changeup: How Baseball's Tech Team Built The Future Of Television," The Verge, August 4, 2015 (www.theverge.com/2015/8/4/9090897/mlb-bam-live-streaming-internet-tv-nhl-hbo-now-espn), Shalini Ramachandran, "MLB's Streaming-Tech Unit Goes Pro," *The Wall Street Journal*, February 23, 2015 (www.wsj.com/articles/mlbs-streaming-tech-unit-goes-pro-1424718022), Craig Edwards, "MLBAM And the Future Of MLB's Revenues," Fangraphs.com, August 6, 2015 (https://blogs.fangraphs.com/mlbam-and-the-future-of-mlbs-revenues/)
35. Maury Brown, "MLB Approves New Digital Media Company Spin-Off That Will Create Billions In New Revenues," Forbes.com, August 13, 2015 (www.forbes.com/sites/maurybrown/2015/08/13/mlb-approves-new-digital-media-company-spin-off-that-will-create-billions-in-new-revenues/#6c1f286b315d), Eric Fisher, "BAMTech Produces Big Payoff," Sports Business Journal, August 14, 2017 (www.sportsbusinessdaily.com/Journal/Issues/2017/08/14/Leagues-and-Governing-Bodies/BAMTech.aspx), The Walt Disney Company Press Release, "The Walt Disney Company To Acquire Majority Ownership Of BAMTech," The Walt Disney Company Press Release, August 8, 2017 (https://thewaltdisneycompany.com/walt-disney-company-acquire-majority-ownership-bamtech/)
36. MLB Press Release, "SiriusXM And Major League Baseball Extend Agreement; Every Game Now Available On Sirius and XM Satellite Radios," MLB.com, August 19, 2013 (www.mlb.com/news/siriusxm--mlb-extend-agreement/c-57494660), Thomas Mentel, "Can Sirius XM's New MLB Deal Boost Revenue?" CheatSheet.com, August 26, 2013 (www.cheatsheet.com/technology/can-sirius-xms-new-mlb-deal-boost-revenue.html/),Dan Orlando, "Sirius XM Reloads On Peanuts And Cracker Jack, Might Never Go Back," New York Business Journal, August 19, 2013 (www.bizjournals.com/newyork/news/2013/08/19/mlb-and-sirius-xm-ink-extension-that.html), Sirius XM Holdings, Inc. Press Release, "SIRIUS and XM Complete Merger," Sirius XM Holdings, Inc., July 29, 2008 (http://investor.siriusxm.com/investor-overview/press-releases/press-release-details/2008/SIRIUS-and-XM-Complete-Merger/default.aspx)

© Debby Wong/Shutterstock.com

Major League Baseball's Salary Structures

Coaching Staff

The salaries of managers and coaches are not included in the Competitive Balance Tax calculation. Managers' salaries can begin in the mid to high six figures and climb to seven figures. Compensation packages can vary for the rest of the coaching staffs based on experience, workload, and name recognition. Hitting and pitching coaches can earn annual salaries between $150,000 and $350,000. A bench coach can earn $150,000-$250,000. First and third base coaches can be compensated between $100,000 and $140,000, with a bullpen coach earning a salary slightly below six figures.[37]

Analytics has challenged front offices to reassess how they interact with managers and coaches. Meaningful experience in the minor leagues as a coach or working in various capacities at the major league level is no longer a primary prerequisite to becoming a manager. If anyone aspires

---

37. David Laurila, "Sunday Notes: Coaching Salaries On The Farm, Bullpen Scatology, Cards STEP, More," Fangraphs.com, February 15, 2015 (https://blogs.fangraphs.com/sunday-notes-coaching-salaries-on-the-farm-bullpen-scatalogy-cards-step-more/) and "Competitive Balance Tax Definition," MLB.com, (http://m.mlb.com/glossary/transactions/competitive-balance-tax)

to manage a major league ball club, there must be an intimate understanding of analytics and a willingness to embrace constant input from the front office.[38]

Players

Every June, Major League Baseball's Rule 4 Draft is held for all amateur baseball players from the United States, Puerto Rico, and Canada. Ball players who are residents of the United States or Canada and have not been previously under contract with a major or minor league ball club are eligible for the draft.[39]

There are three criteria when it comes to draft eligibility. The first applies to ball players who have graduated from high school, but have yet to attend college. The second concerns ball players who have completed one year of junior college. The third applies to ball players who are attending a four-year college and just completed their junior year or are 21 years old.[40]

The Rule 4 Draft covers 40 rounds. Major league ball clubs have an assigned bonus pool for the first ten rounds and there are penalties if ball clubs exceed the thresholds. Every pick in the first ten rounds along with the Compensation and Competitive Balance Rounds picks are assigned a specific slot value.[41]

A ball player drafted in rounds 11-40 can receive a maximum value of $125,000 in terms of a signing bonus without it counting against the ball club's bonus pool. If a ball club outspends the assigned bonus pool between 0 and 5%, they would have to pay a 75% tax on the overage. If they outspend the assigned bonus pool between 5 and 10%, not only are they assessed with a 75% tax on the overage, but they also lose a first-round pick.[42]

The penalties are even harsher when a ball club outspends the assigned bonus pool by more than 10%. If a ball club's overspending falls within the 10-15% range, they lose first and second round draft picks as well as a 100% tax on the overage. Finally, if a ball club's overspending exceeds 15% of the assigned bonus pool, they will lose two first-round draft picks while also dealing with a 100% tax on the overage.[43]

38. Mark Gonzales, "Joe Maddon And Bruce Bochy Believe Baseball Managers Should Be Valued And Compensated Like NFL And NBA Coaches," Chicago Tribune, August 22, 2019 (www.chicagotribune.com/sports/cubs/ct-cubs-joe-maddon-20190822-gev37egvsrhprhexww7k7bsstm-story.html) and Bob Nightengale, "USA TODAY Survey: MLB Power Shift Has Managers' Salaries In Free Fall," USA Today, August 27, 2018 (www.usatoday.com/story/sports/mlb/columnist/bob-nightengale/2018/08/27/baseball-managers-salaries-joe-maddon-dave-roberts-aj-hinch/1102815002/)
39. "Rule 4 Draft Definition," MLB.com, (http://m.mlb.com/glossary/transactions/rule-4-draft)
40. "Rule 4 Draft Definition," MLB.com, (http://m.mlb.com/glossary/transactions/rule-4-draft) and "First Year Player Draft FAQ," MLB.com, (http://mlb.mlb.com/mlb/draftday/faq.jsp)
41. Jim Callis, "Here Are The 2019 Draft Pools And Bonus Values," MLB.com, June 3, 2019 (www.mlb.com/news/2019-mlb-draft-pools-and-bonus-values)
42. Jim Callis, "Here Are The 2019 Draft Pools And Bonus Values," MLB.com, June 3, 2019 (www.mlb.com/news/2019-mlb-draft-pools-and-bonus-values)
43. Jim Callis, "Here Are The 2019 Draft Pools And Bonus Values," MLB.com, June 3, 2019 (www.mlb.com/news/2019-mlb-draft-pools-and-bonus-values)

Latin America and other parts of the world have provided Major League Baseball with extraordinary talent. A cap has been established for ball clubs to spend on international ball players with specific age requirements. A ball player must be at least 16 years old before he signs a contract and must turn 17 years old before September 1st of the following year. Each ball club would start off with at least a $4.75 million bonus pool but if you had a pick in the Competitive Balance Round A of the Rule 4 Draft, you received $5.25 million. If you had a pick in the Competitive Balance Round B of the Rule 4 Draft, you would receive $5.75 million.[44]

There are three keys to international signing bonuses. Ball clubs cannot exceed their assigned their signing bonus pools. Dollar amounts allocated to the pools for the ball clubs can change over time based on the revenues from the industry. Any signing bonus of $10,000 or less does not count toward the ball club's international signing bonus pool.[45]

The signing period begins on July 2nd and goes through June 15th of the following year. Ball clubs can trade international bonus pool money. However, they can only acquire 60 percent of the initial amount distributed to them in the international bonus pool.[46]

The signing period does not apply to professional international ball players. They are exempt from the international bonus pool. A ball player must be at least 25 years old and have played professional baseball for at least six seasons in a foreign league recognized by Major League Baseball.[47]

An important step is to earn a spot on the 40-man roster. This means a ball player is now eligible for membership in the Major League Baseball Players Association and they will see a salary adjustment. Minor league minimum for a ball player signing their first major league contract is $46,000 for the 2020 season. If a ball player is signing their second or subsequent major league contracts, the minor league minimum for a ball player who fits into this category is $91,800 for the 2020 season.[48]

After earning a spot on the major league ball club's 26-man roster there are new aspects of the business regarding compensation, service time, and arbitration. The major league minimum salary for 2020 is $563,500 and this applies to ball players who have yet to qualify for salary arbitration

44. "International Amateur Free Agency and Bonus Pool Money Definition," MLB.com, (http://m.mlb.com/glossary/transactions/international-amateur-free-agency-bonus-pool-money) and Jesse Sanchez, "Here's Where Top International Prospects Are Signing," MLB.com, July 3, 2019 (www.mlb.com/news/international-prospect-signings-july-2-2019)

45. "International Amateur Free Agency and Bonus Pool Money Definition," MLB.com, (http://m.mlb.com/glossary/transactions/international-amateur-free-agency-bonus-pool-money) and Jesse Sanchez, "Here's Where Top International Prospects Are Signing," MLB.com, July 3, 2019 (www.mlb.com/news/international-prospect-signings-july-2-2019)

46. "International Amateur Free Agency and Bonus Pool Money Definition," MLB.com, (http://m.mlb.com/glossary/transactions/international-amateur-free-agency-bonus-pool-money) and Jesse Sanchez, "Here's Where Top International Prospects Are Signing," MLB.com, July 3, 2019 (www.mlb.com/news/international-prospect-signings-july-2-2019)

47. "International Amateur Free Agency and Bonus Pool Money Definition," MLB.com, (http://m.mlb.com/glossary/transactions/international-amateur-free-agency-bonus-pool-money)

48. "MLBPA FAQ – Who Is Eligible For Membership In The Association?" mlbplayers.com, (www.mlbplayers.com/faq), "MLB Minimum Salary Rises $8,500 To $563,500 Next Season," ESPN.com, November 13, 2019, (www.espn.com/mlb/story/_/id/28074687/mlb-minimum-salary-rises-8500-563500-next-season)

(less than three years of major league service). Service time becomes an important issue regarding eligibility for salary arbitration.[49]

There are roughly 187 days during a major league regular season. A ball player needs to accrue 172 days to count as one year of major league service. This covers every day a ball player is on the 26-man roster or injured list. The goal is to reach six years of major league service to qualify for free agency.[50]

After a ball player has accumulated three or more years of service time but less than six years at the major league level, they become eligible for salary arbitration. Eligible ball players and their respective ball clubs engage in salary conversations. The conversations focus on what comparable ball players have received in recent years.[51]

There is a deadline in January in which a ball club and player have come to terms on a contract or neither side could agree on a contract and they must exchange salary figures for the upcoming season. This is in preparation for a hearing that will take place in February in front of a panel of arbitrators. Both parties will present their salary cases to the panel. The arbitrators will then select either the salary figure of the ball player or the ball club. This will become the salary for the ball player in the upcoming season.[52]

Free agency can be an exciting and stressful time in a ball player's life. They finally have the freedom to choose where they want to play in the next phase of their career. Ball players are handsomely compensated in free agency with some even achieving nine figure contracts. (see chart 6)

Chart #6 MLB Minimum And Average Salaries And Annual Payrolls (2015-2019)

Year	Minimum MLB Salary	Average MLB Salary
2015	$507,500	$3,952,252
2016	$507,500	$3,966,020
2017	$535,000	$4,097,122
2018	$545,000	$4,095,686
2019	$555,000	$4,051,490

Sources: Associated Press, "Average MLB Salary Down For First Time Since 2004," ESPN.com, December 21, 2018 (www.espn.com/mlb/story/_/id/25588442/average-mlb-salary-1st-2004), Associated Press, "Average Salary Hits Record $3.2 Million," ESPN.com, December 7, 2012 (www.espn.com/espn/print?id=8724285#), Ronald Blum, "AP News Break: Red Sox, Yanks, Cubs Sent 2019 Luxury Tax Bills," AP News Break, December 18, 2019 (https://apnews.com/1c06039c90703db8c5e9ccef59ab08d3), Associated Press, " Average MLB Salary Drops For Second Straight Year," ESPN.com, December 20, 2019 (www.espn.com/mlb/story/_/id/28341983/average-mlb-salary-drops-second-straight-year)

49. "MLB Minimum Salary Rises $8,500 To $563,500 Next Season," AP-USA Today, November 13, 2019 (www.usatoday.com/story/sports/mlb/2019/11/13/mlb-minimum-salary-rises-8500-to-563500-next-season/40609271/)
50. "Service Time Definition," MLB.com, (http://m.mlb.com/glossary/transactions/service-time)
51. "Salary Arbitration Definition," MLB.com, (http://m.mlb.com/glossary/transactions/salary-arbitration)
52. "Salary Arbitration Definition," MLB.com, (http://m.mlb.com/glossary/transactions/salary-arbitration)

Salary Caps

Major League Baseball is the only professional sports league in the United States that doesn't have a salary cap. Many believe the competitive balance tax (also known as a "luxury tax") serves as a deterrent to spending due to its stringent penalties. So, how does it work? (See chart 7)

Chart #7

MLB CBA 2017-2021

> As stated in Major League Baseball's Collective Bargaining Agreement, there are predetermined base tax thresholds established for each contract year throughout the course of the agreement. Under the current agreement (2017-2021), the following base tax thresholds have been established.
>
> - 2017: $195 million
> - 2018: $197 million
> - 2019: $206 million
> - 2020: $208 million
> - 2021: $210 million

Source: Basic Agreement Between the 30 Major League Clubs And The Major League Baseball Players Association Effective December 1, 2016, art. XXIII, at 106-112, 129-130.

A contract year is the period beginning on December 2nd of one year and running through and including December 1st of the following year. A yearly analysis occurs on all 30 ball clubs' actual club payroll. There is a calculation regarding actual club payroll that is different than a ball player's actual annual salary.[53]

A ball club's actual club payroll comprises the following:

- Benefit costs for the ball players
- Average annual value of guaranteed multiyear contracts
- Outright assignment to a minor league ball club
- Earned performance, award, or other bonuses for the contract year[54]

The average annual value in a guaranteed year:[55]

(Base Salary in each guaranteed year) + (Any portion of a signing bonus attributed to a guaranteed year) + (Any deferred compensation or annuity compensation costs attributed to a guaranteed year) / Number of guaranteed years

---

53. 2016 MLB CBA, art. XXIII, at 106-112, 129-130
54. 2016 MLB CBA, art. XXIII, at 106-112, 129-130
55. 2016 MLB CBA, art. XXIII, at 106-112, 129-130

The base competitive balance tax rates act as a penalty for ball clubs who exceed the base tax thresholds. The tax rate will be applied to the difference between actual club payroll and the base tax threshold. There are three base competitive balance tax rates.

- 20% if a ball club exceeds the base tax threshold a first time.
- 30% if a ball club exceeds the base tax threshold a second consecutive time.
- 50% if a ball club exceeds the base tax threshold a third consecutive time or in more than two preceding contract years.[56]

There are two additional surcharges with even harsher penalties for ball clubs who surpass the Base Tax Threshold by a significant amount of actual club payroll. Here is a breakdown of the thresholds (see chart 8).

Chart #8

- First Surcharge Threshold
  - 2017: $215 million
  - 2018: $217 million
  - 2019: $226 million
  - 2020: $228 million
  - 2021: $230 million

- Second Surcharge Threshold
  - 2017: $235 million
  - 2018: $237 million
  - 2019: $246 million
  - 2020: $248 million
  - 2021: $250 million

Source: Basic Agreement Between the 30 Major League Clubs And The Major League Baseball Players Association Effective December 1, 2016, art. XXIII, at 106-112, 129-130.

If a ball club finishes a contract year with an actual club payroll that exceeds the first surcharge threshold, they will have to pay a 12% surcharge rate on top of the base competitive balance tax rate. The actual club payroll must be above the first surcharge threshold but at or below the second surcharge threshold.[57]

If a ball club finishes a contract year with an actual club payroll that exceeds the Second Surcharge Threshold, they will have to pay an additional 45% surcharge rate on top of the base competitive

56. 2016 MLB CBA, art. XXIII, at 106-112, 129-130
57. 2016 MLB CBA, art. XXIII, at 106-112, 129-130

balance tax rate on the difference between its actual club payroll and the second surcharge threshold. A first-time CBT payor will only be charged a 42.5% surcharge rate on the difference between its actual club payroll and the second surcharge threshold.[58]

A ball club that had an actual club payroll at or above the second surcharge threshold in a contract year, would have their highest draft selection in the following year's Rule 4 Draft moved back ten places in the draft order. The penalty applies to all types of CBT payors (first, second, and third) and even if the ball club has already experienced the penalty in a previous Contract Year.[59]

However, if a ball club has a draft pick within one of the first six selections it will not be moved back ten places. This excludes supplemental selections. Instead, the ball club's second-highest selection will be moved back ten places.[60]

In 2018, the Boston Red Sox amassed an estimated actual club payroll of $239,481,745. The base tax threshold was $197 million while the first surcharge threshold was $217 million, and the second surcharge threshold was $237 million. The Red Sox were an estimated $42,481,745 over the 2018 base tax threshold, which led to the ball club also surpassing both surcharge thresholds.[61]

Since the Red Sox fell under the 2017 base tax threshold of $197 million with an actual club payroll of $189.2 million, they were considered to be first time CBT payors in 2018 even though they had made competitive balance tax payments in the 2015-2016 contract years along with six other occasions dating back to 2004. The Red Sox had to confront four competitive balance tax penalties in 2018: exceeding the base tax threshold, first and second surcharge thresholds, and having their first pick in the 2019 Rule 4 Draft moved back ten places in Draft order.[62]

58. 2016 MLB CBA, art. XXIII, at 106-112, 129-130.
59. 2016 MLB CBA, art. XXIII, at 106-112, 129-130.
60. 2016 MLB CBA, art. XXIII, at 106-112, 129-130.
61. 2016 MLB CBA, art. XXIII, at 106-112, 129-130. Ronald Blum, "Champion Red Sox Owe Nearly $12 Million in Luxury Tax," AP News Break, December 15, 2018 (https://apnews.com/c9825fa95840449cbc66bfc67ef0c2b9). Ronald Blum, "Dodgers Hit With $36.2 Million Tax, Yanks With $15.7 Million," AP News Break, December 19, 2017 (https://apnews.com/245ac5e3fe864a94aa432359b2a5ce7a/AP-NewsBreak:-Dodgers-hit-with-$36.2M-tax,-Yanks-with-$15.7M?utm_campaign=SocialFlow&utm_source=Twitter&utm_medium=AP_Sports). Sports Reference LLC, "2nd Round Of The 2019 MLB June Amateur Draft," Baseball-Reference.com-Baseball Statistics and History, February 9, 2020 (www.baseball-reference.com/draft/?year_ID=2019&draft_round=2&draft_type=junreg&query_type=year_round&from_type_jc=0&from_type_hs=0&from_type_4y=0&from_type_unk=0). "Boston Red Sox," Cot's Baseball Contracts, accessed February 12, 2020, (https://legacy.baseballprospectus.com/compensation/cots/al-east/boston-red-sox/).
62. 2016 MLB CBA, art. XXIII, at 106-112, 129-130. Ronald Blum, "Champion Red Sox Owe Nearly $12 Million in Luxury Tax," AP News Break, December 15, 2018 (https://apnews.com/c9825fa95840449cbc66bfc67ef0c2b9). Ronald Blum, "Dodgers Hit With $36.2 Million Tax, Yanks With $15.7 Million," AP News Break, December 19, 2017 (https://apnews.com/245ac5e3fe864a94aa432359b2a5ce7a/AP-NewsBreak:-Dodgers-hit-with-$36.2M-tax,-Yanks-with-$15.7M?utm_campaign=SocialFlow&utm_source=Twitter&utm_medium=AP_Sports). Sports Reference LLC, "2nd Round Of The 2019 MLB June Amateur Draft," Baseball-Reference.com-Baseball Statistics and History, February 9, 2020 (www.baseball-reference.com/draft/?year_ID=2019&draft_round=2&draft_type=junreg&query_type=year_round&from_type_jc=0&from_type_hs=0&from_type_4y=0&from_type_unk=0). "Boston Red Sox," Cot's Baseball Contracts, accessed February 12, 2020, (https://legacy.baseballprospectus.com/compensation/cots/al-east/boston-red-sox/).

The Red Sox's first pick in the 2019 Rule 4 Draft should have been in the first round (33rd overall). However, due to the Rule 4 Draft Selection penalty for exceeding the second surcharge threshold in 2018, the Red Sox's first pick was in the second round (43rd overall)[63] (see example here and chart 9).

2018 Base Tax Threshold	$197,000,000
2018 Estimated Boston Red Sox Actual Club Payroll	$239,481,745
Estimated Difference	($42,481,745)
20% Competitive Balance Tax For First-Time CBT Payor: $20 Million Difference Between The First Surcharge Threshold ($217 million) and Base Tax Threshold ($197 million)	$4,000,000
20% Competitive Balance Tax For First-Time CBT Payor + 12% Surcharge Rate: $20 Million Difference Between The First Surcharge Threshold ($217 Million) and the Second Surcharge Threshold ($237 Million)	$6,400,000
20% Competitive Balance Tax For First-Time CBT Payor + 42.5% Surcharge Rate For Exceeding the Second Surcharge Threshold ($237 million) on Remaining $2,481,745	$1,551,091
Total	**$11,951,091[64]**

Chart #9

Ball Club	Number of Times CBT Payor	Estimated Competitive Balance Tax Payments (2003-2019)	Percentage of Estimated Total
New York Yankees	16	$347,467,870	59.84%
Boston Red Sox	10	$50,468,570	8.69%
Los Angeles Dodgers	5	$149,589,945	25.76%
Detroit Tigers	3	$8,999,451	1.55%
San Francisco Giants	3	$8,861,255	1.53%
Chicago Cubs	2	$10,560,647	1.82%
Washington Nationals	2	$3,834,287	0.66%
Los Angeles Angels	1	$927,057	0.16%
Estimated Total		**$580,709,082**	

Sources: Maury Brown, "Final MLB Payrolls For All 30 Teams Show Second-Largest Decline Since 2004," Forbes.com, December 17, 2018 and Ronald Blum, "AP News Break: Red Sox, Yanks, Cubs Sent 2019 Luxury Tax Bills," Associated Press, December 18, 2019.

63. Sports Reference LLC, "2nd Round Of The 2019 MLB June Amateur Draft," Baseball-Reference.com-Baseball Statistics and History, February 9, 2020 (www.baseball-reference.com/draft/?year_ID=2019&draft_round=2&draft_type=junreg&query_type=year_round&from_type_jc=0&from_type_hs=0&from_type_4y=0&from_type_unk=0).

64. 2016 MLB CBA, art. XXIII, at 106-112, 129-130. Ronald Blum, "Champion Red Sox Owe Nearly $12 Million in Luxury Tax," AP News Break, December 15, 2018 (https://apnews.com/c9825fa95840449cbc66bfc67ef0c2b9). Ronald Blum, "Dodgers Hit With $36.2 Million Tax, Yanks With $15.7 Million," AP News Break, December 19, 2017 (https://apnews.com/245ac5e3fe864a94aa432359b2a5ce7a/AP-NewsBreak:-Dodgers-hit-with-$36.2M-tax,-Yanks-with-$15.7M?utm_campaign=SocialFlow&utm_source=Twitter&utm_medium=AP_Sports). Sports Reference LLC, "2nd Round Of The 2019 MLB June Amateur Draft," Baseball-Reference.com-Baseball Statistics and History, February 9, 2020 (www.baseball-reference.com/draft/?year_ID=2019&draft_round=2&draft_type=junreg&query_type=year_round&from_type_jc=0&from_type_hs=0&from_type_4y=0&from_type_unk=0). "Boston Red Sox," Cot's Baseball Contracts, accessed February 12, 2020, (https://legacy.baseballprospectus.com/compensation/cots/al-east/boston-red-sox/).

The first $13 million of the proceeds for each contract year will be used to finance the ball club's obligations to fund the Major League Baseball Players Benefit Plan Agreements. Fifty percent of the remaining proceeds will be used to fund contributions to the ball players' individual retirement accounts. The final 50 percent will be given to the ball clubs who did not exceed the base tax threshold during that contract year. Accrued interest will be applied to everything except for the $13 million for the ball players' benefits.[65]

© Matthew Dicker/Shutterstock.com

Major League Baseball's Postseason Financial Structures

Gate receipts are a primary source of revenue during the postseason. There are specific ways how the postseason revenue from gate receipts is distributed among ball clubs and owners. It starts with the creation of a player's pool which covers the World Series, two League Championship Series, four Division Series, and two Wild Card games. The contributions to this pool fall into four distinct categories.[66]

The first category covers the World Series. It incorporates the first four games with 60% of the total gate receipts being added as contributions to the pool. The second category covers the two League Championship Series. It incorporates 60% of the total gate receipts from the first four games of each League Championship Series.[67]

The third category covers the Division Series. It incorporates 60% of the total gate receipts from the first three games of each Division Series. The final category covers the Wild Card games. It incorporates 50% of the total gate receipts from each Wild Card game after the traveling expenses have been deducted for each visiting ball club from the total gate receipts. However, the two visiting ball clubs are only allowed a $100,000 maximum.[68]

65. 2016 MLB CBA, art. XXIII, at 106-112, 129-130.
66. 2016 MLB CBA, art. X, at 39.
67. 2016 MLB CBA, art. X, at 39.
68. 2016 MLB CBA, art. X, at 39.

Once the players' pool has been created, there must be a clear definition of how the money will be distributed as a result of postseason performance. Here is a percentage breakdown[69] (see example and chart 10).

Postseason Finish	Percentage
One World Series Winner	36%
One World Series Loser	24%
Two League Championship Series Losers	24%
Four Division Series Losers	13%
Two Wild Card Losers	3%

Chart #10

2019 - Postseason Players' Pool Total: $80,861,145.74						
Ball Club	Postseason Appearance	Players' Pool	Value Of Full Share	Full Shares	Partial Shares	Cash Awards
Washington Nationals	World Series Champions	$29,110,012.47	$382,358.18	61	14.13	2
Houston Astros	American League Champions	$19,406,674.98	$256,030.16	57	13.580	10
New York Yankees	League Championship Series Runners-Up	$9,703,337.49	$114,367.19	71	13.366	12
St. Louis Cardinals	League Championship Series Runners-Up	$9,703,337.49	$144,024.85	53	13.366	7
Atlanta Braves	Division Series Runners-Up	$2,627,987.24	$33,623.71	63	12.72	36
Los Angeles Dodgers	Division Series Runners-Up	$2,627,987.24	$32,427.60	60	15.282	35
Minnesota Twins	Division Series Runners-Up	$2,627,987.24	$37,186.86	60	9.46	11
Tampa Bay Rays	Division Series Runners-Up	$2,627,987.24	$36,835.39	55	13.766	11
Milwaukee Brewers	Wild Card Game Runners-Up	$1,212,917.19	$14,292.30	62	22.325	1
Oakland Athletics	Wild Card Game Runners-Up	$1,212,917.19	$18,918.89	51	11.667	18

Source: "2019 Postseason Shares Announced," MLB.com, November 26, 2019 (www.mlb.com/press-release/2019-postseason-shares-announced-x8019)

---

69. 2016 MLB CBA, art. X, at 39.

Final Assessment of Major League Baseball's Growth Potential

Major League Baseball's growth potential is based on a variety of factors, but it begins with the implementation of an effective and safe recovery plan from the COVID-19 pandemic that devastated the world in 2020. Revenues were quickly approaching $11 billion even with two consecutive seasons (2018-2019) of attendance failing to eclipse 70 million. Major League Baseball will need to quickly restore confidence among its fans and business partners. At a time of uncertainty and concern, Major League Baseball will need to devise a strategy to ensure long-term profitability amid painful short-term losses.

An extension of the national television rights agreement with Fox Sports beginning in 2022 and running through 2028 at $5.1 billion provides a level of comfort even though media rights deals with ESPN and TBS expire at the conclusion of the 2021 season. An important question going forward is will networks like ESPN and TBS continue to pay between $3 billion and $6 billion over a decade for baseball? Revenue opportunities associated with postseason baseball has exponentially grown in recent years and it is likely that trend will continue going forward.

New opportunities to invest in major league ball clubs will develop due to revised bylaws for ownership, exploding franchise values, billion-dollar local television broadcast deals, and mixed-use development opportunities associated with ballparks. The conversations regarding expansion will pick up in intensity as several attractive cities have already made themselves available to Major League Baseball. It's quite possible to see the addition of two new franchises over the next decade as well as radical realignment in the American and National Leagues.

Major League Baseball Advanced Media (MLBAM) is an incubator for cutting-edge ideas and endless opportunities for innovation. The prominence of live streaming and cord-cutting will continue to challenge Major League Baseball to rethink national and local broadcast strategies. Any growth associated with live streaming will also involve a thorough examination of the current blackout policy.

Besides recovery from Covid-19, a legitimate threat to Major League Baseball's future growth is an acrimonious relationship with the Major League Baseball Players Association (MLBPA). Any negativity surrounding the negotiations of a new collective bargaining agreement could adversely affect growth potential for Major League Baseball.

Case Study

The Tampa Bay Rays (formerly the Tampa Bay Devil Rays) made their regular season debut at Tropicana Field on March 31, 1998 in front of 45,369 fans. Even though they had lost 99 ball games in their inaugural season, the Tampa Bay Rays had ranked 14th out of 30 ball clubs in Major League Baseball in terms of overall home attendance (2,506,293) and average home attendance per game (30,942). Attendance woes would plague the Tampa Bay Rays for the next two decades. The 1998 season would be the only time the Tampa Bay Rays would eclipse 2 million in home attendance through the conclusion of the 2019 season.

Tampa Bay Rays Home Attendance and Average Home Attendance Per Game Versus MLB Average Home Attendance Per Game (1998-2019)

Year	Home Attendance	Average Home Attendance Per Game	MLB Average Home Attendance Per Game
1998	2,506,293	30,942	29,030
1999	1,562,827	19,294	28,887
2000	1,449,673	18,121	29,377
2001	1,298,365	16,029	29,881
2002	1,065,742	13,157	28,006
2003	1,058,695	13,070	27,831
2004	1,274,911	15,936	30,075
2005	1,141,669	14,095	30,816
2006	1,368,950	16,901	31,306
2007	1,387,603	17,131	32,696
2008	1,811,986	22,370	32,382
2009	1,874,962	23,148	30,218
2010	1,864,999	23,025	30,066
2011	1,529,188	18,879	30,228
2012	1,559,681	19,255	30,806
2013	1,510,300	18,646	30,451
2014	1,446,464	17,858	30,345
2015	1,287,054	15,890	30,349
2016	1,286,163	15,879	30,131
2017	1,253,619	15,477	29,908
2018	1,154,973	14,259	28,659
2019	1,178,735	14,552	28,198

Sources: Sports Reference LLC, "Tampa Bay Rays Team History," Baseball-Reference.com-Baseball Statistics and History, March 27, 2020 (www.baseball-reference.com/teams/TBD/), Sports Reference LLC, "Major League Baseball Miscellaneous Year-By-Year Averages And Totals," Baseball-Reference.com-Baseball Statistics and History, March 27, 2020 (www.baseball-reference.com/leagues/MLB/misc.shtml)

Stuart Sternberg spent $65 million on a 48 percent share of the Tampa Bay Rays in May 2004 with the original owner, Vince Naimoli, holding onto a 15 percent stake in the ball club. By October 2005, Sternberg had spent more than an estimated $5 million bonus to take the title of managing partner away from Naimoli. Sternberg immediately began to transform the franchise by hiring Wall Street–trained prodigies such as Matt Silverman and Andrew Friedman to form his leadership team and run the day-to-day operations. In November 2005, the Tampa Bay Rays hired another innovator who was a perfect fit for the changing culture, manager Joe Maddon.

The Tampa Bay Rays had lost more than 100 ball games three times (2001, 2002, 2006) before achieving their first winning season (2008). The newly renamed Tampa Bay Rays had won 97 ball games, American League East title, and pennant in 2008. They lost the World Series in five games to the Philadelphia Phillies but were praised for being well-managed both in the dugout and ownership suite. In total, the Rays have won at least 90 ball games in a season seven times and qualified for the postseason five times since 2008.

Some have questioned the Rays' frugality and the Major League Baseball Players Association (MLBPA) has even filed grievances against them regarding their payroll spending practices as a revenue sharing recipient. According to figures compiled by the Associated Press, the Rays have never had a final 40-man payroll exceeding $82 million through the 2019 season. They have consistently found ways to win ball games through analytics and innovation. The Rays have embraced the concept of using relief pitchers to "open" ball games while mastering the art of defensive shifts.

Tropicana Field has become synonymous with empty seats, unorthodox ground rules involving catwalks, lights, and suspended objects. Between the 2012 and 2019 seasons, the Rays either finished last or next to last in overall home attendance in Major League Baseball. As major league ball clubs have capitalized on the stadium construction and development boom of the 1990s-2000s, the Rays have struggled to make any progress. The Rays do not have the luxuries regarding highly lucrative local revenue opportunities even with a new television deal.

Under Sternberg's leadership, the Rays have been actively pursuing multiple opportunities for a new ballpark beginning in 2007. They have constantly confronted challenges from local politicians regarding site selection, control, and financing. The Rays' existence in Florida depends on the construction of a modern ballpark. This will give them the opportunity to develop new revenue streams which are critical for their economic survival.

In June 2019, the Rays were granted permission by Major League Baseball to explore the possibility of playing a split season between St. Petersburg (Tampa Bay) and Montreal. It is an opportunity for the Rays to review their options since there was not any progress being made toward a new ballpark. The thought was to have a plan in place for the 2024 season at the earliest and play a split schedule beginning in St. Petersburg (Tampa Bay) and then heading toward Montreal during the summer months.

The Rays are locked into a User Agreement with the City of St. Petersburg and Tropicana Field until the conclusion of the 2027 season. The city controls where the Rays can play their home games. The memorandum of understanding (MOU) outlines where the Rays can begin evaluating potential areas to build a new ballpark and it only applies to Hillsborough and Pinellas counties in Florida.

By December 2019, Mayor Rick Kriseman of St. Petersburg sent a memorandum to the City Council that said the Rays and the city have decided to end conversations regarding the shared season concept. If the Rays want to continue the discussion regarding a shared season with Montreal, that must wait until 2028 which marks the conclusion of their agreement with the city of St. Petersburg. Mayor Kriseman said the Rays have rejected the renewal of the MOU based on the concept of looking for a permanent home in the Tampa Bay region.

The city was willing to discuss funding for a new ballpark in St. Petersburg that did not involve a part-time major league ball club. He also informed the Rays of the limited time left on the User Agreement and that they needed to decide soon about their future in Florida. Mayor Kriseman talked about the next steps in beginning to evaluate the land around Tropicana Field for redevelopment purposes. The Rays made it abundantly clear they would not cooperate with the city regarding the redevelopment of the land.

The Rays believe a two-city model can work in the St. Petersburg (Tampa Bay) area and Montreal. Major League Baseball is intrigued by the possibility provided both cities have the appropriate ballparks and revenue streams in place. Could this out-of-the-box idea possibly save Tampa Bay Rays baseball in Florida while also bringing the sport back to Montreal on a part-time basis? Are the decades of attendance woes in Montreal a legitimate concern for the Rays and Major League Baseball? How would the Rays and Major League Baseball handle the salaries of ball players and staff in two different countries?

Review Questions

1. What are the differences between revenue sharing and the competitive balance tax? How have they affected the business decisions of major league ball clubs in large markets?
2. Explain how Major League Baseball Advanced Media (MLBAM) has become a leading innovator in digital technology. How is Major League Baseball embracing the concept of live streaming and confronting inherent challenges regarding consumption preferences?
3. What are the key factors to consider when assessing the value of a major league franchise? How have the concepts of mixed-use development and innovations in ballpark cuisine affected franchise values?

Ten Websites of Interest for Students

1. Baseball-Reference.com (www.baseball-reference.com/)
2. Baseball Savant (https://baseballsavant.mlb.com/)
3. Brooks Baseball (http://www.brooksbaseball.net/)
4. Cot's Baseball Contracts (https://legacy.baseballprospectus.com/compensation/cots/)
5. Fangraphs (www.fangraphs.com/)
6. Forbes Sports Money (www.forbes.com/sportsmoney/)
7. Major League Baseball (www.mlb.com/)
8. Major League Baseball Players Association (www.mlbplayers.com/)
9. National Baseball Hall Of Fame And Museum (https://baseballhall.org/)
10. Society For American Baseball Research (https://sabr.org/)

References

Aramark Press Release. (2019). *New York mets and aramark team with CLEAR and Mashgin to deliver the first fully-automated concessions experience in sports.* September 23, 2019. Aramark Press Release. www.aramark.com/about-us/news/aramark-general/mets-clear-mashgin-automated-concessions

Associated Press. (2018). *Average MLB salary down for first time since 2004.* December 21, 2018. ESPN.com. www.espn.com/mlb/story/_/id/25588442/average-mlb-salary-1st-2004

Associated Press. (2019). *Average MLB salary drops for second straight year.* December 20, 2019. ESPN.com. www.espn.com/mlb/story/_/id/28341983/average-mlb-salary-drops-second-straight-year

Associated Press. (2012). *Average salary hits record $3.2 Million.* December 7, 2012. ESPN.com. www.espn.com/espn/print?id=8724285#

Associated Press. (2005). *Devil rays hire angels coach maddon as manager.* November 15, 2005. ESPN. com. www.espn.com/mlb/news/story?id=2224902

Associated Press. (2005). *Devil rays' ownership transfer approved.* November 17, 2005. ESPN.com. www.espn.com/mlb/news/story?id=2227305

Associated Press and ESPN.com News Services. (2012). *MLB completes New TV deals.* October 2,2012. ESPN.com. www.espn.com/mlb/story/_/id/8453054/major-league-baseball-completes-eight-year-deal-fox-turner-sports

Badenhausen, K., & Ozanian, M. (2019). *Baseball team values 2019: Yankees lead league at $4.6 billion.* April 10, 2019. Forbes.com. www.forbes.com/sites/mikeozanian/2019/04/10/baseball-team-values-2019-yankees-lead-league-at-46-billion/#54d8b86369b2

Blum, R. (2019). *AP news break: Red sox, yanks, cubs sent 2019 luxury tax bills.* December 18, 2019. AP News Break. https://apnews.com/1c06039c90703db8c5e9ccef59ab08d3

Blum, R. (2018). *Champion red sox owe nearly $12 million in luxury tax.* December 15, 2018. AP News Break. https://apnews.com/c9825fa95840449cbc66bfc67ef0c2b9

Blum, R. (2017). *Dodgers hit with $36.2 million tax, yanks with $15.7 million.* December 19, 2017. AP News Break. https://apnews.com/245ac5e3fe864a94aa432359b2a5ce7a/AP-NewsBreak:-Dodgers-hit-with-$36.2M-tax,-Yanks-with-$15.7M?utm_campaign=SocialFlow&utm_source=Twitter&utm_medium=AP_Sports

Cot's Baseball Contracts. (2020). *Boston Red Sox.* https://legacy.baseballprospectus.com/compensation/cots/al-east/boston-red-sox/

Brown, M. T., Rascher, D. A., Nagel, M. S., & McEvoy, C. D. (2010). *Financial management in the sport industry* (pp. 134–136). Holcomb Hathaway Publishers.

Brown, M. (2018). *Final MLB payrolls for all 30 teams show second-largest decline since 2004.* December 17, 2018. Forbes.com. www.forbes.com/sites/maurybrown/2018/12/17/final-mlb-payrolls-for-all-30-teams-show-second-largest-decline-since-2004/#1f0e085ce474

Brown, M. (2015). *MLB approves new digital media company spin-off that will create billions in new revenues.* August 13, 2015. Forbes.com. www.forbes.com/sites/maurybrown/2015/08/13/mlb-approves-new-digital-media-company-spin-off-that-will-create-billions-in-new-revenues/#6c1f286b315d

Brown, M. *MLB extends partnership with youtube TV; MLB network now available on platform.* March 8, 2018. Forbes.com. www.forbes.com/sites/maurybrown/2018/03/08/mlb-extends-partnership-with-youtube-tv-mlb-network-now-available-on-platform/#478330f3702a

Brown, M. (2019). *MLB sees record $10.7 billion in revenues for 2019.* December 21, 2019. Forbes. com. www.forbes.com/sites/maurybrown/2019/12/21/mlb-sees-record-107-billion-in-revenues-for-2019/#2bbc25075d78

Burns, M. J. (2019). *MLB, Facebook scale back streaming deal for 2019 season to 6 non-exclusive games.* March 29, 2019. Morning Consult. https://morningconsult.com/2019/03/29/mlb-facebook-scale-back-streaming-deal-for-2019-season-to-6-non-exclusive-games/

Calcaterra, C. (2019). *A warning about major league baseball's record revenues.* January 7, 2019. NBC Sports. https://mlb.nbcsports.com/2019/01/07/a-warning-about-major-league-baseballs-record-revenues/

Callis, J. (2019). *Here are the 2019 draft pools and bonus values.* June 3, 2019. MLB.com. https://www.mlb.com/news/2019-mlb-draft-pools-and-bonus-values

National Baseball Hall of Fame and Museum. (n.d.). *Alexander Cartwright.* https://baseballhall.org/hall-of-famers/cartwright-alexander

Carp, Sam "MLB Trims Facebook Streaming Deal To Six Games For 2019," Sports Pro, April 1, 2019 (www.sportspromedia.com/news/mlb-facebook-live-streaming-rights-six-games)

Cobb Chamber Of Commerce, "Fiscal Impact Of SunTrust Park And The Battery Atlanta On Cobb County Executive Summary," September 18, 2018 (www.cobbchamber.org/economic-development/suntrust_park_fiscal_impact.aspx)

"Competitive Balance Tax Definition," MLB.com, (http://m.mlb.com/glossary/transactions/competitive-balance-tax)

Diamond, Jared "How To Succeed In Baseball Without Spending Money," *The Wall Street Journal*, October 1, 2019 (www.wsj.com/articles/how-to-succeed-in-baseball-without-spending-money-11569931202)

The Walt Disney Company Press Release, "The Walt Disney Company To Acquire Majority Ownership Of BAMTech," The Walt Disney Company Press Release, August 8, 2017 (https://thewaltdisneycompany.com/walt-disney-company-acquire-majority-ownership-bamtech/)

Edwards, Craig "MLBAM And the Future Of MLB's Revenues," Fangraphs.com, August 6, 2015 (https://blogs.fangraphs.com/mlbam-and-the-future-of-mlbs-revenues/)

Feinsand, Mark "Manfred's Contract Extended Through 2024," MLB.com, November 15, 2018 (www.mlb.com/news/rob-manfred-contract-extended-c300765450)

Feinsand, Mark "Rays To Explore Idea Of TB-Montreal Split Season," MLB.com, June 20, 2019 (www.mlb.com/news/rays-tampa-bay-montreal-split-season)

"First Year Player Draft FAQ," MLB.com, (http://mlb.mlb.com/mlb/draftday/faq.jsp)

Fisher, Eric "BAMTech Produces Big Payoff," Sports Business Journal, August 14, 2017 (www.sportsbusinessdaily.com/Journal/Issues/2017/08/14/Leagues-and-Governing-Bodies/BAMTech.aspx)

Gaydos, Ryan "Nike's Uniform Deal With MLB Worth More Than $1B, Report Says," Fox Business, December 19, 2019 (www.foxbusiness.com/sports/nikes-uniform-deal-mlb-1-billion-report)

Gonzales, Mark "Joe Maddon And Bruce Bochy Believe Baseball Managers Should Be Valued And Compensated Like NFL And NBA Coaches," Chicago Tribune, August 22, 2019 (www.chicagotribune.com/sports/cubs/ct-cubs-joe-maddon-20190822-gev37egvsrhprhexww7k7bsstm-story.html)

Gough, Christina "MLB League And Teams Sponsorship Revenue 2010-2018," Statista, August 30, 2019 (www.statista.com/statistics/380197/mlb-sponsorship-revenue/)

Ham, Eldon L. " Broadcast 90 Years Ago Was First To Help Listeners 'See' Series," Sports Business Journal, October 17, 2011 (www.sportsbusinessdaily.com/Journal/Issues/2011/10/17/Opinion/Eldon-Ham.aspx)

IEG Sponsorship Report, " Sponsorship Spending On MLB Totals $892 Million In 2017 Season, IEG Sponsorship Report, October 23, 2017 (www.sponsorship.com/Report/2017/10/23/Sponsorship-Spending-On-MLB-Totals-$892-Million-in.aspx)

"International Amateur Free Agency and Bonus Pool Money Definition," MLB.com, (http://m.mlb.com/glossary/transactions/international-amateur-free-agency-bonus-pool-money)

Jackson, Barry "The Most Important Negotiation Of Jeter Ownership Hangs In Balance For Miami Marlins," Miami Herald, January 23, 2020 (www.miamiherald.com/sports/spt-columns-blogs/barry-jackson/article239526553.html)

Juliano, William "Looking Under The Hood Of MLB's Revenue Sharing Plan," The Captain's Blog, March 7, 2020 (http://www.captainsblog.info/2020/03/07/looking-under-the-hood-of-mlbs-revenue-sharing-plan-yankees-baseball-red-sox-mets-how-does-baseballs-revenue-sharing-work/25425/)

Keri, Jonah *The Extra 2%: How Wall Street Strategies Took A Major League Baseball Team From Worst To First* (New York: Ballatine Books, 2011), Pages 85-102.

Kriseman, Rick " Moving Forward: Mayor Rick Kriseman's Memorandum To The St. Petersburg City Council," Facebook.com, December 4, 2019 (www.facebook.com/notes/rick-kriseman/moving-forward-mayor-rick-krisemans-memorandum-to-the-st-petersburg-city-council/2922432891101092/)

Laurila, David "Sunday Notes: Coaching Salaries On The Farm, Bullpen Scatology, Cards STEP, More," Fangraphs.com, February 15, 2015 (https://blogs.fangraphs.com/sunday-notes-coaching-salaries-on-the-farm-bullpen-scatalogy-cards-step-more/)

MLB.com, "MLB, DAZN Agree To 3-Year Live Digital Rights Deal," MLB.com, November 15, 2018 (www.mlb.com/news/mlb-dazn-agree-to-3-year-digital-rights-deal-c300774598)

MLB.com, "MLB.TV Out of Market Packages," (www.mlb.com/live-stream-games/subscribe?k-bid=127996)

MLB.com, "2019 Postseason Shares Announced," MLB.com, November 26, 2019 (www.mlb.com/press-release/2019-postseason-shares-announced-x8019)

Major League Baseball, "MLB, YouTube TV Expand Partnership," MLB.com, March 8, 2018 (www.mlb.com/news/mlb-youtube-tv-expand-partnership-c268161958)

Major League Baseball Collective Bargaining Agreement," Pages 39, 106-112, 129-130 (2017-2021 Major League Baseball's Collective Bargaining Agreement

"Major League Baseball Collective Bargaining Agreement," art. XXIV, Pages 130-149, Attachment 22, Pages 226-235, Attachment 26 and art. XXIV (A), (12), (2017-2021 Major League Baseball's Collective Bargaining Agreement

"Major League Baseball Constitution," (https://assets.documentcloud.org/documents/6784510/MLB-Constitution.pdf)

Major League Baseball Press Release, "MLB, Nike And Fanatics Form 10-Year Partnership," MLB.com, January 25, 2019 (www.mlb.com/news/mlb-nike-fanatics-form-10-year-partnership-c303162762)

Major League Baseball Press Release, "MLB And ESPN Reach Eight-Year Broadcasting Agreement," MLB.com, August 28, 2012 (www.mlb.com/news/mlb-and-espn-reach-new-eight-year-broadcasting-agreement/c-37475930)

Major League Baseball Press Release, "SiriusXM And Major League Baseball Extend Agreement; Every Game Now Available On Sirius and XM Satellite Radios," MLB.com, August 19, 2013 (www.mlb.com/news/siriusxm--mlb-extend-agreement/c-57494660)

"MLB Minimum Salary Rises $8,500 To $563,500 Next Season," ESPN.com, November 13, 2019, (www.espn.com/mlb/story/_/id/28074687/mlb-minimum-salary-rises-8500-563500-next-season)

"MLBPA FAQ – Who Is Eligible For Membership In The Association?" Major League Baseball Players Association (www.mlbplayers.com/faq)

"Rob Manfred-Commissioner of Major League Baseball Bio," MLB.com, (www.mlb.com/official-information/executives/rob-manfred)

McCann, David "Baseball CFO Looks To Win With CPM Software," CFO, April 20, 2017 (www.cfo.com/forecasting/2017/04/baseball-cfo-looks-to-win-with-cpm-software-scenario-planning/)

"Memorandum Of Understanding," City of St. Petersburg, January 25, 2016, (https://assets.documentcloud.org/documents/4329865/Memorandum-of-Understanding.pdf)

Mentel, Thomas "Can Sirius XM's New MLB Deal Boost Revenue?" CheatSheet.com, August 26, 2013 (www.cheatsheet.com/technology/can-sirius-xms-new-mlb-deal-boost-revenue.html/)

Monagan, Matt "75 Years Ago Today, The First Major League Baseball Game Was Televised," MLB.com-Cut 4, August 26, 2014 (www.mlb.com/cut4/75-years-ago-the-first-baseball-game-was-televised/c-91371436)

Nightengale, Bob "USA TODAY Survey: MLB Power Shift Has Managers' Salaries In Free Fall," USA Today, August 27, 2018 (www.usatoday.com/story/sports/mlb/columnist/bob-nightengale/2018/08/27/baseball-managers-salaries-joe-maddon-dave-roberts-aj-hinch/1102815002/)

Nike News, "Nike Enters 10-Year Partnership With Major League Baseball," Nike Press Release, January 25, 2019 (https://news.nike.com/news/nike-major-league-baseball)

Nucciarone, Monica "Alexander Cartwright," Society For American Baseball Research, (https://sabr.org/bioproj/person/09ed3dd4)

Oakland Athletics Press Release, "A's Cast On TuneIn Is Now The Exclusive Home Of All Oakland A's Audio Content," Oakland Athletic Press Release, February 18, 2020 (www.mlb.com/press-release/press-release-a-s-cast-on-tunein-is-now-the-exclusive-home-of-all-oakland-a-s-au)

Orlando, Dan "Sirius XM Reloads On Peanuts And Cracker Jack, Might Never Go Back," New York Business Journal, August 19, 2013 (www.bizjournals.com/newyork/news/2013/08/19/mlb-and-sirius-xm-ink-extension-that.html)

Ourand, John and Fisher, Eric "MLB Signs Seven-Year Extension With Fox Worth $5.1 B," Sports Business Daily, November 15, 2018 (www.sportsbusinessdaily.com/Daily/Issues/2018/11/15/Media/MLB-Fox.aspx?hl=Eric+Fisher&sc=0)

Ozanian, Mike "John Sherman Buys Kansas City Royals For $1 Billion," Forbes.com, November 22, 2019 (www.forbes.com/sites/mikeozanian/2019/11/22/john-sherman-buys-kansas-city-royals-for-1-billion/#7e71624a3851)

Ozanian, Mike "Steve Cohen To Buy Mets For $2.42 Billion, Within 1% Of Forbes Valuation Of Team," Forbes.com, September 14, 2020 (www.forbes.com/sites/mikeozanian/2020/09/14/steve-cohen-to-buy-mets-for-242-billion-within-one-percent-of-forbes-valuation-of-team/?sh=-79decf501d21)

Popper, Ben "The Changeup: How Baseball's Tech Team Built The Future Of Television," The Verge, August 4, 2015 (www.theverge.com/2015/8/4/9090897/mlb-bam-live-streaming-internet-tv-nhl-hbo-now-espn)

Ramachandran, Shalini "MLB's Streaming-Tech Unit Goes Pro," *The Wall Street Journal*, February 23, 2015 (www.wsj.com/articles/mlbs-streaming-tech-unit-goes-pro-1424718022)

Ring, Sheryl "The Legal Ramifications Of The Two-City Rays," Fangraphs.com, June 24, 2019 (https://blogs.fangraphs.com/the-legal-ramifications-of-the-two-city-rays/)

Roberts, Daniel "As NFL Falters, MLB Sponsors Spent Record-High $892 Million," Yahoo Finance, November 8, 2017 (https://finance.yahoo.com/news/nfl-falters-mlb-sponsors-spent-record-high-892-million-132837545.html)

Rubin, Shayna "Oakland Athletics Off The Radio Waves In The Bya Area, Commit To A's Cast Stream," The Mercury News, February 18, 2020 (www.mercurynews.com/2020/02/18/oakland-athletics-off-the-radio-waves-in-the-bay-area-commit-to-as-cast-stream/)

"Rule 4 Draft Definition," MLB.com, (http://m.mlb.com/glossary/transactions/rule-4-draft)

"Salary Arbitration Definition," MLB.com, (http://m.mlb.com/glossary/transactions/salary-arbitration)

Sanchez, Jesse "Here's Where Top International Prospects Are Signing," MLB.com, July 3, 2019 (www.mlb.com/news/international-prospect-signings-july-2-2019)

Sandomir, Richard "ESPN Extends M.L.B. Deal, Doubling What It Pays Yearly," The New York Times, August 29, 2012 (www.nytimes.com/2012/08/29/sports/baseball/espn-extends-deal-with-mlb-through-2021.html)

"Service Time Definition," MLB.com, (http://m.mlb.com/glossary/transactions/service-time)

Sirius XM Holdings, Inc. Press Release, "SIRIUS and XM Complete Merger," Sirius XM Holdings, Inc., July 29, 2008 (http://investor.siriusxm.com/investor-overview/press-releases/press-release-details/2008/SIRIUS-and-XM-Complete-Merger/default.aspx)

Smith, Daniel P. "How Sports Stadiums Are Upping Their Foodservice Game," QSR Magazine, May 2018 (www.qsrmagazine.com/menu-innovations/how-sports-stadiums-are-upping-their-foodservice-game)

Solomon, Josh "Hardball: Rays Threaten To Block Redevelopment Of Tropicana Field," Tampa Bay Times, January 29, 2020 (www.tampabay.com/news/st-petersburg/2020/01/30/hardball-rays-threaten-to-block-redevelopment-of-tropicana-field/)

Sports Reference LLC, "Major League Baseball," Baseball-Reference.com-Baseball Statistics and History, March 5, 2020 (www.baseball-reference.com/bullpen/Major_League_Baseball)

Sports Reference LLC, "Major League Baseball Miscellaneous Year-By-Year Averages And Totals," Baseball-Reference.com-Baseball Statistics and History, March 15, 2020 (www.baseball-reference.com/leagues/MLB/misc.shtml)

Sports Reference LLC, "Second Round Of The 2019 MLB June Amateur Draft," Baseball-Reference.com-Baseball Statistics and History, February 9, 2020 (www.baseball-reference.com/draft/?year_ID=2019&draft_round=2&draft_type=junreg&query_type=year_round&from_type_jc=0&from_type_hs=0&from_type_4y=0&from_type_unk=0)

Sports Reference LLC, "Tampa Bay Rays Team History," Baseball-Reference.com-Baseball Statistics and History, March 27, 2020 (www.baseball-reference.com/teams/TBD/)

SunTrust, "The Evolution Of Stadium Financing And Development," (www.suntrust.com/resource-center/wealth-management/article/the-evolution-of-stadium-financing-and-development#.XnfcuYhKjIV)

Swistak, Greg "The Whys And Hows Of Restaurant/Stadium Partnerships," QSRweb, May 21, 2014 (www.qsrweb.com/blogs/the-whys-and-hows-of-restaurantstadium-partnerships/)

"Tampa Bay Rays," Cot's Baseball Contracts, accessed March 29, 2020, https://legacy.baseballprospectus.com/compensation/cots/al-east/tampa-bay-rays/

"Tampa Bay Rays Franchise Timeline," MLB.com (www.mlb.com/rays/history/timeline)

Thorn, John "October 1845: The First Recorded Baseball Games In New York," Society For American Baseball Research (https://sabr.org/gamesproj/game/october-1845-first-recorded-baseball-games-new-york)

Topkin, Marc "Rob Manfred: Rays' Montreal Plan Legitimate, Gaining Momentum," Tampa Bay Times, February 16, 2020, (www.tampabay.com/sports/rays/2020/02/16/manfred-rays-montreal-plan-legitimate-gaining-momentum/)

Treese, Joel D. "President Herbert Hoover And Baseball," The White House Historical Association (www.whitehousehistory.org/president-herbert-hoover-and-baseball)

Wagner, James "M.L.B. Extends TV Deal With Fox Sports Through 2028," The New York Times, November 15, 2018 (www.nytimes.com/2018/11/15/sports/mlb-fox-tv-deal.html)

Zimbalist, Andrew "The Nonprofit Status Of Sports Leagues Is Irrelevant," The New York Times, September 4, 2014 (www.nytimes.com/roomfordebate/2014/09/03/should-pro-sport-leagues-get-tax-breaks/the-nonprofit-status-of-sports-leagues-is-irrelevant)

"2019 Instructions for Form 990 Return of Organization Exempt From Income Tax," IRS.gov (www.irs.gov/pub/irs-pdf/i990.pdf)

CHAPTER 9
Business of Professional Soccer

Scott Hirko

LEARNING OBJECTIVES

- To assess the governance structures of different soccer organizations including FIFA, one of the largest in the world.
- To identify the economic investment areas that are critical for the development of soccer as espoused by FIFA.
- To identify the issues facing the economic parity in salaries and training between male and female soccer players.
- To gain insight on how leagues like the English Professional League (EPL) maintain competitive equity.
- To compare the financials of Major League Soccer and the now-defunct North American Soccer League—and identify what MLS learnt from the NASL.

International football (soccer) is considered the most popular sport in the world and has different leagues in each of many different countries, cultures, and languages. This chapter aims to investigate the complex financial nature of global football, by first looking at the development of the sport under the Fédération Internationale de Football Association (FIFA) with a brief historical introduction. The current structure of FIFA is explained, as well as the major sources of revenue and expenses. The growth of women's football is also explored, including lawsuits filed by the U.S. National Women"s Soccer Team against the U.S. Soccer Federation.

This chapter will then explore several different professional leagues and teams across the world, and how they work together to create and support the global organization. Countries, and cultures, have different concepts of competitive equity interwoven into understanding the competition of football in different leagues and countries. This is explored by learning about the ownership and

© katatonia82/Shutterstock.com

leadership of different professional teams in different leagues. This chapter will also look at the professional Major League Soccer in the United States as a case study about a unique financial model that has succeeded in helping one of the world''s younger professional football leagues.

FIFA: History and Structure

Recognizing the popularity in the late 19th century, football was added as a demonstration sport in the 1900 international Olympics, with Great Britain winning the event (Churchill et al., 1979). Soon after, the Fédération Internationale de Football Association (FIFA) was formed in order to provide a venue for a country to win an international football competition outside the Olympic structure. Eventually, FIFA under President Jules Rimet, created an environment with Uruguay hosting the first every FIFA World Cup in 1930.

The stated mission of FIFA is to "Develop the Game, Touch the World, Build a Better Future." (FIFA, 2020a). Moreover, the vision, stated by the present president of FIFA, Gianni Infantino, is, "for the organisation to help develop football in all regions of the world so that many more can compete at the very highest level." In this chapter, we explore how the financial decisions made by FIFA helped to reach its goals through its mission and vision, while examining why some impediments affected decision-making.

As of 2020, FIFA reported its membership comprised 211 affiliated associations—there are no individual people as members; rather, FIFA is an organization with different country "associations," also known as national soccer programs. To be a member, a country association must belong to a continental collaborative group that helps to organize national contests of countries against each other within their region.

The continental collaborative groups include The Asian Football Confederation in Asia (AFC), Confederation of African Football (CAF) the Football Confederation in North and Central America and the Caribbean (CONCACAF), the South American Football Confederation (CONMEBOL), the European Football Association (UEFA), and the OFC in Oceania (FIFA, 2020a). Each group has its own national team, but each group also sponsors professional leagues. Among these collaborative groups, each country's football association pays no more than $1,000 in dues each year to be a member of FIFA (FIFA, 2019b).

As a member, each country's national football association has the ability to impact the leadership, rules, and direction of FIFA. For instance, FIFA periodically votes on which country will host the World Cup, and how that competition's revenue earned from ticket sales, television rights, and marketing would be shared among the members, to pay administrative expenses.

FIFA's organizational structure has several committees, including a competition committee (to oversee international competition among member association teams, including the World Cup), a medical committee (to oversee the health of athletes in competition), a referees committee (to oversee the enforcement of rules during competition), and a finance committee (to "monitor the financial management and advise the FIFA Council on financial matters and asset management") (FIFA, 2020a), which is a focus of this chapter.

Finances of FIFA

FIFA Revenues

FIFA's primary source of revenues is from its administration and direction of the men's World Cup championship, held every 4 years. From 2015 to 2018, the men's World Cup in Russia generated $5.4 billion in revenue. This is arguably the most prestigious sport championship in the world, watched and celebrated by billions of people each tournament.

In addition, FIFA hosts other annual tournaments for both men and women, including a Club World Cup, Youth World Cup, and Interactive World Cup; FIFA spent $2.6 billion during that same period for a total of 32 tournaments including the men's and women's World Cup (FIFA, 2019a).

FIFA accepts applications from countries who are willing to host this championship, similar to the process of applicants to host the Olympic Games. Nations who apply to host the World Cup should accept the cost for improving facilities (stadiums, locker rooms, media/press needs and telecommunications, etc.), infrastructure (roads, utilities, emergency services such as health, police, and fire), or other costs (taxes, urban redevelopment, etc.). To fund many of the needs for the men's or women's World Cup, nations encumber debt, at a potential opportunity cost of other needs of local or national interest (such as education, transportation, and police).

FIFA's income statements from 2017 and 2018 demonstrate the significant impact of the men's World Cup on its finances, and how the money earned is distributed to its members (see Table 1).

TABLE 1: Summary of key areas from FIFA income statements, 2017–2018, in USD (thousands).

	2018	2017
Total Revenues	$4,640,854	$734,202
Television/Media	$2,543,968	$228,645
Ticket Sales	$689,143	$22,368
Marketing	$1,143,312	$245,277
Licensing	$184,573	$160,211
Total Expenses	–$2,584,265	–$721,445
Competition and Events	–$1,974,317	–$219,373
Development and Education	–$578,469	–$477,507
Football Governance and Administration	–$306,889	–$201,703
NET PROFIT	**$1,831,997**	**–$191,522**

Adapted from FIFA Financial Report, *Consolidated Statement of Comprehensive Income*, 2019, p. 72. https://resources.fifa.com

Similar to the American professional leagues, National Football League, National Basketball League, and the National Collegiate Athletic Association, FIFA's main source of revenue is not ticket sales, nor licensing, but selling television and media broadcast rights during years when the men's World Cup is held. In 2018, FIFA earned $2.54 billion from television and media, more than 10 times the amount of the $229 million earned from media in 2017 without the tournament. Broadcasts of other tournaments funded by FIFA, including the Women's World Cup and youth tournaments (Under-17 and Under-20), made up the bulk of media revenues in years without the men's World Cup (FIFA, 2019a).

More than 2.7 million tickets were sold for games to the 2018 men's World Cup, generating more than $689 million in revenue for FIFA. In the nonmen's World Cup year such as 2017, $22 million was earned in ticket sales. Marketing rights, primarily for sponsorships, also are exponentially higher for the men's World Cup, generating more than $1.1 billion 2018, compared to $245 million in 2017 (FIFA, 2019a).

FIFA Expenses

FIFA has a variety of expenses, including administration, competitions, prize money for competitors, revenue sharing to membership countries and confederations, and youth development and educational programs. The greatest cost to FIFA in 2018 was for $1.97 billion to cover competitions and events, primarily the cost of the 2018 men's World Cup, including $400 million in prize money for competitors (FIFA, 2019a).

FIFA also spends a significant amount on development and education—a total of $578 million in 2018. Development and education includes $364 million for the "Football Forward Programme," used to share revenue with each of the member associations and confederations, $101 million for "Football for Schools" educational programs, and a variety of other development efforts such as women's football promotion, medicine and science, and refereeing assistance (FIFA, 2019a).

The cost of competition is significant compared to the non–World Cup year of 2017 of $219 million. Its administrative expenses totaling $191 million in 2018 included salaries for senior officials including FIFA's president, secretary general, and a congress to vote on rules and selection of a World Cup site each 4 years (FIFA, 2019a). Administration also included a three-step process for rules compliance (accountability to stakeholders, managing risk, and auditing; FIFA, 2020b), created after several international scandals involving corruption and misconduct of millions of dollars by senior officials leading to an indictment by the U.S. Department of Justice in 2015 (McFarland, 2015; Ruiz & Mather, 2015).

FIFA's Community impact

There is significant literature on the economic impact of international sporting events, including the men's and women's World Cups, to local host economies, much of it with mixed opinions on benefits relative to costs (Anderson, 2020; Barrios et al., 2016; Lee & Taylor, 2005; Maennig, 2017; Maennig & Zimbalist, 2012). For instance, it was estimated $13.5 billion dollars was invested by the Brazilian government to host the men's 2016 World Cup, including athletic facility and airport improvements, and other infrastructure and organizing expenses (Herman, 2014; Manfred, 2015; Watts, 2013). Furthermore, while many of the men's World Cup improvements in Brazil are used long term, many economists, officials, and citizens noted the investment was an opportunity cost, meaning the dollars spent were not instead invested in bus and rail projects, hospitals, and education (Anderson, 2020; Herman, 2014; Rapoza, 2014). Conversely, the women's World Cup in Vancouver, Canada was shown to have positive financial impact to the Canadian Soccer Association, which hosted the event on behalf of FIFA. The event generated $82 million in revenue versus $72 million in costs for the CSA (Mackin, 2016).

© Romain Biard/Shutterstock.com

FIFA Women's World Cup

Notably, the women's World Cup is an important source of income for FIFA, but only at a fraction of the revenue generated by the men's: The 2015 Women's World Cup in Canada generated $73 million (Bajana, 2019), while the 2018 men's World Cup in Russia generated $5.4 billion (FIFA, 2019a).

For instance, the 2015 Women's World Cup in Canada cost FIFA $82 million; however, this amount is not much less than the $1.82 billion in expenses for the 2018 World Cup in Russia (FIFA, 2019a). This disparity has led to controversy over whether or not women playing the same game, football, are earning nearly 30 times less the prize money as men. As such, a gender discrimination lawsuit has been filed in the U.S. District Court by the USNWT against the U.S. Soccer Federation (*Alex Morgan et al. v. US Soccer Federation, 2:19-CV-01717*) (Cater, 2020; Cohen et al., 2020).

Yet, in the United States, the women's national soccer team (USWNT)—winner of three World Cups, has been far more successful than the men's soccer team. Moreover, USWNT generated as much or more media interest in America than the men's team in its history. Yet the women athletes were not compensated in the same way as the male athletes. In 2019, after winning the World Cup, the U.S. women's national soccer team sued the U.S. National Soccer Federation, which is a member of FIFA, stating that its members were not compensated fairly, even though they generated more in revenue ($50.8 million) compared to the men ($49.9 million; Hess, 2019).

FIGURE 1: Gender Disparity in World Cup Prize Money, 2018–2019

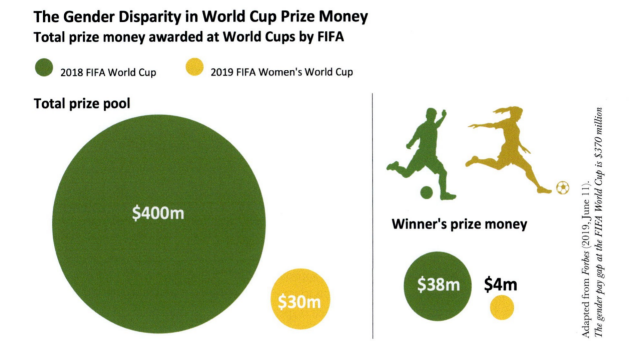

The Gender Disparity in World Cup Prize Money
Total prize money awarded at World Cups by FIFA

● 2018 FIFA World Cup   ● 2019 FIFA Women's World Cup

Total prize pool

$400m

$30m

Winner's prize money

$38m $4m

Adapted from Forbes (2019, June 11).
The gender pay gap at the FIFA World Cup is $370 million

Participants

The participants of the men's and women's World Cup generally compete in their own professional leagues when not representing their country. For instance, superstar Cristiano Ronaldo plays for Real Madrid in the Spanish League, La Liga, but as a citizen of Portugal, he represents Portugal in the World Cup. The schedule of the professional leagues often overlap with the World Cup; however, most professional leagues postpone their play to allow their athletes to represent their own country in the World Cup (the United States' Major League Soccer being an exception).

For competing in the World Cup, participants receive a stipend from their country's national soccer federation, as well as prize money from FIFA for competing in the World Cup. In the 2018 men's World Cup, $400 million was distributed to male participants; and in the 2019 Women's World Cup, $38 million was distributed to female participants (see Figure 1).

Independent Professional Football Leagues

Many countries have their own independent professional football leagues, which is worth exploring to better understand their unique financial models. Examples of professional football leagues around the world include La Liga (Spain), Bundesliga (Germany), English Premiere League, Italy Lega Serie, Campeonato Brasileiro Série A (Brazil), and Major League Soccer in the United States. Most of the teams are privately owned and some are publicly owned (by the community fan-base or stock shareholders). In addition, there are different levels of competitive equity based on the league. Team ownership will be explored in this chapter by reviewing community-owned Real Madrid (La Liga), Manchester United (English Premiere League) owned by shareholders on the public New York Stock Exchange, and the privately owned Seattle Sounders (Major League Soccer). In addition, financial decisions in leagues impacting competitive equity will be explored with the English Premiere League and Major League Soccer.

Public Ownership

La Liga's Real Madrid, among the wealthiest sport organizations in the world with an estimated value of $4.24 billion in 2019 (Khan, 2019), is unique in that it is owned by 91,000 community members in clubs (called "socios") as a nonprofit organization (Srivastava, 2015). In other words, while the players and administration earn money for working for Real Madrid, the team is organized not to make a profit. Each community member pays approximately $150 per year in dues for privileges to be a member, including season tickets, the right to vote for the president and board of directors, and approving the budget (which impacts how much is spent to acquire players; Srivastava, 2015).

This fan-owned football club model is required of every team in Germany's Bundesliga football league, which requires each football club to have a minimum of 51% fan ownership. The purpose of Germany's requirements mirrors that of Real Madrid: to encourage fan direction and interaction over private owners who may make decisions for profit over success (Bundesliga, 2020).

The English Premier League's Manchester United, also among the wealthiest sports organizations at a $3.81 billion value (Khan, 2019), has a history of it being publicly owned through selling stock in the team. In 1991, the affectionately titled "ManU" raised £6.7 million in shares on the London Stock Exchange before American investor Malcolm Glazer bought enough shares to privately own the team and remove it from the exchange (ADVFN, 2020). This changed in 2012, when Glazer decided to sell stock in 10% of the value of the team to have it publicly owned by shareholders on the New York Stock Exchange.

While the Glazer family controls the majority of shares, and thus control the decisions, all others who own stock still have the right to vote on its board of directors and financial decisions at annual meetings similar to that of other publicly traded companies (such as Apple, Nike, or General

Motors). As of December 2020, more than 38.9 million shares in ManU were listed on the NYSE, with a stock market valuation at $2.64 billion (Yahoo Finance, 2020).

League Competitive Equity

Since 2011, the English Premier League (EPL) has seen a growing level of competitiveness among its teams for a variety of reasons, primarily due to massive increases in finances. In the 18 years from 1994, when the EPL top-tier status in England football began, until 2011, four football clubs won the title. In the 9 years from 2012 to 2020, five clubs had won the title. There are several reasons, one of which is the process of "relegation" whereby the three lowest of the 20 clubs in the EPL each year are demoted to a lesser league (the Champions League), to be replaced by the three best teams who are promoted from the Champions League to the EPL. This allows the newly promoted clubs to have access to the revenue streams at the highest level, and improve their talent. And the increase in the value of media contracts demonstrates how the EPL sends payments to the 20 member clubs in an equal share (£34.3 million), for international television (£43.2 million), and commercial revenue (£5.0 million)—giving more revenue to more teams to spend on better talent (English Premier League, 2019; Planet Football, 2020) (Table 2).

Another reason for competitive equity is the overall value of EPL clubs. Because the EPL is by far the wealthiest football league in the world, valued at £5.7 billion, £2 billion more than each of the other leagues in Europe, due primarily to lucrative international media contracts (BeSoccer, 2020). The vast sums of wealth allow the league to encourage a greater depth of talent from around the world to play in the EPL and for international players to earn big paychecks (Goff, 2015). In the EPL, there is no maximum amount ("salary cap") on how much a team can spend on its talent.

Conversely, Major League Soccer (MLS) in the United States is a younger professional league (formed in 1996) compared to the English professional football leagues (formed in 1885), dependent on a process to make teams equal in competitiveness for more exciting games, selling more tickets and earning increasing the value of media contracts. To accomplish competitive equity, MLS has a "reverse order" draft to improve the performance of teams, similar to most other North American professional sport leagues, such as the NFL and NBA. This means those teams who have worse performances 1 year have earlier choices to recruit better talent the next year, and vice versa, those who are most successful are given a lower opportunity to recruit better talent.

North American leagues create rules to make lesser-talented teams more competitive, and subsequently, have better (and more exciting) contests the following season. In addition, MLS has a "salary cap," and as of 2019, no more than $4.2 million could be spent by each team on its roster of 20 players with a maximum salary of $530,000 (Goal, 2019)—as such, the better talent commanding greater salaries is spread among all the MLS teams. More on the MLS and salaries is noted in the following case study.

TABLE 2: Media Payments in the English Premier League, 2018–2019 (in pounds)

	Equal Share	Facility Fees	Merit Payment	International TV	Central Commercial	Total Payment
Manchester City	£34,361,519	£30,104,476	£38,370,360	£43,184,608	£4,965,392	£150,986,355
Liverpool	£34,361,519	£33,461,785	£36,451,842	£43,184,608	£4,965,392	£152,425,146
Chelsea	£34,361,519	£28,985,373	£34,533,324	£43,184,608	£4,965,392	£146,030,216
Tottenham Hotspur	£34,361,519	£30,104,476	£32,614,806	£43,184,608	£4,965,392	£145,230,801
Arsenal	£34,361,519	£28,985,373	£30,696,288	£43,184,608	£4,965,392	£142,193,180
Manchester United	£34,361,519	£31,223,579	£28,777,770	£43,184,608	£4,965,392	£142,512,868
Wolverhampton	£34,361,519	£17,794,343	£26,859,252	£43,184,608	£4,965,392	£127,165,114
Everton	£34,361,519	£21,151,652	£24,940,734	£43,184,608	£4,965,392	£128,603,905
Leicester City	£34,361,519	£17,794,343	£23,022,216	£43,184,608	£4,965,392	£123,328,078
West Ham United	£34,361,519	£18,913,446	£21,103,698	£43,184,608	£4,965,392	£122,528,663
Watford	£34,361,519	£12,198,828	£19,185,180	£43,184,608	£4,965,392	£113,895,527
Crystal Palace	£34,361,519	£14,437,034	£17,266,662	£43,184,608	£4,965,392	£114,215,215
Newcastle United	£34,361,519	£22,270,755	£15,348,144	£43,184,608	£4,965,392	£120,130,418
A.F.C. Bournemouth	£34,361,519	£12,198,828	£13,429,626	£43,184,608	£4,965,392	£108,139,973
Burnley	£34,361,519	£13,317,931	£11,511,108	£43,184,608	£4,965,392	£107,340,558
Southampton	£34,361,519	£12,198,828	£9,592,590	£43,184,608	£4,965,392	£104,302,937
B&H Albion	£34,361,519	£15,556,137	£7,674,072	£43,184,608	£4,965,392	£105,741,728
Cardiff City	£34,361,519	£14,437,034	£5,755,554	£43,184,608	£4,965,392	£102,704,107
Fulham F.C.	£34,361,519	£15,556,137	£3,837,036	£43,184,608	£4,965,392	£101,904,692
Huddersfield Town	£34,361,519	£12,198,828	£1,918,518	£43,184,608	£4,965,392	£96,628,865
Totals	£687,230,380	£402,889,186	£402,888,780	£863,692,160	£99,307,840	£2,456,008,346

Adapted from English Premier League (2019).

Case Study—Major League Soccer

The author thanks Grant Wahl, *Sports Illustrated*, and Matt Pentz, author of *The Sound and the Glory: How the Seattle Sounders Showed Major League Soccer How to Win* (Pentz, 2019).

Grant Wahl, *Sports Illustrated* lead journalist on soccer in the United States, provided a useful way to investigate the finances of Major League Soccer (MLS): "Major League Soccer is unique compared to most other professional sports leagues, particularly in North America: the owners were all in business together when it started, as opposed to a traditional sport league with teams as individual businesses competing against each other." Considering MLS as a business with each sport as a subunit of the league, as opposed to each club as an individual business belonging to a league, is a useful investigation of the rationale to MLS's business model to help it grow. To help understand the MLS's business model, its finances and the different organizations intertwined with MLS will be explored in this chapter.

A theme of this chapter is the impact on finances from the unique needs of soccer as a sport to compete in an already well-grown North American sport environment with the century-plus–old professional sport legacies Major League Baseball (MLB), National Basketball Association (NBA), National Football League (NFL), and National Hockey League (NHL). The exploration of MLS will include an understanding of decisions with respect to the finances of both the revenues (where the money comes from) and the costs (where the money goes) of the league as a single entity. Revenue discussion will include private support, ticket sales, media revenue, and a unique collaboration with the U.S. Soccer Federation. And the expense discussion will include stadium improvements, competitive equity, and sharing of revenue with players through its salary structure.

Notably, because MLS is a private company, it is not required under federal and state laws to share financial information, including revenues and expenses for each club. However, the players' union of MLS does make salary information available in their attempt to gain public support to increase salaries; providing transparency about the decisions made by MLS on salaries helps to better understand the profit motives of MLS. Therefore, much of the information provided in this case study on MLS finances is provided by the MLS Players Association and investigative research by journalists and scholars.

A (brief) financial history of professional soccer in the United States

Unlike many other countries in the world, professionalized soccer (or football, as known in most of the rest of the world), has had its challenges in sustaining as a viable financial model. In other words, owners of soccer teams in which they pay players a salary to play the game, has failed in America on multiple occasions. Early professional soccer in the United States included the Amer-

© Dorti/Shutterstock.com

ican League of Professional Football (in 1894) and the American Soccer League (from 1921 to 1933), but wider economic concerns impacting the sports' financial viability (Litterer, 2015; Phillips, 2010).

Prior to the current MLS, the last professional soccer league in the United States was the North American Soccer League (NASL), from 1968 to 1985. The NASL ceased operations as a result of significant financial issues including salary disputes, lack of major media contracts, and no plan for competitive equity (G. Wahl, personal interview, December 24, 2020; Reed, 1980). At the end of its existence, NASL clubs competed against each other to the extent that most clubs could not afford competing against the few wealthiest clubs with major corporate investors. Without adequate revenue for enough clubs to compete, the NASL folded.

The financial history of the NASL is important to understand the current financial model of the MLS, because current investors in American professional soccer were determined not to repeat recent history of failures. Thus, all MLS clubs are owned by league, with individual owners as "partners" within the MLS system. The creation of the MLS's structure reflects the financial concerns in the competitive American professional sports model. MLS was created in 1995 to support the growth of the sport of soccer in North America, with its hope of eventually creating a league that was financially sustainable and profitable (for once, hoping its revenues would exceed its expenses) (M. Pentz, personal interview, December 23, 2020; G. Wahl, personal interview, December 24, 2020).

As MLS struggled to make a profit in America, the focus of the league was to grow soccer as a sport, including at the amateur level, and including to grow interest in women's soccer. Those involved in soccer as a profession in America have worked to build a business model to profit from the wider greater soccer interest than just the MLS. To meet the desire to profit, in 2004 MLS helped to create a for-profit enterprise, Sports United Marketing (SUM). SUM used a commercialized marketing effort to promote soccer in America, including the MLS, the U.S. Soccer Federation, the men's (USMNT) and women's (USWNT) national team, and youth soccer.

Revenues

Like most professional sport leagues, MLS and its clubs earned money through a variety of sources, raised both by clubs and by the league. Each MLS club earned some of its revenue through ticket sales, sponsorships, sales of merchandise, parking fees, or other local means. However, because the MLS owned every club, most of the revenue earned by each club is shared with the league to be evenly distributed to the other clubs (Ilyas, 2017). Next, we investigate three significant MLS revenues: Sports United Marketing, Franchise Entry Fees, and Player Transfers.

1. Sports United Marketing

In addition to local club revenue, the MLS league also earned revenue through its partnership with Sports United Marketing (SUM) to raise money from media contracts, international contests, national sponsorship and advertising deals, and most merchandise sales. One of the significant revenue streams provided for by SUM was for major media (television) contracts. The importance of the money from MLS selling its rights to broadcast its contests on media networks was notable by pointing at the MLS's stated need improve on its $90 million per year, eight-year deal with ESPN, FOX, and Univision—a deal to be renegotiated upon its expiration in 2022 (Young, 2020).

The revenues created from SUM's marketing efforts come from media, merchandise sales, and from international competitions (for instance, financial rewards from FIFA for the USMNT and USWNT winning games in their respective World Cup). Since its creation, SUM revenues have helped to absorb and pay the expenses of MLS as it grew in popularity. Notably, SUM's profits also help to pay for the U.S. national team members' salaries and costs for competing in international competition, such as the CONCACAF Cup and the World Cup.

As noted earlier in the chapter, in 2019 members of the USWNT sued the U.S. Soccer Federation for lack of equitable compensation compared to the earnings for those competition on the U.S.

men's national team. Players' compensation is one of the major expenses that could be considered as supported from revenues earned by marketing efforts from SUM (M. Pentz personal interview, December 23, 2020; G. Wahl, personal interview, December 24, 2020; Wahl, 2018). Considering the revenues derived from these efforts, and the costs to meet the needs to grow soccer, will help to better understand the impact of MLS growth on its profitability.

2. Entry Fee to the MLS

MLS also charges new clubs with an entry fee to join the league, upon selection. The entry fee has grown from $10 million for a new team in Toronto in 2007 (Yoesting, 2019) to $325 million for Charlotte beginning in 2021 (Dowdeswell, 2020). This high fee, and the nature of the league sharing revenues, has led to some wondering if the MLS is too dependent on entry fees to help keep struggling clubs from deciding to stop competing and quit the league.

3. Player Transfer/Acquisition

In addition, selling a player from an MLS club to a club in other country creates a significant revenue stream for the MLS, such as Miguel Almirón transferring from MLS's Atlanta United to English Premier League's Newcastle United for a $26 million fee collected by the MLS (Mandel, 2019). (Conversely, MLS contributes to the cost to purchase players from other leagues, such as Zlatan Ibrahimović to sign with the LA Galaxy with support from Target Allocation Money provided by MLS.)

Expenses

Here we share two of the most significant expenses by MLS clubs: stadium construction/improvement and salary expenses. The first is the investment in new, soccer-specific stadiums in each club's bid to join MLS and to help the professional sport expand to new areas of North America. By 2020, 18 stadiums were built as MLS-only use since the soccer-only Mapfre Stadium completion for the Columbus Crew in 1998; an additional seven stadiums were expected to be built by 2021, with the most recent being West End Stadium for FC Cincinnati at the cost of $250 million (Reichard, 2019). Construction costs for new stadium developments are complicated, and typically involve financial contributions from a new club and support from the public to support infrastructure, such as road access or sewage and electrical needs. This support typically is in the hundreds of millions of dollars for professional sports, and low interest bonds are made available to investors to help pay the cost to build the stadiums over a 20 to 30 year period (Humphreys & Matheson, 2019; Robertson, 2010).

Player salaries are also among the greatest expenses of any professional team, and these expenses are estimated at 50% or more of total revenues in most American professional leagues. MLS players averaged earning $758,000 per year in Toronto to $290,000 in Cincinnati (Lange, 2020). In 2019, the average MLS salary was $411,926, but a third of MLS players earned below $100,000 (Drager, 2020; Smith, C., 2019a, 2019b). However, in MLS, salaries were limited to only 25% of total team revenues in 2007, which increased slightly to 27% in 2016 (Prockl, 2018). Although MLS clubs share much of their revenue, the big difference in salaries paid by each club relates to the club's ability to pay a higher salary to recruit international players.

In 2006, MLS initiated the Designated Player Rule to allow clubs to spend above a team's maximum allowed pay for all its players (salary cap). Any club was allowed to pay as much as it wanted to an international star to play in the MLS without that player from leaving to join other teams, even the player was offered more money (Siregar, 2016). This was also known as the "David Beckham rule" as he was the first international star to receive the designation to play for the LA Galaxy. Another way to add talent outside of the Beckham rule was Targeted Allocation Money, in which funds from MLS ($1.2 million per year as of 2019) helped pay the salary for a player making more the league-allowed-maximum, and beyond a team's salary cap (MLS, 2017). Though the MLS tries to maximize competitive equity among teams, many clubs with smaller population markets (such as Columbus, Colorado, Minnesota, and Montreal) have greater challenges to generate revenue to improve player rosters as in larger population markets (Chicago, New York, or Los Angeles).

What is an MLS club's value?

Thus, subtracting costs from money made can provide an insight into how much an MLS sport club profits. Profits are one way to determine the value of a sport organization, and it seems reasonable to assume that if a club keeps losing money it is less valuable. However, there are other investments and expenses over time that change how one can perceive the value: revenues like long-term media contracts and ticket sales, or expenses like stadium debt or player salaries. The more revenue is made, the more money to pay the bills. Atlanta United's $78 million of revenue makes it much more valuable than the Colorado Rapids $18 million (see Table 3).

In addition to considering revenues and expenses, there are other ways to place a value (or worth) on an MLS club. A club valuation is not necessarily about how much revenues or how much profit is made, but rather how much an organization is valued. One simple way to determine value is how much an owner is willing to pay or sell a franchise within the MLS. For instance, Joe Mansueto as owner of the MLS's Chicago Fire paid the remaining $204 million of $400 million to purchase the full 100% ownership of the club in September 2019 (Smith, S., 2019). In August 2019, 3.5% share of the MLS's Huston Dynamo was purchased for $15 million by the NBA's James Harden (do the math: $15 million divided by .035 = $428 million valuation). Using information published by *Forbes*

TABLE 3: 2019 Value of MLS Teams with Revenue and Operating Income

Rank	Team	Value ($ million)	Revenue ($ million)	Operating Income ($ million)
1	Atlanta United	500	78	7
2	LA Galaxy	480	64	5
3	LAFC	475	50	–5
4	Seattle Sounders	405	47	1
5	Toronto FC	395	43	–19
6	Portland Timbers	390	47	4
7	New York City FC	385	45	–16
8	Chicago Fire	335	23	–16
9	DC United	330	41	1
10	Sporting Kansas City	325	43	1
11	Minnesota United	300	24	–8
12	Orlando City SC	295	39	–1
13	New York Red Bulls	290	36	–6
14	FC Cincinnati	285	n/a	n/a
15	Houston Dynamo	280	23	–6
16	San Jose Earthquakes	275	35	–5
17	New England Revolution	245	29	–2
18	Philadelphia Union	240	21	–5
19	Real Salt Lake	235	21	2
20	FC Dallas	220	33	–7
21	Vancouver Whitecaps	215	20	–5
22	Montreal Impact	210	18	–12
23	Columbus Crew	200	18	–8
24	Colorado Rapids	190	18	–5

Adapted from Smith, S. (2019). *Forbes.*

from 2011 to 2017, Prockl (2018) this valuation method found the average value of an MLS club was $37.3 million in 2007, then more than doubled from $103.1 million in 2012 to $222.9 million in 2016. By 2019, the average value of an MLS club was estimated at $313 million (Yoesting, 2019).

Another way to determine value may be to review how well a club invests in competitive improvement compared to the outcome of the investment a few years afterward, also known as an "Ambition Ranking." Wahl (2017) determined an MLS club's ambition by investigating investment in players, facilities, and youth development as the primary impact to a club's competitive value.

Ambition Rankings from 2017 were compared to the total success 2 years later in 2019. According to the 2017 Ambition Rankings, Toronto, Seattle, Atlanta, and Portland all were among the top five clubs with investments to improve their on-field success, and each participated in at least one MLS cup from 2017 to 2019; however, each of these clubs also lost more games over the same three-year period in the regular season.

Moreover, the average change in success between teams (from 1 year to the next, e.g., standard deviation) dropped significantly from 2017 to 2019, reflecting greater competitive equity: possibly, more competitive teams were added (LA FC and FC Cincinnati), and/or MLS prioritized decisions to support investment by more clubs in purchasing more quality players (such as Targeted Allocation Money, used by MLS to give to clubs to attract more international talent) (see Table 4).

The following are among the considerations from this analysis: (1) The aforementioned clubs with highest Ambition Rankings in 2017 previously invested in success via player acquisition and facilities, and show positive results (competing in the MLS Cup) with no need for additional investment; (2) other clubs whose 2017 results were not reflected in their Ambition Ranking (LA Galaxy, NY City, and Salt Lake) may soon see the silver lining because their success on the field is greater than the recent financial investments (ambition) of more successful clubs; (3) the reduction in the amount of success (determined by points, the more points one has, the more successful one is) by standard deviation (9.3 in 2017 to 7.1 in 2019) demonstrates greater competitive equity by more clubs across the MLS.

In sum, the data demonstrate in the MLS, the more teams invest in their soccer clubs, the more competitive they will become.

TABLE 4: Change in MLS Regular Season Competitiveness Based on Ambition Ranking, 2017-2019.

2017 Ambition Rankings	2017 MLS Clubs**	2017 Results* (total pts)	2018 Results* (total pts)	2019 Results* (total pts)	2019 Results – 2017 Results
1	Toronto	69.0	33.0	45.8	−23.2
2	Atlanta	55.0	63.3	53.2	−1.8
3	Seattle	53.0	54.1	51.3	−1.7
4	LA Galaxy	32.0	44.0	46.8	14.8
5	Portland	53.0	49.5	44.9	−8.1
6	Kansas City	49.0	56.8	34.8	−14.2
7	Orlando	39.0	25.7	33.9	−5.1
8	NY City	57.0	51.3	58.7	1.7
9	Dallas	46.0	52.3	44.0	−2.0
10	NY Red Bulls	50.0	65.1	44.0	−6.0
11	Vancouver	52.0	43.1	31.2	−20.8
12	Salt Lake	45.0	44.9	48.6	3.6
13	San Jose	46.0	19.3	40.3	−5.7
14	Philadelphia	42.0	45.8	50.4	8.4
15	Colorado	33.0	28.4	38.5	5.5
16	Chicago	55.0	29.3	38.5	−16.5
17	Montreal	39.0	42.2	37.6	−1.4
18	DC	32.0	46.8	45.8	13.8
19	Columbus	54.0	46.8	34.8	−19.2
20	Houston	50.0	34.8	36.7	−13.3
21	Minnesota	36.0	33.0	48.6	12.6
22	New England	45.0	37.6	41.3	−3.8
Median points		*47.5*	*44.5*	*44.0*	*−2.9*
Standard Deviation points		*9.3*	*12.0*	*7.1*	*−2.0*

Table created by author based on Wahl (2017), Major League Soccer (2020).

* Notes: The total points for a club relate to the scoring system of the MLS includes three points for a win and one for a tie: so, in 2017, Toronto with a record of 20 wins, 5 losses, and 9 ties, earned 69 points: (20 wins × 3 points/win) plus (9 ties × 1 point per tie) = 69.

** Notes: Because two teams (LA FC and FC Cincinnati) were added in 2018 (to make 24 teams), points for all teams were weighted in 2018 and 2019 to reflect 2017 league membership (of 22 teams). 1—Toronto, Seattle Participated in 2017 MLS Cup; 2—Atlanta, Portland participated in 2018 MLS Cup; 3—Toronto, Seattle in 2019 MLS Cup.

Review Questions

1. What is the difference in how a professional football (soccer) team profits in different parts of the world and why?
2. Why is competitive equity important, and how does it differ in professional football (soccer) in different leagues? How does competitive equity in MLS differ from other North American professional sports?
3. How would you value a soccer (football) franchise? What matters in how you would value a minor league sport franchise? Why?

Case Study References

Dowdeswell, A. (2020). *MLS: The looming 2023 TV deal vital for league survival*. Fansided. https://mlsmultiplex.com/2020/06/02/mls-looming-2023-tv-deal-vital-league-survival/

Drager, K. (2020, February 6). Major league soccer reaches a deal with its players. *The New York Times*. www.nytimes.com/2020/02/06/sports/soccer/major-league-soccer-reaches-a-deal-with-its-players.html

Humphreys, B., & Matheson, V. (2019). Should the construction of new professional sports facilities be subsidized." *Journal of Policy Analysis and Management, 38* (1), 264-270.

Ilyas, A. (2017, August 29). *How MLS makes money for its owners*. StarsandstripesFC.com. www.starsandstripesfc.com/2017/8/29/16088402/mls-money-owners-sum-major-league-soccer-marketing-usa-mexico-canada

Lange, D. (2020, November 26). *Average player salary in MLS by team 2019*. Statista. www.statista.com/statistics/551765/average-player-salary-in-mls-by-team/

Litterer, D. (2015, March 27). *American league of professional football*. Rec.Sport.Soccer Statistics Foundation. http://www.rsssf.com/usadave/alpf.html

Major League Soccer. (2020). *Standings*. www.mlssoccer.com/

Mandel, Eric. (2019, January 31). "Atlanta United parts with star midfielder, breaking MLS transfer fee record." *Atlanta Business Journal*. https://www.bizjournals.com/atlanta/news/2019/01/31/atlanta-united-parts-with-star-midfielder-breaking.html

Pentz, M. (2019). *The Sound and the Glory: How the Seattle Sounders Showed Major League Soccer How to Win*. ECW Press.

Phillips, B. (2010, June 9). *The secret history of American soccer*. Slate. https://slate.com/culture/2010/06/how-soccer-almost-became-a-major-american-sport-in-the-1920s.html

Prockl, F. (2018). *The economics of major league soccer*. Master's Thesis. Universität Paderborn, Paderborn, Germany.

Reed, J. (1980, December 1). *It's time for trimming sails in the NASL*. Sports Illustrated. https://vault.si.com/vault/1980/12/01/its-time-for-trimming-sails-in-the-nasl-three-franchises-are-on-the-verge-of-going-under-as-the-league-grapples-with-the-effects-of-overexpansion-the-reces-sion-and-union-troubles

Reichard, K. (2019, October 29). Designing new west end stadium for FC Cincinnati: High energy, neighborhood integration. *SoccerStadiumDigest.com*. https://soccerstadiumdigest.com/2019/10/designing-new-west-end-stadium-for-fc-cincinnati-high-energy-neighbor-hood-integration/

Robertson, R. (2010). *The economic impact of sports facilities*. The Sport Digest. http://thesportdigest.com/archive/article/economic-impact-sports-facilities

Siregar, Cady. (2020, January 21). *What is a Designated Player? How MLS star transfers work*. Goal.com; https://www.goal.com/en-us/news/what-is-a-designated-player-how-mls-star-trans-fers-work/12g4zantr3xhj18afa3uxba7p8

Smith, C. (2019a, September 13). *Billionaire Joe mansueto completes purchase of Chicago fire at $400 million valuation*. Forbes. www.forbes.com/sites/chrissmith/2019/09/13/billionaire-joe-mansue-to-completes-purchase-of-chicago-fire-at-400-million-valuation/?sh=2cce00d64709

Smith, C. (2019b, September 30). *Complete 2019 MLS salaries*. The Blue Statement. www.the-bluetestament.com/2019/9/30/20889779/complete-2019-mls-salaries-major-league-soccer-zla-tan-atlanta-sporting-kc-los-angeles-new-york

Smith, S. (2019). *Major league soccer's most valuable teams 2019: Atlanta stays on top as expansion fees, sale prices surge*. Forbes. www.forbes.com/sites/chrissmith/2019/11/04/major-league-soccers-most-valuable-teams-2019-atlanta-stays-on-top-as-expansion-fees-sale-prices-surge/?sh=50b39d4451b5

Wahl, G. (2017, March 3). *2017 MLS ambition rankings: Who strives for greatness the most?* Sports Illustrated. www.si.com/soccer/2017/03/03/2017-mls-ambition-rankings#planet-fut-bol/2017/03/03/lafc-mls-ambition-rankings

Wahl, G. (2018, January 25). *Soccer united marketing fact/fiction: Garber opens up on SUM's role in U.S. Soccer, MLS*. Sports Illustrated. www.si.com/soccer/2018/01/25/sum-soccer-united-mar-keting-garber-gulati-carter

Yoesting, T. (2019, December 17). *Why MLS expansion fees are so damn high but also kind of a great deal*. The18.com. https://the18.com/en/soccer-news/why-mls-expansion-fees-are-so-high-charlotte

Young, J. (2020, February 27). *Major league soccer has a 25-year plan, but it needs to secure huge media deals first*. CNBC.com. www.cnbc.com/2020/02/27/major-league-soccer-has-a-25-year-plan-but-it-needs-to-secure-huge-media-deals-first.html

References

ADVFN. (2020). *Football Clubs you can buy shares in*. https://uk.advfn.com/football

Anderson, N. (2020, March 5). *The economic impact of the FIFA World Cup in Brazil. StoryMaps Arc-gis*. https://storymaps.arcgis.com/stories/c227b86142f04ea7b426b202c4734dff

Bajana, A. (2019). *Everything money: Your guide to the money behind the 2019 women's world cup.* Revenue.

Barrios, D., Russell, S., & Andrews, M. (2016, July). Bringing home the gold? A review of the economic impact of hosting mega-events. *CID Working Paper Series*, 320. Harvard University, Cambridge, MA.

BeSoccer. (2020, April 3). *What are the richest football leagues in the world?* www.besoccer.com/new/what-are-the-richest-football-leagues-in-the-world-816834

Bundesliga. (2020). *German soccer rules: 50+1 explained. ESPN+.* www.bundesliga.com/en/news/Bundesliga/german-soccer-rules-50-1-fifty-plus-one-explained-466583.jsp

Cater, F. (2020, May 2). *Federal judge dismisses U.S. women's soccer team's equal pay claim.* NPR. www.npr.org/2020/05/02/849492863/federal-judge-dismisses-u-s-womens-soccer-team-s-equal-pay-claim

Churchill, J. E., Hacker, J., & Humphrey, E. (Eds). (1979). *Pursuit of excellence: The Olympic story.* Franklin Watts.

Cohen, K., Hays, G., Kaplan, E., & Carlisle, J. (2020, June 3). USWNT lawsuit versus U.S. Soccer explained: Defining the pay gaps, what's at stake for both sides. *ESPN.* www.espn.com/soccer/united-states-usaw/story/4071258/uswnt-lawsuit-versus-us-soccer-explained-defining-the-pay-gapswhats-at-stake-for-both-sides

English Premier League. (2019, May 23). *Premier league value of central payments to clubs 2018/19.* www.premierleague.com/news/1225126

Fédération Internationale de Football Association. (2019a). *FIFA financial report.* https://resources.fifa.com/image/upload/xzshsoe2ayttyquuxhq0.pdf

Fédération Internationale de Football Association. (2019b). *FIFA statutes.* June 2019 edition. https://resources.fifa.com/image/upload/fifa-statutes-5-august-2019-en.pdf

Fédération Internationale de Football Association. (2020a). www.fifa.com

Fédération Internationale de Football Association. (2020b). *Compliance handbook.* October 2020 edition. https://resources.fifa.com/image/upload/compliance-handbook-x8992.pdf?cloud-id=lp015yxfdqesvrleo6ii

Goal. (2019, December 5). *What is the MLS salary cap & how much are U.S. soccer players paid?* www.goal.com/en/news/mls-salary-cap-how-much-us-soccer-players-paid/q015j4su3gb-31bha41zto4fkb#targeted-allocation-money-tam

Goff, B. (2015, December 28). *Growing competitive equality in spite of large income inequality in the English premier league.* Forbes. www.forbes.com/sites/briangoff/2015/12/28/growing-competitive-equality-in-spite-of-large-income-inequality-in-the-english-premier-league/?sh=59b3f8fd2acf

Herman, C. (2014, August 11). *$13.5 billion later, did the world cup help or hurt Brazil?* Diplomatic Courier. www.diplomaticcourier.com/posts/13-5-billion-later-did-the-world-cup-help-or-hurt-brazil

Hess, A. (2019, June 19). *US women's soccer games now generate more revenue than men's—but the players still earn less.* CNBC.com. www.cnbc.com/2019/06/19/us-womens-soccer-games-now-generate-more-revenue-than-mens.html

Khan, Y. (2019, July 24). *These are the 10 most valuable sports franchises in the world in 2019*. Business Insider. https://markets.businessinsider.com/news/stocks/10-most-valuable-sports-franchises-2019-forbes-2019-7-1028380114

Lee, C.-K., & Taylor, T. (2005). Critical reflections on the economic impact assessment of a mega-event: the case of 2002 FIFA World Cup. *Tourism Management, 26*(4), 595–603.

Mackin, B. (2016). *Women's World Cup windfall revealed in CSA financials*. Business in Vancouver. https://biv.com/article/2016/09/womens-world-cup-windfall-revealed-csa-financials

Maennig, W. (2017). *Major sports events: Economic impact*. Hamburg Contemporary Economic Discussions No. 58.

Maennig, W., & Zimbalist, A. S. (Eds.). (2012). *International handbook on the economics of mega sporting events*. Edward Elgar Publishing. Available at SSRN: https://ssrn.com/abstract=2990262 or http://dx.doi.org/10.2139/ssrn.2990262

Major League Soccer (MLS). (2017, February 2). *Targeted allocation money*. www.mlssoccer.com/glossary/targeted-allocation-money

Manfred, T. (2015, March 20). *FIFA made an insane amount of money off of Brazil's $15 billion World Cup*. Business Insider. www.businessinsider.com/fifa-brazil-world-cup-revenue-2015-3

McFarland, K. (2015, May 27). *Everything you need to know about FIFA's corruption scandal*. Wired. www.wired.com/2015/05/fifa-scandal-explained/

Planet Football. (2020). *Club-by-club: A breakdown of the 2019-20 Premier League prize money*. www.planet-football.com/quick-reads/club-by-club-a-breakdown-of-the-2019-20-premier-league-prize-money/

Rapoza, K. (2014, June 11). *Bringing FIFA to Brazil equal to roughly 61% of education budget*. Forbes. www.forbes.com/sites/kenrapoza/2014/06/11/bringing-fifa-to-brazil-equal-to-roughly-61-of-education-budget/?sh=197650f36d62

Ruiz, R., & Mather, V. (2015, September 25). The FIFA scandal: What's happened, and what's to come. *The New York Times*. www.nytimes.com/2015/09/26/sports/soccer/the-fifa-scandal-whats-happened-and-whats-to-come.html

Srivastava, N. (2015, August 13). *Behind the scenes at Real Madrid: How the club is structured and how it functions*. Sportskeeda. www.sportskeeda.com/football/how-real-madrid-club-socios-president-elections-structure-functions

Watts, J. (2013, June 18). Brazil protests erupt over public services and World Cup costs. *The Guardian*. www.theguardian.com/world/2013/jun/18/brazil-protests-erupt-huge-scale

Yahoo Finance. (2020, December 1). *Manchester United*. https://finance.yahoo.com/quote/MANU/key-statistics?p=MANU

CHAPTER 10

Business of Women's Sports and Pay Equity

Jill S. Harris and Jennifer Lee Hoffman

LEARNING OBJECTIVES

- To learn how the individual soccer teams are owned, how they are contracted with the United States Soccer Federation (USSF), and how that may change in 2021 and beyond.
- To discover why young leagues are so dependent on ownership buy-ins, owner's relationship to access to facilities, and why famous investors can elevate a team's profile.
- To learn about how various event staging models and regional leagues are a preferred revenue model compared to more traditional national schedules and franchises.
- To gain an understanding of how the NWHL announced a media coup in 2021 when ESPN decided to broadcast the postseason games for the Isobel Cup, the league championship.
- To study how facilities, teams, and ownership determine subsidies and public–private partnerships.
- To understand the differences in the pay equity discussions between the National Women's Hockey League and the National Women's Soccer League.

Structures and Finances of Three Different Leagues

This chapter examines the financial underpinnings of three higher profile women's pro sports: soccer, softball and hockey. We review the histories, ownership buy-ins, revenue sources and distribution schemes, tax status, partnerships, salary structures and salary caps, and any postseason financial structures for all three sports. We also examine the facility revenue and construction subsidies the sports enjoy (or live without).

© Dmitry Demidovich/Shutterstock.com

The chapter also includes the new optimism around the "growth potential" that many investors are seeing around professional (and some collegiate) sports. The narrative shifted in early 2021, and sports finance enthusiasts would be wise to pay attention to the new opportunities emerging. The issue of pay inequity between women and men in the U.S. labor force is a persistent economic issue and that includes professional sports.

Today, we can point to many positive advances in women's sports compensation and benefits. For example, professional women jockeys in Australia are now eligible for full maternity benefits, such as maternity leave and salary payments between the first trimester and birth (MacLennan, 2020). However, cultivating athletic opportunities, sustaining leagues, and promoting visibility that drive revenue for women's professional athletics all remain a challenge. The inequity in the promotion of women's sports is a key factor in the persistent pay gap between women's and men's professional athletes. (Please see additional content in Chapter 11.)

National Women's Soccer League and U.S. Women's National Team

More than any other sport, the World Cup and Olympic athletes in women's soccer are tied directly to the emergence and success of the National Women's Soccer League. Athletes from the U.S. Women's National Team (USWNT) have taken to boycotts and legal action against the U.S. Soccer Federation (U.S. Soccer) over pay equity. A key question for any observer of elite-level international women's soccer should be, Why are women's salary and compensation decisions based on the potential for revenue instead of performance in head-to-head competition (Walters, 2016) and actual revenue? What really counts for U.S. Soccer's compensation of the U.S. national women's and men's soccer teams?

The growth of soccer in the United States has a mixed history. For men, U.S. soccer grew more slowly, with the North American Soccer League and the United Soccer League taking a lower profile in the broader U.S. sports market for decades. For the women's game, soccer grew swiftly at the youth and college level after Title IX. Despite this disparate appetite for men's professional soccer compared to women's amateur soccer, the U.S. women have outpaced the men on the world stage since the first FIFA Women's World Cup in 1991. Since then, the USWNT has amassed a dominating record of international play, posting 530 wins in 673 in matches, eight CONCACAF titles, four Olympic medals, and winning four of the eight FIFA World Cup tournaments held (U.S. Soccer website; Society for American Soccer History website.).

These wins have also come with expansive viewership and growing revenues for the women's World Cup—the highest level of global soccer competition. The 2019 FIFA Women's World Cup in France drew 1 billion viewers around the globe who tuned in to watch a collective 2.5 billion hours of coverage—twice that of the viewership for the 2015 Women's World Cup in Canada (FIFA, 2019). Fox Sports also reported that their U.S. broadcast earnings for the 2019 FIFA Women's World Cup were 20% higher than the men's 2018 FIFA Men's World Cup Tournament. In addition, in the 3 years, leading up to the women's 2019 FIFA championship, the USWNT generated $50.8 million in revenue, compared to the men, who earned $49.9 million—a gap of nearly $2 million dollars more than the USMNT (Bachman, 2019).

For many, the 1999 Women's World Cup is *the* event that fused women's team sports in the global landscape of elite-level athletics beyond single athletic feats or Olympic medal performances. Both the swiftness of the popularity of the event, with fans filling NFL stadiums across the United States for 3 weeks on the road to the final between the United States and China in front of 90,000 fans in the Rose Bowl and 40 million fans worldwide (Kelly, 2013). Yet, since then, the U.S. Soccer Federation has failed to grow the women's game at the professional level and repeatedly denied the USWNT the same pay and benefits as the men's squad.

Despite the North American success and popularity for women's international play, the work of the U.S. Soccer Federation has not seeded professional opportunities in the United States as quickly as other countries or the men's Major League Soccer. Three women's professional soccer leagues have been launched by U.S. Soccer. The first two failed after two seasons, the current women's professional league, National Women's Soccer League launched in 2013. The NWSL is partially funded by the U.S. Soccer Federation, to support the league's office expenses and the national team player salaries (Jay, 2019), illustrates how the nonprofit model that pairs women's athletic interests with national or amateur sporting interests does not fare much better than professional organizations for elevating women's sports.

Despite the visibility and dominant on-the-field success of the USWNT, U.S. Soccer Federation continues to offer the women's national team less pay than the USMNT. For example, after winning the 2015 FIFA Women's World Cup, the women's team was still paid 25% of what the men's team was paid, yet generated $20 million dollars more in revenue than the men's team in 2015. After filing wage discrimination suit and later, the USWNT received

© Romain Biard/Shutterstock.com

more in pay and bonuses, plus additional travel, maternity, and childcare benefits (Alvarez, 2019).

In March 2019, 28 USWNT players filed a gender discrimination lawsuit under the Equal Pay Act and Title VII of the Civil Rights Act, against the U.S. Soccer Federation, over continued inequity between the men's and women's team in pay and benefits, back pay, and inequity in marketing and promotion (Alvarez, 2019; ESPN News Services, 2019; Morgan et al., Plaintiffs vs. US Soccer Federation, 2020). U.S. Soccer contending that the U.S. women generate less in ticket sales, but does not disclose how much it spends on marketing those games (Alvarez, 2019) or how ticket pricing is determined. Attitudes by the U.S. Soccer Federation over the value of the women's team also appear in court documents before U.S. Soccer reversed their public stance on the ability of women's athletes. The U.S. Soccer Federation first suggested that soccer skill should be judged by speed and strength—with men's soccer requiring a higher level of skill based on speed and strength than women. The women's soccer players contend the comparison should be made by the job requirements between the women's team and the men's team (Morgan versus U.S. Soccer Federation).

To that assumption, Carli Lloyd, a 38-year-old striker, explains that from a skill level, based on athleticism in soccer, there is no difference. She regularly trains against the U-18 team, playing against athletes 20 years younger and contends that she does so with *greater* skill based on soccer athleticism and acumen. The gender difference in speed and strength comes when men mature, gaining more muscle mass, which in turn adds speed to the men's game. However, when skill is based on soccer athleticism and acumen, there are no gender differences at the highest levels of play.

Where the difference between the women's and men's national team can be found is in wins and revenue. The USWNT is better against their opponents in world-class women's tournaments than the USMNT. Today the U.S. women are global leaders in soccer—the U.S. men are not. Why is a nonprofit organization basing its payroll decisions not on performance or organization revenue, but on assumptions over gendered athletic value? And why, in a country that revels in the USWNT as the pinnacle of Title IX's impact on women's athletic successes, is a nonprofit organization discriminating between men and women at all?

While the current pay equity case by the USWNT against the U.S. Soccer Federation is not fully resolved as of this writing, there are some encouraging signs for endorsement compensation and contract structures as women's soccer players continue to fight for pay equity (McCann, 2019, November 8). In 2015, Adidas pledged to pay the same bonus to women and men players they have under endorsement deals in soccer (ESPN News Services, 2019).

In early 2020, Nike offered new maternity clauses in USWNT forward Alex Morgan's endorsement contract. Later that year, Nike signed Norway's Ada Hegerberg to a ten-year endorsement deal, estimated at "'six-figures,'" which is closer to the amount Nike holds with athletes in men's soccer (Becoats, 2020). Like other athletes in Nike's portfolio, Hegerberg is outspoken in her views on equal pay in Norway.

Relationships between Major League Soccer, the United States Soccer Federation, and the NWSL

© Keeton Gale/Shutterstock.com

A game between the Portland Thorns and FC Kansas City on April 13, 2013 kicked off the National Women's Soccer League (NWSL). In front of a crowd of 6,784 fans, the game ended in a 1-1 tie. The first goal was scored by Renae Cuellar—a California native who played college soccer for the University of Oklahoma before debuting with FC Kansas City. Despite the recent legal actions taken by USWNT against USSF, NWSL athletes are playing in a league that is reasonably healthy from a financial perspective. This is due, in large part, to the joint relationships enjoyed by many of the clubs with their MLS counterparts.

Unlike softball and hockey—with fan bases localized in a handful of North American regions—soccer is truly an international sport with fan bases stretching across the globe. Not surprisingly, NWSL is an international affair. Three American teams, two Mexican teams, and two Canadian teams took to the pitch for 4 years until Mexico formed their own women's league in 2017: *Liga MX Femenil*. Why would Mexico want to form its own league? What is in it for them? Ultimately, the name of the game is revenues. Before we survey the nature of revenues earned in league soccer, we review the league structure.

Since 2013, the individual teams own the league even though they are managed under a contract with the United States Soccer Federation (USSF), a 501(c)(3) nonprofit governing organization. This management relationship is under review and expected to evolve in 2021; more responsibility for decision making will be in the hands of league owners. Four of the nine teams (Portland, Houston, Orlando, and Utah) affiliate with MLS teams. Cheryl Bailey, Jeff Plush, and Amanda Duffy have all had the commissioner helm. Lisa Baird (former chief of marketing for New York Public Radio) took over the reins in 2020. Women's soccer, much more so than softball or hockey, is financially positioned for growth and success in the years ahead. They have a reasonably stable slate of teams, they do not rely exclusively on the participation of other countries to feed national team players into the league for sustainability, and they have no rival leagues waiting in the wings.

NWSL ownership is almost between split evenly between affiliates and private owners. Buy-in amounts are closely guarded and not for public consumption.

As of 2021, the current owners include:
- Chicago Red Stars—Arnim Whisler;
- NC Courage—Stephen Malik;
- Gotham FC—Phil and Tammy Murphy, Steven Temares, and Ed Nalbandian;
- Houston Dash—James Harden, Oscar De La Hoya, partners led by Gabriel Brener; and
- Portland Thorns—Merritt Paulson.

Harden's buy-in is a reported 5% stake in the club whose owners claim is worth $475 million. If that is accurate, the buy-in was over $23 million. How much of this was for the Dash? Again, it is difficult to parse out. What is crystal clear is both the Thorns and Timbers are owned by Merritt Paulson (i.e., Henry Merritt Paulson III who is the son of former United States Treasury Secretary Hank Paulson). Olympique Lyonnaiss owns a 89.5% stake of OL Reign. They reportedly invested $3.45 million for their stake in the franchise. The Florida Pride is co-owned by Flávio Augusto da Silva (majority) and Phil Rawlins (minority). Their group owns the MLS team, the new stadium (built with private funds), and the OL Pride. Back-of-the-envelope calculations hint that the buy-in for the OL Pride may be about $12 million.

NWSL benefited from about $18 million dollars from the USSF since the league's inception. Distributed across the teams this translates into a bit more than $277,000 each year. If every dollar of that support showed up in player salaries, athletes would be earning about 11% of revenues. It is unlikely that is the case. Thus, we can safely assume athlete compensation is probably less than 10% of overall revenue. There is a growing body of scholarship about player share of sports revenues. These estimates are well below what you typically find in professional sports leagues. The NWSL under the umbrella of the USSF is a nonprofit 501(c)(3) organization registered in New York and headquartered in Chicago. What additional support does NWSL receive?

Nike was the first official sponsor of NWSL providing apparel and the official game ball. Budweiser and Thorne are also partners. This league, more than the other hockey and softball, may benefit from its stronger ties to MLS. The NWSL has a new multiyear contract with CBS, CBS Sports Network, CBS All-Access, and Twitch. Fans will have to pay $59.99 for the All-Access plan to watch the majority of games. NWSL has a new multiyear agreement with CBS. It is not yet clear how much revenue will ultimately flow back to the league from this arrangement.

NWSL players eagerly await a Collective Bargaining Agreement. A new union formed in 2019, but the players are patiently awaiting the dust to settle after the USSF and NWSL reshuffle management duties. Each team can now carry a maximum of 26 players. The minimum player salary is $16,538 and the maximum salary is $46,200.

The history of NWSL salary caps is captured in Table 1. It shows the team cap more than doubling from 2017 to 2020. The unallocated minimums and maximums have increased, but not

by the same amount. This steady increase is probably the result of MLS influence through joint ownership of NSWL teams, but also in response to the remarkable performance of the USWNT. Still, the cap effectively limits the NWSL from attracting top talent.

Take the case of Florida State University superstar Deyna Castellanos. This college athlete graduated with a degree and over 1 million Instagram followers. She signed with Atlético Madrid for multiples of what she could earn as a draftee in the United States (see photo).

The NWSL Championship is a single elimination tournament. In addition to the championship series, the team with the highest regular season points earns the NWSL Shield. The big revenue event for postseason play in soccer is the World Cup. The 2019 season World Cup final saw 14.3 million U.S. viewers and attracted Budweiser as an official sponsor. However, even though the financial boost from the World Cup is expected to be large, not enough data exists (yet) to verify it.

TABLE 1: NWSL Salary Cap History

Year	Team Cap	Unallocated Min	Unallocated Max
2020	$650,000	$20,000	$50,000
2019	$421,500	$16,538	$46,200
2018	$350,000	$15,750	$44,000
2017	$315,000	$15,000	$41,700

Table adapted from "NWSL announces new 2020 compensation guidelines" by Matthew Levine, 1 November, 2019 on NWSL website.

National Pro Fastpitch

In 1976, three iconic athletes (including Billie Jean King, Janie Blaylock, and Joan Joyce) and two sports entrepreneurs cofounded the International Women's Professional Softball Association (IWPSA). Four intensive, 120 game seasons went in the books before the IWPSA closed up shop. It was 30 years later that the first professional fast pitch crossed home plate in the reorganized National Pro Fastpitch (NPF) league.

© JoeSAPhotos/Shutterstock.com

The current league formed originally in 1997 and operated under the names Women's Pro Fastpitch (WPF) and Women's Pro Softball League (WPSL). In 2004, WPSL shed the old brand and debuted new skin: National Pro Fastpitch (NPF). That same year, Major League Baseball joined as a development partner. This joint venture opened the door for NPF to create community relationships and laid the groundwork for future broadcast contracts. In December 2004, owners of the individual National Pro Fastpitch (NPF) teams announced a plan intended to transition operations of National Pro Fastpitch from the founding Cowles family to an operating group of team owners.

The founding NPF teams included the following.
- Akron Racers
- Arizona Heat
- California Sunbirds
- New England Riptide
- NY/NJ Juggernaut
- Texas Thunder

More recently, the league included the following.
- Aussie Peppers
- Beijing Eagles*
- Canadian Wild
- Chicago Bandits
- Cleveland Comets
- California Commotion (an expansion team slated to play the 2021 season)
- USSSA Pride*

*(*No longer in NPF)*

Players come from the United States, Australia, Canada, and China. In the last 6 years, the NPF seems to have suffered more than its fair share of legal tumult and instability with teams entering and folding faster than a beady-eyed poker player. Much of this is due to the alleged misbehavior of Joel Bartsch, owner of the former NPF Scrap Yard Dawgs (now the Scrap Yard Fast Pitch independent team). NPF sued SY Dawgs, LLC (i.e., Bartsch) in January of 2018 in the Northern District Court of Ohio for violating terms of his franchise agreement with NPF. As of May 2018, the court denied the motion for a preliminary injunction against Bartsch. Even so, in a league with four teams and one promising expansion team, losing the 2017 Champions in such a public break up is difficult.

The NPF is a *franchiser*. Individuals, partnerships, corporations, and government municipalities may own an NPF team. Ownership of or established relationships with event venues are a plus according to the NPF Franchisee application. The structure of the NPF is evolving as worldwide demand for high-caliber softball competition remains focused on the resources in the United States. NPF teams are a mixed bag of private and public ownership. The Village of Rosemont owns the Chicago Bandits while Softball Australia owns the Aussie Peppers and Softball Canada owns The Canadian Wild. At the other end of the spectrum, Craig Stout owns the Cleveland Comets (who were formerly the Akron Racers) and Damon Zumwalt owns the expansion team California Commotion. All paid a $50,000 licensing fee to acquire franchise rights for the teams.

Absent from the roster in 2020 is The Scrap Yard Fast Pitch (who notoriously had the highest paid individual female athlete of record in 2016, pitcher Monica Abbott). The NPF terminated its franchise agreement effective January 29, 2018 due to violations of the team's contract. They are now an independent team.

Longtime player and fastpitch softball ambassador Cheri Kempf serves as the commissioner of the league. Kempf is a four-time National Champion and three-time Hall of Fame Inductee. She represented the United States on Team USA in 1992. Kempf lends her commentary expertise to ESPN, FOX Sports, Comcast Sports, the YES Network, and the MLB Network. She is also President of NPF Media, LLC.

Perhaps future editions of this volume will have more to report on revenue. The NPF website claimed that NPFTV generated almost $50,000 in subscription revenue, but offers no details on how—or even if—that revenue came back to the league. However, without more information about the total size of the NPF pie, it is impossible to know how big a slice player compensation represents. They are searching for partners to take advantage of OPAL (on player ad location) sponsorships. The NPF Coaches Association reported $1,757,128 in revenue for 2017 (the most recent year for which audited financials are available).

National Pro Fastpitch Softball is organized as a 501(c)(3) organization. It has numerous media partners including NPFTV, ESPN+, ELEVEN sports, B/R Live, Flo Sports, MLB.com, and the Olympic Channel. However, this does not prevent some back-of-the-envelope type of estimation.

The NCAA Women's College World Series draws over a million viewers. If just one tenth of that audience continues to follow college players into the NPF, then 100,000 viewers are potentially interested in tuning into one of the broadcast partners streams. Using a very conservative 5% split of subscription fees, the NPF could see $3 per subscriber. This places our estimate at $300,000 in revenue. In reality, the total viewership could be much lower (or higher!) than this and the split could be different.

NPF teams can carry 26 players; only 23 can be active during a given game. Although there is a team salary cap of $175,000, this only applies to the salary itself and not to signing bonuses, performance incentives, or improved living conditions. Minimum player salary is $3,000 per year. Players must be 21 years of age at the time of competition year. NPF maintains rosters of at least 18 players within a salary cap of $175,000—most players make less than $20,000.

NPF teams challenge each other for the Cowles Cup, named for Jane Sage Cowles whose family were financial backers of the former WPSL. Commissioner Kempf announced the organization is adopting a "Series Event Model" to spur growth in attendance and widen exposure. According to Kempf, this model moves away from one-on-one matchups and embraces a multiteam "tournament" where the teams will play each other to determine the winner of each series. This format eliminates the necessity of each team having to bear the expense of hosting games at a home venue (although teams can still opt to play traditional matches as well). Winners will earn points for head-to-head games and series wins. Final points will determine league standings and the Championship Series. To date, there is no financial payday for league Champions.

In 2020, a new professional venture involving softball was launched. Athletes Unlimited Softball changed the entire paradigm around team construction, paying players, and (most surprisingly), eliminated separate coaches. An entire financial structure was built around incentivizing player performance and decision making. A similar concept was launched with women's volleyball and lacrosse. This financial model will be important to pay attention to.

© JoeSAPhotos/Shutterstock.com

National Women's Hockey League

Women's professional basketball and women's soccer leagues are ahead of women's ice hockey both in North America and globally (Donnelly, 2019). However, women's professional ice hockey has had a North American presence since before women's ice hockey first appeared in the 1998 Olympic games. Women's professional hockey can largely be attributed to organizing in Canada with the Central Ontario Women's Hockey League (COWHL). The COWHL predates the 1998 Olympics and helped seed interest and grow the women's game for later professional play (COWHL, n.d.).

Women's professional hockey today begins with the Canadian Women's Hockey League (CWHL), formed by a nearly all women's board. The CWHL was run by the Canadian Association for the Advancement of Amateur of Women's Hockey, which was registered with the Canadian Amateur Athletic Association (CAAA). This affiliation provided insurance and other player benefits from Hockey Canada, but the affiliation with the CAAA, a not-for-profit, tax-exempt organization prohibited player salaries under Canadian law. Instead players received stipends of $2,000–$10,000CAD per season (CWHL, 2019).

© Iurii Osadchi/Shutterstock.com

This affiliation with the CAAA as an amateur organization also prohibited other sources of private revenue such as franchise teams, investments from private equity firms, or merger with a for-profit league (CWHL, 2019), limiting revenue to sponsorships and donations. Despite these financial limitations, this model of women's hockey proved stable over 12 years, growing the women's game with consistent play that also fostered the development of players around the globe competing in the Olympics and U.S. colleges.

Long before these amateurs were drafted into a pro league, they brought home Olympic Gold medals. They competed in 1980 for USA Hockey, and brought home Gold from Nagano, Japan in the 1998 Winter Olympics and again in 2018 from PyeongChang. After the CWHL folded in 2019, NWHL is striving to stake its claim as the top (and only) professional league for female players.

In 2015, a second women's hockey league, the National Women's Hockey League (NWHL), formed in the United States as a professional sports organization. The NWHL's professional model was distinct from basketball and soccer because it operates without the tethers to the NHL that women's basketball has with the NBA or within an NGO as with the U.S. Women's National Team (USWNT) or the National Women's Soccer League (NWSL).

The NWHL permitted player salaries, but the emergence of two leagues created uncertainty by sponsors, which restricted the limited source of revenues in support of either league. Still, the Canada-based CWHL and the U.S.-based NWHL operated with approximately 200 players and in 2019 the CWHL attempted to expand into China with two additional teams in 2017–2018, but later reducing to one.

Still, like their professional league partners in soccer and basketball, financial viability remained a challenge for women's hockey. The CWHL announced at the end of the 2019 season that it would cease operations (CWHL, 2019; Jay, 2019). In its wake, nearly 200 players from both the CWHL and the U.S.-based NWHL formed the National Women' Hockey League Players Association (NWHLPA) and pledged to boycott any future play over concerns that included lack of health insurance and salary contracts as low as $2,000 U.S. dollars (Ayala, 2019b). Additionally, under the newly formed NWHLPA, the player boycott was also in solidarity over issues of overexpansion, more involvement in growing women's hockey, and alliances with the NHL.

The NWHL and NWHLPA agreed to a "50-50 split of revenue from all league-level partnerships—the first such deal in women's professional sports history" and a three-year streaming deal with Twitch (NWHL website). Today, the NWHL has over 100 players mainly from the United States and Canada, with six teams in Boston, Buffalo, Connecticut, New Jersey, St. Paul, and Toronto playing in the 2020–2021 season. The Boston Pride has an alliance with the Boston Bruins of the NHL and the Minnesota Whitecaps have an alliance with the NHL's Minnesota Wild (NWHL website). As of 2020, the NWHL remains women-led, without a formal league-to-league partnership with the NHL (Clinton, 2019).

The NWHL operates exclusively four out of five teams. The NHL provides $100,000 in financial support to the NWHL each year in an annual stipend. As of 2019, the Professional Women's Hockey Players Association—a players' group seeking to create a rival league—has taken the initiative to "do better" by the players. This group formed after the implosion of the CWHL and dissatisfaction on the part of some players with the management of the NWHL. They envision one league—populated by PWHPA players. Although they completed a "Dream Gap Tour" in 2020, a formal league remains just that—a dream.

The NWHL is organized as a 501(c)(6) organization similar to the NHL. The league reported in 2019 it paid athletes $2.5 million over the first four years of operations. This amounts to an average paycheck of $6,250 to $10,000 a year. Players do earn up to 15% profits from jersey sales and will earn a 50/50 revenue split from all media and sponsorship dollars. However, the

© Leonard Zhukovsky/Shutterstock.com

league has yet to earn any media or sponsorship income. In addition to the $100,000 stipend, they do have contract relationships with Twitch, Dunkin' Donuts, and Chipwich. However, the NWHL does not disclose budget or revenue information.

It is interesting to note the NWHL was the first women's pro hockey league to play their players. The Canadian Women's Hockey League paid bonuses, but not salaries before they folded in 2019. The highest announced salary is $15,000. Due to the ongoing expansion into Canada and the tension between NWHL and the PWHPA, salary structures are dynamic and fluid. NWHL has a $100,000 team cap. The lowest paid player in 2019 earned just $2,500. However, the league asserts it has paid over $2.5 million to players over 5 years. Players (for the most part) work other jobs and the sport is a passion, but not the source of any meaningful income.

After six seasons, the NWHL established new benchmarks for league sponsorships, including signing Discover card, Dunkin' Donuts. The league also received more ownership interest in multiple teams, including the Metropolitan Riverters by BTM Partners, and the Connecticut Whale, owned by the owner of Arc Hockey, an equipment and apparel company. In 2021-22, the salary cap will grow from $100,000 to $300,000, a substantial increase (Caron, 2021).

The NWHL teams play for the Isobel Cup. Isobel was the daughter of Frederick Stanley, the 16th Earl of Derby. His name, of course, is on the famed NHL Stanley Cup. For the first time, the Isobel Cup was broadcasted live in concert with NBC sports in 2021. This broadcast exposed a wider audience to the Olympic veterans still playing great hockey in the NWHL. Students of finance should tune in later in 2022 to see what impact the broadcast has on NWHL revenue streams.

Stadium Dilemmas—A Comparison

NPF Softball

Three of the four NPF teams play in publicly funded stadia; one is privately owned. The expansion team is tentatively slated to play at Fresno State University. The fields are not used exclusively for NPF. Youth development programs, high school and college teams play in these complexes as well. It appears that public funding is a bit easier to secure when the public also gets to take advantage of the sports facilities—versus just buying tickets to watch professional teams play.

NWHL Hockey

NWHL hockey teams get a free ride on their NHL sister teams. These ice arenas also host learn-to-skate programs and are leased out to school programs year-round. None of the NWHL teams has to compete with other sports for rink time (similar to an NBA basketball team).

NWSL Soccer

It is a little easier to succeed when you have a steady home field. Playing for spare change on a handful of street corners is exhausting, if not humiliating. Landing a permanent "home" to perform in leads to higher returns for your talent. Indeed, one of the distinguishing features of the sports business is that you cannot play alone. Everyone needs an opponent. As it turns out, having a steady place to play your rivals is correlated with higher revenue streams (see the Portland Thorns Case Study at the end of this chapter).

The NWSL Portland Thorns had an advantage from the start: an award-winning city-owned urban stadium, Providence Park. Evolving from the Multnomah stadium designed and built in 1925, private funds backed a $50 million expansion to accommodate 4,000 more fans. The desire to seat more Portland Timbers (MLS) fans *and* create a place for a second tenant to play was a win-win for the city of Portland.

The OL Reign play in Cheney Stadium (a minor league baseball stadium). The stadium has to convert for soccer play before each game. A new soccer-specific stadium (shared by both the Reign and Tacoma Defiance) is being built next door with plans to be opened in 2021.

The Royals play in Rio Tinto stadium—a soccer-specific venue shared with the men's team. $110 million dollar stadium, $35 million from Utah House Bill from 15% of hotel taxes in Salt Lake County to support construction ($2 million a year).

Facilities probably cannot break a team or league, but they can go a long way toward making a team or league successful. About half of the teams receive some form of public support in their home venues (11 of 21 teams in the three leagues). This is not unusual in the sports public finance domain; many studies show that municipalities are eager to woo teams with subsidies and the promise of increased tax revenues from an influx of visitors. Typically, the same elected officials are not around when the construction cost over runs are tallied, the promised visitor counts never materialize, or the team folds before the first pitch is thrown (see Table 2).

Table 2 summarizes the facilities, construction subsidies, and ownership of the venues in the NPF, NWHL, and NWSL leagues.

© Keeton Gale/Shutterstock.com

TABLE 2: Facility Subsidies and Ownership by League and Team (NPF, NWHL, and NWSL)

Sport/Team	Facility	Subsidies	Ownership
NPF Aussie Peppers	Franklin Rogers Park	Local city sales tax; $3 million from city of Mankato $1.5 million from the minor league team (Source: www.mankatomn.gov)	Joint between city of Mankato and Mankato Moon Dogs
NPF Chicago Bandits	The Ballpark at Rosemont	Leased (Source: https://chicago.cbslocal.com/2011/06/15/brand-new-ballpark-for-bandits-womens-softball-team/)	Village of Rosemont
NPF Cleveland Comets	Firestone Stadium	City of Akron $3.5 million renovation (Source: https://www.beaconjournal.com/article/20180128/SPORTS/301289804)	City of Akron
NPF Canadian Wild	Rent One Park	Miners and Southern Illinois University provide housing and training facilities (Source: https://datelinemarion.com/covid-complications-sideline-canadian-wild-for-npf-season-p4257-109.htm)	Jayne Simmons
NPF California Commotion*	TBD Fresno State University	N/A	N/A

Sport/Team	Facility	Subsidies	Ownership
NWHL Boston Pride	Warrior Ice Arena	Part of Boston Landing mixed use development New Balance Warrior Sports Brand (Source: https://stadiumjourney.com/stadiums/warrior-ice-arena-boston-pride)	NB Development Group, HYM Investment Group, LLC
NWHL Buffalo Beauts	Northtown Center	Leased (Source: https://buffalonews.com/sports/hockey/buffalo-beauts-moving-home-games-to-northtown-center/article_958b039a-6f26-5235-a226-4b259c231a4c.html)	City of Amherst, New York
NWHL Connecticut Whale	Danbury Ice Arena	Leased (Source: https://thehockeywriters.com/connecticut-whale-welcome-addition-danbury-ice-arena/)	Diamond Properties
NWHL Metropolitan Riveters	ProSkate Ice Arena	Leased (Source: www.nwhl.zone/team-info)	Private Ownership
NWHL Minnesota Whitecaps	TRIA Rink	Leased (Source: www.nwhl.zone/team-info)	Paul Port Authority and Hempel Properties
NWHL Toronto*	TBD	TBD	TBD
NWSL Houston Dash	BBVA, multipurpose	$35 million by city of Houston $60 million by Dynamo (Source: www.nwslsoccer.com/news/article/houston-dynamo-football-club-and-houston-dash-unveil-new-club-initiatives-brand-identity-and-primary-badges)	Harris County owns 50% of land & 50% of stadium
NWSL Chicago Red Stars	SeatGeek Stadium, soccer-specific	$100 million cost (Source: https://chicago.curbed.com/2019/5/9/18556610/chicago-fire-soldier-field-return-bridgeview)	Village of Bridgeview; operated by Spectra—a division of Comcast Spectacor
NWSL Florida Pride	Exploria Stadium, soccer-specific	Privately funded (Source: http://www.orlandosentinel.com/sports/orlando-city-lions/os-orlando-city-stadium-0731-20150730-story.html)	$156 million in private funds leveraging EB-5 visa program

Sport/Team	Facility	Subsidies	Ownership
NWSL Kentucky Proof*	Lynn Family Stadium, soccer specific	$30 million financing plan from city (Source: www.courier-journal.com/story/sports/soccer/louisville-city-fc/2020/04/21/nwsl-proof-louisville-fc-moniker-under-reconsideration/2996740001/)	Louisville City FC
NWSL NC Courage	WakeMed Soccer Park, soccer specific	$14.5 million from hotel and prepared food county taxes (Source: www.nccourage.com/stadium)	Land owned by state leased to county then leased to town of Cary who sublet to Triangle Professional Soccer
NWSL OL Reign	Cheney Stadium,* multipurpose	New soccer specific stadium under construction (Source: www.thenewstribune.com/sports/soccer/article225264695.html)	TBD
NWSL Portland Thorns	Providence Park, soccer-specific	$50 million privately funded expansion (Source: www.timbers.com/post/2020/10/29/providence-park-expansion-project-recognized-aia-oregon-architecture-awards)	City of Portland
NWSL Gotham FC	Red Bull Arena, soccer-specific	Leased for $1.3 million to town of Harrison (Source: www.frontrowsoccer.com/2019/08/18/record-crowd-9415-watch-sky-blues-1-1-draw-with-reign-fc/)	Hudson County Improvement Authority; operated by Red Bull GmbH
NWSL Spirit	Audi Field, soccer-specific	$150 million from city plus $43 million in tax credits (Source: www.washingtonpost.com/news/soccer-insider/wp/2018/04/24/washington-spirit-to-play-one-nwsl-match-at-audi-field-this-summer/)	District of Columbia; operated by D.C. United
NWSL UT Royals	Rio Tinto, soccer-specific	$35 million from state plus 15% hotel tax Salt Lake County totaling $2 million per year (Source: https://www.deseret.com/2017/12/4/20636791/questions-linger-about-decade-old-real-salt-lake-stadium-deal)	Dell Loy Hansen

Source: Jill S. Harris

Conclusion

In 2021, a new movement emerged in women's sports. As if a light switch was flipped, the amount of money pouring into ownership of women's pro sports franchises, investment in women in promotion and marketing, and TV viewership numbers outperformed even the most optimistic projections. With new financial tools like SPACs (special purpose acquisition companies) and minority ownership in women's professional franchises exploding, it feels as if women's sports have begun to evolve.

What is most telling about this trend is the narrative has changed. It used to be that women's sports were assumed to be a money-losing proposition that had a limited fan base and owners who saw little chance of their investments growing. In 2021, the conversations surrounding women's sports began to be far more optimistic. Terms like "growth opportunity" and "a chance to create a different paradigm" for owners and players are bandied about. Companies like The Fan Project are building different metrics to measure financial and media success, believing that in today's hypersocial world, the old measures just don't work.

Promoting women's interests and protecting pay equity in established sports such as hockey and soccer remain an issue despite their athletic success. However, there are examples to turn to in emerging sports, where women are treated equally in compensation and as ambassadors for raising the profile of their sport. In 2020, surfing was scheduled to appear in the Tokyo Olympics for the first time. With the 2020 worldwide pandemic halting competition and the Olympics on hold, the World Surfing League (WSL) quickly turned to its athletes to fill the void left from live competitions and continued promotion of surfing.

Already compensating women and men equally in prize earnings (Townes, 2019), the WSL 2019 podcast launch also gave similar promotion to women and men from the start. This promotion continued in their marketing during the Covid suspension of WSL tour events (Moran, 2020), freeing up women athletes to promote their sport without the burden of fighting for equal pay or visibility. Also, in 2021, the NCAA will no longer prohibit athletes monetizing their publicity rights. This policy change, coupled with the growth of media technology like Twitch and Tik Tok for women's sports, signals that women athletes accustomed to building following based on their athleticism are not going to be as willing to be paid less in salary, revenue sharing, and player benefits.

Case Study

Caught Doing It Right: Portland Thorns

Downtown Portland is colorful any day of the week. If it is soccer game day, visitors north of Goose Hollow and Downtown Portland will see red. A lot of it. Caitlin Murray pointed this out for *The New York Times* in her story from October 2017. She argued then the Portland Thorns might be the most successful professional women's sports team in the world. What would cause her to make this claim?

© Keeton Gale/Shutterstock.com

When owner Merritt Paulson acquired the expansion MLS Timbers in 2011, he decided to support a women's team when the new NWLS debuted in 2013. From the beginning, fan support has been united—not divided. The Timbers have sold out more than 100 home games and Thorns attendance has grown every year since the league's inception. More than 17,000 fans show up on average for the Thorns. Murray points in her piece that is more fans than 15 NBA teams, 13 NHL teams, and at least one MLB team.

The city of Portland has been soccer-friendly since 1975 when the Timbers were seedlings. It supported the conversion of an urban stadium to a soccer-specific venue for the Timbers (and later the Thorns). Geography helps; Providence Park is walkable from most of Portland's dense neighborhoods and reachable by public transit for others. Fans do not have to choose between lots of competing options. The Trail Blazers are the only other game in town. Soccer matches do not overlap much with the NBA season—another plus!

The Thorns benefit from the joint production of both MLS and NWLS games. Office staff, general management, administrative facilities, ticket sales, merchandising, and marketing all have economies of scope in production. Marketing is key; the Thorns marquis does not get lost in the noise at the stadium. They are not an afterthought. Paulson and his team want to make sure women's soccer is here for the long run. They initiated a profit-sharing plan with the rest of the league.

But what of teams that do not have an owner equally vested in the MLS? Are they doomed to mediocrity or failure? Other observers point to another unique feature of the Thorns model: they eschew a minor league mentality. Indeed, four of the 23-player USWNT squad came from the Thorns in 2019. NWLS is not some sort of development program for the big show. In Portland, the Thorns are the show. The players know it, the fans know it, and the owners celebrate it.

Review Questions

1. Does a close financial relationship with an established team or league (i.e., the NHL and the NWHL) guarantee successful outcomes? Why or why not? Use a specific example from two of the three leagues considered in this chapter.

2. How would you test the validity of your response to question number one? What data would you need? Write out an empirical model with revenues as the dependent variable and as many relevant independent variables you can justify on the right-hand side. What signs do you expect on the estimated coefficients in this model? Why?

3. You are the new commissioner of National Pro Fastpitch. What three courses of action will you recommend to the league to increase attendance and drive revenue growth in the sport? Provide a paragraph of explanation for each recommendation.

References

Ayala, E. A. (2019a). *NWHL releases attendance numbers, hints at new initiatives in 2018-2019 in review.* https://ericalayala.com/2019/03/29/nwhl-releases-attendance-numbers-in-2018-19-season-in-review-kendall-coyne-schofield/

Ayala, E. (2019b, May 6). "We're not going to play": Will a player boycott save women's hockey … or harm it? *The Guardian.* www.theguardian.com/sport/2019/may/06/womens-hockey-boycott-north-america-nwhl-cwhl

Bachman, R. (2019, June 17). US. women's soccer games outearned men's games; the 2015 world cup title was a catalyst to boost women's game revenues, which in recent years exceeded the men's. *Wall Street Journal (Online).* https://search.proquest.com/docview/2241258000?accountid=14784

Becoats, K. (2020, June 8). Nike Signs Soccer Star Ada Hegerberg Away From Puma With 'Game Changer' Step Toward Equal Pay. *Forbes.* www.forbes.com/sites/kellenbecoats/2020/06/08/nike-signs-ada-hegerberg-lyon-equal-pay/

Canadian Women's Hockey League. (2019, July 2). *Final public communication.* www.thecwhl.com/

Caron, Emily (2021, May 27). *Women's Hockey League Branches Out As Private Owners Step In.* Sportico.com. https://www.sportico.com/leagues/hockey/2021/nwhl-womens-hockey-private-team-ownership-1234630711/

Central Ontario Women's Hockey League. (n.d). *History page.* http://www.cs.toronto.edu/~andria/cowhl/history.html

Clinton, J. (2019, November 22). *The NHL's stance hasn't changed and the NWHL isn't folding. Where does that leave the PWHPA?* The Hockey News. https://thehockeynews.com/news/article/the-nhls-stance-hasnt-changed-and-the-nwhl-isnt-folding-where-does-that-leave-the-pwhpa

Donnelly, P. (2019, June 9). North American women's ice hockey players struggle for a league of their own. *The Conversation.* http://theconversation.com/north-american-womens-ice-hockey-players-struggle-for-a-league-of-their-own-117581

ESPN News Services. (2019, March 8). *USWNT suing U.S. Soccer for discrimination*. ESPN.com. www.espn.com/espnw/sports/article/26189867/uswnt-suing-us-soccer-discrimination

FIFA.com. (2019, October 18). *FIFA Women's World Cup 2019 watched by more than 1 billion*. www.fifa.com/womensworldcup/news/fifa-women-s-world-cup-2019tm-watched-by-more-than-1-billion

Jay, M. (2019, September 3). *How the Canadian Women's Hockey League fell apart*. SBNation.com. www.sbnation.com/2019/9/3/20804377/cwhl-womens-hockey-league-history-collapse

Kelly, C. (2013, August 20). *The summer that changed women's soccer*. The New Yorker. www.newyorker.com/sports/sporting-scene/the-summer-that-changed-womens-soccer

MacLennan, L. (2020, May 30). *Female jockeys eligible for maternity leave in SA for first time*. www.abc.net.au/news/2020-05-31/female-jockeys-eligible-for-maternity-leave-in-south-australia/12296954

McCann, Michael. (2019, November 8). *Judge Favors USWNT in Class Certification Ruling, but U.S. Soccer Maintains Defenses in Equal Pay Case*. SI.com. https://www.si.com/soccer/2019/11/08/uswnt-class-certification-us-soccer-equal-pay-gender-discrimination

Moran, E. (2020, April 7). *World surf league turns to athletes for content efforts*. Front Office Sports. https://frntofficesport.com/world-surf-league-athletes/

Morgan et al., *Morgan v. U.S. Soccer Fed'n, Inc.*, 445 F. Supp. 3d 635 (C.D. Cal. 2020)

Townes, C. (2019, December 31). *A decade of fighting for equal pay in sports*. Forbes. www.forbes.com/sites/ceceliatownes/2020/12/31/a-decade-of-fighting-for-equal-pay/

Walters, J. (2016, April 1). A lawsuit from the US women's soccer team reveals deeper issues with gender equity in sports. *Newsweek*. www.newsweek.com/womens-soccer-suit-underscores-sports-gender-pay-gap-443137

CHAPTER 11
Business of the NBA and WNBA

David Berri and Stephen Engst
Pay Equity in the WNBA: *Jennifer Lee Hoffman*

LEARNING OBJECTIVES

- To learn about the growth process for the NBA league over the past half century.
- To learn about the league's management structure and the role of the commissioner.
- To learn about the exceptional relationship between the NBA's television revenue and owner's ability to meet the payroll cap.
- To gain insight into the tremendous impact the American Basketball Association had on player salaries, and the inception of the Oscar Robertson rule.
- To understand the long history of women's basketball in the United States, and the role that the NBA played in establishing and growing the WNBA.
- To compare the revenue streams and player salaries of both the NBA and WNBA.

The Basketball Association of America (BAA) was launched on November 1, 1946 when the New York Knicks and the Toronto Huskies took the court. We don't know how many people showed up to watch the all-white team from New York defeat the all-white team from Toronto by two points.[1] We do know that the average BAA team that first season attracted 3,142 fans per game.[2] We also know that when the BAA merged with the National Basketball League in 1949 to form the National Basketball Association (NBA), five of the original eleven BAA teams were not around. And only three teams—the Knicks, Boston Celtics, and Philadelphia Warriors[3]—still exist today.

Today, the NBA is a global presence and its players are international celebrities. People around the world know the names Michael Jordan, Kobe Bryant, LeBron James, Shaquille O'Neal, and Steph

---

1. Earl Lloyd became the first black player in the NBA history in October 1950 (History.com Editors, 2019). This means the BAA was an all-white league for its entire three-year existence.
2. "NBA/ABA Home Attendance Totals." www.apbr.org/attendance.html
3. The Philadelphia Warriors eventually became the Golden State Warriors.

Curry. Perhaps many also know that these players followed in the footsteps of such legends as Elgin Baylor, Oscar Robertson, Bill Russell, and Wilt Chamberlain. But when we look back at the league's attendance history, we know that those early legends often played in front of very few fans.[4] As Table 1 indicates, average attendance in the NBA did not reach 5,000 fans until the 1958–1959 season. And it was not until the late 1960s that average attendance in the NBA began to come close to the average attendance we have seen recently in the Women's National Basketball Association (WNBA).

To understand the current economics and finance of professional basketball in North America, we have to understand the history of these leagues. People tend to look at the popularity of the NBA today and think it was always like that. Likewise, people look at how the WNBA is less popular today than the NBA and conclude that tells us something about the consumer demand for women's sports in general. When we take a historical perspective, though, we see that demand for the NBA took decades to develop, and it is likely that the same story will apply to the WNBA.

All of this gets at a fundamental nature of demand for sports. It takes time for people to form an emotional connection to a sport, its teams, and its players. Often, this connection is inherited from a person's parents. This means it often takes generations for demand for a sport to develop.

Once we see that point, we see that the economic and financial conditions of a league depend on where the league is at in time. The economic and financial conditions of the NBA in its first few decades were different from the economic and financial conditions we see today. Likewise, the economic and financial conditions of the WNBA are also different from today's NBA (see Table 1).

---

4. "NBA/ABA Home Attendance Totals." www.apbr.org/attendance.html

TABLE 1: Attendance in the WNBA, and first years of NBA

Year of League	NBA Season	Per-game Average NBA Attendance	WNBA Season	Per-game Average WNBA Attendance
1	1946–1947	3,142	1997	9,661
2	1947–1948	4,049	1998	10,869
3	1948–1949		1999	10,205
4	1949–1950		2000	9,080
5	1950–1951	3,576	2001	9,110
6	1951–1952		2002	9,237
7	1952–1953	3,210	2003	8,826
8	1953–1954	3,583	2004	8,588
9	1954–1955	3,345	2005	8,171
10	1955–1956	4,498	2006	7,480
11	1956–1957	4,895	2007	7,740
12	1957–1958	4,824	2008	7,949
13	1958–1959	5,077	2009	8,039
14	1959–1960	5,008	2010	7,857
15	1960–1961	5,494	2011	7,955
16	1961–1962	4,566	2012	7,457
17	1962–1963	5,054	2013	7,531
18	1963–1964	5,266	2014	7,578
19	1964–1965	5,371	2015	7,318
20	1965–1966	6,019	2016	7,655
21	1966–1967	6,631	2017	7,716
22	1967–1968	6,749	2018	6,746
23	1968–1969	6,484	2019	6,528

Source: www.apbr.org/attendance.html

This chapter will review these differences. We will begin with a discussion of the NBA that will include a brief review of the history behind what we see today and then continue to a discussion of the league's revenues and salaries. We will then turn to a similar discussion of the WNBA.

A Brief History of the National Basketball Association

The Basketball Association of America was founded on June 6, 1946 (Schwartz, 2003). Thirteen teams were part of the league that June, but before the season started, the teams in Buffalo and

Indianapolis dropped out. The team with the best record that year was the Washington Capitals, coached by the legendary Red Auerbach. Despite this initial success, the Capitals, like seven other BAA[5] teams, was out of business five years later.

The outcome for the Capitals was the typical outcome for the early franchises in BAA and NBA history. From 1946 to 1949, 23 different franchises participated in the BAA and/or the NBA. Of these, though, 15 went out of business by the mid-1950s. In other words, the franchise failure rate in men's professional basketball was 65% during its first ten years.[6]

The NBA consisted of just eight franchises for the 1955–1956 season. All eight of these still exist today. But only two of these eight teams—the New York Knicks and Boston Celtics—still play in the same city today. Franchise movement has been a recurring theme in NBA history. Of the current 30 franchises, 14 are playing in a different location from where they started, and five of these franchises have played in three or more cities. The leader in the latter group is the Sacramento Kings, who have also played home games in Rochester, Cincinnati, Kansas City, and Omaha.

As we have noted, it took a long time for attendance to grow. But as Table 2 makes clear, in the last thirty years there has not been much change in average attendance. This is not because interest in the NBA has been stagnant. This issue is that basketball attendance has a clear ceiling. Because the court—relative to other sports surfaces (i.e., like soccer, baseball, and American football)—is relatively small, arena attendance can't get very large. Average per game attendance reached 17,000 for the first time in 1995–1996 and more than twenty years later the league still hasn't reached 18,000 in average attendance. In 2018–2019, 11 teams played before capacity home crowds every night and another seven teams averaged 95% of capacity or more. In sum, capacity constraints mean attendance can't grow much more (see Table 2).

TABLE 2: NBA League Revenue in Select Years: 1950 to 2019

Season	Average Attendance per game	Revenue in Nominal Terms (in millions of dollars)	Revenue in 2019 dollars (in millions of dollars)
1950–1951	3,576	$1.5	$14.8
1970–1971	7,648	$32.3	$199.9
1989–1990	15,690	$606.3	$1,162.0
1999–2000	16,870	$2,316.0	$3,369.1
2009–2010	17,150	$3,805.0	$4,370.3
2018–2019	17,830	$8,759.0	$8,759.0

Source: Table adapted from Rodney Fort's Sports Business Data Pages.

---

5. Five of these first eleven BAA teams folded in 1947. www.basketball-reference.com/teams/

6. This failure rate is just of franchises in the BAA and NBA. There is a very long list of failed professional men's basketball leagues in North America.

The same story, though, cannot be told about revenue. Prior to 1989–1990, revenue data is available sporadically. We do know from congressional testimony—reported at Rodney Fort's Sports Business Data Pages—that the NBA had $1.5 million in revenue in 1950–1951 (first year we have any data). In 2019 dollars, those dollars from 1950–1951 would be worth $14.8 million.[7] So—once again—the NBA began as a very tiny operation. By 1970–1971, per game attendance had more than doubled. The increase in revenue, though, went far beyond the increase we see in attendance. That season—again according to congressional testimony—revenue had grown substantially to nearly $200 million in 2019 dollars.

Unfortunately, data on revenue does not appear to be available for much of the next two decades. In 1989–1990, a publication called *Financial World* began publishing revenue data for sports leagues. According to that publication, in 1989–1990, NBA revenue was more than $600 million (or more than $1 billion in 2019 dollars).[8]

As noted, in the 1990s, the growth rate in attendance slowed considerably. But in 2019 dollars, NBA revenue more than tripled in the last decade of the 20th century. Although revenue grew across the next decade, the rate of increase in the first decade of the 21st century was less impressive. In the last 10 years, though, we once again see substantial growth in league revenue. In 2018–2019 NBA revenue—according to *Forbes*—approached $9 billion.

A big reason the NBA has grown is that its market has expanded tremendously. When the BAA began in 1946 the teams only employed white players and the teams were generally located in the East. The furthest to the west the league went was St. Louis, and except for Toronto, all of the teams were in the United States.

As Martinez (2015) notes, the NBA began the process of racial integration in 1950 when Earl Lloyd, Chuck Cooper, and Nathaniel Clifton began playing in the NBA (Lloyd was technically the first to play). There was only a handful of black NBA players in the early 1950s. But across the next three decades, the NBA changed dramatically with respect to race. By the late 1980s, 75% of the NBA was black (Lapchick et al., 2008).

The search for talent in the NBA went beyond racial integration. The search for talent in the NBA is increasingly on a global scale. As Figure 1 illustrates, the NBA had few international players in the 1960s and 1970s. Starting in the 1980s, though, the percentage of players born outside of the United States began to increase dramatically.

---

7. The Consumer Price Index reported by the Minneapolis Federal Reserve was used to calculate 2019 dollars. www.minneapolisfed.org/community/financial-and-economic-education/cpi-calculator-information/consumer-price-index-and-inflation-rates-1913
8. *Financial World* no longer exists. Its findings are reported at Rodney Fort's Sports Business Data Pages.

Based on opening night rosters for each NBA team this year, 108 players—or 24.5% of players in the league—come from a record-tying 42 countries outside of the United States. Cash and Gal (2018)

The search for talent across the globe mirrors the move to broadcast the NBA brand worldwide. Patrick Murray (2019) reported a few numbers highlighting the NBA's global reach:

- For the 2017–2018 season, NBA programming reached 1 billion unique viewers.
- More than 35% of those who visit NBA.com (the official website of the NBA) come from outside of North America.
- The top three markets for the NBA (outside the United States) are China, Australia, and Brazil.

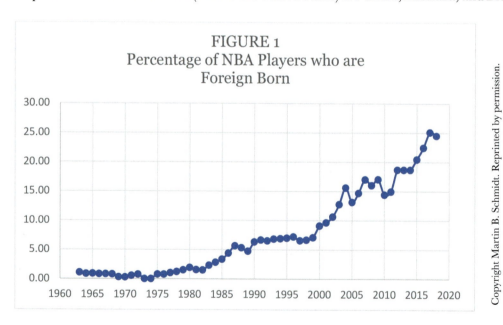

FIGURE 1
Percentage of NBA Players who are Foreign Born

Again, in the late 1940s, professional basketball in the BAA and NBA was an all-white affair primarily located in the Eastern United States. Few people paid much attention to the NBA in its early history and many of its teams struggled to survive. Seventy years later, the NBA is an international business with games broadcast around the world. Not only can you find NBA fans everywhere, the talent the NBA employs also comes from around the globe.

League Organization

Although the playing talent increasingly comes from around the globe, the leader of this organization— or the league commissioner—has consistently been the same race, gender, and nationality. Across the history of the NBA, only five white males (all Americans) have worked as the league commissioner.[9]

- Maurice Podoloff (1946 to 1963)
- Walter Kennedy (1963 to 1975)
- Lawrence O'Brien (1975 to 1984)
- David Stern (1984 to 2014)
- Adam Silver (2014 to the present)

Although the commissioner technically leads the league, it is important to remember the commissioner also answers to the league's owners. Ultimately, it is the league's owners who collectively own the league.

The NBA follows the norm in professional team sports. The thirty teams are organized in a league, which the teams jointly own. As Leeds and von Allmen (2010) explain, leagues serve several functions. As they note, in North America these include:

- Setting the rules of competition in the league's games;
- Limiting entry of teams to maintain league monopoly power[10];
- Marketing the league's games and products;
- Creating mechanisms to share revenue and limit salaries. These are generally created in the name of competitive balance.

All of these functions are managed by the commissioner. And once again, that person answers to the league owners.

League Revenues

The stability we see in the league commissioner officer likely reflects the consistent growth we have seen in the NBA across the last few decades. We have already noted that today the NBA's revenue

---

9. https://sportsecyclopedia.com/nba/comish/nbacomish.html/

10. It is a different story in European sports leagues, where the system of relegation means teams move up and down the league rankings. If this existed in the NBA, the top G-league teams (the NBA's minor league) would be promoted each year into the NBA, while the worst NBA teams would move to the G-league.

is approaching $9 billion per year. Although gate revenue is a significant part of this total, media revenues are also very important.

In 2014, the NBA signed a new television deal with ESPN and Turner Broadcasting (see Lewis, 2014, 2017). The deal—scheduled to start with the 2016–2017 season—called for the NBA to be paid $24 billion across nine seasons. That works out to $2.66 billion per year. As Table 3 makes clear, this was a 187% increase on the previous broadcasting deal.

TABLE 3: National Broadcasting Revenue from 1998 to 2025

Years	Media Partners	Annual Rights Fees (million)
1998 to 2002	NBC, Turner	$615
2002 to 2008	ESPN, Turner	$765
2008 to 2016	ESPN, Turner	$930
2016 to 2025	ESPN, Turner	$2.66

Source: Lewis (2014)

Obviously, it is television ratings—or more precisely, the expectation of ratings—that drives these deals. But all teams don't have the same impact on these ratings. Teams in larger markets, like the New York Knicks and Los Angeles Lakers, are far more likely to appear than teams from smaller markets (like the Indiana Pacers or Sacramento Kings). In addition, teams that employ such stars as LeBron James, Steph Curry, James Harden, and Kevin Durant are more likely to have games broadcasted.

Although teams do not have the same impact on ratings, they all receive the same share of these deals (Helin, 2012). As Table 3 indicates, from 2008 to 2016 the NBA's 30 teams split $930 million per season. That means each team received $31 million per year from the national broadcasting contract. Beginning with the 2016–2017 season, that per-team payout increased to $88.9 million.

As we will note momentarily, the NBA has a payroll cap (commonly called a "salary cap") that limits how much a team can spend on its players. In 2019–2020, that cap was $109.1 million (Goldberg, 2020). Given the size of the broadcasting deal, we can see that NBA teams can pay 81% of the value of the payroll cap before the team sells a single ticket.

Beyond ticket sales and national television deals, NBA teams also are able to exploit several other revenue streams. According to Leeds and von Allmen (2010) and Carr (2019), the list includes local broadcasting deals; merchandise sales; stadium revenues such as concessions, luxury box sales, and/or arena naming rights; and corporate sponsorships. To this list, Carr (2019) notes that the NBA is increasingly looking to earn revenue from streaming services, sports betting, and aggressive expansions into markets outside the United States.

In 2012 the NBA began a new revenue sharing plan. As Helin (2012) notes, the NBA requires each team to contribute approximately 50% of its local revenue[11] into a pool. Teams then receive in return the average team payroll in the league. This means a team that contributes more revenue than the average team payroll end up being a contributor to the league revenue sharing plan. Teams that contribute less local revenue than the average team payroll end up being a recipient.[12]

League Salaries

The NBA doesn't just share revenue among its teams. Revenue is also obviously shared with its players. Historically there has been some variation in the percentage of revenue that is given to players.

We have already noted that when the NBA began it didn't attract particularly big crowds. The NBA also didn't have the national media contracts we see today to supplement its lack of gate revenue. Consequently, as Table 4 indicates, league revenues were quite low.

In 1957, the NBA reported to Congress its total income and payroll for each season from 1951–1952 to 1956–1957. This report gives us a clear picture of the financial health of the NBA in its early years. As one can see, total league income at this time was less than $2 million and the average player made less than $10,000 per year (see Table 4).

TABLE 4: Income and Payroll in the NBA from 1951 to 1957

Season	Total Income	Total Payroll	Number of Players	Average Salary	Percentage Paid to Players
1951–1952	$1,533,457	$530,475	116	$4,573	34.6%
1952–1953	$1,648,544	$650,614	124	$5,247	39.5%
1953–1954	$1,559,567	$682,592	110	$6,205	43.8%
1954–1955	$1,578,064	$733,332	105	$6,984	46.5%
1955–1956	$1,798,884	$745,728	92	$8,106	41.5%
1956–1957	$1,776,181	$768,972	99	$7,767	43.3%

Source: Rodney Fort's Sports Business Data Pages. Originally taken from the Committee on the Judiciary. House of Representatives. Organized Professional Team Sports. 85th Cong. 1st sess. Part 3. 1957. P. 2928.

Of course, these dollar figures are from 1950. According to the Minnesota Federal Reserve, prices have risen nearly 10 times since this decade. But even when we convert the dollar figures in Table 4

---

11. As Helin (2012) notes, local revenue includes ticket sales, concessions and parking revenue at arenas, and local broadcasting deals.
12. Consider this example from Helin (2012): imagine average team payroll is $58 million. If a team contributes $70 million to the revenue sharing pool, they will end up making a $12 million payment (i.e., $70 million minus $58 million). If a team contributes just $45 million, then when the $58 million payment is made they come out $13 million ahead.

into 2019 dollars (as is done in Table 5), it is still clear that the NBA was a very small business in the first years of its existence. In 2019 dollars, total revenues in the NBA in the first years of its existence were less than $20 million and average salaries were less than $100,000 (see Table 5).

TABLE 5: Income and Payroll in the NBA in 2019 Dollars from 1951 to 1957

Season	Total Income	Total Payroll	Average Salary
1951–1952	$15,080,960	$5,217,021	$44,974
1952–1953	$15,847,094	$6,254,211	$50,437
1953–1954	$14,879,899	$6,512,641	$59,206
1954–1955	$15,000,408	$6,970,743	$66,388
1955–1956	$17,163,233	$7,115,024	$77,337
1956–1957	$16,697,407	$7,228,902	$73,019

We can also see across this time period how much revenue was going to player payroll. In 1951–1952, only about 35% of league revenue went to players. But that percentage jumped to nearly 40% the next year and remained above 40% the remaining years in the sample. When we turn to the WNBA, we will revisit these numbers.

Unfortunately, the NBA didn't keep reporting its data to Congress (or anyone else). But we do have some idea that player salaries took a significant jump in the late 1960s. Consider the following salary information for John Havlicek published in *The New York Times* (Montgomery, 1976) (see Table 6).

TABLE 6: John Havlicek's Salary from 1967 to 1976

Season	Salary
1966–1967	$32,000
1967–1968	$50,000
1968–1969	$55,000
1969–1970	$140,000
1970–1971	$140,000
1971–1972	$140,000
1972–1973	$250,000
1973–1974	$250,000
1974–1975	$250,000
1975–1976	$250,000

The 1968–1969 season was Havlicek's seventh year in the NBA. Across those 7 years, Havlicek had been to four All-Star games and played on six teams that won an NBA championship. Despite that resume, his pay in 1968–1969 was only $5,000 more than what it had been the previous season.

And then suddenly, his pay more than doubled. What caused that to happen?

In 1967, the American Basketball Association began playing and suddenly the NBA faced competition for talent. Rick Barry was an NBA All-Star in 1967 with the San Francisco Warriors. For the 1968–1969 season, though, he was an ABA All-Star with the Oakland Oaks. To encourage him to make the jump, the Oaks gave Rick Barry a contract that paid him $75,000 per season and also gave him 15% ownership stake in his new ABA team (DeFord, 1967). As *The Washington Post* reported in 1977, prior to Barry's move, NBA stars like Bill Russell and Wilt Chamberlain were paid $100,000 a year. After Barry made his move and set off a salary war, even "fringe players" were getting Chamberlain money (Attner, 1977).

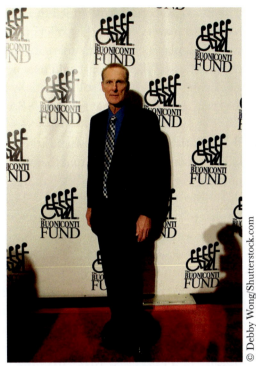

© Debby Wong/Shutterstock.com

Montgomery (1976) reports in 1976 that in 1974–1975 the New York Nets of the ABA had gross receipts of $2,326,925 (more than $2 million of that was gate receipts) and a team payroll of $1,350,000. This means the Nets were paying 58% of their revenue to their players. This is essentially the percentage of revenue the NBA claimed it was paying its players for the 1982–1983. In 1983, David DuPree reported in *The Washington Post* the NBA was paying 59% of its revenue to its players.

This may seem odd. The ABA ceased playing in 1976. However, to merge the two leagues, the NBA had to institute what was known as the Oscar Robertson rule.[13] Prior to this rule, the NBA operated under what was known as the "reserve rule". This clause was first instituted in Major League Baseball. The clause gave a team the right to re-sign a player after the player's contract expired. Because the new contract the team gave the player also had the clause, theoretically the team could just keep doing this for as long as they liked. Hence, the reserve clause bound a player to a team for as long as a team wanted the player.[14]

---

13. www.oscarrobertson.com/oscar-robertson-rule

14. As detailed in Berri (2018b), the reserve clause was ended in baseball by the Messersmith-McNally arbitration case. In baseball the reserve clause specifically said a team could re-sign a player for one year. Baseball had always interpreted that to mean the team could just keep re-signing the player since each one-year contract still had the clause. The arbitrator in this case—Peter Seitz—ruled that one year really just meant one year. This ended baseball's reserve clause.

The Oscar Robertson rule ended this clause for NBA players in 1976. Prior to 1976, professional basketball players could solicit offers from the ABA and NBA. With the ABA gone, professional basketball players in North America could only negotiate with the NBA teams. By removing the reserve clause, NBA players could now negotiate with more than one team. Hence—even with the ABA gone—NBA players still potentially faced a labor market with more than one entity bidding for their services. And that gave the NBA players much more bargaining power.

By 1983, though, the NBA owners argued players had too much power. Once again, David DuPree (1983) reported at this time that the NBA was paying 59% of its revenue to the players, and consequently—according to the NBA—many teams were losing money.[15] It is important to emphasize the phrase "according to the NBA." The NBA's teams are privately owned and do not produce reports of revenues and costs to shareholders. This means that it is not possible for us to know if they are losing money or not. All we have are their claims. This point is going to be important as we tell the story of the NBA's salary institutions and then again when we move on to the WNBA.

Although no one independent of the NBA can confirm the league was in financial trouble in 1983, the NBA's argument that the league was in trouble led to the creation of a payroll cap; or what became known as a salary cap (we will note in a moment that "payroll cap" is a more helpful description). This was not the first time the NBA had employed such a cap. As Robert Bradley (n.d.) noted, in 1946–1947 the league capped team payrolls at $55,000. Of course, this was the first season of league existence. The 1983 cap was the first payroll cap for a more mature league. This cap guaranteed that pay for players would be between 53% and 57%. In sum, the payroll cap reduced the pay of the NBA's players.

It is important to note that the NBA's payroll cap is a "soft" cap. This means it is possible for a team to exceed the cap. For example, there is an exemption known technically as the "Qualifying Veteran Free Agent Exemption," but more commonly as the "Larry Bird Exemption" (Cronin, 2010). In 1983, Larry Bird's contract was expiring and the Boston Celtics wished to re-sign him. The impending salary cap, though, might have restricted the offer the Celtics could make to keep their star. Thus, an exemption was put in the payroll cap that allowed a team to re-sign a veteran player on their roster for an amount that would put place the team's payroll above the payroll cap.[16]

One should see this exemption as keeping in the intended spirit of the payroll cap. The NBA argued a cap on payrolls was necessary because—again, according to the NBA—the league was in financial trouble. There was, though, another argument. The league argued that a cap on payrolls was necessary to promote competitive balance in the league. The story is simple enough

---

15. At this point, the NBA was in its 37th season and average NBA attendance was only 10,202 fans per game. "NBA/ABA Home Attendance Totals." http://www.apbr.org/attendance.html

16. As Cronin (2010) notes, this exemption was not applied to Larry Bird in 1983. Thus, the popular name is inaccurate.

to follow. There are large market teams (i.e., teams in New York and Los Angeles) and teams in small markets (i.e., teams in San Antonio and Detroit). The argument is that if teams can spend whatever they like on talent, the large markets—who have much larger revenues—will employ all the top talents. Consequently, large market teams will win all the time and the small market teams will both lose on the court and eventually financially. A cap on payrolls prevents this from happening.

There is a vast amount of research on competitive balance and sports. As summarized in Berri (2018b), there simply isn't much of a link between market size and team success in sports. Yes, the New York Yankees have generally been successful. But other big market teams—like the New York Knicks and Los Angeles Clippers—have been persistent losers. Since the Knicks last won a title in 1973, teams in smaller markets—like the Portland Trail Blazers, Seattle Supersonics, San Antonio Spurs, Detroit Pistons, and Cleveland Cavaliers—have all won titles. Furthermore, as Berri (2018) notes,[17] salary controls are not linked to changes in competitive balance. In sum, restricting player salary just transfers money from the players to the owners. It doesn't appear to make the league more competitive.

Prior to the payroll cap in 1983, the Boston Celtics and Los Angeles Lakers had won the title in 1980, 1981, and 1982. After the cap was instituted, those teams combined to win the next five titles. Thus, as the more extensive study of competitive balance indicated, the payroll cap didn't appear to change the balance of power in the NBA. Nevertheless, the NBA didn't stop trying to cap salaries.

© lev radin/Shutterstock.com

In 1995, the NBA imposed a cap on the pay of rookies. The impetus for the rookie cap is believed to be the contract negotiations for Glenn Robinson, the first overall pick in the 1994 draft. It was believed Robinson was holding out for a $100 million contract. In the end he settled for $67.5 million over 10 years (Rowe, 2016). To put that in perspective, Michael Jordan was only paid $3.85

17. As Berri (2018b) notes, competitive balance is primarily about the underlying population of talent the league employs. Consider the history of baseball. In the early years of the 20th century, competitive balance in baseball was quite poor. This is because the league only employed white males from the United States. After the league integrated in 1947 and the search for talent became global, baseball became more competitive. The supply of truly talented stars increased and consequently more and more teams could field competitive rosters. This same story explains why the NBA has never been very balanced. Even with a global search, there is a short supply of tall people in the world. And finding seven-footers who are also athletic … well, that is very difficult!

million for the 1995–1996 season.[18] That means Robinson, a player who had never played in the NBA, was being paid more than the best player in the game.[19] The rookie cap very much worked to stop deals like the contract given to Robinson. In 2017–2018, the salary of the first pick in the NBA draft was $5,855,200. Thus, more than twenty years after Glenn Robinson signed his rookie deal, the top pick in the NBA draft was still receiving a nominal salary below the average salary Robinson received across his rookie contract.[20]

Despite the payroll cap and the rookie cap, the NBA still claimed it had problems. According to the NBA, in 1997–1998 player pay was once again more than 57% of league revenue (Staudohar, 1999). And once again, the NBA argued that teams were losing money and the solution was yet another cap!

Veteran NBA players did not seem to object much to a rookie salary cap. In 1999, though, the NBA proposed something that would impact the pay of veterans. It is believed this was motivated by the six-year contract Kevin Garnett signed in 1997 that was valued at more than $120 million (Smith, 1997). After this contract, the NBA owners decided the league needed a cap on the pay of individual veterans.

This was not easy to impose. For the first time in NBA history, the NBA lost games due to a labor dispute. But after a lengthy lockout, the NBA and its players agreed to a cap on individual salaries. As Paul Staudohar (1999) reported, "For players with up to 5 years of service, the maximum salary will be $9 million. The figure is $11 million for players with 6 to 9 years of service and $14 million for 10-year veterans and up."

Staudohar (1999) also noted that although a soft cap existed for each team, the cap for the entire league would now be a hard cap. This was accomplished via an escrow tax. If player pay exceeded the agreed-upon threshold of league revenues, all players would be taxed to restore the cap. For example, in years 4 through 6 of the agreement, players were to be paid 55% of league revenue. If the pay went beyond that threshold a tax would be imposed to bring salaries back to 55% of league revenue.

The 1999 collective bargaining agreement also included one last method to limit player salaries. As Berri (2018b) explains, because the soft cap was not limiting team spending enough, the NBA began imposing a luxury tax on spending. A luxury tax imposes a penalty on a team whenever its payroll exceeds a certain threshold.

---

18. www.basketball-reference.com/players/j/jordami01.html

19. Robinson's career only lasted 11 seasons. In his last season, he only played nine games. In essence, he barely played beyond this rookie contract. www.basketball-reference.com/players/r/robingl01.html

20. See Larry Coon (http://www.cbafaq.com/scale17.htm). In 2019-20, the first-year pay for the first pick in the draft had surpassed $8 million. So today it is finally the case that the first pick in the NBA can do better,—in nominal terms, than the first pick in the 1994 draft. But adjusted for inflation, and the massive increase in league revenues, rookies are paid quite a bit less than Robinson.

From 1999 to 2012 this luxury tax did result in a few high payroll teams paying a penalty. Larry Coon reports[21] that no team paid a luxury tax penalty until 2003. In 2003, though, thirteen teams combined to pay $169.2 million in luxury taxes. The next season, ten teams combined to pay $154.1 million. But after that, the penalties declined. From 2005 to 2011, the average luxury taxes paid by all teams in a given year was $70.1 million. That suggests teams were doing a good job of controlling their spending on talent.

Despite the luxury tax, the NBA argued in 2011—as it argued back in 1983—that spending on players was out of control and the NBA was definitely losing money. This argument was met with skepticism by Berri (2011) at HuffPost (formerly The Huffington Post) and by Nate Silver (2011) at *The New York Times*. At this time, the NBA claimed that it had been losing money every year since a collective bargaining agreement in 2005 was signed. But in a league where player salaries were already collectively fixed and revenues often quite easy to forecast, that claim seemed hard to believe. Given that the 2005 agreement was reached without any sort of labor dispute, it was hard to believe that the NBA agreed to something that would instantly result in significant losses for the teams.

Nevertheless, after a lockout the NBA players agreed to a salary cut. The NBA players' share of revenue fell from 57% to 50%. The NBA also imposed a very punitive luxury tax with the 2013–2014 season.

Perhaps nothing illustrates this better than the luxury tax the Brooklyn Nets paid in 2013–2014. The threshold for that season was $71.7 million. The Nets payroll that year—before any taxes were imposed—was $101.3 million. For exceeding the luxury tax threshold by a bit less than $40 million, the Nets were charged a tax of $83.3 million![22] Yes, the Nets—by themselves—paid more in luxury taxes than the league average from 2005 to 2011.

With player salaries reduced, caps on rookie and veteran pay, and a strong luxury tax it appeared player compensation was very much under control. In addition, as noted earlier, the NBA landed a major broadcasting deal in 2016 that substantially increased league revenues. Therefore, the NBA had to be profitable. Right?

Well, according to the NBA in 2017 it was still the case that "nearly half" the NBA teams were still losing money (Windhorst & Lowe, 2017). Once again, no one has seen the financial record that clearly established this claim. The NBA simply told ESPN that many of its teams—despite substantial controls on player salaries and a significant increase in revenues—were still losing money.

---

21. Coon, Larry (http://cbafaq.com/blog/?p=117)
22. As Berri (2018b) states, the luxury tax that season increased for each $5 million a team exceeded the threshold. For the first $5 million a team paid $1.50 for each $1 over the threshold. That payment than increased to $1.75, $2.50, $3.25, $3.75, and $4.25.

Again, there is some reason to be skeptical of the NBA's claims. One should note, though, that if NBA teams were all clearly making a profit that a clear rationale for that menu of salary controls would be weakened. In other words, the NBA has a clear incentive to claim that profits are scarce. This claim helps their bargaining position with its players.

© Elliott Cowand Jr/Shutterstock.com

That bargaining power was exhibiting during the Covid pandemic of 2020. The pandemic led the NBA to stop playing in March of 2020 before the season was completed. When the league finally did return, the regular season was very much cut short. In fact, teams that were not in playoff contention were not even allowed to return.

What the NBA did bring back was the playoffs. This is significant because player salaries are paid for the regular season. There is a playoff pool that compensates the teams in the playoffs, but it is quite small compared to pay of NBA players. As Reynolds (2020) reports, for 2020 the entire playoff pool was $23.2 million. This was split across all teams. The Milwaukee Bucks finished with the best regular season record, so they were granted $1.6 million of this pool for having the top won-loss mark. Had the Bucks gone on to win the title (they did not), that share would have risen to $6.8 million.

It is important to note, that playoff share is not just split by the players. At least, it doesn't have to be. Teams can also share this money with other members of the organization (Kleps, 2018). Thus, the amount the Bucks players could have theoretically split could have been less than $6.8 million. When we consider the fact that six different players on the Bucks were paid more than $6.8 million for the 2019–2020 season. we can see how truly small the playoff pool is for the players.[23]

This means the players essentially came back in a pandemic to make sure a competition would happen that didn't necessarily make many of the players much richer. It did, though, help the owners who needed to have the playoffs happen to justify their television deal. Again, it appears NBA owners have substantial bargaining power with respect to the players. Thus, perhaps it is not surprising to see how the pandemic played out in 2020 for the NBA.

23. www.basketball-reference.com/teams/MIL/2020.html

League Growth Potential

Basketball was only invented in 1891. Less than sixty years later, the NBA began as a very small sports league in North America. As stated before, initially the league struggled financially. In 1951, Lou Pieri purchased the Boston Celtics for just $50,000, or about $480,000 in today's dollars. In 1965, the Celtics sold for $3 million, or about $24 million in today's dollars.[24] Today, *Forbes* argues that very same franchise is worth $3 billion.[25]

The Boston Celtics have been to the playoffs 57 times in its history and won 17 NBA titles (more than any franchise in the league). In contrast, the Los Angeles Clippers have only been to the playoffs 15 times in its history and have never even appeared in a conference final. Thus, it was somewhat surprising that Steve Ballmer was willing to pay $2 billion for the Clippers in 2014. At the time of the sale, though, Ballmer made it clear he thought this investment was justified (Schwartz, 2014).

> Lots of people run lots of numbers. I feel like I paid a price I'm excited about. It obviously was a price that was negotiated and I feel very good about it. It's not a cheap price, but when you're used to looking at tech companies with huge risk, no earnings and huge multiples, this doesn't look like the craziest thing I've ever acquired …. And compared to some of the public traded companies, there are great companies out there like Amazon with absolutely no earnings and huge market caps and lots of risk. There's much less risk. **There's real earnings in this business. There's real upside opportunity.**

Yes, the NBA insists that making a profit in this sport is difficult. The people buying the franchises, though, seem to be disagreeing. And there is reason to think the owners like Ballmer are right.

Today, basketball is the second most popular sport in the world.[26] And the NBA—who played a huge role in expanding the popularity of the sport—is an international entity.

Once again, the NBA has a growing fan base around the world. As noted earlier, more than one-third of people who visit NBA.com come from outside the United States. Clearly there is a growing fanbase for the league internationally. And the NBA continues to work to increase the number of global fans. In 2019 the NBA announced a new 12-team basketball league in Africa (Karimi, 2019).

Given what we have seen in recent years, the growth potential for the NBA appears impressive. The NBA is not only securing talent from around the world. The NBA is also marketing to fans across the world. As the NBA expands into more and more markets, its revenues—and yes, profits—will continue to grow. The NBA may never admit it is profitable. But we can expect the people buying the franchises to continue to behave as if those profits really exist!

24. Rodney Fort's Sports Business Data Pages
25. www.forbes.com/nba-valuations/list/#tab:overall
26. "25 World's Most Popular Sports (ranked by 13 factors)," Total Sportek. www.totalsportek.com/most-popular-sports/

A Brief History of the Women's National Basketball Association

The story of James Naismith inventing basketball at Springfield College in 1891 has been frequently told. The story of how women began playing basketball at Smith College (just 25 miles from Springfield) in 1892 is perhaps told a bit less frequently. The person responsible for first bringing this game to women was Senda Berenson (Jenkins, 1997). And because of Berenson, women have been playing basketball nearly as long as men.

Of course, women have not quite had the same support. As Lewis (2020) reports, in 1908, the American Athletic Union (AAU) argued women shouldn't play in public. In 1914, the American Olympic Committee said women shouldn't play at the Olympics. And in the 1920s, the Women's Division of the National Amateur Athletic Federation said women shouldn't play basketball anywhere.

Nevertheless, women persisted. Women continued to play basketball despite a lack of organizational support. But with the passage of Title IX in 1972, women's basketball became far more common in high school and colleges in the United States. And in 1976, women's basketball was finally added as a sport at the Olympics (Lewis, 2020).

After the 1976 Olympics, a number of professional basketball leagues for women were founded and failed. As Lewis (2020) reports, the list includes the Women's Basketball League (founded 1978, last game in 1981), the Ladies Professional Basketball Association (founded and failed in 1980), Women's American Basketball Association (founded and failed in 1984), National Women's Basketball Association (founded and failed in 1986), Liberty Basketball Association (founded and failed in 1991), and Women's Basketball Association (founded in 1993 and failed in 1995).

By 1995, women had seen at least six different professional leagues start and fail in the United States in less than twenty years. As Becker (1990) reported, opportunities to play professionally did exist in Europe and Asia. But women had no professional leagues in the United States.

That would soon change. The same year the Women's Basketball Association failed the American Basketball League (ABL) was formed. The next season the ABL began playing games and then the Women's National Basketball Association (WNBA) was formed. Both of these leagues were well-financed and had hopes of being a league that would outlast their many short-lived predecessors. As Agha and Berri (2020) report, unfortunately the ABL—despite sponsorships from companies like Nike—did not have the resources to compete with the WNBA. Consequently, by 1998 the ABL also folded.

The WNBA, though, persisted. Credit for the WNBA is often given to NBA commissioner David Stern. Val Ackerman, the WNBA's first commissioner, had this to say when David Stern retired as NBA commissioner in 2014 (Voepel, 2020a):

Without his vision and engagement, the league wouldn't have gotten off the ground. He was the mastermind, and the WNBA was really in line with his vision about how sports and society are intertwined.

As Mechelle Voepel (2020a) noted, Stern observed the WNBA would face headwinds that the NBA never saw. A league built around black women would face issues of sexism, racism and homophobia. None of this deterred Stern from getting the WNBA launched. As Ackerman observed (Mullen, 2020),

He was our biggest champion. Nobody pushed him around. WNBA critics were sort of top of list of people he fought off at every turn. He was our biggest defender.

Stern was very much correct. The WNBA is a league where obviously the players are women. In addition, the majority of these players are black. And unlike what we see in men's sports, the players who are homosexual in the WNBA are often quite open about this. Consequently, as Stern noted, this league does face sexism, racism, and homophobia.

Despite these issues, it has continued far longer than any of the other North American professional leagues in women's basketball. One key factor behind the WNBA's relative success is Stern's plan to connect the WNBA and NBA. Stern's initial plan was to have each franchise in the WNBA linked to a corresponding NBA. Those first sixteen franchises—and their corresponding NBA team in parenthesis—are listed below with the year they were added:[27]

The 1997 teams (first season in league history)
- Charlotte Sting (Hornets)
- Cleveland Rockers (Cavaliers)
- Houston Comets (Rockets)
- Los Angeles Sparks (Lakers)
- New York Liberty (Knicks)
- Phoenix Mercury (Sun)
- Sacramento Monarchs (Kings)
- Utah Starzz (Jazz)

The 1998 expansion teams
- Detroit Shock (Pistons)
- Washington Mystics (Wizards)

---

27. https://www.topendsports.com/world/lists/popular-sport/totalsportek.htm

The 1999 expansion teams
- Orlando Miracle (Magic)
- Minnesota Lynx (Timberwolves)

The 2000 expansion teams
- Miami Sol (Heat)
- Portland Fire (Trail Blazers)
- Seattle Storm (Super Sonics)
- Indiana Fever (Pacers)

As one can see, from 1997 to 2000 the WNBA doubled in size. As we noted in the early history of the BAA/NBA, of the 23 franchises started in the early history of these leagues, fifteen completely failed. The WNBA's failure rate was not quite that bad. Of these first sixteen franchises, six teams failed (Charlotte, Cleveland, Houston, Sacramento, Miami, and Portland).[28] Thus, the failure rate was just 37.5%. Of course, the NBA was backing the WNBA. Consequently, one should expect the failure rate to be lower.

In 2002, that model changed and outside ownership was allowed (Voepel, 2016). Today, only six WNBA teams are owned by people who also own an NBA team.[29] Thus, the WNBA has moved away from a model where the NBA fully owns each and every franchise. That said—as we note in the case study to this chapter—the NBA is still very much involved in this league. Yes, as the case study to this chapter makes clear, the league organization of the WNBA is … unique!

League Revenues

Previously we noted that the NBA's revenue, in 2019 dollars, was less than $20 million in the first few years of its existence. By 1970–1971, when the league was 25 years old, revenue had grown to nearly $200 million in 2019 dollars.

Both sets of numbers come from Congressional testimony. Unfortunately, the WNBA has not been asked to report its revenues to Congress. And national publications like *Forbes* have not formally

28. Three other franchises—Utah, Detroit, and Orlando—eventually moved someplace else but still exist today.
29. The six franchises owned by NBA owners are as follows (NBA team noted): New York Liberty (Brooklyn Nets), Washington Mystics (Washington Wizards), Indiana Fever (Indian Pacers), Minnesota Lynx (Minnesota Timberwolves), Phoenix Mercury (Phoenix Suns), Los Angeles Sparks (Los Angeles Lakers).

tried to tabulate revenues and franchise values for each WNBA team. This means our knowledge of league revenue—relative to the NBA—is more limited. That said, we do know something.

In 2018, two pieces of information were reported regarding WNBA revenue (Berri, 2018a). In 2016 it was reported that ESPN pays $25 million per year for the right to broadcast WNBA games (Ourand, 2016). This deal runs through the 2022 season. In addition, in 2018, the average team, as noted earlier, attracted 6,712 fans per game. Given the minimum ticket prices for each team, minimum gate revenue was $24.4 million (Berri, 2018a).

Given the ESPN television deal and minimum gate revenue, WNBA revenue was at least $49.4 million in 2018. There are, though, other revenue sources. For example, the WNBA League Pass allows one to see broadcasts of games throughout the league. Subscriptions were priced at $16.99 in 2016 (Perez, 2016) and that hasn't changed. Unfortunately, although it was reported that subscriptions rose 40% from 2017 to 2018 (Philippou, 2018), we don't know what the number of subscriptions was in either year, and thus we don't know how much the league earns from League Pass.

The WNBA and its teams also earn revenue from merchandise sales, local television and radio deals, and websites like FanDuel and Tidal. In addition, games are also broadcast on Twitter and in 2019 CBS Sports signed an agreement—for an undisclosed sum—to start broadcasting games on its cable sports channel.

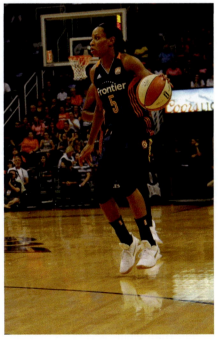

And then there are corporate sponsorships. The Connecticut Sun reported[30] that the team earned 40% of its revenues just from corporate sponsorships. If this were true for all teams and all teams only earned revenue from ESPN and the minimum figure reported for gate revenue, the league revenue would be $82.3 million.

Unfortunately, we don't know that what the Sun reports is true for all teams. In fact, we are clearly lacking specifics with respect to much of what the WNBA earns in revenue. It was reported in 2018 that a league source indicated a conservative estimate of league revenue was $60 million or $5 million per team (Berri, 2018a). Again, that is conservative and, in the case of the Sun, clearly would give us a team figure that is far too low.

© Keeton Gale/Shutterstock.com

---

30. Front Office Sports. (2018). "WNBA Teams Find Success Through Creative Partnerships." https://frontofficesports.com/wnba-creative-partnerships/

League Salaries

Let's take the $60 million revenue figure as given. How much of that is going to the players? It was reported in 2018 that average salary in the WNBA was $77,878. Given the number of players, total payroll in the league was $12.3 million. That works out to 20.3% of league revenue (Berri, 2018a). This is a far smaller percentage than anything we saw in NBA history. In sum, there is a substantial gender-pay gap between the NBA and WNBA.

When the gender-pay gap was noted in *Forbes* in 2017 (Berri, 2017), several players responded. For example, Kelsey Plum—the first player chosen in the 2017 draft—offered this thought:

> I'm tired people thinking that us players are asking for the same type of money as NBA players. We are asking for the same percentage of revenue shared within our CBA. NBA players receive around 50% of shared revenue within their league, whereas we receive around 20 percent
>
> Ellentuck (2018)

Skylar Diggins-Smith—a WNBA All-Star—also noted the clear difference between the WNBA and NBA.

© Keeton Gale/Shutterstock.com

> Players in the NBA get about 50% of the revenue. For women, the percentage is in the twenties. So before we even talk about base salary or anything like that, we don't even get paid the same percentage of the revenue that we bring in, which is kind of unbelievable. People try to hijack this issue and say that women's basketball may not be as interesting a game, because they disparage women in sports, period. But we don't even make the same percentage of revenue!
>
> Wealthsimple (2018)

The lack of pay in the WNBA has led many players to play international basketball. According to Agha and Berri (2020), 48% of the WNBA's players played in basketball leagues in Europe and Asia in 2019. These same authors note that pay in leagues outside the WNBA is often much higher than what players are paid in the United States.

The case of Diana Taurasi famously illustrates this issue. According to Prada (2015), UMMC Ekaterinburg agreed to pay Taurasi's 2015 WNBA salary if she agreed to skip the 2015 WNBA season. This pay was on top of the $1.5 million UMMC Ekaterinburg was already paying Taurasi. Taurasi is not the only player to be paid substantially better outside the WNBA. It was reported by Gaines (2014) that Brittney Griner, Maya Moore, and Sylvia Fowles were all paid $600,000 to play the 2014 season in the Women's Chinese Basketball Association.

Salary is capped in the WNBA and the top salary in 2019 was less than $120,000. As Agha and Berri (2020) note, it is not uncommon for even non-stars to be paid better than this in Asia or Europe. Consequently, as Candace Parker has noted, the primary job for WNBA players is their work in other nations. The WNBA is just their summer job.[31]

After the 2019 season, the WNBA and its players came to a new collective bargaining agreement. As Berri (2020) reported, this new agreement is supposed to increase average wages to $130,000. Yes, that is an increase in pay. But as Berri (2020) notes, it appears WNBA players are still being paid less than their NBA counterparts.

> Let's say that the WNBA again employs 156 players next year. If average salaries are $130,000, then the players will be paid $20,280,000. If revenues were only about $40 million, that would give the players about 50% of revenue. But again, a conservative estimate of WNBA revenue places that figure at about $60 million. And that means that if average salaries are $130,000, the WNBA is only paying about 34% of its revenue to its players.

As previously noted, the NBA gives 50% of its revenue to its players. Thus, again, a gender-wage gap persists. If revenues are $60 million, average salary in a league with 156 players must be $192, 308 for the players to receive 50% of salaries. But as Table 7 indicates, only the players earning the "Supermax" in the WNBA would get at least that amount. In fact, it is not until 2022 that the "Regular Max" surpasses what average pay has to be for the WNBA players to share in 50% of the league's revenue (see Table 7).

TABLE 7: Regular and Super Maximum Salaries in the WNBA

Year	Regular Max	Supermax
2020	$185,000	$215,000
2021	$190,550	$221,450
2022	$196,267	$228,094
2023	$202,154	$234,936
2024	$208,219	$241,984
2025	$214,466	$249,244
2026	$220,900	$256,721
2027	$227,527	$264,423

Source: Mox (2020).

---

31. TooFab Staff. (2020, February 3). Candace Parker tells Steve Harvey WNBA players make '10-20 times more' overseas. TooFab. https://toofab.com/2020/02/03/candace-parker-steve-harvey-wnba-pay-gap/

Once again, all of that is based on a very conservative estimate of league revenue. If league revenue is more than $60 million, then the gender-wage gap looks even worse. In addition, it appears this new agreement will not stop players from playing outside the WNBA.

In 2019, Breanna Stewart—the Most Valuable Player of the 2018 WNBA season—was hurt while playing for Dynamo Kursk in Russia. Stewart's injury caused her to miss the entire 2019 WNBA season (Voepel, 2020b). Despite this injury, in February of 2020 Stewart again signed to play in Russia. As Stewart noted (Voepel, 2020b),

> For me, it's something that makes sense financially. Playing EuroLeague is a very high level. And my window is short. Maybe when I'm 30, I won't want to [play overseas]. But right now I want to play as much as I can.

Stewart's comment indicates the new collective bargaining agreement in the WNBA is not going to stop the league's assets from risking significant injury in other leagues. In sum, the persistent gender-wage gap in the WNBA imposes significant costs on the league.

League Growth Potential

NBA Commissioner Adam Silver was asked in 2015 about where the WNBA was after 19 seasons. Silver's response indicated he wasn't entirely pleased with the WNBA's progress. As Silvers said, he thought the league would be "further along" (Mensheha, 2015). This seems an odd response given the relative attendance of the NBA and WNBA. After 19 seasons, as Table 1 indicates, the NBA was only drawing 5,371 fans per game. WNBA average attendance at this point was nearly 2,000 more fans per contest.

From just the perspective of average attendance, it appeared the WNBA was doing quite well in 2015. The league's success is even more remarkable when we consider the many factors working against the league, even in addition to the sexism, racism, and homophobia noted by David Stern. Beyond those issues, the WNBA—like all women's sports—is simply not as likely to be covered by the male-dominated sports media. As Cooky et al. (2015) noted, women's sports receive less than 5% of the coverage in the sports media. This result is not surprising given that these same authors note that men comprise about 90% of the sports media.

The lack of sports media coverage is not the only issue facing the WNBA. Consider for a moment Major League Soccer (MLS). This league was formed in 1996. Hence it is about the same age as the WNBA. However, whereas the WNBA is the elite professional league in women's basketball, the MLS is very much a minor soccer league in the world (Berri, 2018c). Despite the minor league status of the MLS, Baade and Matheson (2012) report that this league has received more than

$800 million in public subsidies. In addition, it was reported in 2019 that the expansion fee for a new MLS team in Charlotte was $325 million (Negley, 2019). If the WNBA received the same level of both public and private investment, the gender-wage gap would certainly be much easier to resolve.

The WNBA hasn't just suffered from a lack of public and private investment. The WNBA's television deal also doesn't seem to reflect its ratings. It was reported that on average, 246,000 people tuned in for television broadcasts of MLS games in 2019 (Carp, 2019). Meanwhile, for the first half of the 2019 season it was reported by Moran (2019) that on average 318,000 people tuned in to see television broadcasts of the WNBA. And then in 2020 it was reported that WNBA television attendance had risen 68% relative to the previous season (Negley, 2020).

Despite the WNBA apparently having a larger television audience, the MLS has a much larger television contract. As noted, the WNBA is only paid $25 million per year by ESPN. According to Young (2020), though, ESPN and Univision are paying the MLS $90 million per year. Yes, the MLS—with apparently less viewers on television—gets more than three times the television money of the WNBA. Again, men dominate the sports media and it seems likely the gender of the decision makers played a role in deciding the television contracts for the MLS and WNBA.

The growing television numbers for the WNBA suggest an audience exists for this league. It is expected, though, that the attendance numbers are not going to reflect that growth. Obviously the COVID pandemic reduced in-game attendance in 2020 to zero. The 2021 version of the WNBA showed substantial increases in attendance along with some sell-outs. However, just two years earlier, attendance dropped. Why? The issue is where two of the 12 teams have decided to play.

The Atlanta Dream announced in 2019 it was moving into the Gateway Center Arena. The capacity of this arena[32] is only 3,500, or as Levin and Broughton (2019) report, more than 700 fans less than the Dream's 2019 average attendance. A similar story can be told about the Washington Mystics. In 2019 the team moved into the St. Elizabeth's East Entertainment and Sports Arena. In 2018, the Mystics attracted 6,126 fans per game (Karp, 2018). The team's new arena has a capacity of only 4,200. Thus, in 2019, the Mystics's attendance declined.

32. https://dream.wnba.com/news/atlanta-dream-announces-new-home-court-at-gateway-center-in-college-park/

© Keeton Gale/Shutterstock.com

As noted, the WNBA and NBA after 23 years had similar attendance. But the moves made by the Mystics and Dream suggest it is going to be difficult for the WNBA to grow in attendance as the NBA did after its first quarter-century. With only 12 teams in the league, artificially limiting the attendance of two teams will have a significant impact on average league attendance. Thus, when we look at the popularity of the WNBA in the future, our focus might have to be more on the television ratings and less on the artificially constrained attendance numbers.

And those television numbers suggest the WNBA is reaching an audience. Yes, that audience is currently smaller than the NBA. But once again, the WNBA is a much younger league. When we compare the WNBA to what the NBA was at the same age, it appears the WNBA—contrary to Silver's 2015 assertion—really is quite far along.

Government Subsidies of the NBA and WNBA

As noted in Chapter 9, the MLS has received over $800 million in public subsidies. Although impressive, this pales in comparison to the NBA. As Baade and Matheson (2012) report, from 1990 to 2010 the NBA received more than $3.1 billion in public subsidies to finance the building and rehabilitation of NBA arenas. After 2010, the subsidies continued. Matheson (2020) reports that the Atlanta Hawks, Milwaukee Bucks, Detroit Pistons, and Sacramento Kings combined to receive more than $1 billion in public subsidies from 2016 to 2018. In all, across the past three decades, nearly 40% of the cost of NBA arenas has been paid by taxpayers and the NBA has benefitted from more than $4 billion in public subsidies.

Public subsidies for the WNBA tend to happen via their connections with the NBA. For example, the Talking Sticks Resort Arena was renovated in 2020. This is home to the Suns of the NBA and the Mercury of the WNBA. According to a published report[33], $80 million of the renovations will be paid for by the Suns leaving the city of Phoenix to pay the remaining $150 million cost. Obviously, both the Mercury and Suns benefits from this subsidy.

A similar story can be told about the new home of the Mystics. According to Neibauer (2015), Washington D.C. funded nearly half of the expense of building this arena. Not only did this arena serve as a home for the Mystics but it is also a practice facility for the Washington Wizards. In other words, taxpayers in D.C.—just as we saw in Phoenix—are subsidizing both the WNBA and NBA.

In general, the subsidy game tends to benefit the NBA far more than the WNBA. Once again, men's sports tend to receive both more public and private investment than women's sports. This has to be remembered when we consider the development of women's sports.

Despite the relative lack of investment, though, it does appear that the WNBA is doing about as well as the NBA at a similar point in its history. And that means we can likely conclude that the future of both leagues can be described in a similar fashion. In sum, we can expect the future of both leagues to be quite bright indeed!

---

33. https://arizonasports.com/story/2021136/phoenix-mercury-play-veterans-coliseum-talking-stick-resort-renovation/

Case Study: When Is Ownership Not Ownership—The WNBA Story

League ownership in professional sports tends to be simple to understand. The teams are owned by individuals, partnerships, or sometimes corporations, and those teams collectively own the league. In discussing the WNBA, though, the NBA often emphasizes that it owns 50% of the league. That would mean that the owners of the WNBA teams somehow only collectively own half of their league. How exactly does that work?

NBA, Inc owns WNBA Holdings, LLC., which "owns" 50% of WNBA Enterprises, LLC (an LLC is a limited liability company). Put differently, WNBA Enterprises is a subsidiary of WNBA Holdings. A holding company is a type of financial organization that owns a controlling interest in other companies, which are called subsidiaries. Holding companies are protected from losses accrued by subsidiaries; if a subsidiary goes bankrupt, its creditors can't go after the holding company (Berkshire Hathaway, Alphabet, and Goldman Sachs are large holding companies). To be a subsidiary, more than half of that business' equity must be controlled by another business. WNBA Holdings and WNBA Enterprises (the league) are both LLCs. In a limited liability company, or LLC, the owners are not personally responsible for the company's debts or liabilities. LLCs are a hybrid of a corporation and a partnership or sole proprietorship.

The other half of WNBA Enterprises is "owned" by the 12 franchises. We put "owned" in quotes because we suspect that this is the agreed-upon split of league revenue and league costs—half to the WNBA franchises and half to WNBA Holdings (NBA, Inc.).

Both the NBA and the WNBA are franchise systems. Franchisors grant licenses and rights to operate to the franchisee. One can think of this like fast-food franchises like McDonalds or Subway. Team owners are franchisees and the league is the franchisor. It's important to note that franchise-generated revenues (ticket sales, local TV deals) go to the team while league-generated revenues (national TV deals, apparel and licensed merchandise sales) are split evenly among the teams.

All of this was likely set up by the NBA to attract investment to the WNBA. Whereas men have shown with respect to league like the MLS that they are willing to invest hundreds of millions in a league that doesn't tend to earn a profit (Smith, 2019), historically there has not been a similar level of commitment to women's sports. By agreeing to cover some of the WNBA's losses, the NBA has helped ensure investment in the WNBA.

An Analysis of Pay Equity in the WNBA and Women's Professional Basketball

By Jennifer Lee Hoffman

© Keeton Gale/Shutterstock.com

Women's basketball has a long history well before today's WNBA. While women's basketball started famously with Senda Berenson at Smith College alongside the men's game, university administrators pushed the college women's game along a recreational detour that would not end until the 1960s (Hoffman, 2011). However, early women's basketball leagues were not constrained by the limits on athleticism that colleges and universities administrators placed on the women's college and high school game. Instead, early industrial leagues, community and church organizations, as well as ethnic clubs sponsored competitive women's basketball in the 1920s (Festle, 1996; Grundy & Shackelford, 2005). The American Athletic Union (AAU) was also an early adopter of women's basketball teams. Women's basketball in these early years were closely tied to local communities and their economic interests. As such, women's leagues found community support and sponsorship from local businesses such as department stores, car makers, oil companies, grocery stores, and insurance agencies. Unfortunately these community ties did not persist into post-war World War II America, and the women's game stalled (Grundy & Shackelford, 2005).

The first U.S. women's national professional basketball league, Women's Professional Basketball League (WBL) began in 1978 but quickly faced the challenge of media promotion and coverage that focused almost exclusively on men's sports. While some players, mostly white, had endorsements, the limited coverage of women's sports, made developing the financial infrastructure to grow the women's game impossible. After three seasons, the WBL folded and it would not be until the American Basketball League (ABL) in 1996 when women's professional basketball would return. A year later the NBA announced it would start a women's professional league as well.

By 1998, the ABL was a fledgling professional league, facing the earlier problem of visibility and still trying to solidify its North American television exposure to build league wide attendance and financial stability. Securing the broadcasting contracts and advertising sponsorship necessary to drive revenue were early challenges for the ABL. In 1998, the WNBA launched its first season, with eight teams tethered to their NBA franchises in Charlotte, Cleveland, Houston, New York, Los Angeles, Phoenix, Sacramento, and Utah (wnba.com). This arrangement created two women's professional leagues and a tenuous arrangement. The WNBA had greater attendance, sponsorship, and player salaries but the ABL had more talent and autonomy over growth of the women's game. Neither league solved the problem of player pay. Women basketball players in both leagues continued to sign contracts and play overseas. With each league vying for the same revenues and the WNBA backed by the assets of the NBA, women's independence in the game ended with ABL's abrupt mid-season financial collapse.

Today the WNBA has 12 women's teams in two conferences. The Eastern Conference has teams in, in Atlanta, Chicago, Connecticut, Indiana, New York, and Washington. The Western Conference has teams in Dallas, Las Vegas, Los Angeles, Minnesota, and Phoenix. Only five teams are directly tethered to an NBA team by sharing the same market, ownership, and arena. Seven teams are independently owned.

One of the early decisions by the NBA was to adjust the women's schedule, so that women would get access to the larger arenas for games, but in an alternate or 'off-season' from the typical basketball season—essentially giving the women's teams the gym when the NBA did not need the arenas. The WNBA also plays a compressed summer schedule with 36 games and an eight team playoff (wnba.com), compared to the NBA's 30 teams playing in 82 regular season games, and a 16 team playoff (nba.com).

From the outset of the WNBA, many players play overseas because of the excellent salary opportunities (Baker, 2008; D'Arcangelo, 2018). WNBA players go overseas to supplement their income, improve their game, and try to increase their personal player visibility (D'Arcangelo, 2018). The WNBA's shortened season, combined with player's competing overseas during the peak of the American basketball game's visibility, and the WNBA's limited marketing budget (Alvarez, 2019; Publicis, 2020; Wallis, 2020) further limits promotion of the US women's professional game. This in turn contributes to pay inequity by severely limiting the infrastructure growth necessary to build visibility and attention that would infuse revenue to support player salaries and revenue sharing.

These factors continue to put the athletes, especially younger women's players, and the league in a position of having to balance growing the women's game and mediating player overuse and injury. In 2016, Diana Taurasi took the season off from the WNBA, foregoing her then WNBA $107,000 salary. Instead she rested during the WNBA season so she could be ready for her international season where she earned $1.5 million (Walters, 2016). In April 2019, Brianna Stewart, whose Seattle Storm team won the 2018 WNBA title and she took league and playoff MVP honors, would be lost for the entire 2019 season after tearing her Achilles tendon while playing overseas (Alter, 2019). The WNBA simply cannot grow its league revenues when its best players are not willing or able to play.

Today WNBA direct player compensation comes in many forms, from team salaries, to revenue sharing, player benefits, and team-related accommodations and services. This also includes benefits such as health insurance, medical care, including maternity leave and childcare, training, and travel resources. Player compensation also includes third party endorsement opportunities. As is customary with professional sports, player compensation is regulated in partnership between the league and the players' union.

Formed in 1998, the Women's National Basketball Players Association (WNBPA) represents the 144 WNBA players (Women's National Basketball Players Association, n.d.). Like other professional sports organizations, the WNBPA represents player interests in contract negotiations, such as base pay, minimum and maximum salaries, rookie contracts, free agency, and salary caps in a collective bargaining agreement (CBA) contract. The WNBPA negotiates with the WNBA to establish the CBA to for player other benefits such as health insurance, pregnancy and childcare benefits, and player-related expenses such as travel accommodations, meals, and air travel (wnba. com/cba). The 2020 CBA negotiated by the WNBA and the WNBPA is scheduled to last until 2027 and includes new salary structures that would bring the highest-paid players an estimated $500,000 in cash compensation in addition to benefits, in particular improvements to travel and increased childcare resources (Voepel, 2020a). Later, the WNBA opted to pay rookies health benefits before the start of training camp and 100% of player salaries during the shortened 2020 season due to coronavirus (Feinberg, 2020; Voepel, 2020b).

League revenues are drawn from ticket sales, media contracts, advertising, and merchandising. Direct comparison figures between the WNBA and the NBA are difficult to draw, but some estimates suggest that although the WNBA has made recent gains in player benefits, namely in the areas of pregnancy/child care and travel accommodations, there is likely a growing gap in salary and revenue sharing (Berri, 2017). Revenue sharing is a key element of player compensation and building financial power within the sports industry. NBA player salaries are roughly 50% of league revenue, compared to approximately 20% to 25% of revenue sharing for WNBA player salaries. While revenue sharing is expected to rise closer to 50% for WNBA player salaries under the latest CBA, growth in overall league revenues remains challenging given the lack of media coverage of women's sports (Lough, 2018; Alvarez, 2019) and the ways in which overseas play limits the attention women's basketball players can garner at home when attention for basketball is at its highest.

The financial backing of the NBA buoyed the start of the WNBA and has sustained its initial growth, but the long-term implications for pay equity remain. Despite the increased visibility and relative independence from the NBA that the WNBA enjoys today, the issue of pay equity cultivates a long-standing question in the gender separate structure of sports—should women's sports organizations be separate from men's and instead women-led and women-owned? The tethering of women's basketball to the NBA has not narrowed the gap in pay equity, benefits, or equal access to endorsement and other revenue for women's professional basketball players. If the ABL had continued and had the opportunity to build out women's basketball visibility along with the popularity of the women's college game, what would have been the impact on women's salaries and benefits today?

Conclusion

As noted in Chapter 10, the climate in 2021 seems to be shifting toward viewing the WNBA as a "buy option" in the world of finance. The player's visible social justice movement and a new collective bargaining agreement that more appropriately divides marketing opportunities between the League and the players is embraced by the fans. More financial investment is coming into the league from other high-profile athletes and business owners, indicating they see a real upside in women's sports. The WNBA is poised to take advantage of this moment.

Review Questions

1. In looking at the per-game attendance of the NBA and the WNBA from Table 1, what do you think caused the NBA's attendance to take off? Is it possible for the WNBA to replicate that model?
2. The franchise valuation for an NBA team has skyrocketed in recent years. List three reasons as to why that has occurred.
3. If you were the WNBA Commissioner, what strategies would you use to grow the League from 12 to 16 teams over the next several years?

References

Agha, N., & Berri, D. (2020). Gender differences in the pay of professional basketball players: The role of owner motivation. In A. Bowes & A. Culvin (Eds.). *Women's Sports in a Professional Era*. Emerald Studies in Sports and Gender Series. idrottsforum.org.

Alter, A. (2019). *Breanna Stewart's injury is a blow to the Storm-and the WNBA*. Seattle PI. www.seattle-pi.com/sports/storm/article/What-does-Breanna-Stewart-s-injury-mean-for-the-13774925.php

Alvarez, A. (2019, May 9). I thought the main issue in women's sports was equal pay. I was wrong. *The Guardian*. www.theguardian.com/sport/2019/may/09/i-thought-the-main-issue-in-womens-sports-was-equal-pay-i-was-wrong

Attner, P. (1977, December 13). Pioneer of big money in sport. *The Washington Post*. www.washingtonpost.com/archive/sports/1977/12/13/pioneer-of-big-money-in-sport/633a84dc-f762-4079-ad2a-2a8f48eefefc/

Baade, R., & Matheson, V. (2012). Financing professional sports facilities. In Z. Kotval & S. White (Eds.). *Financing Economic Development in the 21st Century* (2nd ed., pp. 323–342). M.E. Sharpe Publishers.

Baker, C. A. (2008). *Why she plays: The world of women's basketball*. University of Nebraska Press.

Becker, D. (1990, September 14). More career possibilities for the elite. *USA Today*, p. 1C.

Berri, D. (2011, September 8). Skepticism and solutions to imaginary problems in the NBA. *Huffington Post*. https://www.huffpost.com/entry/skepticism-and-solutions-_b_954524

Berri, D. (2017, September 20). Basketball's growing gender wage gap: The evidence the WNBA is underpaying players. *Forbes*. www.forbes.com/sites/davidberri/2017/09/20/there-is-a-growing-gender-wage-gap-in-professional-basketball/

Berri, D. (2018a, September 4). WNBA players are simply asking for a greater share of WNBA revenues. *Forbes.com*. www.forbes.com/sites/davidberri/2018/09/04/what-wnba-players-want/#72e2d54133eb

Berri, D. (2018b) *Sports Economics*. Worth Publishers/Macmillan Education.

Berri, D. (2018c, March 25). In the sports marketplace, politicians are helping men's sports leagues win the race. *Forbes.com*. www.forbes.com/sites/davidberri/2018/03/25/in-the-sports-marketplace-politicians-are-helping-mens-sports-leagues-win-the-race/#1743b4f178b5

Berri, D. (2020, February 22). Basketball's gender wage gap narrows (but doesn't vanish!). *WNBA Insidr*. https://winsidr.com/2020/02/12/basketballs-gender-wage-gap-narrows-but-doesnt-vanish/

Bradley, R. (n.d.). Labor pains nothing new to the NBA. *APBR.org*. http://www.apbr.org/labor.html

Carp, S. (2019, October 9). ESPN's MLS ratings up 2% for 2019 regular season. *Sports Pro Magazine*. www.sportspromedia.com/news/mls-espn-regular-season-tv-ratings-social-impressions

Carr, H. (2019, December 18). The multiple revenue streams of the NBA. *Businessing*. https://businessingmag.com/9825/money/nba/

Cash, M., & Gal, S. (2018, October 16). NBA's trend of increasing number of international players appears to be slowing down. *Business Insider*. www.businessinsider.com/growing-number-of-foreign-born-players-in-nba-slows-2018-10

Coon, L. (2015). *Larry Coon's NBA salary cap FAQ*. http://www.cbafaq.com/salarycap.htm

Cooky, C., Messner, M. A., & Musto, M. (2015). It's dude time!" A quarter century of excluding women's sports in televised news and highlight shows. *Communication & Sport*, pp. 1–27.

Cronin, B. (2010, May 5). Sports legends revealed: How did the "Larry Bird exception" to the NBA salary cap get its name? *Los Angeles Times*. https://latimesblogs.latimes.com/sports_blog/2010/05/sports-legends-revealed-how-did-the-larry-bird-exception-to-the-nba-salary-cap-get-its-name.html

D'Arcangelo, L. (2018). "There's no break": Overseas double duty is an offer many WNBA stars can't refuse. *The Guardian*. www.theguardian.com/sport/2018/may/19/theres-no-break-overseas-double-duty-is-an-offer-many-wnba-stars-cant-refuse

DeFord, F. (1967, August 14). The education of Mr. Barry. *Sports Illustrated*. https://vault.si.com/vault/1967/08/14/the-education-of-mr-barry

DuPree, D. (1983, March 15). NBA: Red ink and a bleak future. *The Washington Post*. www.washingtonpost.com/archive/sports/1983/03/15/nba-red-ink-and-a-bleak-future/198bd65f-4062-4372-95e4-388b22c77666/

Ellentuck, M. (2018, August 16). *Liz Cambage tells us 5 ways the WNBA is failing its players*. SB Nation. www.sbnation.com/wnba/2018/8/16/17693052/liz-cambage-interview-wnba-players-problems-fixing

Feinberg, D. (2020, April 29). *WNBA rookies to begin receiving health benefits this week*. AP NEWS. https://apnews.com/54b0e79c3dbdb99b981472655876de5a

Festle, M. J. (1996). *Playing nice: Politics and apologies in women's sports*. Columbia University Press.

Fort, Rod. *Rod Fort's Sports Business Data*. https://sites.google.com/site/rodswebpages/codes

Gaines, C. (2014, April 21). Brittney Griner makes 12 times as much money playing basketball in china. *Business Insider*. www.businessinsider.com/brittney-griner-basketball-china-2014-4

Goldberg, R. (2020, January 30). Report: Updated 2020-21 NBA salary cap, luxury-tax projections revealed. *Bleacher Report*. https://bleacherreport.com/articles/2873875-report-updated-2020-21-nba-salary-cap-luxury-tax-projections-revealed#

Grundy, P., & Shackelford, S. (2005). *Shattering the glass: The remarkable history of women's basketball*. The New Press.

Front Office Sports. (2018). *WNBA teams find success through creative partnerships*. https://frontoffice-esports.com/wnba-creative-partnerships/

Helin, K. (2012, January 24). *Details emerge of league's new revenue sharing plan*. NBC Sports. https://nba.nbcsports.com/tag/nba-revenue-sharing/

History.com Editors. (2019, October 29). *Earl Lloyd becomes first black player in the NBA*. History. A&E Networks. www.history.com/this-day-in-history/earl-lloyd-becomes-first-black-player-in-the-nba

Hoffman, J. L. (2011). "Each generation of women had to start anew": A historical analysis of Title IX policy and women leaders in the extracurriculum. In P. Pasque & S. Errington (Eds.), *Empowering women in higher education and student affairs: Theory, research, narratives, and practice from feminist perspectives* (pp. 32–46). Stylus Publishing. http://stylus.styluspub.com/Books/BookDetail.aspx?productID=205835

Jenkins, S. (1997, July 3). *The history of women's basketball*. WNBA.com. www.wnba.com/news/history-of-womens-basketball/

Karimi, F. (2019, February 17). *NBA to start African basketball league with 12 teams across the continent*. CNN.com. www.cnn.com/2019/02/17/africa/nba-africa-basketball-league/index.html

Karp, A. (2018, August 28). WNBA sees record low attendance as liberty's move hurts figures. *Street & Smith's Sports Business Journal*. www.sportsbusinessdaily.com/Daily/Issues/2018/08/28/Leagues-and-Governing-Bodies/WNBA-gate.aspx

Kleps, K. (2018, June 12). Cavs' players will split more than $3.8 million from NBA playoff pool. *Crain's Cleveland Business*. www.crainscleveland.com/article/20180612/blogs06/164911/cavs-players-will-split-more-38-million-nba-playoff-pool

Lapchick, R., Elkins, C., & Mathew, R. (2008, May 29). *The 2008 Racial and Gender Report Card: National Basketball Association*. https://43530132-36e9-4f52-811a-182c7a91933b.filesusr.com/ugd/7d86e5_6d817aabf4b44630abad6c4f7dc190c2.pdf

Leeds, M., & von Allmen, P. (2010). *The economics of sports* (4th ed.). Prentice-Hall.

Levin, A., & Broughton, D. (2019, September 10). WNBA turnstile tracker: Attendance down at end of regular season. *Street & Smith's Sports Business Journal*. www.sportsbusinessdaily.com/Daily/Issues/2019/09/10/Research-and-Ratings/WNBA-Turnstile-Tracker.aspx

Lewis, J. (2014). NBA announces 9-year extension with ESPN, Turner, through 2025. *Sports Media Watch*. www.sportsmediawatch.com/2014/10/nba-tv-deal-espn-abc-tnt-nine-year-deal-2025-24-billion-lockout/

Lewis, J. (2017). Is the NBA worth all that TV money. *Sports Media Watch*. www.sportsmediawatch.com/2017/04/nba-tv-deal-billions-espn-turner-ratings-layoffs/

Lewis, J. J. (2020). History of women's basketball in America. *ThoughtCo.* February 11. thoughtco.com/history-of-womens-basketball-in-america-3528489

Lough, N. (2018, August 9). *The case for boosting WNBA player salaries*. The Conversation. http://theconversation.com/the-case-for-boosting-wnba-player-salaries-100805

Martinez, J. (2015, April 3). *Chuck Cooper and the little-known history of the NBA's first black players*. Complex.com. www.complex.com/sports/2015/04/chuck-cooper-and-the-little-known-history-of-the-nba-first-black-players/

Mensheha, M. (2015, September 18). Silver says he thought WNBA would be further along after nearly two decades. *Street & Smith's Sports Business Journal*. www.sportsbusinessdaily.com/Daily/Issues/2015/09/18/Game-Changers/Silver-WNBA.aspx

Montgomery, P. (1976, March 21). Top NBA stars were subsidized. *The New York Times*. p. 153. www.nytimes.com/1976/03/21/archives/top-nba-stars-were-subsidized-court-records-here-show-nba.html

Moran, E. (2019, August 2). *First half viewership spike has WNBA optimistic about 2019 and beyond*. Front Office Sport. https://frntofficesport.com/wnba-viewership-growth/

Mox, J. (2020, June 29). *WNBA CBA and salary cap explained. Base salary basics*. Her Hoop Stats. https://herhoopstats.substack.com/p/wnba-cba-and-salary-cap-explained-ca9

Mullen, L. (2020, January 27). Commissioner did more for women than just start WNBA. *Street & Smith's Sports Business Journal*. www.sportsbusinessdaily.com/Journal/Issues/2020/01/27/David-Stern-Tribute/Women.aspx

Murray, P. (2019, January 20). *Insider the NBA's efforts to reach a global audience. Forbes.com*. www.forbes.com/sites/patrickmurray/2019/01/20/inside-the-nbas-attempts-to-reach-a-global-audience/#160c60597dd2

Negley, C. (2019, December 16). Charlotte's MLS expansion fee a reported $325 million—Two-thirds more than recent expansions. *Yahoo.com*. https://sports.yahoo.com/charlotte-will-reportedly-become-30th-mls-franchise-for-record-325-m-twothirds-more-than-recent-expansions-212710659.html

Negley, C. (2020, October 1). *WNBA average viewership grows 68 percent during a season focused on social justice*. Yahoo.com. https://sports.yahoo.com/wnba-average-viewership-up-68-percent-national-tv-windows-marketing-growth-210452911.html

Neibauer, M. (2015, September 21). Verizon Center 2.0? Arena League Football? First look at the deal that will bring the Wizards, Mystics to St. E's. *Washington Business Journal*. www.bizjournals.com/washington/breaking_ground/2015/09/verizon-center-2-0-arena-league-football-first.html

Ourand, J. (2016). ESPN's new deal doubles rights fee. *Street & Smith's Sports Business Journal*. May 9. www.sportsbusinessdaily.com/Journal/Issues/2016/05/09/Media/ESPN-WNBA.aspx

Perez, J. (2016). WNBA unveiling revamped league pass, including single-game, team packages. *Street & Smith's Sports Business Journal*. www.sportsbusinessdaily.com/Daily/Issues/2016/05/09/Media/WNBA-League-Pass.aspx#

Philippou, A. (2018). The storm draws a big crowd, but elsewhere, why aren't more WNBA fans attending games?" *The Seattle Times*. www.seattletimes.com/sports/storm/storm-attendance-up-wnba-shows-upswing-except-for-fans-showing-up-at-games/

Prada, M. (2015, February 3). *A Russian team paid Diana Taurasi to sit out 2015 WNBA season*. SB Nation. www.sbnation.com/nba/2015/2/3/7973177/diana-taurasi-sit-out-wnba-season-russian-salary

Publicis Media, https://www.mi-3.com.au/23-01-2020/womens-sport-conversation-needs-shift-equal-pay-equal-marketing

Reynolds, T. (2020, August 17). 10 Things to know as 2020 playoffs begin. Associated Press. www.nba.com/article/2020/08/17/10-things-know-playoffs-begin

Rowe, D. J. (2016). *It's time to retire the NBA's rookie salary scale*. Duke University—School of Law. www.sportslaw.org/docs/Time_to_Retire_NBAs_Rookie_Salary_Scale_Rowe.pdf

Schmidt, M. B. "The Competitive Returns to a Global Search for Talent: Professional Sports Markets and Foreigners," J*ournal of Economic Inquiry Vol 59,* No.1, January 2021, pp 396-419. https://onlinelibrary.wiley.com/doi/epdf/10.1111/ecin.12947

Schwartz, L. (2003, November 19). *Basketball association of America is born*. ESPN.com. http://www.espn.com/classic/s/moment010606BAAopens.html

Schwartz, N. (2014, August 12). Steve Ballmer explains why he paid $2 million for the clippers. *USA Today*. https://ftw.usatoday.com/2014/08/steve-ballmer-2-billion-clippers

Silver, N. (2011, July 5). Calling foul on the NBA's claims of financial distress. 538 Blog (*The New York Times*). http://fivethirtyeight.blogs.nytimes.com/2011/07/05/calling-foul-on-n-b-a-s-claims-of-financial-distress/

Smith, C. (2019, November 4). Major league soccer's most valuable teams 2019: Atlanta stays on top as expansion fees, sales prices surge. *Forbes*. www.forbes.com/sites/chrissmith/2019/11/04/major-league-soccers-most-valuable-teams-2019-atlanta-stays-on-top-as-expansion-fees-sale-prices-surge/#f462a451b580

Smith, S. (1997, October 2). *Garnett hits jackpot of $123 million*. Chicago Tribune. www.chicagotribune.com/news/ct-xpm-1997-10-02-9710020351-story.html

Staudohar, P. (1999). Labor relations in basketball: the lockout of 1998-99. *Monthly Labor Review* (April), pp. 3–9.

Voepel, M. (2016). WNBA oral history: Moving the ball forward. *ESPN.com* (May 16). www.espn.com/wnba/story/_/id/15561974/moving-ball-forward

Voepel, M. (2020a, January 14). *WNBA, union reach "groundbreaking" new CBA*. ESPN.com. www.espn.com/wnba/story/_/id/28480768/new-wnba-cba-include-salary-bump-other-cash-compensation-increases

Voepel, M. (2020b, June 12). *Sources: WNBA offers players full salary in '20.* ESPN.com. www.espn.com/wnba/story/_/id/29303544

Wallis, B. (27 Jan 2020). *Women's sport: The conversation needs to shift from equal pay, to equal marketing.*

Walters, J. (2016, April 1). A lawsuit from the US. women's soccer team reveals deeper issues with gender equity in sports. *Newsweek.* www.newsweek.com/womens-soccer-suit-underscores-sports-gender-pay-gap-443137

Wealthsimple. (2018, August 21). *Skylar Diggins-Smith wants to be paid like a man and isn't afraid to say it.* Wealthsimple. www.wealthsimple.com/en-us/magazine/skylar-diggins-smith

Windhorst, B., & Lowe, Z. (2017, September 19). *A confidential report shows nearly half the NBA lost money last season. Now what?* ESPN.com. www.espn.com/nba/story/_/id/20747413/a-confidential-report-shows-nearly-half-nba-lost-money-last-season-now-what

Women's National Basketball Players Association. (n.d). *Collective bargaining agreement.* https://wnbpa.com/cba/

Young, J. (2020, February 27). *Major league soccer has a 25-year plan, but it needs to secure huge media deals first.* CNBC.com. www.cnbc.com/2020/02/27/major-league-soccer-has-a-25-year-plan-but-it-needs-to-secure-huge-media-deals-first.html

CHAPTER 12
Business of the National Football League

Derek Helling

LEARNING OBJECTIVES

- To understand the structures of the 32 NFL franchises and how one becomes an owner of a team.
- To describe the various revenue streams teams use to maximize their home stadium opportunities and the expenses that offset them.
- To gain an understanding of the various tax liabilities and salary structures embedded in players and coaches contracts.
- To understand how the salary cap works and the postseason financial structures.

Over the past century, the National Football League has become the most lucrative North American professional sports league in terms of annual revenue (Colangelo, 2019). The heads of the first four clubs to create the American Professional Football Conference in 1920 likely never imagined their league would one day regularly play games on two continents and number its fans in the millions (Professional Football Hall of Fame, year unknown).

It would have been hard for those representatives of the Akron Pros, Canton Bulldogs, Cleveland Indians, and Dayton Triangles to foresee the role that stadium subsidies and television would play in growing the value of their enterprise. A hundred years later, that's what the NFL can attribute much of its value to.

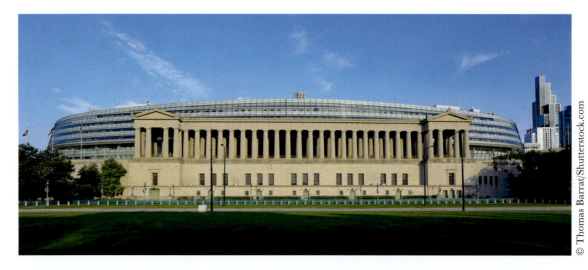

A Brief History of the National Football League

After those four clubs formed the APFC in 1920, the conference added more clubs and rebranded to become the NFL in 1922 (Encyclopedia Britannica, 2019). Though there were other leagues through the 1930s and 1940s, the NFL outlasted them all into the middle of the 20th century (BBC History Magazine, 2019).

In 1960, the first serious threat to the NFL's dominance of professional American football emerged. The fourth iteration of the American Football League established itself by signing talent like George Blanda and Len Dawson away from the NFL (Coniglio, A. 2020). The AFL also made waves by negotiating broadcast rights deals with ABC and NBC in the United States (Brulia, 2004).

Six years later, the two leagues merged into the version of the NFL fans know today (History.com Editors, 2020). Although that merger didn't take full effect until 1970, 1966 saw the first Super Bowl between the NFL's Green Bay Packers and the AFL's Kansas City Chiefs for the championship of both leagues.

The next two decades saw enormous growth of the league under NFL Commissioner Pete Rozelle. By the time, Rozelle retired in 1989, the league had grown to 30 clubs and all of its games were broadcast on local or national television.

New Commissioner Paul Tagliabue oversaw the NFL's journey into the age of the Internet (McClain, 2017). Under his leadership, the NFL spread to two more markets—Charlotte, NC and Jacksonville, FL (Litsky, 1993). The league also signed a landmark broadcasting deal with DirecTV to create its popular "Sunday Ticket" package (Effectives, 2018).

In 2006, Tagliabue gave way to current Commissioner Roger Goodell. With Goodell at the helm, the league has seen the values of its broadcast contracts balloon to billions (Reuters, 2018). The NFL started playing regular-season games in the UK (Thomas, 2019). The league also navigated issues like a landmark concussion lawsuit filed by former players (ESPN, 2013).

The NFL's Structure

The NFL is technically a trade association for its 32 member franchises (Schallhorn, 2017). Until 2015, it was listed as a 501(c)(6) organization, a status that it voluntarily forfeited (Myers, 2015). Up until that point, it faced governmental pressures to make the move (Internet Archive, 2012).

The majority stakeholders in those franchises delegate power to the league through a list of by-laws (NFL, 2019b). Almost all of that power is vested in the Office of the Commissioner, including hiring a league secretary and treasurer.

All but one of the league's clubs are for-profit corporations that are privately owned. The Green Bay Packers are the lone exception, which is the only publicly held nonprofit professional sports franchise in North America (Green Bay Packers, 2020).

The league does have the ability to act in proxy of those individual clubs on certain matters. It has the authority to negotiate broadcast rights contracts and a collective bargaining agreement with the labor unions for game officiants and players, for example.

The heads of the 32 clubs do hold authority on matters like rule changes, ownership changes, club expansion and relocation and have the final authority on the CBAs the league negotiates. The owners also have the authority to replace the commissioner.

Although the NFL is involved in the daily operations of its clubs and players in a supervisory role, the players are technically employees of their member franchises and not the NFL. The current CBA between the league and the National Football League Players Association governs that relationship.

Outside of the aforementioned exceptions, member franchises largely handle their own operations. This includes broadcast deals for preseason games, which players to sign contracts with and negotiating sponsorship deals with other corporations in accordance with league rules.

League rules also play a big part in dictating who can own a club and whether that stake amounts to actual control of the team. The market has raised the bar for the cost of such ownership over time as well.

Ownership Buy-In Amount

In the realm of ownership stakes in an NFL franchise, there are two different models. The first model is employed by 31 of the 32 franchises. The other is used by the Green Bay Packers.

For the other 31 clubs, there is one individual, family, or trust who holds a controlling interest. The cost of acquiring that has varied greatly throughout the years and in different markets.

Those majority owners have worked with various numbers of minority owners over the decades as well. Like for their controlling partners, the cost of acquiring a stake has fluctuated with market conditions but also relied heavily upon how much equity was bought.

Most of the publicly available information on the topic of the cost of minority ownership is both inexact and recent. As privately held corporations, these 31 franchises are under no obligation to expound upon any of their financial details to the public.

The most recent example of a sale of a minority stake in an NFL franchise involved the Tennessee Titans in 2020. A one-third stake in the franchise went for $515 million (Ozanian, 2020).

In 2019, Arthur Blank sold a 10% stake in the Atlanta Falcons for $3 million (Bassam, 2019). The Falcons confirmed one new partner and two existing partners at the same time, so it's uncertain how that 10% stake was divided and how much of that $3 million each party contributed.

16 years earlier, Daniel Snyder sold three shares in the Washington Football Team for more than $200 million (*The Washington Times*, 2013). Again, there were no specific details about how much each share cost or what percentage of the whole that gave the parties.

What's common about minority stake transactions is that they give the buyers no control over the operations of the clubs. The majority owners retain full authority, with their less-invested partners essentially playing a silent role.

Despite their silence, all transactions are still subject to the approval of the league. More accurately stated, the majority owners of the other franchises must ascent to any sale of any stake in a club, regardless of how small.

The winding story of buying a majority stake in a club is much more well-documented. The following chart shows who the current majority owner of all 31 clubs besides Green Bay is, what they paid for that controlling interest, and when they did so (partial list).

Team	Majority Owner	Purchase Price	Year of Purchase
Arizona Cardinals	The Bidwell Family	$50,000	1932
Atlanta Falcons	Arthur Blank	$545 million	2002
Baltimore Ravens	Stephen Biscotti	$600 million	2004
Buffalo Bills	Terry and Kim Pegula	$1.4 billion	2014
Carolina Panthers	David Tepper	$2.275 billion	2018
Chicago Bears	McCaskey Family	$100	1920
Cincinnati Bengals	Michael Brown	$8 million	1967
Cleveland Browns	Jeremy Haslam	$1 billion	2012
Dallas Cowboys	Jerry Jones	$150 million	1989
Denver Broncos	The Bowlen Family	$78 million	1984
Detroit Lions	William Clay Ford	$4 million	1964
Houston Texans	The McNair Family	$700 million	1999
Indianapolis Colts	James Irsay	$15 million	1972
Jacksonville Jaguars	Shahid Kahn	$770 million	2012
Kansas City Chiefs	The Hunt family	$25,000	1960

Chart created by Karen Weaver, adapted by: McKinney, J. (2014, June 10). Purchase Price and Current Value of Each NFL Franchise, https://www.thephinsider.com/2014/6/10/5796114/purchase-price-and-current-value-of-each-nfl-franchise; Pitts, B. (2012, October 28). Shahid Khan: from Pkistan to Pro-Football. CBSNews: 60 minutes. https://www.cbsnews.com/news/shahid-khan-from-pakistan-to-pro-football/; Wogton, N. (2019) How Terry Pegula went extra mile to buy Bills. https://billswire.usatoday.com/2019/09/11/terry-pegula-went-extra-mile-to-buy-buffalobills/

League rules generally state that the majority owners must control at least 30% of the interest in a club. A family member can account for one-third of that stake, however (Davenport, 2013). If the controlling interest in a franchise is held by the same individual or family by over a decade, league rules allow the controlling interest in that club to represent as little as a 10% stake.

The Packers, as a publicly held nonprofit organization, are exempt from those rules because their ownership structure predates them. Green Bay has always existed in this structure, with the first sale of shares in 1923 for $50. Similar to publicly traded commodities, the cost to acquire a share can fluctuate based on the value of the franchise at the time of the transaction.

Unlike publicly traded commodities, however, shares in the Packers aren't available on a continual basis. The last time shares became available was 2011 and that sale was limited to 250,000 shares (Associated Press, 2011). The cost of each share was $250 and no individual could buy more than 200 shares. The sale was open to individuals only and shares can only be transferred within immediate families. The 2011 sale was the fifth in the club's history and the first since 1997. The other two prior sales happened in 1935 and 1950.

Also unlike publicly traded commodities, Packers stocks pay no dividends and have no resale value, and the value of the stocks won't go up with the value of the franchise or the NFL. Shareholders elect officers to represent them in league affairs.

Although shareholders don't take part in the revenue the Packers produce, the Packers still participate equally in NFL revenue distributions. Like with ownership, there are many league policies governing that and time has seen it become much more lucrative.

Revenue Distribution

Although all 32 clubs have an equal part in steering the NFL's future, that doesn't mean all 32 franchises produce revenue equally. There are several components that each club operates independently and thus revenue can vary greatly within a fiscal year from one franchise to the next. Examples include:

- Preseason and regular-season ticket pricing and sales;
- Sponsorships of in-game and venue content;
- Concessions and merchandising at stadiums; and
- Investing in nonfootball business ventures.

As previously mentioned, the clubs give the NFL the authority to negotiate terms for them collectively on some matters. This includes broadcasting rights for regular-season and playoff games and the licensing of merchandise. The NFL also operates the postseason structure. Revenue from those sources is dispersed equally to the 32 teams.

The most single significant source of revenue for NFL franchises is their share of the league's broadcast rights income. The rights are currently owned by AT&T, Comcast, Disney, Fox, and ViacomCBS (Sherman, 2020). Those contracts are set to expire in 2022, though it's possible they could be renewed prior. At press time, the NFL announced a massive set of new media deals totalling over $100 billion, while adding a 17th regular season game (Belon, K. and Draper, K., 2021).

The NFL parcels out access to different products between those parties, who pay different amounts based on the package they have contracted for (Travis, 2017). The breakdown is as follows.

- AT&T: $1.5 billion for exclusive out-of-market streaming rights for regular-season games subject to blackout rules, aka DirecTV's "Sunday Ticket" package
- Comcast: $1.18 billion for Sunday Night Football, five Thursday Night Football games and select playoff games
- Disney: $2 billion for Monday Night Football and one wild card playoff game each season
- Fox: $1.1 billion for NFC regular-season games and all the NFC playoff games not given to Comcast or Disney
- ViacomCBS: $1.23 billion for the AFC version of Fox's package plus five Thursday Night Football games

Comcast, Fox, and ViacomCBS rotate coverage of the Super Bowl as well. Splitting those revenues up 32 ways amounts to $219.06 million for each club.

The other league revenue, which mostly comes from licensing and league-level corporate sponsorships, is also split evenly between franchises. For FY2019, the league's total shared revenue came to $8.78 billion. From that, each team got a disbursement of approximately $274.3 million (Erby, 2019). That equated to an increase of 6.8% from the previous year ($255.9 million) and growth of a third ($187.7 million) over 2013.

The single bargaining block the NFL represents in these regards has a great benefit for all 32 franchises. It acts as a "rising tide that lifts all ships." The chart shows that effect for three different franchises at various levels of the NFL ecosystem (see NFL Valuations).

NFL Valuations (in millions)

The foregoing values are in millions of dollars. All valuations are estimates by *Forbes* and Sportico. The Cowboys represent the most valuable NFL franchise in all years depicted. The Atlanta Falcons

© Leonard Zhukovsky/Shutterstock.com

Cowboys, Falcons and Bengals

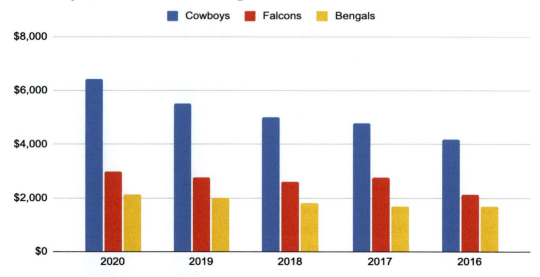

Graph created by Derek Helling, adapted by: Sportico (2020) National football league interactive franchise valuations; Ozanian, Mike. (2016, September 14) The NFL's Most Valuable Teams. Forbes.com. https://www.forbes.com/sites/mikeozanian/2016/09/14/the-nfls-most-valuable-teams-2016/?sh=579ad7853068; Badenhausen, K. (2017) The Dallas Cowboys head the NFL's most valuable teams at $4.8 billion; Ozanian, Mike. (2018, September 20) The NFL's Most Valuable Teams: The Yardage Gets Tougher on Prices. Forbes.com. https://www.forbes.com/sites/sportsmoney/2018/09/20/the-nfls-most-valuable-teams-the-yardage-gets-tougher-on-prices/?sh=2acd0a34737f

were the franchise whose value was closest to the mean in 2020 and the Cincinnati Bengals were the least valuable team in 2020.

The teams control all other aspects of their business and also pull in revenue from those sources. These individual-franchise level sources of revenue can vary wildly from one club to the next in a given year.

For example, the Dallas Cowboys pulled in an additional $675.7 million in revenue on top of their league disbursement in FY2019 (Gough, 2020d). During the same time frame, the then-Oakland Raiders only added $82.7 million to their take in league revenues.

One of the most prominent sources of that revenue is preseason and regular-season ticket sales, though that percentage is somewhat fluid from year to year. In 2015, the take at the gate accounted for 16.45% of the whole while in 2018, it only represented 15.47% (Gough, 2020).

As all of the NFL's clubs besides the Packers are privately held corporations who do not share their financials liberally, it's difficult to accurately ascertain exactly how much of teams' revenues come from what sources. Green Bay's latest filing provides some insight into that franchise, however.

The Packers added $203.7 million to their $274.3 million payment from the NFL in FY2019 (Ryman, R., 2019). That money came from concessions, ticket sales, merchandise sales at Lambeau Field, local sponsorships and from leasing out the attached Atrium to other businesses and for events.

That last item is an example of what really separates the "haves" from the "have-nots" in the NFL. Using the on-field product to leverage investments in nonfootball business ventures is a big part of what made Dallas the NFL's "revenue king" in FY2019, for example.

Legends Hospitality, which the Cowboys co-own the majority interest of along with the New York Yankees, sold a minority stake to a private equity firm in May of 2017 for $700 million (Ozanian, 2017). Given the fact that the sale was not the result of a bidding process but rather a strategic move to integrate the minority partner New Mountain Capital, the stake in the business likely came at a discount. In FY2019, revenue from Legends likely added many millions of dollars to Dallas's total.

Teams also experience a bump in revenue from their on-field performance. That affects gameday sales most drastically, as evidenced again by the Packers' financials. Packers President and CEO Mark Murphy said after the 2018 season that there's a "definite spike" from postseason success. He also shared that visits to the Packers Hall of Fame, sales at the team's Pro Shop and general spending at the Atrium were down. Green Bay missed the playoffs in 2017 and 2018.

The best ways for NFL franchises to maximize their values are consistently competing for championships and diversifying their revenue streams so that a portion of the income isn't dependent on the on-field product. While it's a simple formula, achieving that success is difficult.

The other major distribution that the NFL does annually with its revenue is the NFLPA. The players association through the current collective bargaining agreement gets a share of several sources of the NFL's revenue on nearly an equal footing with the team's owners. Player benefits and salaries figure heavily into that equation, however.

For example, the NFLPA received $61.54 million from NFL Ventures in 2017, up from $55.8 million in 2016 from NFL Ventures (Gough, 2019). NFL Ventures handles the league's advertising and broadcasting arms.

Another difficulty that NFL clubs often encounter is managing their stadium situations. While a new facility can tremendously boost the value of a franchise, getting to that point often requires a lot of capital and effort.

Facility Revenue, Subsidies, and Construction

The NFL is one of the biggest businesses in the United States that is largely dependent on brick-and-mortar facilities. While digital streaming rights and online merchandise sales certainly present

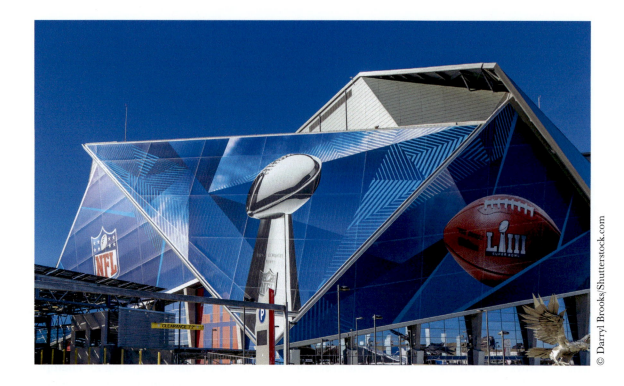

a significant component of the league's revenue, the NFL would be unable to sell its primary product of American football games without such facilities.

The most important of those facilities are venues for those games. These can represent a tremendous cost for NFL clubs but also present several opportunities for revenue in and of themselves. These include but aren't limited to:

- Selling signage in and around the stadiums;
- Naming rights for the facilities;
- Personal seat licenses;
- In-stadium sponsor activations;
- Branded guest offerings; and
- Experiential activations.

Costs for these facilities are significant. The greatest of those, in terms of one-time expenditures, is construction. Significant renovation of existing facilities falls right alongside that expense, although what is and isn't a significant renovation is somewhat subjective.

As with construction on anything else, costs rise with time. This isn't just due to simple inflation but the never-ending "arms race" to create a venue with the biggest attractions, latest innovations and most impressive design elements.

The construction cost estimate of SoFi Stadium in Inglewood, CA that will host the Los Angeles Chargers and Rams is currently up over $4 billion (Kaplan, 2018). There are several unique elements to this situation, like state requirements for such facilities to theoretically be able to withstand earthquakes.

Allegiant Stadium, which has hosted Las Vegas Raiders games since 2020, is the most recent example of completed construction costs at $1.9 billion. The venue boasts a translucent roof and sliding doors that can open to provide a view of Las Vegas's famous Strip (Associated Press, 2019a). Part of that cost can be attributed to a 2018 surge in the cost of construction materials brought on by tariffs and an increase in the cost of gasoline (AGC.org, 2018).

That cost represents an increase of about $300 million, or about 15.8%, from the $1.6 billion construction cost of the last such facility, Mercedes-Benz Stadium in Atlanta, GA (Caldwell, 2016). The home of the Atlanta Falcons opened in 2017. The year prior, U.S. Bank Stadium opened to Minnesota Vikings fans at the cost of $1.1 billion (Murphy, 2016). Rises in costs haven't always been linear with the passage of time, however.

Stadium amenities, design and location have more impact on construction costs than inflation over time. In 2010, MetLife Stadium in East Rutherford, NJ opened with a price tag of $1.6 billion (Craven, 2015). Despite being built 7 years earlier than Mercedes-Benz, construction costs were equitable partially for the home of the New York Giants and Jets because New Jersey boasts the third-highest pay in the nation for construction workers (US News & World Report, 2020).

To further emphasize the point of amenities and design playing a major role, AT&T Stadium in Arlington, Texas began hosting Dallas Cowboys games in 2009 after developers spent $1.3 billion. AT&T Stadium is home to the world's largest high-definition television and covers 73 acres with a capacity of 111,000.

Capacity and size also determine the price tag of major renovations to existing facilities. The costs to update Soldier Field in Chicago, Ill., the home of the Chicago Bears, came to $802 million in 2003. Soldier Field has a capacity of almost 50,000 fewer people than AT&T Stadium.

After facilities are complete, the operation and maintenance costs begin. Those are year-round costs, not only applicable during the NFL season. Like construction costs, these costs vary greatly from facility to facility based on the markets they inhabit and design elements of the venues.

Lincoln Financial Field in Philadelphia, PA, cut down on these costs during the construction phase by installing 11,000 solar panels and 14 wind turbines. While that helped balloon the cost to build the facility to $650 million in 2003, the implements produce almost a third of the energy required to operate the stadium.

Other operational and maintenance costs include personnel, property taxes, sanitation, security and supplies. Whether or not NFL clubs incur those costs depends heavily on whether they own the stadiums they play in or simply act as anchor tenants.

That situation can be the subject of confusion for fans at times. For example, the New England Patriots technically do not own Gillette Stadium, rather they pay between $2 and $3 million in annual rent to the stadium's owner, the Kraft Group (*Las Vegas Review Journal*, 2017). However, the Kraft Group also owns the Patriots. A similar situation applies to the future home of the Los Angeles Rams, as Kroenke Sports & Entertainment owns both the Inglewood stadium and the Rams.

Four other current NFL stadiums are owned by private corporations or individuals, they are as follows.

- Bank of America Stadium in Charlotte, NC, which is owned by Panthers Stadium LLC
- FedEx Field in Landover, MD, which is owned by Washington Football Team owner Daniel Snyder
- Hard Rock Stadium in Miami, FL, which is owned by Miami Dolphins owner Stephen Ross
- MetLife Stadium in East Rutherford, NJ, which is owned by the Meadowlands Stadium Corporation

All other NFL stadiums are owned by city, county or state governments. The terms of those leases vary greatly from one jurisdiction to another. For example, the Baltimore Ravens pay the Maryland Stadium Authority no rent but the Ravens cover the cost of all maintenance and utilities along with the hourly wages and salaries of all the workforce necessary to operate the facility year-round. Of those who pay a flat fee per year to play their games in the stadiums, the rent ranges from zero (the Cleveland Browns to the City of Cleveland) to $24.5 million (the San Francisco 49ers to the Santa Clara Stadium Authority). Most teams pay around $2 million in annual rent.

Just as the terms of these leases can vary greatly from jurisdiction to jurisdiction, the path to financing the construction of these facilities that led to the creation of those leases can be wildly different. For example, the state of Maryland financed the entire $220 million cost of the 1998 M&T Bank Stadium for the Baltimore Ravens. Municipal authorities contributed just $750 million or about 39.5% of the $1.9 billion construction cost of Allegiant Stadium, however (Barrabi, 2020).

Using Allegiant as an example for private–public partnerships, the NFL kicked in $400 million toward the construction costs while Raiders themselves contributed $500 million (Gutierrez, 2017). Bank of America provided financing for the other $250 million.

Just as the terms of the agreements in these partnerships dictate how each party contributes to construction/renovation and maintenance costs, they also determine how parties collect and split revenues generated by usage of the facilities. As expected, these terms are highly individualized for each venue.

Continuing to use Allegiant as an example, the Raiders collect all revenues generated by the usage of Allegiant in exchange for managing the facility. So far, the Raiders have collected $400 million in selling personal seat licenses and between $20 and $25 million in naming rights fees.

While operating and/or owning facilities can represent great expenses, there is somewhat of a benefit to that for tax purposes. Owners can claim depreciation of the facilities for tax purposes. For example, the Kraft Group reported a 3.5% depreciation of Gillette Stadium for 2020 (Schwartz, 2020).

Operators and owners of these venues have started to monetize their physical space in conjunction with gambling companies. The Denver Broncos have a deal in place with Betfred to offer fans a "sports betting lounge" during games, for example (Cohen, 2020). The area is not a fully-fledged retail sportsbook, but rather a themed area that has many of the aesthetic components of a sportsbook but all wagering takes place online. On the NFL side, this is just another way to pull revenue from the acreage on game days.

Banks, government leaders and NFL franchise owners weigh projected costs of doing business against their projected revenues when making these decisions. It is the ability of individuals to accurately predict these figures that spell failure or success. For more information on stadium financing, see Chapter 5.

Financial Forecasting

Producing a financial forecast regarding an NFL franchise is essentially the same as doing so for any other for-profit corporation. The purpose of the forecast drives the process of production.

Corporations that have operated for decades and largely followed a reliable operations plan generally do so when considering a serious decision. Forecasts help them choose between several options.

The NFL is approaching such a decision within the next 2 years with the expiration of its broadcasting rights contracts. As previously mentioned, the league has the power to negotiate and execute those deals on the behalf of its member franchises.

The simplest way to produce a forecast is through the use of historic figures and trends to predict future growth or lack thereof. An example of this is taking revenue totals from the last 5 years, finding the mean and adding 5%. For a company the size of the NFL and with billions of dollars at stake, however, that's far too simplistic.

Using the example of broadcast rights, NFL personnel will try to design a forecast to answer several questions for themselves. Examples include the following.

- What is the value of a package of our games to a broadcast partner?
- Is a shorter or a longer term for these broadcast contracts more advantageous?
- How does the day and time of those games affect that value, for example, how much more valuable are day games on Sundays than Thursday night games?
- Is it more lucrative for us if we parcel out the product as opposed to selling all the rights in one package?
- What's the optimal way to parcel out the product if we go that route?
- Is it more lucrative to include streaming rights with broadcast rights or sell those separately?

In 2017, ad revenue for the NFL's broadcast partners was worth $3.5 billion (Badenhausen, 2017). That represented a 5% uptick from 2015 and it was one of the worst seasons for television ratings of NFL broadcasts in recent memory with an 8% drop-off from 2016. Ratings have rebounded since, while traditional cable and satellite television customers continue to cancel their subscriptions (Porter, 2018). Assuming 5% growth each year since 2017, the NFL's broadcast partners paid about a 46.8% premium for access in 2019.

Five percent year-over-year is a solid conservative growth estimate for the value of broadcast packages because of all those factors. That projection has ad revenues for NFL broadcasts in total worth over $6.9 billion by 2032. That's assuming the same model as these contracts currently operate on, however, which isn't a safe assumption.

A big part of why that's a dangerous assumption to make is the aforementioned effect of "cord-cutting." Like with other broadcast entertainment forms, that makes traditional broadcast rights less valuable while increasing the value of streaming rights. Factoring that into a revenue forecast requires the NFL to make a decision about whether to separate those two products and to what extent. So far, the NFL has largely decided to incorporate those two products. Because of the continued trend of cord-cutting, however, they may opt to take a different course in the future.

That may act to decrease potential bidders' interest in traditional broadcast rights but the countereffect is it brings more potential bidders in. Instead of dealing with just the big broadcast partners like Comcast and Disney, companies like Amazon and Google may factor into the conversation as well.

Because such competition benefits the NFL and the scarcity of its product, it's safe to assume that bidders will be likely to pay above market value for the product. That doesn't mean the sum of the parts will be greater than the whole, however. There is another consideration the NFL must account for in its broadcast contract negotiations. That is protecting the value of the in-stadium experience.

Ticket revenue is a small component of the overall pie, especially in comparison to the value of broadcast contracts, but full crowds in stadiums are part of the aesthetic for television broadcasts. Because of that, contracts will contain blackout restrictions that apply to both broadcast and streaming rights. For streaming rights, that means out-of-market viewing restrictions while for broadcast components, that means stadium sellouts will continue to dictate local coverage in NFL markets.

Because that facet of the status quo remains constant, there is no need to adjust forecasted revenue up or down to account for it. The element of parceling out the broadcast rights that works most strongly in the NFL's favor is that not all of those rights need be exclusive for certain components.

An example is the contingent of Thursday Night games. Currently, both Comcast and ViacomCBS have rights to broadcast them on broadcast and streaming services. The NFL could continue to let

© DCStockPhotography/Shutterstock.com

multiple broadcast partners handle that aspect while selling the streaming rights, with blackout and geographic exemptions, to a third party like Amazon or Google. The NFL has done this exact thing before, allowing Amazon to stream Thursday Night games on its Prime video service and Twitch (Wolf, 2018). Amazon paid $130 million for such access in 2018 and 2019, so following the same 5% year-over-year growth formula forward would put the value of those rights at $208 million by 2032. For more information on sports media, see Chapter 2.

Going through this exercise with these parameters suggests that the NFL could simply replicate much of the current terms of its broadcast deals and expect to get over $10 billion in annual revenue for its broadcast rights if it assumes the ad revenue is worth $6.9 billion by 2032. Modifying one or two variables, like decreasing or increasing the number of bidders for those rights, will accordingly adjust that number.

For example, as Disney now owns streaming media powerhouse Hulu and thus can add its live streaming product to its buffet, it might contend with Amazon for Thursday Night streaming rights. That could increase the take on that element because it should make the eventual winner of that bidding war more likely to pay more than market value for the product.

In summation, creating a financial forecast for businesses like the NFL is not complicated in terms of the math involved but rather in taking into account the various factors that influence the situation and assigning some value to those factors. One of those factors taken into account when creating forecasts could be how a certain decision will affect the tax liabilities of the league and/or one of its clubs.

Tax Status and Liabilities

Until 2015, the NFL was classified as a 501c6 organization. At that time, it changed its registration with the federal government to become a privately held for-profit corporation. Although it saved about $10 million a year from that previous status, there was a tremendous value gained in changing its status (Isidore, 2015).

That benefit is the protection from public disclosure laws that all such corporations enjoy. Prior to the change, federal law required the NFL to publish its financial details each year. Those included the salaries of each employee and other expenditures. How much tax the NFL pays is a private matter now, but it's likely very little because of how the league is structured.

The NFL disperses almost all of its revenue to its member franchises, likely keeping just enough on the books to fund employee salaries and league operations. Because of that, it likely shows a loss on its tax filings for the IRS and the state of New York each year.

NFL franchises take a page out of that book as often as they can. Some stadium subsidies come in the form of property tax breaks, such as that which the Atlanta Falcons enjoy with the State of Georgia (Kass, 2019). Although the Falcons manage Mercedes-Benz Stadium, the agreement between the club and the stadium's owner, the Georgia World Congress Center Authority, absolves them of paying taxes to the state on the property.

Although NFL franchises are theoretically taxed on all their revenue, they can claim a number of deductions like most other privately owned corporations in the United States. Those have diminished over the past few years, however, largely due to recent changes in the federal tax code enacted in 2018 (Scharf, 2018).

For example, the ability of clubs to deduct the cost of money paid to the league in the form of dues vanished in 2018. That may affect the price tag of future expansion or relocation fees paid to the league, although it's possible that accountants for the teams may find a way to reclassify such an expense so it's at least partially deductible.

While keeping up with changes to the federal tax code is a full-time job for league and team employees, the same also have to concern themselves with local and state taxes as well. The rates and terms of those can vary broadly from jurisdiction to jurisdiction.

For example, four states that house NFL franchises do not assess any taxes on their residents' incomes. Those are Florida, Nevada, Texas, and Washington. Tennessee has also progressively limited its assessment on residents' income, although it still technically has an income tax (Sraders, 2018). That affects NFL teams' business models significantly.

One way is that teams that reside in such jurisdictions can often offer personnel lower salaries and/ or signing bonuses because of the lower cost of living that such personnel will incur in those states. Some jurisdictions counteract that benefit, however, with what's become known as a "jock tax."

The "jock tax" is a tax levied by some cities, counties and states on income made by nonresidents while performing their business within their jurisdictions. For example, when a player of another team plays a road game at Heinz Field against the Pittsburgh Steelers, the City of Pittsburgh assesses them three percent on the income they made while working there (De Lea, 2019).

While those requirements fall upon individuals, it affects NFL clubs' finances because they have to account for such costs in the salaries of personnel. The biggest source of tax liability for each franchise and the league is their revenue, much of which comes from partnerships with other corporations.

Revenue Sources and Partnerships

The NFL has three primary sources of revenue.

- Broadcast rights contracts
- Corporate sponsorships
- Licensing

The league does not handle corporate sponsor contracts for its member franchises. They do that themselves. As previously mentioned, however, the league does negotiate broadcast rights for all 32 clubs as a whole. In a similar way, the league does have some authority to handle licensing for teams' brands.

In the 2019–2020 season, sponsorship dollars brought over $1 billion to the NFL (Forsdick, 2020). Almost half of that revenue came from just two partners, AB InBev and Verizon. Verizon paid $300 million to the league while AB InBev, whose beverage brands include Budweiser beer, paid $230 million.

Sponsorship revenue of more than a billion dollars is a plateau that the league has lived on for several years. For example, the league hit a then-record high of $1.25 billion in 2016 (Heitner, 2017). That record didn't stand long, as it rose to $1.32 billion for 2017 and then $1.39 billion in 2018 (Gough, 2020).

Part of the value of the NFL's sponsorship value comes in concert with its licensing arm (Associated Press 2019b). Nike, which has an eight-year deal with the NFL to design its player uniforms and have its logo on all such gear, paid $120 in 2019 for that privilege. In similar fashion, Fanatics paid $50 million to the league in 2019 for the right to distribute and manufacture NFL apparel and novelties.

The NFL licenses much more than clothing, however. A multitude of companies from video game manufacturer Electronic Arts to gambling companies like DraftKings and tech manufacturers like Microsoft pay the NFL to have their products used by the league and/or its franchises or to use the logos of the NFL and its 32 clubs on their merchandise.

Within the past year, licensing out club and league trademarks to gambling companies has become another revenue source. The league has a contract with DraftKings along these lines while numerous individual franchises have made their own deals with DraftKings and its competitors (Associated Press, 2019).

© Lori Butcher/Shutterstock.com

In 2014, the NFL together with Major League Baseball accounted for half of the sales of licensed merchandise in North America measured by revenue (Transparency Market Research, 2016). Retail sales of NFL-licensed merchandise rose by 5.2% year-over-year in 2014. The total value of sport officially licensed merchandise worldwide was estimated to surpass $48 billion by 2024.

Reporting since then points to that estimate being accurate. In 2017, the NFLPA reported its share of the league's licensing and merchandise revenue was $167 million (Kaplan, 2017). The NFLPA also reported that revenue from that source had grown by 79% since 2013.

That year, EA paid $47 million to the NFLPA to use player images, likenesses and names in its popular Madden video game franchise. The Panini America Corporation also paid the union $25 million to use the same properties for its digital and physical trading cards along with other forms of marketing and memorabilia. The league likely received similar payments from those companies as the products also require the use of trademarks the NFL and its clubs own.

Clubs also negotiate their own sponsorship contracts for in-stadium signage, in-game activations and the rights to use their trademarks in conjunction with business' products and services. Individual franchises benefit greatly from suite rentals and ticket sales. For example, the Dallas Cowboys brought in over $200 million in premium seating and sponsorship dollars in 2019 (Ozanian, 2019).

© Postmodern Studio/Shutterstock.com

All the revenue from licensing, merchandise, and sponsors pales in comparison to revenue from the primary method of consumption of its product, mass media. Broadcast delivery of games is a big part of that, but not the sum total.

Media Revenues

In 2019, the NFL brought in over $7 billion for the rights to broadcast its games. While that's the largest slice of its media revenues by far, there are other components.

The NFL is also in the media business for itself. These components include:

- NFL Network;
- NFL.com and league social media sites;
- NFL Game Pass; and
- Officially licensed data feeds.

One of the great perks of being the size of the NFL is that many media companies produce media for the league at their own expense. This comes in the forms of products who use NFL trademarks in their marketing, NFL-centric blogs and sports journalists. There is constantly new content that NFL fans can consume that the NFL has spent no overhead on the production of.

The NFL does bear some cost in content creation, however, with its various digital properties. NFL Ventures is responsible for those operations and collects that revenue. As it is a privately held corporation, it does not share its financials. These outlets do present great opportunities to supplement the broadcast rights revenue as digital real estate.

Game Pass is a limited OTT video service that operates on a subscription model and also sells ad space within the content. The content includes access to audio feeds of live games, game replays, NFL Network content, and episodes of HBO's "Hard Knocks" series. The league also sells advertising with NFL.com, NFL Network, and social media content.

One of the newest forms of media revenue for the league is in licensing official data feeds for gambling companies. In 2015, Sportradar became the exclusive and official game statistics and information system distributor for the NFL (Sportradar Press Release, 2015). Sportradar collects and distributes that information to daily fantasy games and sportsbook operators around the world. The value of that partnership has not been disclosed.

Individual clubs follow a similar pattern in regards to media revenues. They can partner with local broadcasters for coverage of preseason games and have digital real estate to sell within their own properties. Those include team social media accounts and websites. Like with in-stadium signage and in-game activations, the value of that real estate varies from club to club and many factors like market size influence it.

The cost of production of that media is a common expense for all the franchises along with the league. Another common expense for all clubs is personnel and while that's somewhat arbitrary, there are some measures to control those costs in the NFL CBA. The NFL benefits from a long standing partnership with NFL Films, the archival and storytelling arm of the league.

Salary Structures

Most NFL franchises sign members of their coaching staffs and players to detailed, lengthy contracts that cover not only the duration of the contract but spell out the compensation and the duties of both parties to the other. While constantly evolving culture and technology makes it necessary for these contracts to be broad and living documents on some terms, the experience of NFL teams in their business makes them experts at this craft (National Football League, n.d.).

There are some similarities between these contracts for coaches and players. They both often contain several different types of compensation.

- Allowances for living expenses like per diems for road games
- Base salary broken down by annual figures
- Benefits such as life insurance
- Definitions of acceptable conduct
- Pension contributions
- Performance incentives that the coach/player can earn
- Signing bonuses
- Termination clauses

Coaches and players receive their base salaries on a biweekly basis throughout the years they are under contract with teams. Benefits and pensions are paid by clubs throughout the year as well (Sample NFL Player Contract, year unknown). The years for those purposes begin with the first regular-season games each year.

The terms of individual contracts dictate exactly how a coach/player can earn bonuses, the dollar amount for each incentive and when those are paid if earned. Signing bonuses are paid when all parties agree to the terms of the contract, though league rules allow teams to apply them equally over the length of a contract for salary cap purposes.

Coaches and players receive their per diems on a weekly basis, with veteran players receiving more than rookies (Kuharsky, 2018). In 2018, the veteran per diem was $1,900 and the rookie edition was $1,075. The franchises pay those and those figures are just for the duration of preseason and regular-season games.

In the NFL there are few rules about minimum and maximum durations of contracts. Most contracts are for at least one calendar year, although there are exceptions. The CBA dictates that players' rookie contracts can cover their first four seasons in the league, although it does not require teams to sign them to contracts of that length.

Players with at least three accrued seasons reach restricted free agent status if their contracts expire (NFL, 2019). In that situation, the last teams that employed those players can get exclusive rights to negotiate a new contract with those players provided they make a qualifying offer to those players. To get a first right of refusal, teams must submit an offer that meets a minimum dollar amount corresponding to whether or not the player entered the league via the draft and if so, how highly a team selected him.

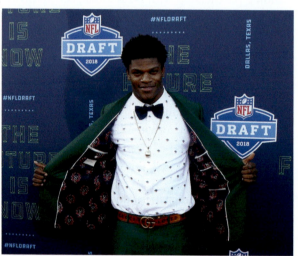

© Debby Wong/Shutterstock.com

In 2019, for example, teams had to extend an offer sheet of at least $2.025 million or 110% of the 2018 First-Round Draft Pick salary, whichever was higher, to get the first right of refusal with a former first-round selection. Teams can offer lower salary amounts but they will not secure a first right of refusal with restricted free agents. In those circumstances, an RFA is able to negotiate with any team he wishes and if the player signs with another team, the team he played for last will receive compensation via a draft pick from the player's new team.

Players whose contracts expire and have at least four accrued seasons become eligible for unrestricted free agency. Those players are free to negotiate with any team they wish immediately and their last teams won't receive any compensation from their new teams if they don't re-sign.

Even with players who are set to hit unrestricted free agency, teams do have options to minimize the effects of losing them, however. In the NFL, those are the franchise and transition tags.

Each offseason, a team can designate one franchise or one transition player. Franchise tags are exclusive and transition tags are nonexclusive. The exclusive tag prohibits that player from negotiating with any other team. In exchange, the team must compensate that player the average of the five highest salaries at his position for the approaching season. The nonexclusive tag requires a team to extend an offer sheet equal to at least 120% of the player's previous year's salary and if he signs with another team, the former team receives compensation of two first-round draft picks from the new team.

There are usually buyout clauses for both parties in coach and player contracts, along with guidance for how much if any compensation is due the coaches, players and teams if either party desires to terminate the contract early.

While there are no caps in the NFL in regards to how much teams can compensate members of their coaching staffs, with Las Vegas Raiders head coach Jon Gruden recently having eclipsed the $10 million in annual compensation mark, there are clear rules about how much teams can spend on players. Like with per diems, there is a separate system for rookie and veteran players.

Salary Caps

The NFL imposes a maximum amount that teams can spend on player payroll from one season to the next. Those figures escalate each season on a percentage basis based on revenues it expects to receive during the season. The league also has a standard annual minimum contract value.

In 2019, the salary cap was $188.2 million and the minimum contract was $495,000 (Gough, 2020). That salary cap represented a 5.9% increase from 2018, which sat at $177.2 million. 2018's figure was 5.2% ($9.2 million) higher than 2017. Teams that are under the cap during one season can carry that gap over to following seasons and they have to be in compliance on the first day of the league year. Only players' base salaries and signing bonuses count toward the cap. For cap purposes, teams can spread the value of signing bonuses over the length of players' contracts.

Although rookie players count toward roster limits, rookie contracts with players selected in the NFL Draft each year do not count toward the salary cap. The value of undrafted rookie contracts do count toward the cap, however.

Teams contribute money into a pool for draft pick compensation and then that money is distributed back to the clubs based on how many picks they control and where those picks fall among the seven rounds (Badenhausen, 2019). Contracts for rookie players taken in the Draft are slotted. The compensation decreases as the draft proceeds.

For example, 2019 first overall selection Kyler Murray was slotted to receive a four-year deal worth $35.2 million while the final pick of the first round, N'Keal Harry, was set to make $10.1 million over the value of his four-year deal. Like the veteran salary cap, these values go up each year based on expected revenues. 2018 top overall selection Baker Mayfield's four-year deal was worth $33.1 million (Belzer, 2018).

All that compensation revolves around the offseason, preseason and regular season. For the players on the 12 teams (as of the 2019–2020 season) who qualify for the NFL playoffs each year, there is more money at stake.

Postseason Financial Structures

The NFL takes over player compensation when the playoffs begin. While coaches and players may earn bonuses from their individual franchises alongside their shares of postseason revenue, all players receive standard monetary bonuses for qualifying for and advancing in the NFL playoffs from the league.

Most players on playoff teams receive the same share of the NFL's dedicated postseason fund regardless of their actual time on the field during playoff contests. Generally speaking, to qualify for a full share a player must be on a team's 53-man roster for each successive round and have been on that roster for the three most recent games that team has played (Corry, 2020). Both postseason and regular-season games qualify for that requirement. Players who are on teams' postseason rosters who have been added more recently usually receive half-shares.

In the system last employed before the 2020–2021 season, which was unique due to the COVID-19 pandemic, the top two seeds in each conference received a first-round bye. Players on those teams do not get paid a share of the postseason fund for wild card games. The higher seeds in wild card games do receive more than the lower seeds, however. Players on teams who win games in each round do not receive more than the players on losing teams, with the exception of the Super Bowl.

In 2019, a full share in each successive round amounted to the following.

- Wild card round—low seeds: $27,000
- Wild card round—high seeds: $29,000
- Divisional round: $29,000
- Conference championship round: $54,000

In 2020, each eligible player on the Kansas City Chiefs roster got an $118,000 bonus as the winners of Super Bowl LIV while their counterparts on the San Francisco 49ers took home $59,000 for reaching the game (Caron, 2019).

These bonuses were up about 11% compared to 2017, when the lowest bonus was $24,000 for being on a lower-seeded wild card team and the highest was $107,000 for winning Super Bowl LII (Barrabi, 2017). A select group of players, whether their teams reached the playoffs or not, earned another kind of postseason bonus.

The Pro Bowl is the NFL's annual "All-Star Game" and while many players have incentives for qualifying for the event in their contracts, the league also gives such players a bonus. In 2019, players on the winning team received $67,000 while the league gave each of their opponents $34,000 (Inabinnett, 2019). That was an uptick from the previous season, when the winners got $64,000 and the losers got $32,000 (Breech, 2018).

In an interesting dichotomy, as many players make most of their money during the regular season, the league thrives on its championship structure. The NFL maximizes the value of seating capacity while teams do the same with other stadium amenities during the playoffs.

For example, tickets for the divisional playoff game that sent the Tennessee Titans to Baltimore to take on the Ravens in January of 2020 averaged $347 (The Ticket Club, 2019). During the preceding regular season, the average ticket price for a Baltimore Ravens home game was $103.59 (Gough, 2020). The NFL collects 100% of ticket revenues for all playoff games and the Super Bowl. It all goes into the pot that the league distributes to all 32 member clubs evenly.

Teams who host playoff games do get to keep 100% of the revenue generated by amenities like parking and sales of concessions and merchandise during those games, however, save any percentage that they may have to pay to stadium owners due to the terms of their leases. The league also provides each team with a stipend to cover expenses.

The playoffs are also the biggest time of the year for the NFL's largest driver of growth in coming years. The explosion of legalized gambling in many states should drive interest in the league.

Final Assessment of Growth Potential

As there doesn't seem to be any expansion in terms of more clubs on the horizon for the NFL, growing into new markets isn't a shortcut to expansive growth in the near future. The NFL intends to continue its series of regular-season games outside the United States, but the potential growth from that series may not be explosive.

Another sure path to growing revenue would be expanding upon the existing product from a quantity of games played angle. That remains a possibility, as the recently ratified CBA gives the league the option to add a 17th regular-season game and expand the playoffs to 14 teams. In order to maximize the value of its next round of broadcast rights contracts, the league may do so. If it can make that happen, the increased value of those rights will be significant (Caron, 2019).

Perhaps the greatest potential for growth is the NFL's embracing of legalized gambling, specifically legal wagering upon its games. As of the onset of 2021, 25 states and Washington, D.C. had legalized sports betting in some form. Many of those jurisdictions contain venues where NFL teams play their home games within their borders.

Goodell set a goal for the NFL to reach $25 billion in annual revenue by 2027 (Kaplan, 2016). To get there, the league has to maximize the value of its existing fans worldwide by converting them into regular customers who open their wallets and devote their time to the league and its franchises in a number of ways. If the league can negotiate a substantial increase for its broadcasting rights and similarly increase the cost of sponsorships, it is on pace to achieve that goal.

NFL Case Study

One of the best ways for the NFL and its franchises to ensure dependable revenue that grows over time is the same way any individual can do the same thing—diversify their investments. The more revenue they are able to bring in that doesn't depend on the success of the on-field products and television ratings, the better situated they are for the long haul.

Both the NFL and NFLPA have endeavored to do that with venture capital funds (Kaplan, 2011). The league did so in 2011, requiring every team to contribute $1 million toward the initial fund. The fund was directed toward startup entertainment, media, and technology companies that tie into its sport.

The NFLPA mirrored those actions in 2016, creating the One Team Collective (Brown, 2016). The Collective has used its greatest asset, the intellectual property of NFL players, to leverage stakes in startups. One of the most successful products that the Collective has assisted in developing is the WHOOP Strap (WHOOP Press Release, 2017).

The WHOOP Strap is a wearable device that measures a number of biometrics and has gone through a number of iterations and expansions of its business since the investment of the Collective and the NFLPA. For example, in 2018 it launched a subscription service and is poised to get a piece of the action (Shieber, 2018). Some estimates peg the value of that market at $57 million by the end of 2022 (PR Newswire, 2020).

While the NFLPA may have been ahead of the trend in wearable technology, the decisions of the NFL haven't always been so spot on in how it spends its capital. Its 2013 concussion lawsuit settlement and the management of that since is a great example of the league's missteps.

When the league originally negotiated the settlement, it did so as an uncapped agreement. It may have been necessary for the class of plaintiffs to agree to drop its complaint but the projected cost was far too conservative, putting the fund on the "brink of collapse" in 2019 (Hohler, 2018). It only took 2 years for claims to hit half of the projected cost for the 65-year term of the settlement (Associated Press, 2018). If the NFL had insisted on a capped settlement and made more concessions in other areas of the agreement, it might have been able to control the cost better.

The story of another genre of investment and return in the NFL remains to be written. That particular vertical is the NFL's relationship with legal gambling. While the NFL was originally party to lawsuits that sought to keep wagering upon sports illegal in most of the country, the attitude of the league has changed drastically since the U.S. Supreme Court ruled in *Murphy v. NCAA*.

The NFL has not been as active in lobbying on this issue as other professional sports leagues like Major League Baseball and the National Basketball Association. Regardless, it has some questions it has to answer in the near future.

- What extra steps, if any, does the league need to take to insure consumer confidence in the integrity of its product as legal gambling continues to expand?
- How does the league convert bettors into fans who open their wallets to the league in other ways?
- Will the NFL allow casinos and sportsbook operators to buy stakes in teams?

Another area where the league can and must adapt in order to maintain its place of prominence in North American professional sports is content delivery. Mobile devices are increasingly becoming the primary viewing device for consumers and shorter-form content is also becoming more preferential. The NFL must deliver condensed, engaging, and regular content along these lines or it risks losing its foothold.

Adaptation to what customers desire and staying competitive in a crowded entertainment industry will always require investment for the NFL and its member franchises. It has been the most successful professional sports league in North America because of its ability to take advantage of a societal passion for its game. As long as it is able to deliver a high-quality on-field product, it should continue to occupy that top spot.

Review Questions

1. One of the biggest single licensing revenue sources each year for the NFL and the NFLPA is Electronic Arts' spend on licensing for its Madden video game franchise. As the video game industry continues to grow, how can the NFL take advantage of this partnership to reach and monetize new fans?
2. The NFL negotiates broadcasting rights on the behalf of all 32 teams and each member franchise shares in that revenue equally. Other leagues, like MLB, allow each club to negotiate its own rights. While some clubs may be able to get more from going it alone, others might actually see a loss if they tried to sell their own package in comparison to the share they get now. Do you think the NFL's "socialist" policy in this regard discourages teams' improving their on-field products in terms of wins and losses?
3. The NFL is the most popular professional sports league in North America but its popularity fades on other continents quickly. Would increasing the number of regular-season games played on other continents be a prudent investment for the league?

References

AGC.org. (2018). Construction material costs increase 7.4 percent, as contractors continue to be squeezed by tariffs and rising fuel prices.

Associated Press. (2011). Green Bay packers plan stock sale, fifth in team history.

Associated Press. (2018). Claims in NFL concussion settlement hit $500 million in less than 2 years.

Associated Press. (2019a). Cost of raiders stadium in Las Vegas rises to $1.9 billion.

Associated Press. (2019b). NFL partners with draftkings for daily fantasy sports.

Badenhausen, K. (2017). NFL TV Ad revenue hits record $3.5 Billion despite drop in ratings.

Badenhausen, K. (2019). 2019 NFL draft first round rookie salary projections: What Murray, Bosa, and Williams will make.

Barrabi, T. (2017). Here's how much NFL players earn in the playoffs.

Barrabi, T. (2020). Las Vegas raiders' allegiant stadium, by the numbers.

Bassam, T. (2019). Atlanta falcons minority stake sale values franchise at US $3bn.

BBC History Magazine. (2019). History of American football facts: From invention to the Super Bowl.

Belson, K. and Draper, K. (2021, May 26). *N.F.L. Signs Media Deals Worth Over $100 Billion. New York Times*. https://www.nytimes.com/2021/03/18/sports/football/nfl-tv-contracts.html

Belzer, J. (2018). 2018 NFL draft 1st round rookie salary projections: What mayfield, barkley, and darnold will make.

Breech, J. (2018). Here's why Pro Bowl paychecks can actually be bigger than Super Bowl payout.

Brown, C. (2016). NFL players union launches startup accelerator and venture fund.

Brulia, T. (2004). A chronology of pro football on television: Part 1.

Caldwell, C. (2016). Officials: Mercedes-Benz stadium cost rises to $1.6 billion—Atlanta business chronicle.

Caron, E. (2019). How much do NFL players make in playoffs? 2019 postseason payout.

Cohen, A. (2020). Denver Broncos' mile high stadium will feature Betfred sports betting lounge.

Colangelo, M. (2019). The NFL made roughly $16 billion in revenue last year.

Coniglio, A. (2020). History of the American Football League—1960.

Corry, J. (2020). Agent's take: Inside the NFL's postseason pay; how much players are paid for the playoffs.

Craven, K. (2015). Construction costs most expensive NFL stadiums.

Davenport, G. (2013). What does it take to be the owner of an NFL franchise?

De Lea, B. (2019). Pittsburgh's jock tax triggers lawsuit from pro athletes, player's associations.

Effectives, A. (2018). When does Directv NFL sunday ticket start?

Encyclopedia Britannica. (2019). National Football League | History and Teams.

Erby, G. (2019). Eagles earn $274.3M of record $8.78B revenue split between NFL teams.

ESPN. (2013). NFL, players reach concussion deal.

Forsdick, S. (2020). NFL 2019-20 sponsors: Analysing the biggest deals for the season.

Gough, C. (2019). NFLPA merch and licensing revenue 2016-2017.

Gough, C. (2020a). Baltimore Ravens average ticket price 2006-2019.

Gough, C. (2020b). Minimum NFL salary 2020.

Gough, C. (2020c). NFL league and team sponsorship revenue 2010-2020.

Gough, C. (2020d). NFL revenue by team.

Gough, C. (2020e). NFL ticket/gate receipts revenue share 2010-2019.

Green Bay Packers. (2020). Green Bay Packers Shareholders.

Gutierrez, P. (2017). Raiders find new financing for Las Vegas stadium.

Heitner, D. (2017). NFL sponsorship soars to $1.25 billion, up 4.3% year-over-year.

History.com Editors. (2020). NFL and AFL announce merger—HISTORY.

Hohler, B. (2018). Billion-dollar NFL concussion settlement 'on the brink of collapse'.

Inabinnett, M. (2019). Pro Bowl winners' checks bigger than Super Bowl losers'.

Internet Archive. (2012). NFL targeted by Oklahoma Senator for 'not for profit' tax status.

Isidore, C. (2015). NFL gives up tax exempt status.

Kaplan, D. (2011). NFL plans to start venture capital fund.

Kaplan, D. (2016). NFL halfway to $25B goal.

Kaplan, D. (2017). NFLPA reports increase in licensing, merch revenue.

Kaplan, D. (2018). Los Angeles Rams stadium costs top $4 billion—LA Biz

Kass, A. (2019). Fulton residents say Mercedes-Benz Stadium should be paying taxes.

Kuharsky, P. (2018). How players are paid during training camp | News.

Las Vegas Review Journal. (2017). Stadium and rent details for all 32 NFL teams.

Litsky, F. (1993). PRO FOOTBALL; NFL Expansion Surprise: Jacksonville Jaguars.

McClain, J. (2017). Paul Tagliabue's stint as NFL commissioner had ups, downs.

Murphy, B. (2016). U.S. Bank Stadium by the numbers.

Myers, G. (2015). NFL no longer non-profit after giving up tax exempt status.

National Football League. (2019a). 2019 NFL Free Agency FAQ.

National Football League. (2019b). 2019 Official playing rules of the national football league.

National Football League. (n.d.). Sample NFL Player Contract.

Ozanian, M. (2017). Legends hospitality scores rich valuation with new mountain capital deal.

Ozanian, M. (2019). Dallas cowboys' 2019 valuation.

Ozanian, M. (2020). Tennessee titans sale puts team in compliance with NFL bylaws and indicates values not harmed by pandemic.

Porter, R. (2018). TV long view: NFL ratings up while broadcast nets bleed viewers.

PR Newswire. (2020). Wearable technology market size is expected to reach USD $57,653 millions by the end of 2022, with a CAGR of 16.2 | Valuates.

Professional Football Hall of Fame. (n.d.). Timeline Detail.

Reuters. (2018). Fox reaches 5-year deal with NFL to broadcast Thursday Night Football.

Ryman, R. (2019). Green Bay Packers report record revenue, record expenses.

Schallhorn, K. (2017). NFL's "tax breaks" targeted by Trump: A look at the league's tax status today.

Scharf, Y. (2018). new tax law is a curveball for the sports industry | Economic intelligence.

Schwartz, Peter (2020, August 25). National Football League Franchise Valuations. https://www.sportico.com/valuations/teams/2020/nfl-valuations-data-viz-1234611955/

Schwartz, P. (2020). Sportico 2020 NFL franchise valuations report.

Sherman, A. (2020). NFL TV rights up for renewal in 2022, and big media will pay more.

Shieber, J. (2018). Super wearable WHOOP launches $30 subscription service—wearable totally included.

Sportradar Press Release. (2015). NFL tabs sportradar as new exclusive statistics distribution partner.

Sraders, A. (2018). Seven states without income tax and what you need to know.

The Ticket Club. (2019). NFL playoff tickets—Divisional round prices and trends.

The Washington Times. (2003). Redskins in process of selling a minority stake in franchise.

Thomas, J. (2019). Why does the NFL play games in London?

Transparency Market Research. (2016). Licensed sports merchandise market to reach US$48.17 billion by 2024—A new research report by transparency market research.

Travis, C. (2017). How much do the NFL and TV partners make a year?

US News and World Report. (2020). Construction worker salary.

WHOOP Press Release. (2017). WHOOP strikes landmark deal as the officially licensed recovery wearable of the NFL players association.

Wolf, J. (2018). Thursday NFL games to be streamed on twitch.

CHAPTER 13
Business of the National Hockey League

Carol Schram

LEARNING OBJECTIVES

- To follow the long history of the NHL through North America, and learn about the "Original Six" franchises.
- To understand the role of franchise expansion and why owning an NHL franchise has become more lucrative today than ever.
- To learn why NHL owners and players are savvy about income tax and exchange rates in managing their finances.
- To analyze the postseason player bonus pool and how the leagues regular season payrolls differ from other professional leagues.

A Brief History

The National Hockey League (NHL) was first established in Montreal, Quebec on November 26, 1917. It was the successor to the National Hockey Association (NHA) and was founded by a group of NHA owners who were no longer willing to continue working with one of their counterparts, but couldn't expel him under the terms of the old league's constitution.

The NHL's original four franchises were the Montreal Canadiens, the Montreal Wanderers, the Ottawa Senators, and the Toronto Arenas. Quebec City also held a franchise, but chose not to operate in the 1917–1918 season.

Over the next 25 years, the league grew to as many as 10 teams as franchises came, went, and changed identities. The Toronto Arenas became the Toronto St. Patricks in 1919 before changing

© Kendall Hunt Publishing Company.

their name to the Maple Leafs in 1927. The Boston Bruins became the NHL's first American franchise when they joined in 1924. The Senators enjoyed a period of dominance during the 1920s, including four Stanley Cup wins. They folded in 1934, during the Great Depression.

The Stanley Cup was originally offered up by Lord Stanley of Preston in 1892 to "the champion hockey team in the Dominion of Canada," as a memento of his time as Canada's governor general. From 1893 to 1906, the winner was determined through challenge games between Canada's top amateur teams. In 1907, the Montreal Wanderers became the first professional team to win. In 1910, the NHA started a tradition of interleague championships when it took control of the Cup, giving U.S. teams the opportunity to compete for the trophy for the first time.

In 1917, the Seattle Metropolitans of the Pacific Coast Hockey Association became the first U.S. Stanley Cup champion. Later that year, the NHL was born. Its top team continued to play the top team from the western professional leagues for the Stanley Cup until 1926, when the Victoria Cougars of the Western Canada Hockey League lost to the NHL's Montreal Maroons.

Though no non-NHL team competed for the Stanley Cup after that year, it wasn't until 1947 that the Cup's trustees officially entered into an agreement that granted control of the trophy to the NHL.

By 1942, the NHL had established its "Original Six" franchises, which all survive to this day—the Montreal Canadiens, Toronto Maple Leafs, Boston Bruins, Chicago Blackhawks, Detroit Red Wings, and New York Rangers. That structure remained unchanged for 25 years.

In 1967, the league underwent an unprecedented expansion, doubling in size from six to 12 teams. Expansion continued during the 1970s, and the World Hockey Association (WHA) sprung up in 1972 as a competing league.

When the WHA folded in 1979, the NHL absorbed four of its franchises as expansion teams—the Hartford Whalers, Quebec Nordiques, Winnipeg Jets, and Edmonton Oilers, who had the greatest player in the history of the game already under contract in 18-year-old Wayne Gretzky.

Gretzky's goal-scoring exploits made headlines throughout the 1980s. The only news bigger was his blockbuster trade from the Oilers to the Los Angeles Kings in 1988, putting the face of the National Hockey League on a team outside the league's traditional geographic strongholds of Canada and the northern United States.

With the Kings, Gretzky raised the profile of hockey in Southern California, which, in turn, helped fuel expansion over the next 10 years into other nontraditional markets like Florida, Anaheim, and Nashville. "The Great One" also went on to play for the St. Louis Blues and New York Rangers before retiring in 1999 as the league's all-time leading scorer with 894 goals and 1,963 assists for 2,857 points in 1,487 NHL games.

Two other important events took place in the early 1990s: in 1992, original NHL Players' Association head and player agent Alan Eagleson was forced to resign and eventually sent to jail after it was revealed that he had swindled and misled the very players he had been assigned to represent. And as the league adjusted to its new post-Eagleson reality, a 38-year-old lawyer named Gary Bettman was hired away from the NBA to become the new NHL commissioner on February 1, 1993.

Bettman's tenure has been a period of growth for the league, both functionally and monetarily. Early on, he oversaw the first wave of Sunbelt expansion. More recently, he has successfully brought in expansion franchises in Las Vegas and Seattle, with previously unimaginable expansion fees going into the pockets of owners.

Bettman has also overseen the improvement of the league's broadcast rights footprint in both Canada and the United States, has shepherded the move into the digital age, and has built long-lasting relationships with blue-chip sponsors on both sides of the border, while delivering cost certainty for his league's owners.

He is criticized for the three lockouts that have occurred during his tenure, which caused the league to lose half a season in 1994–1995, the full 2004-2005 season and half a year in 2012-2013. In the face of escalating player wages, he delivered a hard salary cap in 2005, then significantly increased the owners' share of total revenues under that cap in 2013 (Wyshynsk, 2019).

Bettman was inducted into the Hockey Hall of Fame in November of 2018.

In September of 2019, with the league on a growth curve and players and owners enjoying the spoils of ever-increasing revenues, both sides elected not to exercise their respective options to re-open the collective bargaining agreement that was signed in 2013, which could have triggered another work stoppage in 2020 if a new agreement was not reached.

Instead, the two sides committed to attempting to negotiate a CBA extension without a strike or lockout.

League Structure

In the 2019–2020 season, the NHL comprised 31 clubs, divided into two conferences and four divisions. Three divisions had eight teams; one had seven.

A 32nd franchise, the Seattle Kraken, has been approved beginning in the 2021–2022 season. The Seattle club is slated to join the Pacific Division and the Arizona Coyotes are slated to move to the Central Division, creating four balanced eight-team divisions.

EASTERN CONFERENCE

Atlantic Division

Boston Bruins
Buffalo Sabres
Detroit Red Wings
Florida Panthers
Montreal Canadiens
Ottawa Senators
Tampa Bay Lightning
Toronto Maple Leafs

Metropolitan Division

Carolina Hurricanes
Columbus Blue Jackets
New Jersey Devils
New York Islanders
New York Rangers
Philadelphia Flyers
Pittsburgh Penguins
Washington Capitals

WESTERN CONFERENCE

Central Division

Chicago Blackhawks
Colorado Avalanche
Dallas Stars
Minnesota Wild
Nashville Predators
St. Louis Blues
Winnipeg Jets

Pacific Division

Anaheim Ducks
Arizona Coyotes
Calgary Flames
Edmonton Oilers
Los Angeles Kings
San Jose Sharks
Vancouver Canucks
Vegas Golden Knights

Ownership Buy-In Amount

NHL franchise valuations have been on an upward trajectory ever since 1967, when the league grew from six to 12 teams (Forbes, 2013). The cost was $2 million for clubs in Philadelphia,

Pittsburgh, Los Angeles, St. Louis, Minnesota, and Oakland to join the league at that time—the equivalent of just $15.62 million dollars in 2020, when adjusted for inflation.

When the Vancouver Canucks and Buffalo Sabres joined in 1970, the expansion fee had tripled to $6 million, a number that grew to $7.5 million when the four WHA teams joined at the end of that decade.

The next wave of expansion came in the 1990s, with an exponential jump in franchise valuations. Five teams joined early in the decade with price tags of between $45 and $50 million. Expansion fees then rose to $80 million for the Nashville Predators, Atlanta Thrashers, Columbus Blue Jackets, and Minnesota Wild as the new millennium dawned.

After that, no new franchises were added until Bill Foley handed over $500 million for the Vegas Golden Knights in June of 2016. Just eighteen months later, the owners of NHL Seattle agreed to pay $650 million for their expansion franchise—a premium of 30 percent over Foley's price. (see link: www.tsn.ca/a-look-at-the-nhl-s-expansion-history-1.1220677)

While team ownership around the league has been relatively stable over the last decade or so, two existing franchises have changed hands in recent years. In June of 2019, *Forbes* estimated the value of the Arizona Coyotes' sale of a majority stake to businessman Alex Meruelo at approximately $300 million. *Forbes* reported the value of Tom Dundon's purchase of the Carolina Hurricanes in January of 2018 at $420 million.

© oasisamuel/Shutterstock.com

Revenue Distribution

According to *Forbes*, revenues for the NHL's 31 teams totaled $5.084 billion in the 2018–2019 season—a massive increase over 10 years compared to $2.9 billion in the 2009–2010 season (Wyshynski, 2019).

Speaking very generally, these revenue streams include gate receipts, broadcast and digital rights, licensed clothing and merchandise, concessions, premium suites and luxury boxes, and parking in club-operated facilities (ESPN, 2020).

Facility Revenue, Subsidies, and Construction

Some clubs are independent organizations, with lease agreements with the arenas where they play. Some clubs own their arenas, and some are part of larger conglomerates that can include other teams in other sports as well as ownership of the arena.

© Pinkcandy/Shutterstock.com

Examples of each:

The New York Rangers are owned by The Madison Square Garden Company, which also owns the Madison Square Garden arena and other venues, including Radio City Music Hall and the Beacon Theatre, as well as the NBA's New York Knicks and the Rangers' minor-league affiliate, the Hartford Wolf Pack of the American Hockey League.

The Vancouver Canucks are owned by Canucks Sports and Entertainment (CSE), a private company that is part of the family-run Aquilini Investment Group. The Aquilinis' other sports holdings include Rogers Arena, the Vancouver Warriors of the National Lacrosse League, and two esports teams.

The Carolina Hurricanes are owned by Hurricanes Holdings, LLC, with majority owner Tom Dundon and 14 minority investor groups. Hurricanes Holdings has a contract to operate the PNC Arena facility, which also includes more than 8,000 parking spaces.

The NHL has a revenue-sharing program, outlined in the Collective Bargaining Agreement as "The Player Compensation Cost Redistribution System" (NHL, n.d.). The purpose of the program is to allow higher-revenue teams to help cover the player salaries of the league's lower-revenue teams. The goal is to help keep the talent gap between teams at a minimum, ultimately increasing parity and keeping all franchises around the league competitive, regardless of their individual revenue streams.

Funding for this system is provided as follows.

- Fifty percent from the income of the 10 highest-grossing teams
- Thirty-five percent from the gate receipts of all participating playoff clubs
- The remainder, if needed, from centrally generated league revenues (ESPN NHL attendance, 2020)

The 50/50 revenue split between players and owners as directed by the collective bargaining agreement is used to determine which teams are eligible to receive these revenue-sharing funds. If half of a team's gross revenues are insufficient to cover the Targeted Team Player Compensation as set by the league in any given season, the club will receive additional funds through the cost redistribution system (Forbes Team Valuations).

The NHL also operates an Industry Growth Fund. It is used to fund leaguewide marketing and promotional initiatives, and to make funds available to lower-revenue teams to provide "supplemental support to allow them to make long-term improvements in their revenue generating potential and operational efficiency given their particular circumstances."

The newest NHL arena currently in operation is Little Caesars Arena, the home of the Detroit Red Wings. It opened on September 5, 2017, at a reported cost of $863 million, nearly double the original estimate of $450 million. $324 million of that cost was covered by public funding.

Groundbreaking for T-Mobile Arena in Las Vegas took place on May 1, 2014. The arena opened on April 6, 2016, at a cost of $375 million, as a privately funded joint venture between AEG and MGM Resorts International. The Vegas Golden Knights franchise was awarded on June 22, 2016, and the team began play in October of 2017.

Three new facilities are currently in the works:

The New York Islanders are expected to move into their new arena at Belmont Park in October of 2021. Groundbreaking for the $1.3 billion redevelopment, which also includes a hotel and a retail village, took place on September 23, 2019. The project is being undertaken by New York Arena Partners, a joint venture between Sterling Equities, the Scott Malkin Group, and the Oak View Group. Malkin is one of the primary owners of the Islanders.

Through a public-private partnership, the developers are also helping to fund a new full-time station for the Long Island Rail Road in Elmont, near the Belmont Park site.

In Seattle, the NHL's 32nd franchise was approved after the Oak View Group committed to a redevelopment of the old Key Arena at Seattle Center. The facility has been completely gutted, preserving only its historic roof. In April of 2019, cost estimates for the project were revised to more than $900 million, well above the project's initial projection of $600 million, and the target date for completion was bumped back from October of 2020 to the summer of 2021.

The Calgary Flames are expected to move into their new arena in time for the 2024–2025 NHL season. The team's parent company, Flames Sports and Entertainment, has reached an agreement with the City of Calgary in December of 2019 to split the cost of the new facility, which is estimated at CDN$550 million.

The project is expected to break ground in 2021.

Some older facilities have undertaken extensive updates in order to keep their buildings up-to-date. The biggest was for Madison Square Garden (MSG), home of the New York Rangers. By far the oldest NHL arena, MSG opened in 1968. In 2013, a three-year renovation was completed, valued at $1 billion.

© littlenySTOCK/Shutterstock.com

Financial Forecasting

Leading up to the league's "pause" due to the coronavirus pandemic in March 2020, the NHL was stable as an organization and franchise valuations were climbing (Ozanian, 2019).

No team had relocated since the Atlanta Thrashers moved to Winnipeg during the summer of 2011. Even the Arizona Coyotes, who had been under constant threat of relocation since leaving Winnipeg in 1996, appeared to be entering a period of stability under new owner Alex Meruelo, who took over ownership of the team during the summer of 2019.

In *Forbes*'s 2019 franchise valuation rankings, all 31 franchises showed a positive one-year change in valuation, though none of the increases kept pace with the market in a boom year where the S&P500 was up by 30%. Valuation increases ranged from 1% (Winning Jets, $420 million; Vegas Golden Knights, $580 million; Vancouver Canucks $740 million) to a high of 21% (New Jersey Devils, $550 million).

On average, franchise valuations increased by 66.75% between 2013 and 2019, to an average valuation of $667 million if the expansion Vegas Golden Knights are factored in.

By comparison, the S&P500 increased from 1,685.73 on July 1, 2013 to 2,980.38 on July 1, 2019—an increase of 1,294.65, or 76.80%.

Ten NHL owners beat that rate of return, but on average, during a six-year bull market, investors would have made more money in a market-index fund than by owning an NHL franchise.

Tax Status and Liabilities

Though Canada is the birthplace of hockey and its residents have historically had an insatiable thirst for the sport, five of the six clubs with the lowest growth in their valuations between 2013 and 2019 hail from north of the border.

Exchange rates have been an issue. The vast majority of these teams' revenues are collected in Canadian dollars, while player salaries and some other expenses are paid out in U.S. currency.

On July 1, 2013, it cost CDN$1.0492 to buy one U.S. dollar. On July 1, 2019, it cost CDN$1.3134. All other things being equal, that shift effectively diminished the buying power of Canadian teams by 25%.

In addition, provincial and state taxes vary dramatically in markets around the league.

According to a tax calculator provided by hockey wealth specialists The Gavin Group, effective tax rates are lowest for players in U.S. locales where there is no state tax, such as Nevada (Vegas Golden Knights), Texas (Dallas Stars), Tennessee (Nashville Predators), and Florida (Florida Panthers and Tampa Bay Lightning). Rates rise in all jurisdictions as salaries increase. Check out this link to learn more about how taxes affect salaries.

https://gavingroup.ca/nhl-tax-calculator/

At the other end of the spectrum, Canadian teams play in some of the most highly taxed jurisdictions. Players in the United States with the highest tax rates play for the New York Rangers or New York Islanders (42.15%) or one of the three teams in California (41.58%).

Tax rates are a consideration for unrestricted free agents, who have the freedom to decide where they want to play. In July of 2016, Steven Stamkos chose to forsake the overtures of the Toronto

Maple Leafs, instead signing an eight-year, $68 million contract to remain with the team that originally drafted him, the Tampa Bay Lightning.

Because he re-signed with his current club, Stamkos was permitted to sign for one additional year—in this case, an eighth season at a cap hit of $8.5 million rather than a maximum of 7 years if he'd signed with Toronto. He also saved $9.8 million in taxes—$1.4 million for each of the first 7 years—of the contract by staying in Florida, rather than moving back to his home province of Ontario.

For more information on tax implications, log onto the tax calculator below.

https://gavingroup.ca/nhl-tax-calculator/

As part of their pitch to Stamkos, the Maple Leafs invited him to a meeting in Toronto that included team brass as well as mayor John Tory and Michael B. Medline, the CEO of major retailer and long-time hockey sponsor Canadian Tire. It's believed that Stamkos was presented with a proposal outlining how he'd be able to match or exceed his net earnings with the Lightning through sponsorship opportunities with Canadian Tire and, potentially, other businesses, if he chose to play in Canada's biggest market.

Broadly speaking, hockey players are low-key personalities who often prefer to live their lives out of the spotlight. Following the hard-sell meeting in Toronto, Stamkos immediately instructed his agent to cancel scheduled meetings with other interested teams and accept the Lightning's offer to remain in Tampa Bay.

Stamkos set a precedent—but 2 years later, John Tavares broke it. Another Toronto native, selected first overall by the New York Islanders in 2009, Tavares and his representatives went through a full set of meetings with NHL teams before he reached unrestricted free agency on July 1, 2018.

Though the Islanders had apparently presented an eight-year offer worth $91 million ($11.375 million per season), Tavares ultimately decided to return home to Toronto on a seven-year deal worth $77 million ($11 million per season). He absorbed an additional tax hit of about $440,000 per year in addition to accepting a lower total contract value and a lower average annual value per season.

One consideration was Tavares's desire to return home. Another could have been the instability of the Islanders franchise, which had relocated to Barclays Center in Brooklyn in 2015. Playing in an arena that wasn't well-suited to hockey, and far away from the Islanders' core fan base on Long Island, the club announced 5 months before Tavares's departure that, starting in 2018–2019, it would start splitting games between Barclays and its old home, a now-renovated Nassau Coliseum on Long Island, until the new Belmont Park arena was completed.

At a team level, partnerships with local government can be crucial. After rejecting various arena proposals for years, which led to the eventual departure of the NBA's Seattle SuperSonics in 2008, Seattle City Council got on board with the Oak View Group's proposal to renovate KeyArena in 2017. With a new arena confirmed, the NHL expansion franchise was approved one year later, and since then, the team has continued to work in concert with the municipality.

For example, in February 2020, the club announced that it would be subsidizing free public transit passes as well as entering into a partnership with the Seattle Monorail to help get fans to games in an efficient, environmentally friendly fashion.

Tampa Bay Lightning owner Jeffrey Vinik has also taken his partnership with Hillsborough County to another level. Since purchasing the Lightning for $170 million in 2010, he and the county have committed to total investments of $100 million each in renovations to county-owned Amalie Arena by 2030.

Vinik and Cascade Investment LLC are also behind Strategic Property Partners, who are spearheading the $3 billion, mixed-use Water Street Tampa district that is being developed adjacent to the arena.

Revenue Sources and Partnerships

Statista shows that 36.6% of the NHL's revenues were derived from regular-season gate receipts in 2018–2019—down from 41.81% in 2010–2011, but still traditionally higher than other major sports. In 2017–2018, gate receipts accounted for 37% of NHL revenue, but only 27% in MLB, 22% in the NBA, and 16% in the NFL.

Gate receipt revenues and average revenue per ticket varies dramatically from team to team—from a high of $156.91 per ticket in Boston to a low of 31.27 in Florida in 2018–2019.

Even more important than ticket sales—concessions and merchandise. In 2017–2018, a total of 75.4% of league revenues were estimated to have come from those three areas. Teams have increased their commitment to maximizing these revenue streams by broadening their offerings and making their arenas desirable destinations for eating, drinking and socializing at both the premium and casual levels.

Sponsorships at both the league and team levels have also been on the rise. According to a 2018 report from ESP Properties, total NHL sponsorship revenue rose from $409 million in 2013–2014 to $559.5 million in 2017–2018—37% overall growth, with an uptick of more than 10% in the

2017–2018 season alone. That growth was fueled primarily by the out-of-the-box success of the expansion Vegas Golden Knights and a new seven-year deal with Adidas to supply team uniforms and licensed apparel that was reportedly valued at $70 million, more than twice the amount paid by Reebok in the league's previous contract.

The NHL also expects to see increased revenue from sports betting, which has been rolling out on a state-by-state basis ever since the U.S. Supreme Court struck down the federal ban in 2018.

Within less than 6 months of the Supreme Court announcement, the league had entered into partnerships with three different sports betting entities: MGM Resorts, FanDuel and William Hill.

Terms vary in each agreement. The deal with MGM Resorts includes exclusive access to "previously unseen enhanced NHL proprietary game data that will be generated by the League's state of the art tracking systems currently under development. Access to this data will allow MGM Resorts to provide its customers with specialized NHL game insights, as well as unlocking new and innovative interactive fan engagement and betting opportunities for its U.S. customers wherever legally available."

The league's new puck-and-player-tracking system, intended to provide additional support for broadcasters as well as sports betting partners, was previewed at the 2020 All-Star Game in St. Louis and was also used in the 2020 NHL playoffs.

In regions where sports betting has been legalized, some clubs were quick to add that to their in-arena experience. By the 2019–2020 season, the New Jersey Devils had entered into partnerships with William Hill, Caesars, Unibet and FanDuel, the most visible of which is their sportsbook-style William Hill Sports Lounge inside their arena, the Prudential Center, where fans can place bets via the William Hill mobile app.

In October of 2019, Washington Capitals owner Ted Leonsis announced plans to open a full sports betting parlor inside Capital One Arena, also in partnership with William Hill.

Expansion fees are not classified as Hockey Related Revenue. Fees for both Vegas and Seattle were divided equally among the league's 30 incumbent teams, so each owner received $16.67 million when the Golden Knights joined the league and will get $21.67 million from Seattle.

Media Revenues

On a league level, broadcast revenues are generated from television, Sirius XM satellite radio and out-of-market digital sports packages through NHL Live.

In the United States, the NHL will be negotiating a new broadcast rights deal starting with the 2021–2022 season, following the conclusion of a 10-year deal with NBC Sports that began in 2011–2012 and was worth $200 million per season (McCarthy, 2019).

Bidding for the new deal could get competitive, which will drive up the final value and could see broadcast rights split across more than one network, like we've seen with other sports. In 2019, Brooks Melchior of Sports By Brooks predicted that the new deal could come in somewhere between $400 and $450 million per season.

In Canada, Rogers Media snatched away the national NHL broadcast rights from longtime rightsholder TSN/BellMedia in November of 2013, signing a 12-year deal worth CDN$5.2 billion that kicked off in the 2014–2015 season. Longtime Hockey Night in Canada rightsholder CBC and French-language network TVA were also partners in the deal—essentially, paying for the rights to show games, but with little opportunity to generate revenue from the broadcasts (Ladurantaye, 2013).

Rogers pays the NHL in Canadian dollars for this deal. When signed, CDN$1 was worth 95.82 U.S. cents., but by early 2016, it had dropped as low as 68 cents before rebounding to the 75 to 80 cent range in subsequent seasons.

As such, the league has been receiving annual payments from Canada worth between 15% and 30% less than when the agreement was originally signed. Visit these currency conversion charts to learn more: https://www.bankrate.com/calculators/investing/currencycalc.aspx.

Payments to the league were pegged to start at CDN$300 million in the first year and rise to $500 million by the end of the deal. As one of Canada's primary telecommunications providers, part of Rogers' goal in acquiring the NHL rights was to secure content that would boost other sectors of their business, driving cable subscriptions and creating synergies with its mobile unit, Rogers Wireless.

The NHL has also continued to expand its broadcast footprint outside North America. As one example, in September of 2019, it partnered with Russia's leading internet search provider, Yandex, to stream all games for free in Russia.

In 2015, the NHL made an important move in the digital sphere when it signed a six-year deal with MLB Advanced Media, the company that handles streaming video and other digital properties for Major League Baseball. The deal, which also included additional components, generated $100 million per year in rights fees for the NHL as well as an equity stake of nearly 10% in the tech spinoff BAMTech, which was valued at $3.75 billion in 2017 following a significant investment by Disney.

At the team level, broadcast revenues vary widely. In 2013, *Forbes* reported that the Toronto Maple Leafs led the pack with $41 million in broadcast revenues for their regional games, broadcast across TSN, Sportsnet and Leafs TV. At the other end of the spectrum, the Florida Panthers reportedly inked a 10-year extension with Fox Sports Florida in 2012, which was worth just $115 million in total or $11.5 million per season—an improvement over their previous contract, but still worth barely a quarter of what the Maple Leafs earn each year (Settini, 2013).

Salary Structures

The NHL operates under a hard salary-cap system. Once a revenue projection is established by the league, a midpoint is set.

The upper limit (salary cap) is set at 115% of the midpoint, and the lower limit (salary floor) is set at 85%. All teams' total player salaries must fall within this window at the end of the year.

No individual player may earn more than 20% of the upper limit in any given season, and league minimum salaries are set by the collective bargaining agreement. In the 2019–2020 and 2020–2021 seasons, the minimum is set at $700,000. In 2021–2022, it rises to $750,000.

Connor McDavid of the Edmonton Oilers carried the largest cap hit in the 2019–2020 season at $12.5 million, in the second year of an eight-year deal worth $100,000,000. His deal was worth 16.7% of the upper limit when it was signed. Also in 2019–2020, Alex Ovechkin of the Washington Capitals was in the 12th year of a 13-year contract, signed under the previous collective bargaining agreement when longer contract lengths were permitted. Ovechkin's cap hit is $9.538 million per season, but his contract was worth a whopping 19% of the upper limit when it was signed.

The type of contract a player receives depends on his years of service in the league.

Entry-level contracts can range from one year to a maximum of 3 years. They are capped at a maximum base salary of $925,000 per season. Players on entry-level contracts can be eligible for performance bonuses, as laid out in their individual contracts. For select superstar players, those bonuses can total as much as $2.85 million per season.

Once a player has completed his entry-level period, he signs a standard contract, which can range from 1 year to 8 years in length. Contracts can be structured to include signing bonuses or different cash payouts in different years but for purposes of the salary cap, the final total is averaged to create a consistent salary-cap hit throughout the duration of the contract (Capfriendly, 2020).

After a player reaches the age of 35, he signs a 35+ contract. These deals are typically short, as players are nearing retirement age. Bonuses are allowed, so 35+ contracts often carry a relatively modest base salary with the opportunity for the player to earn more through bonuses.

All contracts can be one-way or two-way. On a one-way contract, a player receives his standard salary whether he plays in the NHL or is demoted to the minor-league American Hockey League. On a two-way contract, he receives his full salary when playing in the NHL, but a lower minor-league salary when playing in the AHL.

Example: Carsen Twarynski signed his entry-level contract on March 11, 2018 after being drafted in the third round by the Philadelphia Flyers in 2016. He played his first full pro season with the Lehigh Valley Phantoms of the AHL, earning his two-way salary of $70,000 for the year.

In 2019–2020, he was called up for 15 games with the Flyers, where he would have earned his NHL salary of $742,500, pro-rated to the number of days he was with the Flyers. During his time in the NHL, he would also be accruing stats that could potentially be applied toward $132,500 worth of performance bonuses.

Twarynski also received a signing bonus of $92,500 in each season, regardless of where he played.

If a team wishes to part ways with a player who is under contract, the player can be bought out. If the player is under 26, he will receive one-third of the remaining value of his contract. Players who are 26 or over receive two-thirds of the value of their contract. The cap hit for contracts that are bought out is spread over twice the length of the contract and may not be the same in each season, depending on how the contract was structured.

When a player's contract expires, he becomes a free agent. Early in his career, he is a restricted (Group 2) free agent, which means his team retains his negotiating rights. Once he has accumulated more years of service, he earns arbitration rights that give him additional leverage.

Once a player reaches age 27 or 7 years of service, whichever comes first, he can become an unrestricted (Group 3) free agent who is free to sign with any team, further increasing his bargaining power.

In order to maintain the 50/50 revenue balance between players and owners, the league withholds a portion of each player's paychecks and places it in an escrow account. Once the final accounting for each season is complete—typically, about one year after the season's completion—the players' total revenue share is compared against the amount that was actually paid out in net salaries (base salary minus escrow). If there's a shortfall, players receive a refund from the escrow account, thus balancing the books.

Over the years, escrow withholdings have been significant, and have been a bone of contention among the players. During the 2019–2020 season, 14% of each paycheck was withheld and placed in the escrow account.

Salaries for top NHL coaches increased significantly after Mike Babcock negotiated an eight-year, $50-million deal to become the head coach of the Toronto Maple Leafs during the summer of 2015. Not all salaries are disclosed, but other veteran coaches like Joel Quenneville of the Florida Panthers, Claude Julien of the Montreal Canadiens, and Todd McLellan of the Los Angeles Kings were making about $5 million a year in the 2019–2020 season. Coaches at the low end of the spectrum included Travis Green of the Vancouver Canucks ($1 million) and Rick Tocchet of the Arizona Coyotes ($1.5 million).

Salary Cap

The NHL operates under a hard salary cap, with owners and players each receiving 50% of Hockey Related Revenue (HRR) each season.

According to the HRR Reporting Package amended to the collective bargaining agreement signed in 2013, HRR comprises the money earned by the NHL and its individual clubs through games and other NHL-related events.

Once the NHL sets its salary-cap midpoint each year, the NHL Players' Association then has the opportunity to utilize an "escalator" to increase that number by up to 5%, in order to provide a larger pool of funds for the players who are looking to sign new deals during the offseason.

The salary cap ceiling started at $39 million when it was first introduced following the 2004–2005 lockout. It grew to $64.3 million by the 2011–2012 season, setting the stage for another half-season lockout, and had risen to $81.5 million by the 2019–2020 season (see chart). www.capfriendly.com/faq#upper-lower-limit

Unless an extension is reached beforehand, the NHL's current Collective Bargaining Agreement is set to expire on September 15, 2022.

Postseason Financial Structures

In the NHL playoffs, the league and its teams make money, but the players mostly do not.

Player salaries are paid out only through the regular season—players do not receive regular paychecks during training camp, preseason, or the playoffs.

There is a playoff bonus pool, which is paid out to teams round-by-round, and which each team distributes at its own discretion. When the current CBA took effect in 2013, the total bonus pool for that season doubled to $13 million.

Team shares were broken down as follows—with individual shares based on payouts to 25 players, a ballpark figure that varies from team to team.

- Presidents' Trophy winner (best regular-season record): $500,000 ($20,000 per player)
- First-round losers (eight teams): $250,000 per team ($10,000 per player)
- Second-round losers (four teams): $500,000 per team ($20,000 per player)
- Conference Final losers (two teams): $1.25 million per team ($50,000 per player)
- Stanley Cup Final loser (one team): $2.25 million ($90,000 per player)
- Stanley Cup Final winner (one team): $3.75 million ($150,000 per player)

Relative to most players' salaries, these bonuses are relatively inconsequential. But players on all teams do benefit from the Hockey Related Revenue that is generated during the NHL's two-month-long postseason marathon.

Typically, NHL teams who have a chance at reaching the playoffs will connect with season-ticket holders well before the regular season ends, asking for deposits on postseason tickets at prices that are well above regular-season levels and that increase round-by-round.

When authorized, ticket holders' credit cards are typically charged for the maximum number of home games (four) in each of the first two rounds. A second payment will go through if the club reaches the Conference Final or Stanley Cup Final.

Ticket prices are rarely made public, but the Toronto Maple Leafs published a grid in 2002 that gives an idea of the type of round-by-round price increases that fans can expect to absorb if their team goes on a run—although base ticket prices would now be much higher (see chart in link here: www.nhl.com/mapleleafs/news/maple-leafs-announce-playoff-ticket-prices/c-458956).

Playoff ticket commitments are also usually tied into season-ticket renewals for most teams. If a team doesn't advance, or doesn't play four home games in any round, payments for unplayed games are typically applied against a fan's season tickets for the following season, rather than being refunded.

According to the CBA, up to 50% of the league's revenue-sharing monies, based on its redistribution agreement, can come from playoff revenues. Teams that host playoff games are required to remit 35% of their gate receipts to the league for potential redistribution.

Secondary markets drive prices even higher. For Game 7 of the 2019 Stanley Cup Final between the St. Louis Blues and the Boston Bruins in Boston, secondary-market prices started at nearly $1,500 and were listed as high as $10,000 each for tickets close to the action.

Playoff games are included in the NHL's agreements with its broadcast partners and its major sponsors, but additional revenue-generating activations can be made during the postseason. In recent years, the NHL has done an outstanding job of leveraging its first-ever Stanley Cup Finals in two entertainment hubs—in Nashville in 2017 and in Las Vegas in 2018.

Final Assessment of Growth Potential

Though the NHL's reach in the United States falls well short of the NFL, NBA, and Major League Baseball, the league has been successful in expanding outside its traditional regional bases over the last quarter-century, under the guidance of Commissioner Gary Bettman.

The league has seen significant growth in revenues, including from broadcast rights, merchandise and sponsorships. It has also tweaked its on-ice product to deliver a game that's faster and more exciting than ever before. Additionally, the NHL has been proactive in exploring digital media and has worked to expand its global footprint.

Case Study

The NHL's expansion to Las Vegas in 2017 has been a tremendous success, but was considered risky when discussions first began. The desert location was an unlikely fit for a sport played on ice, the population of the city itself was much lower than other NHL markets, and Las Vegas had previously been passed over by sports leagues because of its connection to the gambling industry.

Examine:

- How owner Bill Foley and the Vegas community presented a case that put those concerns to rest.
- How the landscape of gambling legalization shifted at just the right time.
- How the Golden Knights took advantage of their market's unique characteristics to bring innovation to NHL live game presentation.
- How the team's hockey operations staff manipulated its expansion-draft terms and utilized its available salary-cap space to build a winner in its first season of operation.
- How the Golden Knights' template paved the way for the NFL's arrival in Las Vegas.

Review Questions

1. Choose a current NHL player. Research how his present contract is structured, then calculate how much he receives in his pocket from each paycheck after deductions for taxes and escrow. Players are paid twice a month through the regular season, beginning on October 15.
2. Explain why a local government would or would not wish to invest in or offer tax breaks for construction of a new NHL arena in their jurisdiction.
3. Based on historical numbers, project how the NHL's salary cap ceiling will change over the next 5 years.

References

CapFriendly. (2020). *Frequently asked questions*. www.capfriendly.com/faq#upper-lower-limit

ESPN. (2020). *NHL attendance report 2018-19*. http://www.espn.com/nhl/attendance/_/year/2019

Forbes. (2013). Forbes announces 2013 NHL team valuations. November 25. www.forbes.com/sites/forbespr/2013/11/25/forbes-announces-2013-nhl-team-valuations/#3544b2f14874

Jessiman, E. (2020, March 21). *NHL Sponsorships: Richer than they think*. The Hockey News – Money and Power 2019.

Ladurantaye, S. (2013, November 26). *A game changer for Canada's game*. The Globe and Mail. www.theglobeandmail.com/report-on-business/rogers-reaches-12-year-broadcast-deal-with-nhl-worth-52-billion/article15600412/

McCarthy, M. (2019, October 3). *How will NHL's TV talks play out? We ask the experts*. Front Office Sports. https://frntofficesport.com/nhl-tv/

NHL. (n.d.). *NHL collective bargaining agreement, September 16, 2012-September 15, 2022, Section 50.12.A.* http://www.nhl.com/nhl/en/v3/ext/CBA2012/NHL_NHLPA_2013_CBA.pdf

Ozanian, M., Badenhausen, K., & Settimi, C. (2019, December 11). *NHL's most valuable teams 2019: Though buried in standings, New York rangers remain on top*. Forbes. www.forbes.com/sites/mikeozanian/2019/12/11/the-nhls-most-valuable-teams-2019-new-york-rangers-on-top-at-165-billion/#3d0bc8e47163

Settimi, C. (2013, November 25). *The NHL's richest local television deals*. Forbes. www.forbes.com/sites/christinasettimi/2013/11/25/nhls-richest-local-television-deals/#7a3cc7fc523f

The Gavin Group (n.d.). NHL tax calculator. https://gavingroup.ca/nhl-tax-calculator/

Wyshynski, G. (2019, August 22). *How the NHL has changed in the past 10 years ... and what's next*. ESPN. www.espn.com/nhl/story/_/id/27432037/how-nhl-changed-10-years-next

CHAPTER 14

Business of the Olympics

James T. Reese Jr.
Spiro G. Doukas

LEARNING OBJECTIVES

- To understand the structural membership of the International Olympic Committee, the national governing bodies, the international federations, and organizing committees and how they work together to host an Olympics every quadrennium.
- To assess where the Summer and Winter Olympic revenues come from, how broadcast rights are managed, and the unique relationship with the host city and organizing committee.
- To learn about the exclusive relationship the Olympic Partners program has with venues, athletes and sponsors.
- To consider why hosting an Olympic Games can generate enormous backlash for the host city.

Introduction

The Olympic Games began in Ancient Greece almost 3,000 years ago, in 776 B.C. Almost 1,000 years later, in 393 AD, Greece was under Roman rule and the Olympics were banned by Roman Emperor Theodosius, accusing them of being pagan cults as Christianity was becoming a dominant religion in the Mediterranean. In 1896, French aristocrat Baron Pierre de Coubertin revived the Olympics with the first modern Olympic Games taking place in 1896 in Athens, Greece. One major difference between the original Olympics and the modern Olympics is that the modern Olympics happens in a different country every 4 years (Leading the Olympic Movement, 2020; Who We Are, 2020). What's known today as the Paralympics was founded by neurologist Sir Ludwig Guttmann in 1948 as a rehabilitation program for World War II veterans. Competitions were established between different hospitals to coincide with the London Games that same year. Guttmann's program gained in popularity and in 1960, he brought approximately 400 wheel-

chair athletes from 23 countries to Rome to compete (History of the Paralympics, 2008). Now, the Paralympics has grown to include more than 4,300 athletes, from 159 countries, participating in 528 events, at the 2016 Games in Rio (Dehghansai et al., 2017).

The encompassing phrase that includes the Olympic Games, the Paralympic Games, as well as all associated language (Olympism, The Olympic Motto, etc.), symbols, and activities is referred to as The Olympic Movement. The Olympic Movement is governed internationally by the International Olympic Committee (IOC). The IOC is an international nongovernmental organization that is the final authority on the Olympic Movement. The IOC is guided by the Olympic Charter, a set of rules and bylaws first created in 1908 and revised as recently as 2019 (Olympic Charter, 2019; Olympic Charters, 2020). The IOC also owns the rights to items such as the Olympic Rings, the Olympic flag, anthem, and motto (Who We Are, 2020).

Organizational Structure

The IOC is governed by an executive board that performs numerous duties and legislative functions of the organization. The executive board carries the responsibility of "enacting all regulations necessary for the full implementation of the Olympic Charter" (Olympic Charter, 2019; Olympics and International Sports Law Research Guide, 2018). There are various commissions that assist the executive board with its administrative functions including ethics, sport and law, and television rights and new media.

The internal structure of the IOC includes this executive board, which is responsible for making decisions for the organization and enacting legislation, as well as more than 100 members who

© Leonard Zhukovsky/Shutterstock.com

represent the IOC within their individual countries (Olympics and International Sports Law Research Guide, 2018). These members are volunteers and are elected to four-year terms of service. Although these members represent their countries as Olympic ambassadors, they do not serve as official delegates within the IOC. The IOC also includes approximately 50 honorary members (Members, 2020). Finally, the IOC consists of more than 30 different commissions, which serve like traditional organizational committees, as well as sessions, normally similar to annual corporate meetings (Olympics.org, 2020; IOC Commissions, 2020).

The IOC is supported by numerous independent organizations, including international federations (IFs), national Olympic committees (NOCs), national governing bodies (NGBs), and organizing committees of the Olympic games (OCOGs). In return for the governance and administrative support from each, the IOC provides varying levels of financial support so that all can work together to execute successful events.

International federations (IF) are nongovernmental organizations that are responsible for administering one or more sports on the international level. The IOC collaborates with IFs to ensure they comply with the Olympic Charter. The technical control of each sport is the responsibility of the applicable federation. An example of this is the Fédération Internationale de Basketball (FIBA), the international federation for the sport of basketball. FIBA sets the policies, procedures, and rules for international competitions such as the FIBA Basketball World Cup (International Sports Federations, 2020).

Each of the more than 200 nations that participate in the Olympics or Paralympics has its own National Olympic Committee (NOC). These NOCs govern and promote the growth of their sports and Olympic-caliber athletes. The NOCs also make the final selection of which athletes in their respective country will represent the country at the Olympic Games. An example of this is the

United States Olympic Committee. Another responsibility of the NOCs is that they will also nominate host cities for the International Olympic Committee to select from. Currently there are 205 National Olympic Committees (National Olympic Committees, 2020).

Each nation's NOC is supported by national governing bodies (NGBs), which govern each nation's individual sports, and organizing committees of the Olympic Games (OCOGs), which support the host cities for the Games. For example, the United States Olympic & Paralympic Committee (USOPC) has nearly 50 NGBs governing sports across the nation (Leading the Olympic Movement, 2020). The next time the Games will be held in the United States is 2028 in Los Angeles. Los Angeles's OCOG, the Los Angeles Organizing Committee, is currently helping to prepare the city for the Games (Games Concept, 2020).

The last link in the Olympic organizational structure are these Organizing Committees for the Olympic Games (OCOGs). The formation of each OCOG is the responsibility of the respective host country's NOC, in conjunction with the host city. However, once an OCOG has been formed, and the city has been officially identified as a host city, the OCOG then reports directly to the IOC for the duration of that city's Games (Organising Committees for the Olympic Games, 2020).

Revenues

Overall, the IOC has two primary sources of revenue: broadcast partnerships and sponsorship revenue from The Olympic Partners (TOP) program. The TOP program was implemented in 1985 to develop a consistent base of revenue to support the Games and the Olympic Movement. Broadcast partnerships account for 73% of total revenue. That equates to approximately $4.1 billion. In contrast, the TOP program generates 18% of total revenue, or roughly $1 billion (Baccellieri, 2018; Olympic Marketing Fact File, 2020). However, the IOC allows OCOGs to retain local broadcast rights and revenue generated from OCOG sponsorships, as well as the majority of ticketing and local licensing revenue (Baade & Matheson, 2016). This can add up to an almost equal amount of revenue in some cases as that received from the IOC. Using the 2012 Summer Games in London as an example, the IOC generated $3.2 billion in revenue, while the London Organizing Committee generated $3.3 billion (Baade & Matheson, 2016).

Corporate Sponsorship and Partnership Revenue

As mentioned previously, 18%, or approximately $929 million, of the IOC's overall revenue comes from TOP partners, with an additional 9% coming from other revenues and rights sources such as merchandising and tickets (Olympic Marketing Fact File, 2020). See **Table 1** for a current list of organizations participating in the IOC's TOP program.

TABLE 1: IOC TOP Members

Organizations
Airbnb
Alibaba Group
Atos
Bridgestone
Coca-Cola
Dow
General Electric
Intel
OMEGA
Panasonic
P&G
Samsung
Toyota
Visa

International Olympic Committee, 2020a, p. 16; International Olympic Committee, 2020bInternational Olympic Committee. (2020a). *The Olympic Studies Centre.* www.olympic.org/olympic-studies-centre/collections/official-publications/olympic-charters International Olympic Committee. (2020b). *The Olympic Partner Programme.* www.olympic.org/partners

Not surprisingly, the IOC is very protective of their sponsors. Protections help against issues such ambush marketing. In the bidding process, the IOC is looking at what the potential host city will do to protect against nonsponsors trying to unethically associate with the Olympics. Becoming a TOP sponsor costs millions of dollars, but in return, sponsors provide valuable resources such as technical support, financial investment, media exposure, and in-kind services.

Olympic sponsorship has become one of the most dynamic forms of marketing, with dual benefits for both the corporations and the Olympic movement. Olympic sponsorship launched with the 1984 Los Angeles Olympic Games. These were the first Olympics to generate a profit, and the Los Angeles Games cleared $200 million (Cordova, 2015). Prior to the 1976 Montreal Olympic Games, the TOP sponsors included dozens of companies. After 1976, the IOC lowered the number of TOP partners to around 9 to 12, which included some of the richest companies in the world. By reducing the number of partners, the IOC created a greater sense of exclusivity among sponsors. This is similar to a high profile restaurant or club's allowing few patrons inside to make those allowed in to enjoy a sense of exclusivity; these elites

could potentially pay a large premium for this privilege. What do TOP sponsors receive for paying hundreds of millions of dollars to be a sponsor? Thousands of tickets, platforms, hospitality, and marketing, which help elevate their visibility and investment (Olympic Marketing Fact File, 2020, p. 15).

Media Revenue

As mentioned previously, 73% of the IOC's revenue comes from Olympic broadcast partnerships. The Olympics were broadcast for the first time in 1936, at the Berlin Summer Games, when Germany was the only country to broadcast the games. Since the 1936 Berlin Summer Games were first broadcast, the number of countries broadcasting the Games has increased steadily until the Games were distributed by 214 countries for the Atlanta Summer Games in 1996. At the Sydney

Games in 2000, broadcasting the Games became a global event. Please see **Tables 2 and 3** for data on Olympic broadcast coverage for the Summer and Winter Games from 1936 to 2018 (Olympic Marketing Fact File, 2020, p. 24).

© Leonard Zhukovsky/Shutterstock.com

TABLE 2: Countries Broadcasting the Olympics—Summer Games 1936-2016

Olympic Broadcast Partnerships	Number of Countries/Territories Broadcasting
1936 Berlin	1
1948 London	1
1952 Helsinki	2
1956 Melbourne	1
1960 Rome	21
1964 Tokyo	40
1968 Mexico City	N/A
1972 Munich	98
1976 Montreal	124
1980 Moscow	111
1984 Los Angeles	156
1988 Seoul	160
1992 Barcelona	193
1996 Atlanta	214
2000 Sydney	Global
2004 Athens	Global
2008 Beijing	Global
2012 London	Global
2016 Rio	Global

("Olympic," 2020, p. 24) International Olympic Committee. (2020). *The Olympic Studies Centre.* www.olympic.org/olympic-studies-centre/collections/official-publications/olympic-charters

TABLE 3: Countries Broadcasting the Olympics—Winter Games 1956-2018

Olympic Winter Games	Number of Countries/Territories Broadcasting
1956 Cortina	22
1960 Squaw Valley	27
1964 Innsbruck	30
1968 Grenoble	32
1972 Sapporo	41
1976 Innsbruck	38
1980 Lake Placid	40
1984 Sarajevo	100
1988 Calgary	64
1992 Albertville	86
1994 Lillehammer	120
1998 Nagano	160
2002 Salt Lake City	160
2006 Turin	Global
2010 Vancouver	Global
2014 Sochi	Global
2018 Pyeongchang	Global

("Olympic," 2020, p. 24) International Olympic Committee. (2020). *The Olympic Studies Centre.* www.olympic.org/olympic-studies-centre/collections/official-publications/olympic-charters

Not surprisingly, just as media distribution has increased, so has media revenue. For example, the $1.2 million in media revenue generated in 1960 by the Summer Games in Rome has grown to $2.9 billion at the Rio Games in 2016. See **Tables 4 and 5** for data on broadcast revenue for the Summer and Winter Games from 1960 to 2018 (Olympic Marketing Fact File, 2020, p. 27).

TABLE 4: IOC Broadcast Revenue—Summer Games 1960-2016

Olympic Summer Games	Total Broadcast Revenue in Millions (USD)
1960 Rome	1.2
1964 Tokyo	1.6
1968 Mexico City	9.8
1972 Munich	18
1976 Montreal	35
1980 Moscow	88
1984 Los Angeles	287
1988 Seoul	403
1992 Barcelona	636
1996 Atlanta	898
2000 Sydney	1,332
2004 Athens	1,494
2008 Beijing	1,739
2012 London	2,569
2016 Rio	2,868

("Olympic," 2020, p. 27) The International Olympic Committee. (2020). *The Olympic Studies Centre*. www.olympic.org/olympic-studies-centre/collections/official-publications/olympic-charters

TABLE 5: IOC Broadcast Revenue – Winter Games 1960-2018

Olympic Broadcast Partnerships	Total Broadcast Revenue in Millions (USD)
1960 Squaw Valley	1.2
1964 Tokyo	1.6
1968 Mexico City	9.8
1972 Munich	18
1976 Montreal	35
1980 Moscow	88
1984 Los Angeles	287
1988 Seoul	403
1992 Barcelona	636
1996 Atlanta	898
2000 Sydney	1,332
2004 Athens	1,494
2008 Beijing	1,739
2012 London	2,569
2016 Rio	2,868

("Olympic," 2020, p. 27) International Olympic Committee. (2020). *The Olympic Studies Centre*. www.olympic.org/olympic-studies-centre/collections/official-publications/olympic-charters

Ticket Revenue

Ticketing for the Olympic Games is the responsibility of each respective OCOG, with the assistance of the IOC. This includes the creation of ticket policies, establishment of ticket prices, and distribution of tickets to fans. The last Summer Games in Rio in 2016 generated $321 million in ticket revenue for the Organizing Committee of the Olympic and Paralympic Games. See **Tables 6 and 7** for data on ticket sales revenue for the Summer and Winter Games from 1984 to 2018 (Olympic Marketing Fact File, 2020, p. 33).

TABLE 6: Ticket Sales—Summer Games 1984-2016

Olympic Summer Games	Tickets Available (in millions)	Tickets Sold (in millions)	% Tickets Sold (in millions)	Revenue to OCOG (in millions)
1984 Los Angeles	6.9	5.7	82	156
1988 Seoul	4.4	3.3	75	36
1992 Barcelona	3.9	3.0	77	79
1996 Atlanta	11	8.3	75	425
2000 Sydney	7.6	6.7	88	551
2004 Athens	5.3	3.8	71	228
2008 Beijing	6.8	6.5	96	185
2012 London	8.5	8.2	97	988
2016 Rio	8.8	6.2	91	321

("Olympic," 2020, p. 33) The International Olympic Committee. (2020). *The Olympic Studies Centre*. www.olympic.org/olympic-studies-centre/collections/official-publications/olympic-charters

TABLE 7: Ticket Sales—Winter Games 1988-2018

Olympic Winter Games	Tickets Available (in millions)	Tickets Sold (in millions)	% Tickets Sold (in millions)	Revenue to OCOG (in millions)
1988 Calgary	1.9	1.6	84	32
1992 Albertville	1.2	0.9	75	32
1994 Lillehammer	1.3	1.2	92	26
1998 Nagano	1.4	1.3	89	74
2002 Salt Lake City	1.6	1.5	95	183
2006 Turin	1.1	0.9	81	89
2010 Vancouver	1.5	1.5	97	250
2014 Sochi	1.1	1.0	90	205
2018 Pyeongchang	1.3	1.1	85	143

("Olympic," 2020, p. 33) International Olympic Committee. (2020). *The Olympic Studies Centre*. www.olympic.org/olympic-studies-centre/collections/official-publications/olympic-charters

Licensing Revenue

In 2018, the Winter Games in PyeongChang produced $79 million, the most in recent history for the Winter Games. Licensing in PyeongChang included 1,500 different products including plush toys, commemorative stamps, coins, and bank notes, to name a few. For the Summer Games, Beijing 2008 and London 2012 led the way in licensing revenue with $163 million and $119 million, respectively. See **Tables 8 and 9** for data on licensing sales for the Summer and Winter Games from 1988 to 2018 (Olympic Marketing Fact File, 2020, p. 33; Stewart, 2007).

TABLE 8: Licensing Sales—Summer Games 1988-2016

Olympic Summer Games	Licensees	Revenue to OCOG (in millions)
1988 Seoul	62	19
1992 Barcelona	61	17
1996 Atlanta	125	91
2000 Sydney	100	52
2004 Athens	23	62
2008 Beijing	68	163
2012 London	65	119
2016 Rio	59	31

("Olympic," 2020, p. 36) International Olympic Committee. (2020). *The Olympic Studies Centre*. www.olympic.org/olympic-studies-centre/collections/official-publications/olympic-chartersTable 9: Licensing Sales—Winter Games 1994-2018

TABLE 9: Licensing Sales – Winter Games 1994-2018

Olympic Winter Games	Licensees	Revenue to OCOG (in millions)
1994 Lillehammer	30	24
1998 Nagano	190	14
2002 Salt Lake City	70	25
2006 Turin	32	22
2010 Vancouver	48	51
2014 Sochi	49	35
2018 Pyeongchang	4	79

("Olympic," 2020, p. 36) The International Olympic Committee. (2020). *The Olympic Studies Centre*. www.olympic.org/olympic-studies-centre/collections/official-publications/olympic-charters

Expenses

The IOC is a nonprofit organization; thus 90% of their revenues are redistributed from the Games and go back into sport and athlete development. The IOC provided $965 million toward the Athens 2004 Games, $1.25 billion toward the Beijing 2008 Games, $1.374 billion toward the London 2012 Games, and $1.531 billion toward the staging of the Olympic Games for Rio 2016. These contributions by the IOC help lessen the financial drain on the city hosting the Games. Starting from Athens 2004 to Rio 2016 (Summer Games), and from Salt Lake City 2002 to PyeongChang 2018, there has been a financial shift by the IOC. The IOC started increasing its financial involvement to host cities to help the Olympics succeed. This increase in financial support rose 60% from 2002 to 2018.

In addition to supporting the OCOGs of host cities, the IOC also distributes revenue to NOCs and IFs. For example, $215 million was allocated to NOCs worldwide in conjunction with the 2018 Winter Games in PyeongChang (Olympic Marketing Fact File, 2020, p. 10). Similarly, the IOC supports IFs to assist in running annual world championship events in the different Olympic sports. In conjunction with the PyeongChang Games, IFs received the exact same amount of money as their colleagues at NOCs, $215 million (Olympic Marketing Fact File, 2020, p. 11). Although NOCs and IFs generate revenue on their own, most agree that without the financial support of the IOC, it would be extremely difficult to maintain the current level of quality for global Olympic sport governance (Olympic Marketing Fact File, 2020, p. 8).

The World Anti-Doping Agency (WADA), located in Montreal, Canada, is a foundation created by the IOC that promotes and coordinates the struggle against illegal substances in sports. The IOC provides 50% of WADA's budget. The other 50% comes from governments around the world. The intention with WADA and the IOC is to make an antidoping ecosystem where safety and a level playing field are possible.

Supporting athletes is at the heart of the Olympic Movement. This is done during the Olympic Games, through the whole Games-time experience for athletes, the Olympic Village, travel grants, and all the support athletes receive throughout the 17 days of competition. But beyond the Games, the IOC's funds are used to finance the network of athletes' commissions across the globe, which promotes the empowerment of athletes and enables their voices to be heard (Funding, 2020).

Benefits of Hosting the Olympic Games

Successful hosting a megaevent like the Olympic Games can result in a variety of benefits for a host city. According to Scandizzo and Pierleoni (2017), some of these benefits include increases in tourism, job creation, labor supply, living standards, and personal income. Additional tangible financial benefits can include increases in philanthropic donations, opportunities for new start-up businesses, and urban regeneration (Scandizzo & Pierleoni, 2017).

An example of an Olympic city that reflects some of these benefits is Barcelona, which hosted the 1992 Olympic Summer Games. Leading up to the Games, the city of Barcelona invested heavily in infrastructure, including transportation and hotels, as part of a long-term post-Olympic plan. The efforts appear to be very successful. For example, approximately 3 million people traveled through Barcelona's airport in 1991; by 2002, that number had grown to 21 million (Fickling, 2002). In addition, tourism in Barcelona during the Games included approximately 10 million visitors. By 2001, 9 years after the Games, tourism in Barcelona had more than doubled, reaching approximately 21 million visitors. By hosting the 1992 Olympic Games, the city of Barcelona created a legacy and became known worldwide as a legitimate tourism destination (Gratton & Preuss, 2008; Zonzilos et al., 2015). According to Sakamoto et al. (1999), Japanese undergraduate students' perceptions of foreign nations increased during the Barcelona Olympic Games. Spain, the host country, had the highest increase in positive perceptions. Spain enjoyed the greatest increase in positive perception during the period before and after the 1992 Olympic Games (Sakamoto et al., 1999, p. 274).

Another example is Salt Lake City. Although the 2002 Salt Lake City Winter Games included bribery scandals and was the most expensive in Winter Games history at a price of $2 billion, the

© lazyllama/Shutterstock.com

Games generated a profit of $100 million. In addition, infrastructure added for the games, such as faster lifts and more slopes, resulted in a 37% increase in traffic for the six-year period following the Games (Schlotterbeck, 2012).

The 1996 Atlanta Olympic Games generated approximately $1.8 billion in commercial sponsorship, virtually ensuring the Games would, at a minimum, break even (Schlotterbeck, 2012). However, perhaps the greatest benefit of the 1996 Atlanta Olympic Games is how the city regenerated the downtown urban area, including the addition of 293,000 new jobs, an increase of 0.2% (Hotchkiss et al., 2003). Planning for the Games also assisted in the regeneration by addressing several serious infrastructure issues such as a faulty sewer system and poor water quality. In addition, 16 lower-income neighborhoods were part of the "Olympic Ring" redevelopment efforts (French & Disher, 1997; Schlotterbeck, 2012).

Originally referred to as the "Recession Games" by local residents, the London Summer Games in 2012 are now considered a great success. The Games were able to rejuvenate Eastern London and improve upon its already excellent infrastructure (Rossingh, 2018). In addition, excellent planning has resulted in the continued use of Olympic facilities to host mega sports events such as IAAF World Athletics Championships, the Para Athletics World Championships, and the Triathlon World Grand Final. These three events combinedly created 105 million pounds of economic impact for the city of London (Rossingh, 2018).

Public Opposition to the Olympic Games

Public perception and image is important for all institutions, and typically indirectly influences the financial endeavors of an organization. This is especially important in the sport industry, which is estimated to be a $500 billion industry worldwide. Much of this stems from the perceptions of the residents of an Olympic host city. Why do the perceptions of the residents of an Olympic host city matter? The answer involves a tourism term, the "community approach": "The involvement of local residents is often regarded as the key to sustainable development yet these same residents are expected to be part of the tourism product and to share the benefits as well as they will share the costs" (Taylor, 1995, p. 487). Money spent to bid and host a mega event such as the Olympic Games is justifiably concerning for some local communities. Although enhancing a city's infrastructure is almost always part of preparation for a host city, there have been examples of financial failures, and residents know that a poor outcome could negatively impact the city in a variety of important areas such as an increase in taxes, lower funding for schools, a reduction in salaries and resources for first responders, decreased funding for social services, and a drop in existing fundraising programs, such as lotteries, due to competition for disposable income (Scandizzo & Pierleoni, 2017; Warrell, 2007). These concerns are similar to the concerns voiced by local residents of cities

© JustPixs/Shutterstock.com

with professional sports teams, where cities spend millions on sports facilities to ensure teams do not relocate.

Once a city has successfully hosted the Olympics, residents could resent the increased tourism to their city, as what happened to an extent with Barcelona (1992 Summer Olympics) and Athens (2004 Summer Olympics; Scandizzo & Pierleoni, 2017). According to Burgen (2018), some local citizens of Barcelona experienced difficulties in their daily lives due to the city's high volume of tourism. This led to protests in the city by the local population. Sydney faced several protests before the 2000 Games and many other cities bidding for the Olympic Games have encountered objections by local residents. One of Sydney''s anti-Olympic alliances was the "People Ingeniously Subverting the Sydney Olympic Farce" (PISSOF).

Some watchdog groups position themselves as useful monitors for Olympic spending. Anti-Olympic alliances, such as "Bread Not Circuses" (BNC) based out of Toronto, were fighting against Toronto's 2008 bid. The main argument behind "Bread Not Circuses" was that "the public money spent for the Games would be taken from other more important sectors (e.g. education, health, environment, prosperity)" (Kasimati, 2003, p. 14). A similar concern happened with Quebec City and the 2002 Winter Olympic Games. Residents who opposed the bid for the 2002 Winter Olympic Games called for a referendum on the issue because residents feared that Quebec City would face debts analogous to those that Montreal had in the 1976 Summer Olympic Games (Joppe, 1996, p. 477).

Vancouver's 2010 Winter Games had the " Impact of the Olympics on Community Coalition" (IOCC), which labels itself as a "community watchdog" and not as an anti-Olympic group (Kasimati, 2003). Their goal is to "ensure that the environmental, social, economic and civil rights issues remain outstanding and the Olympic benefits apply to everybody" (Kasimati, 2003, p. 14). Countries such as Greece (2004 Summer Olympics), Russia (2014 Winter Olympics), Brazil (2016 Summer Olympics) do not have forceful community watchdogs, alliances or community coalitions that are as influential as those in Canada, the United States, and Australia. Others, like China (2008 Summer Olympics), have no community watchdogs, alliances, or community coalitions.

Drawbacks of Hosting the Olympic Games

As Barcelona, Atlanta, Salt Lake City, and London have shown, there are many tangible and long-term benefits of hosting the largest sports event in the world. However, Billings and Holladay (2012) studied the longitudinal perspective on revenue, spending, and post-Olympic impacts for Olympic host cities from 1950 through 2005 and determined there was no long-term positive impact from the perspective of population growth, real gross domestic product, or trade (Billings & Holladay, 2012).

Unfortunately, some Olympic endeavors have resulted in financial disaster. For one of the most notorious Olympic failures, Montreal budgeted US$120 million to host the 1976 Montreal Summer Games. Due primarily to overruns on construction costs, the Montreal Games lost US$846 million. In fact, the financial situation was so bad that Olympic Stadium was not even complete by the start of

© Joanna K Drakos/Shutterstock.com

the Games. Between the money lost on the Olympic Games and funds necessary to convert Olympic Stadium to a home for the Montreal Expos Major League Baseball team, it took the city 30 years to pay off the debt, which by 2006, with principal and interest, ended up costing US$2.8 billion (Dove, 2014; Schlotterbeck, 2012).

Another Canadian city, Vancouver, had debt of approximately US$1 billion at the conclusion of the 2010 Winter Games. However, more than US$730 million was due to an extenuating circumstance: The developer of Vancouver's elaborate green-themed Olympic Village ran into financial trouble, and the city was forced to finance the project. It is estimated that $170 million owed to purchase the land for the Olympic Village may never be recovered (Dove, 2014; Schlotterbeck, 2012).

Most fans familiar with Olympic history, especially Americans, remember the 1980 Winter Games in Lake Placid for the success of the U.S. hockey team. However, from a financial perspective, the Lake Placid Games were a bust. For example, the initial budget of $80 million almost doubled to $150 million by the start of the games. Several logistical mistakes contributed to problems, including poor planning for ticket sales, as well as difficulties with transportation and accommodations. When the Games were completed, Lake Placid, with a community tax base of approximately 3,000 residents, was in debt anywhere from $6 million to as much as $8.5 million, to around 1,600 creditors. Fortunately, the city was able to transfer ownership of several facilities, such as the Olympic Fieldhouse, to the State of New York in order to erase the debt (Dove, 2014; Schlotterbeck, 2012).

Realistically, the current size and scope of the Olympic Games make it difficult for most cities to serve as hosts. Between the cost of bidding, upgrading infrastructure, and constructing facilities alone, cities must invest billions of dollars. The last two host cities of the Summer Games, London and Rio, each spent a little more than $11 billion (Baade & Matheson, 2016). For the most recent Winter Games in 2018, PyeongChang spent close to $13 billion (Settimi, 2018). These enormous financial commitments make it difficult for developing countries to compete as a possible host city.

Bidding for the Olympic Games

The financial challenges experienced by some former host cities, and the low possibility of experiencing meaningful net benefits, have resulted in a serious problem for the IOC. Fewer cities are now involved in the bidding process for future Olympic Games (Ludacer, 2018). So, why do some countries continue to host? Baade and Matheson (2016) propose three possibilities. First, just submitting a bid to host the Games brings community leaders together for a shared cause. Even if bidding is unsuccessful, this can lead to future collaborations for city improvement projects. Second, hosting the Games may have nothing to do with money, but everything about making a statement about political and economic power. For example, China spent $45 billion on hosting the 2008 Games in Beijing, the highest in Olympic history. Finally, some cities may feel they are in a better position to negotiate with the IOC if fewer bidders are available. In theory, this could provide a better opportunity for overall financial success.

Case Study

Fraud in Sports: A Global Concern

After a preliminary investigation, the International Olympic Committee (IOC) has uncovered what appears to be widespread fraud by executive board members of the National Olympic Committee of the fictional country known as Zamunda (ZOC). Approximately, $5 million of the budget is unaccounted for. In addition, the numerous allegations of unethical and fraudulent behavior, including board members receiving illegal benefits, skimming money, and fixing the outcomes of games, appear to have merit. This case study will review the issue to determine how the behavior may have occurred, as well as to provide recommendations to avoid similar behavior in the future.

Keywords: Bribing, budgeting, cheating, corruption, economics, ethics, illegal, finance, fixing, fraud, morality, Olympics, and Paralympics

Anytime money is involved, the possibility of fraud is present and the sport industry is no exception. This includes sport at any level, including youth, interscholastic, intercollegiate, professional, as well as the Olympic Games and Paralympic Games (Keiper et al., 2017).

About Olympic Governance and the ZOC

What's referred to as the Olympic movement is governed internationally by the IOC. The IOC is supported by more than 200 national Olympic committees (NOCs), such as the ZOC, around the world. Finally, each nation is supported by national governing bodies (NGBs), which govern each individual summer, winter, and Paralympic sport. The ZOC, NOCs, and NGBs operate independent of each other with separate boards and executive committees (Team USA, 2020).

As a small northern African nation, Zamunda qualifies an average of 20-30 athletes to each summer Olympic Games, and 3-5 athletes to the Paralympic Games. The ZOC operates on a four-year budget of approximately $50 million. However, the ZOC has been unstable recently due to allegations of fraud, Zamunda's disputed presidential election, and numerous reports that the government has been interfering with the autonomy of NGBs by appointing members rather than holding elections (Associated Press, 2011). This instability has created an environment conducent to financial fraud.

Allegations of Fraud

Allegations of bribing and fixing professional soccer matches by the ZOC are not surprising, since sports such as soccer, rugby, and tennis in Europe, as well as professional baseball in Taiwan, have experienced the same issue (Kihl, Misener, Cuskelly, & Wicker, 2017). Governing bodies such as the International Football Federation (FIFA) and the European Football Association (UEFA) have recently established systems to try and detect the influence of gambling in their sports. Other fraudulent activities include skimming money from organizational budgets, and for those with positions of power, as in the example of the 2002 Winter Olympic Games in Salt Lake City, accepting gifts in return for favorable influence (Hamilton, 2010).

Fraud Behavior Patterns and Strategies for Reform

We all like to trust people and believe that our colleagues and people in positions of authority will do the right thing. Unfortunately, that doesn't always happen due to a variety of factors. So, why does financial fraud occur? Several factors may contribute to it. Here are a few common themes related to fraudulent behavior.

Common Behavior Related to Fraud

According to Gardiner et al. (2017), integrity is an undertheorized concept within our society. An organization's values, policies, and internal control systems should discourage fraudulent activity and encourage proper procedure by all employees (Moeller, 2016). Failure to behave proactively and aggressively in regard to financial fraud will not only contribute to the continued degeneration of values and morality in society but could lead to public desensitization in regard to corrupt practices and create cynicism about the role of sport in society (Chien, Kelly, & Weeks, 2016; Kihl, Skinner, & Engelberg, 2017).

Next, the person perpetrating the crime is typically someone the person or organization is familiar with (Keiper et al., 2017). In fact, many times it's a person considered trustworthy and in a position of power within the organization. For individual athletes, when money is unaccounted for, the most common perpetrator is typically their business manager (Prewitt, 2019). A business manager is in a very influential position since they manage income and expenses, and believe they can hide fraudulent transactions. When dealing in cash, this can be true due to a lack of a financial paper trail.

Another common theme related to fraud is a lack of financial controls in place to prevent inappropriate behavior (Keiper et al., 2017). Financial controls include limiting who has access to financial resources, always having a check-in balance system in place, requiring that every transaction has a paper trail, and adopting a constant system of monitoring to identify any financial abnormalities within the organization (Prewitt, 2019).

The last identifiable theme related to instances of fraudulent behavior is a lack of background checks during the hiring process (Keiper et al., 2017). There may be some positions within an organization where background checks are less necessary. However, any candidate being considered for a position with access to financial resources must undergo a rigorous background check. Spending a few dollars on the front end is well worth avoiding fraudulent behavior in the future (Keiper et al., 2017).

Now, let's take a look at administrative practices sport organizations can put in place to reduce the likeliness of fraudulent activities. The simple fact that these safeguards are in place will automatically deter fraudulent behavior, since the likelihood of being caught increases.

Accounting Policies and Procedures

Sport organizations must utilize a sound financial internal control system that includes a series of checks and balances. No one person should have sole budgetary control, or be able to circumvent the internal control system (Keiper et al., 2017). Although this creates an added layer of supervision, the benefits far outweigh the drawbacks (Keiper et al., 2017).

Proper Communication

An organization can have the best policies and procedures in place to avoid fraud, but if they are not communicated properly they will fail to maximize effectiveness. All administrators and employees should have access to policies and procedures, and clear expectations should be communicated in regard to expected behavior (Keiper et al., 2017). Ideally, employees should be required to completed online training modules to avoid any confusion on behavioral expectations down the road (Maurer, 2013).

Summary

Sport organizations must adopt some of the principles presented in this case study in order to ensure they avoid the impact of financial fraud. Perhaps the most import steps are to establish financial policies and procedures, enforce them rigorously and consistently, and communicate behavioral expectations to all employees. No system is foolproof, but proper preparation will likely reduce the possibility of experiencing a financial loss.

Discussion Questions

1. When $5 million is embezzled from a country as small as Zamunda, who are some of the stakeholders that are directly affected?
2. What are some of the factors that may have led to fraud at the ZOC?
3. What are your recommendations on how the ZOC can minimize the risk of financial fraud in the future?

Review Questions

1. The Olympic Games generate billions for the IOC and the OCOG of the respective host city. How does the IOC allocate the different types of revenue?
2. What produces more annual revenue for the IOC: the TOP sponsorship program or media revenues?
3. The IOC relies on a variety of organizations to govern the Olympics on a global perspective. Some of these organizations include OCOGs, NOCs, and IFs. How does the IOC assist these organizations in maintaining the worldwide development of sport?
4. Which host city, for the Summer or Winter Games, do you consider the most successful, and why?

References

Baade, Robert A., and Victor A. Matheson. 2016. "Going for the Gold: The Economics of the Olympics." *Journal of Economic Perspectives, 30*(2): 201-18.

Baccellieri, E. (2018, February 13). *Where does the IOC's money go?* Deadspin. https://deadspin.com/where-does-the-iocs-money-go-1822983686

Billings, S., & Holladay, J. (2012). Should cities go for the gold: The long-term impacts of hosting the Olympics. *Economic Inquiry, 50*(3), 754–772. https://doi.org/10.1111/j.1465-7295.2011.00373.x

Burgen, S. (2018, August 30. How Tourism is Killing Barcelona. *The Guardian.* https://www.theguardian.com/travel/2018/aug/30/why-tourism-is-killing-barcelona-overtourism-photo-essay

Cordova, A. J. (2015). Assessing the economic impact of hosting the Olympic Games. *KAHPERD Journal, 52*(2), 22–27. https://search-ebscohost-com.ezproxy1.apus.edu/login.aspx?direct=true&AuthType=ip&db=s3h&AN=108749750&site=ehost-live&scope=site

Dehghansai, N., Lemez, S., Wattie, N., & Baker, J. (2017). A systematic review of influences on development of athletes with disabilities. *Adapted Physical Activity Quarterly, 34*, 72–90. https://doi:10.1123/APAQ.2016-0030

Dove, L. L. (2014, January 19). *10 Olympic Games that nearly bankrupted their host countries.* HowStuffWorks. https://entertainment.howstuffworks.com/10-olympic-games-bankrupted-host-countries.htm

Fickling, D. (2002, December 7). Barcelona and Sydney: The hosts who got the most. *The Guardian.* www.theguardian.com/politics/2002/dec/08/athletics.olympics2012

French, S. P., & Disher, M. E. (1997). Atlanta and the olympics: A one-year retrospective. American Planning Association. *Journal of the American Planning Association, 63*(3), 379–392. https://dx.doi.org.ezproxy1.apus.edu/10.1080/01944369708975930

Funding. (2020). *The International Olympic Committee.* www.olympic.org/funding

Games Concept. (2020). LA2028. https://la28.org/en/games-plan.html

Gratton, C., & Preuss, H. (2008, December). Maximizing Olympic impacts by building up legacies. *International Journal of the History of Sport, 25*(14), 1922–1938. https://doi.org/10.1080/09523360802439023

History of the Paralympics. (2008, September 4). *Disability sport.* http://news.bbc.co.uk/sport2/hi/other_sports/disability_sport/7582206.stm

Hotchkiss, J., Moore, R., & Zobay, S. (2003). Impact of the 1996 summer Olympic games on employment and wages in Georgia. *Southern Economic Journal, 69*(3), 691–704. https://doi.org/10.2307/1061702

International Sports Federations. (2020). *The International Olympic Committee.* www.olympic.org/ioc-governance-international-sports-federations

IOC Commissions. (2020). *The International Olympic Committee.* www.olympic.org/ioc-commissions

Joppe, M. (1996, November). Sustainable community tourism development revisited. *Tourism Management, 17*(7), 475–479. https://doi:10.1016/S0261-5177(96)00065-9

Kasimati, E. (2003, November). *Economic aspects and the summer Olympics: A review of the related research.* Department of Economics and International Development. University of Bath. https://doi:10.1002/jtr.449

Leading the Olympic Movement. (2020). *The International Olympic Committee.* www.olympic.org/the-ioc/leading-the-olympic-movement

Ludacer, R. (2018, February 6). No one wants to host the Olympics anymore—will they go away? *Business Insider.* www.businessinsider.com/future-olympics-no-country-wants-to-host-games-2018-2

Members. (2020). *The International Olympic Committee.* www.olympic.org/ioc-members-list

National Olympic Committees. (2020). *The International Olympic Committee.* www.olympic.org/ioc-governance-national-olympic-committees

Olympic Charter. (2019, June 26). *The International Olympic Committee.* https://stillmed.olympic.org/media/Document%20Library/OlympicOrg/General/EN-Olympic-Charter.pdf#_ga=2.125302538.1078486186.1585371836-1332274046.1584586569

Olympic Charters. (2020). *The International Olympic Committee.* www.olympic.org/olympic-studies-centre/collections/official-publications/olympic-charters

Olympic Marketing Fact File 2020 Edition. (2020, January). *The International Olympic Committee.* https://stillmed.olympic.org/media/Document%20Library/OlympicOrg/Documents/IOC-Marketing-and-Broadcasting-General-Files/IOC-Marketing-Fact-File-2020-v2.pdf#_ga=2.74774033.2036757079.1587499867-1332274046.1584586569

Olympic Movement (n.d.). https://olympics.com/ioc/olympic-movement

Olympics and International Sports Law Research Guide. (2018, October 22). *Georgetown Law Library.* https://guides.ll.georgetown.edu/c.php?g=364665&p=2463479

Organising Committees for the Olympic Games. (n.d.). *The International Olympic Committee.* www.olympic.org/ioc-governance-organising-committees

Rossingh, D. (2018, July 29). *How the London Olympics still generate $176 million six years on from opening ceremony*. Forbes. www.forbes.com/sites/daniellerossingh/2018/07/29/how-the-london-olympics-still-generate-176-million-six-years-on-from-opening-ceremony/#13f8d3831111

Sakamoto, A., Murata, K., & Takaki, E. (1999, June). The Barcelona Olympics and the perception of foreign nations: A panel study of Japanese university students. *Journal of Sport Behavior, 22*(2), 260–278. https://search-ebscohost-com.ezproxy1.apus.edu/login.aspx?direct=true&AuthType=ip&db=s3h&AN=1909327&site=ehost-live&scope=site

Scandizzo, P. L., & Pierleoni, M. R. (2017, June). Assessing the Olympic Games: The economic impact and beyond. *Journal of Economic Surveys*. https://doi:10.1111/joes.12213

Schlotterbeck, B. (2012, January 19). *Olympic cities: Booms and busts*. CNBC. www.cnbc.com/2012/01/19/Olympic-Cities:-Booms-and-Busts.html?page=10

Settimi, C. (2018, February 8). *By the numbers: The 2018 Pyeongchang Winter Olympics*. Forbes. www.forbes.com/sites/christinasettimi/2018/02/08/by-the-numbers-the-2018-pyeongchang-winter-olympics/#65c3e0307fb4

Stewart, B. (2007). *Sport funding and finance*. Elsevier.

Taylor, G. (1995, November). The community approach: Does it really work? *Tourism Management, 16*(7), 487–489. https://doi:10.1016/0261-5177(95)00078-3

Warrell, H. (2007, December 5). How the 2012 Olympics continue to eat into the sector's lottery funding. *Third Sector, 501*, 1. https://search-proquest-com.ezproxy2.apus.edu/docview/231717018?accountid=8289

Who we are. (2020). *The International Olympic Committee*. www.olympic.org/about-ioc-olympic-movement

Zonzilos, N., Demian, E., Papadakis, E., Paratsiokas, N., & Danchev, S. (2015). The impact of the 2004 Olympic games on the Greek economy. *Foundation for Economic and Industrial Research*. http://iobe.gr/docs/research/en/RES_05_F_15012015_REP_EN.pdf

CHAPTER 15

Future Trends in Sports Finance

Karen Weaver and Michael Cummings

When we look at the future of sports finance, there are various trend lines running through the industry that students should pay attention to. We believe that nearly every one of the sports, organizations, and businesses will not look the same in 2030 as it did in 2020 because of the disruption from COVID-19 pandemic, and the emergence of 5G and other technologies, while debating who owns the data collected, and the rise in the billionaire class willing to invest in sports.

Future Trends

Invariably, when someone writes about predicting the future, they trot out a well-worn quote that has been variously attributed to baseball player Yogi Berra, movie studio chief Samuel Goldwyn or physicist Niels Bohr. "It's tough to make predictions, especially about the future."

The quote is so ubiquitous because it is so true. When gazing into our crystal ball to predict the future of the sports business in 2021 and beyond, it requires a healthy dose of humility. Consider if we had written a similar chapter back in 2010. With the rise of Netflix, YouTube, Hulu, and Prime Video, folks were already predicting the demise of the linear cable bundle in America and hence the move of sports rights to digital only platforms. As of 2021, though, no major sports league has signed an exclusive, digital-only deal with an "over-the-top" provider.

Consider if we had written about the future of professional sports in the year 2000. At the time, "extreme sports" epitomized by ESPN's X-Games were considered the trendy new sport that would dethrone football. (Who is currently the hot young sport about to dethrone football? Esports, of course.) Yet, two decades on, the NFL remains the major sports league in terms of interest

Text, charts, and tables reprinted by permission of Michael Cummings, chapter co-author.

and popularity in America. Soccer—the other football—rules the rest of the world. And both will likely retain their thrones a decade from now.

The difficulty in predicting the future boils down to not just what will happen, but also how fast it will take place. Esports could become the fifth major professional sport, or they go the way of extreme sports. And that could happen gradually or all of a sudden. Sports leagues could choose to make their own "over-the-top" apps, partner with current streamers like ESPN+ and DAZN, or stick with the current bundle.

Our approach will be to look for trends in general, and then analyze the factors that could accelerate or decelerate their adoption. We'll be cautious with our estimates, both on what will happen and how quickly it could come to pass. We've divided this section into three parts. First, we'll evaluate "demand"—revenue driving parts of the financial model—and then "supply"—costs to sports leagues owners. However, as we started writing this chapter the Coronavirus pandemic began and spread around the globe. We will therefore also discuss—in even more cautious terms—how COVID-19 pandemic's impact could change the sports business.

Demand

As the previous chapters have illustrated, the sports business has been good for investors this century. Through 2015, the four major American sports leagues each had a better return on investment than putting money in the S&P 500 (see Major League Sport Teams Compounded Annual Growth Rate chart here).

Major League Sports Teams Compounded Annual Growth Rates
*Through 2015 for NFL and NHL teams
Values compiled from *Forbes* and *Financial Times*

	91–00 (%)	01–10 (%)	11–16* (%)	91–16* (%)
MLB	9.3	7.2	19.8	10.5
NBA	12.1	6.9	27.6	12.7
NFL	15.1	9.5	17.4	12.5
NHL	16.5	5.4	21.3	12.3
S&P 500	16.6	0.1	9.2	7.0
DOW	16.6	-0.9	6.7	7.4
Nasdaq	28.4	-2.8	11.3	10.1
Russell 2000	14.7	1.9	5.8	8.2

Adapted from *Forbes* and *Financial Times*

More and more billionaires are seeing sports ownership as a lucrative investment better than the stock market. Look for more Special Purpose Acquisition Companies (SPAC) to emerge. Sportico wrote, "**Nearly 20** special purpose acquisition companies (SPACs) with ties to sports and entertainment have filed to go public since the beginning of August 2020. This will likely only increase the opportunities for sports-related investments." Investors cite the value of the sports eco-systems critical to their thought processes (see link for more information https://onlinebusiness.syr.edu/blog/billionaires-invest-major-league/).

One of the key drivers of this has been the growth in rights for professional and amateur games. While it's worth looking at the whole revenue pie, the primary driver in the last two decades has been the increase in the cable bundle for consumers, and the value of live rights in supporting the cable bundle. The future of this business and its potential disruption by digital rights are the story of the 2020s.

Broadcast Rights and "Traditional" Distribution

The place to start is with "broadcast" rights for live sports (Armour, 2014). Calling it "broadcast rights," though, is an anachronism that helps illuminate the huge disruption facing how media is distributed. Almost no one in America actually uses over-the-air broadcast frequencies to watch television. The majority instead have a subscription to a cable or satellite provider who provides a stream of channel. (Even broadcast is now done in digital HD, instead of analog signals.)

Traditional broadcast and cable business models are being disrupted by digital platforms going "over-the-top" through the Internet. The business challenge for sports leagues and teams is to reach both digital and traditional customers to maximize their revenue while growing a new generation of fans.

This challenge is difficult for sports leagues because, while digital disruption is clearly the future, the value of sports broadcast rights for traditional linear TV has never been higher. Sports are the one piece of the content pie that are "DVR proof," meaning they drive live or nearly live viewing. When looking at the ratings of broadcast and cable companies, over the last decade sports have taken more and more of the top sports. Visit the chart titled "most watched Prime Time Telecasts" for Nielsen's top 25 programs in 2019, and they're almost entirely sports (or shows premiering after a sports event)

Most Watched Prime Time Telecasts of 2019 (Total Viewers) (College Football Playoff Revenue Distribution, n.d.)

Rank	Program (network)	Viewers (in thousands)	Date aired
1	Super Bowl LIII Patriots versus Rams (CBS)	98,820	February 3, 2019
2	AFC Championship; Patriots versus Chiefs (CBS)	54,399	January 20, 2019
3	NFL Playoffs; Rams versus Cowboys (FOX)	33,651	January 12, 2019
4	Academy Awards (ABC)	30,541	February 24, 2019
5	NFL Playoffs; Cowboys versus Seahawks (FOX)	29,690	January 5, 2019
6	College Football Championship; Clemson versus Alabama (ESPN)	24,945	January 7, 2019
7	The Big Bang Theory, "The Change Constant"/ "The Stockholm Syndrome" (Series Finale) (CBS)	24,755	May 16, 2019
8	NFL Sunday Night Football: Saints versus Cowboys (NBC)	24,373	September 29, 2019
9	World's Best (Post-Super Bowl) (CBS)	23,544	February 3, 2019
10	World Series Game 7: Nationals versus Astros (FOX)	23,309	October 30, 2019

Adapted from https://www.nielsen.com/us/en/insights/article/2019/tops-of-2019-television-2/

As a result, sports rights deals continue to break records, even accounting for inflation. In 2019, the PGA signed an extension of their current deal, increasing yearly revenue from $400 million per year to $700 million. NFL ratings are expected to break similar levels when they are signed in 2022. These trends can be seen in the table titled "Major Media Rights Deals Expiring Soon," a list of major sports rights deals signed in the last decade.

Sports rights have a 5.3% combined average growth rate this century. The growth rate would be the envy of most businesses that aren't social media or tech companies (see Timeline of Sports Media Rights Deals; entertainmentstrategyguy.com, 2019).

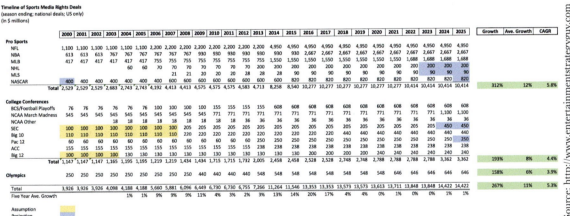

Timeline of Sports Media Rights Deals
(season ending; national deals; US only)
(in $ millions)

	2000	2001	2002	2003	2004	2005	2006	2007	2008	2009	2010	2011	2012	2013	2014	2015	2016	2017	2018	2019	2020	2021	2022	2023	2024	2025	Growth	Ave. Growth	CAGR
Pro Sports																													
NFL	1,100	1,100	1,100	1,100	1,100	1,100	2,200	2,200	2,200	2,200	2,200	2,200	2,200	2,200	4,950	4,950	4,950	4,950	4,950	4,950	4,950	4,950	4,950	4,950	4,950	4,950			
NBA	613	613	613	767	767	767	767	767	767	767	930	930	930	930	930	930	2,667	2,667	2,667	2,667	2,667	2,667	2,667	2,667	2,667	2,667			
MLB	417	417	417	417	417	417	755	755	755	755	755	755	755	755	1,550	1,550	1,550	1,550	1,550	1,550	1,550	1,550	1,688	1,688	1,688	1,688			
NHL					60	60	70	70	70	70	70	70	70	70	200	200	200	200	200	200	200	200	200	200	200	200			
MLS								21	21	21	20	20	20	28	28	90	90	90	90	90	90	90	90	90	90	90			
NASCAR	400	400	400	400	400	400	400	600	600	600	600	600	600	600	600	820	820	820	820	820	820	820	820	820	820	820			
Total	2,529	2,529	2,529	2,683	2,743	2,743	4,192	4,413	4,413	4,575	4,575	4,575	4,583	4,713	8,258	8,540	10,277	10,277	10,277	10,277	10,277	10,277	10,414	10,414	10,414	10,414	312%	12%	5.8%
College Conferences																													
BCS/Football Playoffs	76	76	76	76	76	76	100	100	100	100	155	155	155	155	608	608	608	608	608	608	608	608	608	608	608	608			
NCAA March Madness	545	545	545	545	545	545	545	545	545	545	771	771	771	771	771	771	771	771	771	771	771	771	771	771	1,100	1,100			
NCAA Other				18	18	18	18	18	18	18	18	18	36	36	36	36	36	36	36	36	36	36	36	36	36	36			
SEC	100	100	100	100	100	100	100	100	205	205	205	205	205	205	205	205	205	205	205	205	205	205	205	205	450	450			
Big 10	110	110	110	110	110	110	110	110	220	220	220	220	220	220	220	220	220	220	440	440	440	440	440	440	440	440			
Pac 12	60	60	60	60	60	60	60	60	60	60	60	60	60	250	250	250	250	250	250	250	250	250	250	250	250	250			
ACC	155	155	155	155	155	155	155	155	155	155	155	155	155	238	238	238	238	238	238	238	238	238	238	238	238	238			
Big 12	100	100	100	130	130	130	130	130	130	130	130	130	130	130	130	130	200	200	200	200	240	240	240	240	240	240			
Total	1,147	1,147	1,147	1,165	1,195	1,195	1,219	1,219	1,434	1,434	1,715	1,715	1,732	2,005	2,458	2,458	2,528	2,528	2,748	2,748	2,788	2,788	2,788	2,788	3,362	3,362	193%	8%	4.4%
Olympics	250	250	250	250	250	250	250	250	250	440	440	440	440	548	548	548	548	548	548	548	646	646	646	646	646	646	158%	6%	3.9%
Total	3,926	3,926	3,926	4,098	4,188	4,188	5,660	5,881	6,096	6,449	6,730	6,730	6,755	7,266	11,264	11,546	13,353	13,353	13,573	13,573	13,613	13,711	13,848	13,848	14,422	14,422	267%	11%	5.3%
Five Year Ave. Growth					1%	1%	9%	9%	9%	11%	4%	3%	2%	3%	13%	14%	20%	17%	4%	4%	0%	1%	0%	0%	1%	1%			

Assumption
Projection

The question is when these rights would peak in value. As the foregoing table shows, sports rights are on a trend line to outpace inflation for the foreseeable future. Sports remain valuable for linear channels and will be valuable for whichever streaming platform grabs their rights. These factors alone likely indicate that sports rights will continue to climb. Some estimates place the growth of rights fees in the first part of 2020 up to $85 billion globally (Entertainmentstrategyguy.com, 2019; Pearson, 2018).

However, despite the upside of digital distribution in boosting the next round of rights fees, it has risks as well. Primarily, digital platforms may be unable to capture the same share of customer wallets as the MVPDs grabbed. Cable was largely a local monopoly without more than two to three options per household. This meant that the MVPDs could use the value of sports to charge expensive subscription fees to all their subscriber bases. As a result, ESPN was the most highly valued network by subscription fee (see chart "Subscribers TV Network Summary" and "TV Network Summary." Subscribers are in millions).

Subscribers TV Network Summary

NETWORK NAME	COUNTRY OF OPERATION	NETWORK TYPE	GENRE	2020Y	2021Y	2022Y	2023Y	2024Y
YES Network (US)	USA	RSN	Sports	7.1	6.5	6.0	5.6	5.2
FOX Sports Southeast (US)	USA	RSN	Sports	6.4	5.7	5.1	4.7	4.4
MSG Network (US)	USA	RSN	Sports	5.7	5.3	4.9	4.6	4.3
FOX Sports Southwest (US)	USA	RSN	Sports	5.7	5.0	4.4	4.0	3.6
MSG+ (US)	USA	RSN	Sports	5.7	5.2	4.8	4.5	4.3
SportsNet New York (US)	USA	RSN	Sports	5.6	5.1	4.7	4.4	4.1
FOX Sports South (US)	USA	RSN	Sports	5.4	4.8	4.4	4.0	3.7
Longhorn Network (US)	USA	RSN	Sports	5.3	4.6	4.0	3.6	3.2
Mid-Atlantic Sports Network (US)	USA	RSN	Sports	4.8	4.3	3.8	3.5	3.3
FOX Sports Sun (US)	USA	RSN	Sports	4.7	4.2	3.8	3.5	3.3
FOX Sports Florida (US)	USA	RSN	Sports	4.6	4.1	3.8	3.5	3.2
FOX Sports West (US)	USA	RSN	Sports	4.4	3.9	3.5	3.2	3.0
Prime Ticket (US)	USA	RSN	Sports	3.8	3.4	3.0	2.7	2.5
Spectrum SportsNet (US)	USA	RSN	Sports	3.4	3.1	2.8	2.6	2.4
Marquee Sports Network (US)	USA	RSN	Sports	3.3	3.0	2.7	2.5	2.3
New England Sports Network (US)	USA	RSN	Sports	3.3	3.0	2.8	2.6	2.5
NBC Sports Washington (US)	USA	RSN	Sports	3.2	2.9	2.6	2.3	2.2
Pac-12 Los Angeles (US)	USA	RSN	Sports	3.1	2.9	2.6	2.4	2.3
Spectrum SportsNet LA (US)	USA	RSN	Sports	3.0	2.7	2.4	2.2	2.1
NBC Sports Chicago (US)	USA	RSN	Sports	3.0	2.7	2.4	2.2	2.1
NBC Sports Boston (US)	USA	RSN	Sports	2.9	2.7	2.5	2.3	2.2
NBC Sports Bay Area (US)	USA	RSN	Sports	2.9	2.5	2.1	1.9	1.7
ROOT SPORTS Northwest (US)	USA	RSN	Sports	2.8	2.5	2.3	2.1	2.0
AT&T SportsNet Southwest (US)	USA	RSN	Sports	2.8	2.4	2.1	1.8	1.7
AT&T SportsNet Rocky Mountain (US)	USA	RSN	Sports	2.7	2.4	2.2	2.0	1.8
NBC Sports California (US)	USA	RSN	Sports	2.5	2.3	2.1	1.9	1.8
FOX Sports Carolinas (US)	USA	RSN	Sports	2.5	2.2	2.0	1.8	1.7
AT&T SportsNet Pittsburgh (US)	USA	RSN	Sports	2.4	2.2	2.0	1.8	1.7
FOX Sports Ohio (US)	USA	RSN	Sports	2.4	2.2	2.0	1.8	1.7
FOX Sports Midwest (US)	USA	RSN	Sports	2.4	2.1	1.9	1.7	1.6

NETWORK NAME	COUNTRY OF OPERATION	NETWORK TYPE	GENRE	2020Y	2021Y	2022Y	2023Y	2024Y
FOX Sports Detroit (US)	USA	RSN	Sports	2.4	2.1	1.9	1.8	1.7
SportsTime Ohio (US)	USA	RSN	Sports	2.2	2.0	1.8	1.7	1.6
NBC Sports Philadelphia (US)	USA	RSN	Sports	2.2	2.0	1.9	1.8	1.7
Pac-12 Bay Area (US)	USA	RSN	Sports	2.1	2.0	1.8	1.7	1.6
FOX Sports North (US)	USA	RSN	Sports	2.1	1.9	1.7	1.5	1.4
FOX Sports San Diego (US)	USA	RSN	Sports	1.7	1.5	1.4	1.2	1.2
FOX Sports Arizona (US)	USA	RSN	Sports	1.6	1.4	1.3	1.1	1.1
NBC Sports Northwest (US)	USA	RSN	Sports	1.5	1.4	1.3	1.2	1.1
FOX Sports Kansas City (US)	USA	RSN	Sports	1.5	1.3	1.2	1.1	1.0
Cox Sports Television (US)	USA	RSN	Sports	1.2	1.1	0.9	0.8	0.7
FOX Sports Wisconsin (US)	USA	RSN	Sports	1.2	1.1	1.0	0.9	0.8
Pac-12 Washington (US)	USA	RSN	Sports	1.1	1.0	1.0	0.9	0.8
Altitude Sports & Entertainment (US)	USA	RSN	Sports	1.1	1.0	0.8	0.7	0.7
Pac-12 Mountain (US)	USA	RSN	Sports	1.1	1.0	0.9	0.8	0.7
FOX Sports Tennessee (US)	USA	RSN	Sports	1.0	0.9	0.8	0.7	0.7
FOX Sports Oklahoma (US)	USA	RSN	Sports	0.8	0.7	0.6	0.6	0.5
FOX Sports Indiana (US)	USA	RSN	Sports	0.8	0.7	0.6	0.6	0.5
Pac-12 Arizona (US)	USA	RSN	Sports	0.8	0.7	0.6	0.6	0.5
Pac-12 Oregon (US)	USA	RSN	Sports	0.6	0.6	0.5	0.5	0.5
FOX Sports New Orleans (US)	USA	RSN	Sports	0.4	0.4	0.3	0.3	0.3

TV Network Summary

NETWORK NAME	COUNTRY OF OPERATION	NETWORK TYPE	GENRE	2020Y	2021Y	2022Y	2023Y	2024Y
FOX Sports Oklahoma (US)	USA	RSN	Sports	5.04	5.22	5.51	5.83	6.21
Spectrum SportsNet (US)	USA	RSN	Sports	4.96	5.28	5.63	6.02	6.43
FOX Sports Arizona (US)	USA	RSN	Sports	4.81	6.27	6.66	7.12	7.58
MSG Network (US)	USA	RSN	Sports	4.78	5.05	5.35	5.67	6.00
FOX Sports Detroit (US)	USA	RSN	Sports	4.63	6.85	7.85	8.33	8.80
YES Network (US)	USA	RSN	Sports	4.38	6.84	7.14	7.48	7.80
FOX Sports Midwest (US)	USA	RSN	Sports	4.15	5.90	6.25	6.67	7.08
FOX Sports Kansas City (US)	USA	RSN	Sports	4.09	5.70	5.99	6.35	6.70
FOX Sports Wisconsin (US)	USA	RSN	Sports	3.94	5.80	6.15	6.56	6.97
Spectrum SportsNet LA (US)	USA	RSN	Sports	3.84	5.83	6.26	6.76	7.28
FOX Sports Ohio (US)	USA	RSN	Sports	3.81	6.35	6.67	7.04	7.41
NBC Sports Philadelphia (US)	USA	RSN	Sports	3.71	5.46	5.78	6.12	6.47

Prime Ticket (US)	USA	RSN	Sports	3.66	3.73	3.89	4.67	4.91
MSG+ (US)	USA	RSN	Sports	3.31	3.43	3.57	3.71	3.86
ROOT SPORTS Northwest (US)	USA	RSN	Sports	3.06	4.88	5.18	5.53	5.89
FOX Sports Tennessee (US)	USA	RSN	Sports	3.06	3.19	3.38	3.73	3.92
AT&T SportsNet Pittsburgh (US)	USA	RSN	Sports	3.04	4.42	4.68	4.98	5.27
New England Sports Network (US)	USA	RSN	Sports	3.02	5.10	5.43	5.80	6.17
NBC Sports Chicago (US)	USA	RSN	Sports	2.92	5.00	5.36	5.77	6.18
FOX Sports North (US)	USA	RSN	Sports	2.92	4.22	4.86	5.18	5.50
FOX Sports Indiana (US)	USA	RSN	Sports	2.85	3.53	3.70	3.90	4.13
FOX Sports Southwest (US)	USA	RSN	Sports	2.61	4.34	4.55	4.84	5.10
Marquee Sports Network (US)	USA	RSN	Sports	2.57	4.26	4.50	4.76	5.02
FOX Sports San Diego (US)	USA	RSN	Sports	2.55	3.88	4.18	4.52	4.86
FOX Sports West (US)	USA	RSN	Sports	2.53	4.10	4.38	4.72	5.07
FOX Sports New Orleans (US)	USA	RSN	Sports	2.46	2.63	2.89	3.04	3.19
FOX Sports Carolinas (US)	USA	RSN	Sports	2.29	2.58	2.73	2.90	3.17
NBC Sports California (US)	USA	RSN	Sports	2.24	3.58	3.80	4.06	4.64
SportsNet New York (US)	USA	RSN	Sports	2.19	3.22	3.35	3.50	3.64
FOX Sports Sun (US)	USA	RSN	Sports	2.19	3.18	3.33	3.70	3.86
SportsTime Ohio (US)	USA	RSN	Sports	2.18	3.52	3.80	4.91	5.20
Mid-Atlantic Sports Network (US)	USA	RSN	Sports	2.14	3.19	3.37	3.57	3.77
FOX Sports South (US)	USA	RSN	Sports	2.14	3.34	3.52	3.72	3.92
NBC Sports Washington (US)	USA	RSN	Sports	2.04	2.16	2.29	2.45	2.61
NBC Sports Bay Area (US)	USA	RSN	Sports	1.99	3.22	3.41	3.66	3.88
NBC Sports Northwest (US)	USA	RSN	Sports	1.91	2.14	2.18	2.22	2.25
FOX Sports Florida (US)	USA	RSN	Sports	1.86	3.07	3.26	3.49	3.72
FOX Sports Southeast (US)	USA	RSN	Sports	1.68	2.38	2.49	2.63	2.76
AT&T SportsNet Rocky Mountain (US)	USA	RSN	Sports	1.66	2.61	2.99	3.20	3.41
AT&T SportsNet Southwest (US)	USA	RSN	Sports	1.62	3.11	3.30	3.55	3.78
NBC Sports Boston (US)	USA	RSN	Sports	1.43	1.51	1.60	1.70	1.79
Altitude Sports & Entertainment (US)	USA	RSN	Sports	1.42	2.01	2.22	2.34	2.46
Pac-12 Washington (US)	USA	RSN	Sports	0.86	0.98	1.11	1.25	1.39
Pac-12 Arizona (US)	USA	RSN	Sports	0.80	0.91	1.04	1.17	1.31
Pac-12 Bay Area (US)	USA	RSN	Sports	0.71	0.80	0.91	1.02	1.13
Pac-12 Los Angeles (US)	USA	RSN	Sports	0.64	0.73	0.82	0.93	1.04
Pac-12 Oregon (US)	USA	RSN	Sports	0.50	0.52	0.54	0.55	0.57
Pac-12 Mountain (US)	USA	RSN	Sports	0.50	0.52	0.54	0.55	0.57
Longhorn Network (US)	USA	RSN	Sports	0.42	0.44	0.46	0.53	0.56
Cox Sports Television (US)	USA	RSN	Sports	0.31	0.34	0.36	0.38	0.41

The ESPN example is illustrative of some of the challenges sports broadcasters will face as they shift to digital only. As DVDs were replaced by digital purchases, the common complaint by film studios was that they were replacing physical dollars with digital pennies. ESPN will face the same issue with digital distribution. As the foregoing table shows, ESPN collected $9.50 for nearly *every household that had cable*. Right now, ESPN+ only costs $5 per month (in 2020), but goes to a fraction of households. Either ESPN will have to drastically increase prices to replace the lost revenue, or figure out a way to get carried in nearly every household again.

After cable subscription fees, the other risk is for "regional sports networks" (RSNs), as discussed earlier in the text. We've likely already hit "peak RSN." The worst potential sign for RSNs was the sale of 21 Fox-owned RSNs as part of the Walt Disney-Fox merger. Forced to divest the RSNs as part of their merger agreement, Disney hoped to sell the RSNs for around $20 to $22 billion and ended up selling them for only $14 billion. Worse, later Dish Network refused to carry the RSNs, further eroding their value. Late in 2019, Sinclair purchased the RSNs for $10 billion.

Both of these issues have the same root cause: cable customers are fleeing high-priced bundles for cheaper options. As a result, cable providers need to cut costs and regional sports networks are one of the first options to trim the bundle.

Digital Distribution and Disruption

These customers leaving are increasingly "cutting the cord," the catch-all term for folks ending cable subscriptions to opt for digital over-the-top services.

Moffett and Nathanson predict Netflix will remain the strongest OTT (Over The Top) video player, reaching 70 million subscribers in 2024, followed closely by Amazon Prime at 65 million, Hulu at 58 million, and Disney+ at 53 million. They report, "Netflix will have the strongest pricing power, with average domestic monthly rates rising by $4 to $17 in 2024, driven by the depth of Netflix's content library and its leading market position."

In 2020, analysts predicted a "ceiling for sports fans" when it comes to paying to watch sports. When it comes to cable, satellite and streaming, fans are accelerating their "cord-cutting" and signing on to more subscription services (or bites). In early 2021, Bloomberg reported that Amazon made a bid for Italy's Serie A TV rights, to be made available on its Amazon Prime platform. Serie A is home to superstars Cristiano Ronaldo and Zlatan Ibrahimović, and they are looking for $4.2 billion from 2021 to 2024.

The term actually describes several different groups. "Cord-shavers" are folks who opt for smaller bundles of cable channels, bolstered by over-the-top streamers. These folks make RSNs in particular less valuable. "Cord-nevers" are younger customers who never subscribe to cable in the first place. The last category of folks are "cord-shifters" who are folks who drop cable subscriptions for "virtual MVPDs" like Hulu Live TV and YouTube TV, which offer similar bundles as traditional cable or satellite, but at reduced prices. The gateway to cutting the cord is actually "cord-adders," who are folks with cable subscriptions who add on streaming bundles.

When someone does cut the cord, they still have a few different options. While streaming video services like Netflix, Hulu, and Amazon's Prime Video provided the first alternatives to cable, new digital-only services have started to disrupt these disruptors (see Chapter 2).

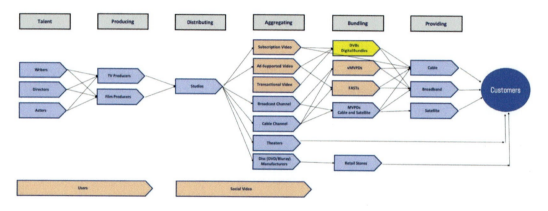

Source: http://www.Entertainmentstrategyguy.com

Each of the aforementioned platforms could play a role in digital disruption. ESPN+ and DAZN are SVODs that are bidding on live rights. AVODs like Yahoo and Twitter have bid for live sports rights. FASTs are also looking for lower tier rights, like Fubo TV. And Apple and Amazon have the deepest pocketbooks of any business. Meanwhile vMVPDs already advertise their live sports, with Hulu using the catchphrase "Hulu has Live Sports."

Likely, different leagues will pursue different partnerships, each trying to maximize revenue and reach. Some will launch their own "owned" SVODs, while others are happy to sell to ESPN+ and DAZN, while keeping their vMVPD rights. Whether this digital disruption results in significantly higher revenue in the medium-to-long term remains to be seen. In the near term, in the bid for rights, cash rich firms like Amazon and Apple could help drive rights higher. As for the long term, it remains to be seen.

Digital rights do bring one significant downside regardless of platform: piracy. Social platforms like Reddit routinely feature live streams of games that cord-cutters can access for free. While some leagues like the NBA are sanguine about the piracy problem, others like the EPL have warned that if piracy does not abate they will lose revenue. (And if piracy remains rampant, large digital firms are unlikely to pay as high of rates.)

Live Events

Attendance at sporting events is a "Tale of Two Cities" type of problem, as in "it was the best of times; it was the worst of times." The "worst of times" comes from attendance issues at most major sporting venues in America.

On the one hand, attendance has slumped at many arenas. Many college venues in particular have suffered from a lack of fan engagement, except for a handful of elite institutions (Alabama and the SEC in college football; Kentucky in college basketball). Yet prices for tickets have skyrocketed in certain markets (Dosh, n.d.). Some of this is driven by the resale market, that helps boost prices but can also price out many traditional fans who can no longer afford top tickets. The challenge is how to price tickets to both maximize revenue while still enabling everyday fans to attend games. Stadium designers and current occupants of stadia around the country are already re-configuring the seating spaces to anticipate a post-COVID-19 era, considering ideas like more suites, dividers between sections of seats, and larger open spaces to limit crowding. Already, there has been an acceleration in introducing "contactless" payments and ticketing to fans, and heightened awareness of demonstrating facility cleanliness. With the advent of 5G both inside and outside arenas, expect more direct communication to spectators via mobile phone push notifications, such as directing fans to restrooms with shorter lines.

Advertising and Sponsorship

Most sports leagues—as seen in previous chapters—make a small percentage of total revenue from sponsorships. However, while small it absolutely helps individual franchises to bolster their bottom lines.

The challenge for most advertisers in the 2020s will be tying traditional sports advertising—in-game advertising, sponsorship deals, and logos on uniforms—to sell-through metrics as digital advertising allows. Direct-to-consumer platforms can leverage digital advertising to tell not just how many people see an advertisement, but all the data around that engagement from demographics to whether a person served an advertisement actually clicked through to a website.

Traditional stadium and linear channel advertising and sponsorships cannot match this level of data. As sports teams and leagues enter the 2020s, their biggest competitor for potential advertiser dollars will be digital and social platforms (Oz, 2018). However, on the side of traditional leagues and teams is the fact that their sports continue to command eyeballs. As long as this is the case, the limited inventory for sponsorship deals will mean sports advertising partnerships and sponsorships will continue into the next decade.

Another growth area is expected to be the second screens so prevalent with sports fans. As mentioned earlier, these screens (think phone, tablet) can be used for gambling information, statistics, or social conversations with fans around the world. These platforms are ripe for advertising.

International Growth

While the majority of this textbook has been focused on the U.S. sports leagues—which is indeed where the vast majority of revenue still originates—in the future, sports leagues are increasingly looking to global revenue streams to boost their value.

In front of this trend are UEFA leagues and teams, such as the EPL, Bayern Munich, Real Madrid, and Barcelona. Professional soccer leagues generate global interest in their matches and players have global followings. As such, the EPL can charge increasingly large fees for their rights around the globe.

American professional leagues such as the NFL, NBA, and MLB would like to capitalize on this. Arguably, the NBA is in front of this trend, with lucrative global deals, in particular with China. The NFL has played games in London for many years and all leagues are experimenting with partnerships in Latin America (ESPN, 2021).

China, in particular, represents a unique opportunity and challenge for domestic leagues. As the NBA discovered in 2019,

© zhangjin_net/Shutterstock.com

the Chinese political system does not always match American political values. As a result, protests in Hong Kong led to social media outrage, which meant NBA games were banned from air. Further, while China represents a huge revenue opportunity, it also is an incredibly difficult place to do business for foreign firms. It can be hard to pull profits from China; the country also has been accused of stealing intellectual property from business partners.

Supply

The future of supply and cost issues facing sports leagues is much less severe than the issues facing revenue streams. However, two big drivers could impact costs of professional sports leagues: stadiums and athletes.

Stadiums and Public Push Back

After years of public–private partnerships for building or renovating stadiums, the last few years in America and around the globe have seen public resistance to government funding for stadiums. The driver behind this trend is the growing body of evidence that the economic impact of stadiums often fails to exceed the costs borne by local and state governments. In other words, the return on investment for building stadiums just isn't there for local governments.

What impact could this have on stadiums? It's unclear. On the one hand, this could be a trend pushing private ownership groups to fund their own stadiums without public backing. In Los Angeles, the Los Angeles Rams ownership group is building their own stadium and development in Inglewood, California estimate to cost $4 billion. At the same time, the local government plans to host the Olympics in 2028 with minimal building of stadiums.

Not every market can support that type of investment. Los Angeles is one of the top three markets in America for live sports due to the size and wealth of the population. Smaller markets like Oklahoma City, Charlotte, New Orleans, and Milwaukee have and will continue to threaten their local governments with moving their sports franchises if they can't build new or renovate old stadiums. From the chapter on mega recreational complexes, students might consider the potential for stadiums to be included in those projects.

Despite some high-profile wins for local governments fighting public funding, concerns about governments financing expensive stadiums dates back to at least the late 1990s. Yet local cities and states continue to pay for these stadiums. For more information about the cost to local communities, read Chapter 5 on Stadium Financing.

Youth and Amateur Athletics

Two trends have become public issues both of which impact how young people learn the various games.

First, America has seen a decline in participation across various youth sports, leading to hyperbolic articles about the "death of athletics." While youth athletics is definitely still popular, it is not growing, indicating a risk that future potential fans are turning elsewhere. Also, the fewer children who grow up playing a sport means the supply of potential future athletes is smaller. For more information about the finances of Youth Sports and Mega-Recreational Sports Complexes, read Chapters 4 and 6.

The forces driving this are varied and not well-proven. While some would claim the decline on cultural factors ("Young kids don't like being yelled at."), in other cases it could be because club athletics has made an increasingly unequal playing field. Further, the cost to participate in club athletics has seen tremendous growth. In some sports, it can cost parents tens of thousands of dollars to play club soccer or softball. This trend is likely exacerbated by income inequality and the push to get children into top colleges. On top of all this, digital video games and social media provide alternative means to socialize with friends, a role previously filled by athletics.

Second, as youth athletes become amateur athletes, the biggest trend sweeping America is the move to allow college athletes the ability to monetize their "Name, Image, and Likeness." Now that Names, Images and Likenesses monetization is permitted for all NCAA athletes, the NCAA is awaiting a national standard to unify the competing state regulations currently in place in 2021. After California passed a sweeping law in 2019, many states adopted similar measures, some who have placed laws on the books in 2020 to allow athletes to proceed in 2021 with monetizing their NILs without interference from their governing organizations. The National Federation of High Schools came out strongly against high school athletes monetizing their NILs, while the NAIA permitted all of their athletes to begin monetizing their brands in October 2020. Chloe Mitchell, an Aquinas College women's volleyball player, was one of the very first to execute a sponsorship activation. Look for more chaos around this issue in the next few years.

The impacts of the NIL movement cannot be understated for the NCAA and college athletics. At the very least, it will require colleges to allow third-party payments to student athletes at some level. After that, the impacts could reach into the millions of dollars for high profile or highly creative athletes.

Professional Athletes

A few issues confront professional athletes in the current climate.

First, athlete safety is a particular emphasis, particularly in football. Studies in traumatic brain injuries could influence how much the sport is able to continue and whether other sports with similar violent collisions (lacrosse, rugby, and hockey) have similar concerns.

Second, athletes will continue to demand a higher share of total revenue from ownership groups. As mentioned earlier, sports continue to be a tremendous investment driven by increasing broadcast rights and potentially global revenue. Yet, during union negotiations, the NBA and NFL, in particular, will always say their member teams are losing money. (These teams then invariably sell for multiples higher than they were purchases.) (Hinnen, 2012)

Third, athletes are increasingly owning their own brands outside of league and team control through social media. The emergence of technology and the data collected on each athlete and who owns that data will be a significant factor in collective bargaining agreements going forward. This data is worth billions to equipment manufacturers, apparel companies that will weave 5G fabric into athlete's uniforms, and cameras and sensors that track every waking hour of an athlete's day. Visit https://www.statista.com/statistics/647392/most-followers-instagram-athletes/ to find out why Lebron James no longer needs the NBA to help build his brand.

© insta_photos/Shutterstock.com

Coronavirus—Does this "change everything" or will things "go back to normal"?

How will the post-pandemic era affect sports business? Frankly, we don't know. But we propose three different potential impacts: pandemic recovery, economic recovery, and changes in customer/sports behavior.

For the first category, folks in the future will understand how this played out. Either countries around the globe will figure out ways to slow and stop the spread of the coronavirus, or shelter in place orders will continue for the foreseeable future. As long as this is the case, live events with thousands of fans will be nearly impossible. However, sports leagues may find creative ways to still host the sporting events to provide the live TV. The ratings for those first games back could be huge, once their personal economic worries subside.

Economic Recovery

A much tougher prediction is trying to forecast how the economy will recover in 2020 and beyond. Given the uncertainty with the pandemic recovery and the general difficulty in predicting the economy even in the best of circumstances.

However, we know that certain economic trends are bad for professional sports leagues. First, in recessions or depressions, advertising is the first casualty. When firms are worried that customers aren't spending, their first cuts go to their advertising budgets—everything from feature films to consumer-packaged goods, to car companies will pull back on advertising. This could hurt league sponsorship revenue and the advertising revenue on cable and digital platforms.

Meanwhile, ticket prices will also see an impact. Even if coronavirus worries are completely abated, we know that recessions would impact the entire economy, and customers would pull back on discretionary spending. This absolutely includes attending live sporting events, which can run a family of four over $500.

Unemployment exacerbates these trends as well.

Customer Behavior— Change Everything or Nothing?

As we write this in the midst of the global pandemic, many, many journalists are willing to declare that the coronavirus "changes everything." CEOs of major corporations have said this, too. We've seen predictions that Americans will be afraid to ever go back to a stadium or movie theater in the future, predicting Americans will decide to stay inside even after the all-clear.

© Abscent/Shutterstock.com

Some have pushed back on this. (And we count ourselves in the latter category.) We believe that as soon as it is "safe" to be in groups—Americans will flock to live events.

So, which is it? A medium course advocated by some thinkers like Scott Galloway or Kevin Drum that the coronavirus will likely accelerate certain trends seems to make sense. For instance, online learning was already growing, and the coronavirus will likely accelerate that trend. The same goes for food, grocery delivery, and even the wider acceptance of working from home.

What about live events? While there is some evidence that live event attendance has stalled, ticket prices have grown at large rates. Meaning, the rise in ticket prices could be stalling out attendance, not actual demand. Reduced ticket pricing may help attract fans back to the stadium.

As for everything else, it is as likely to "snap back" as it is to "change forever." Maybe youth athletics would forever be harmed as fearful parents refuse to take their kids to soccer practice. Alternatively, maybe youth athletics would have a renaissance as bored/cooped-up kids flock to outdoor activities.

Conclusion

If you had looked at sports in 2010s and made bold, sweeping declarations about the future in 2020, you'd mostly have been wrong. Sports in 2020 looked a lot like sports in 2010, and even somewhat like sports in 2000.

The next decade will look very different. There has been both a disruption and an acceleration of acceptance of behaviors for large portions of fans that would have seemed "extreme" in 2018. Having a vaccine stamp or QR code on your phone to get into a game or a building? Sure. Bars and restaurants with hand sanitizers and sparkling clean floors? Expect to see it. Second screens with gambling and statistical information available for every player on the field or court? Some college athletes becoming millionaires monetizing their name, image, and likeness? Count on it. 5G available absolutely everywhere?

This will be one of the most interesting times to be involved in sports finance. A skilled practitioner will need to stay abreast of all of the sectors and trends in the sports industry, while paying close attention to the ecosystem that surrounds sports. Stay tuned.

© Keeton Gale/Shutterstock.com

Case Study—A Reinvention of How to Look at Women's Sports

How can financial specialists help their organizations maximize their franchise values?

The WNBA is the longest standing professional team sports organization for women in our history. Ownership, league officers, and players all realize they have hit a ceiling with regard to revenues; their new era began with envisioning their Collective Bargaining Agreement differently, and creating new opportunities for the players themselves, their media partners, and their corporate partners

On the CNN podcast, "Boss Files," WNBA's commissioner, Cathy Engelbert, discussed the strategy of "Going Bold." Simply stated, if the league didn't consciously change their mindset, there wouldn't be a league in 5 years.

She formulated a three-part equity (or buy-in) plan for the league and its players:
1. Player First Agenda. When it was time to negotiate a new CBA, she believed (as did the owners) that she had to address player concerns first. That led to a very forward-thinking agreement, including:
   a. 53% salary increase for all players,
   b. Tripled salaries for top players,
   c. Full paid parental leave,
   d. Single rooms on the road,
   e. Charter flights when going west to east during the playoffs,
   f. 2 BDR apartments (if they have a child),
   g. Fertility benefits and adoption benefits,
   h. Off-season employment opportunities—coaching, front office, back office—which give them opportunities to learn about corporate jobs that might work for them.

Obviously, these salaries and benefits affect the bottom line, so the league had to design revenue strategies to pay for them. It was a huge sign to the players that they were a valued partner in this new endeavor. The players thought to themselves, "Cathy gets it—she's been a player" (she played basketball in college), and they understood the leaguewide imperative to maximize the highest level of performance on the court during the playoffs, the most widely watched event.

2. Owner Success. Owners realized they had to two things in order to grow the valuation of their asset (the team):
   a. Market the players as role models that women and companies could get behind.
   b. Leverage the player diversity and their robust social media platforms to partner with sponsors and causes.

Engelbert believes this should attract more sponsorship interest. Narrative-focused media as well as sponsors need to be shown how to value and monetize this content. By activating their built-in diversity and inclusion platform (which the WNBA has the talent to showcase), those initiatives are valuable for companies looking to demonstrate how their products or services align with today's focus on sustainability, diversity and inclusion, ultimately driving trust in consumer products and financial institutions. In Engelbert's mind, sponsoring an elite women's professional league and/or player should be a no-brainer. Companies rarely think of sponsorship activation with women players as a value-added commodity; the 140 WNBA players have millions of followers and most are amazing role models. The league has to focus on getting companies to see the benefit in the partnership. If she can execute that strategy, she expects the new revenues coming to the league will be significant.

3.   Fan Engagement

In Engelbert's estimation, the narrative around women's team sports has not been told in the correct way. Women's sports assets should be measured differently. Algorithms are traditionally assessed on a jersey patch, an ad placement on the court, on media rights, usually drawn from men's sports. When franchise valuations are made, they are typically done via a qualitative analysis on spreadsheets with algorithms built on male sports numbers. Only 5% of sponsorships go to women's team sports. Less than 4% of media dollars go to women's sports, even less to women's team sports. There is substantial room for growth. In her estimation, it's a built-in bias, as the traditional metrics of viewership and attendance are disadvantageous for women's team sports. Even on newer digital platforms, those platforms are coded by people who don't think women's sports belong on the top menu.

Take, for example, searching for women's sports on a digital platform. If you look at the foregoing picture, you'll see the WNBA mixed in with "lower profile sports" on the ESPN.com platform. Engelbert believes the coding for what content is prominently featured is driven by fan attendance and media ratings metrics. Assuming that, she wants to put more money behind superstars and rivalries. Both drives interests and stories, leading to household names, which further drive media viewership. Ultimately, more viewers drives the value of the franchise higher. The "W" loosened free-agency rules creating conversations in the offseason, and potentially leading to "Super Teams"—dynastic franchises that become synonymous with winning and success (think Golden State Warriors in the NBA). Fans love to talk about super teams.

The owners created the "Changemaker" platform—a new way to value team sports, using the model outlined earlier. As of early 2020, the WNBA had signed up three companies looking for more synergy with women consumers. After all, 84% of people like to watch women's sports. Whether it is the value of a franchise, patch or media rights, corporate sponsorship, the league's goal is to increase franchise values that allow for more expansion and ownership investment.

Both the NBA and the WNBA want the owners to be successful, and for players to become role models and household names. It's essential to change the narrative around professional women's sports.

Review Questions

1. Make a list of the ways that 5G could impact the fan experience. Now do the same with the athlete's experience.
2. How will the college athlete's ability to monetize their name, image, and likeness change the fabric of college sports?
3. Think about the ways the WNBA's model of Player First, Owner Success, and Fan Engagement could be applied to other smaller leagues currently looking to grow their profiles, like the National Pro Fastpitch or National Women's Hockey League.

References

Armour, N. (2014, May 7). *NBC universal pays $7.75 billion for olympics through 2032*. www.usatoday.com/story/sports/olympics/2014/05/07/nbc-olympics-broadcast-rights-2032/8805989/

College Football Playoff Revenue Distribution. (n.d.). *College football playoff revenue distribution*. https://collegefootballplayoff.com/sports/2017/9/20/revenue-distribution.aspx?utm_source=listrak&utm_medium=email&utm_term=https%3a%2f%2fcollegefootballplayoff.com%2f-sports%2f2017%2f9%2f20%2frevenue-distribution.aspx&utm_campaign=bang-mult-nl-pac-12-hotline-nl

Dosh, K. (n.d.). *College football playoff payouts*. https://businessofcollegesports.com/college-football-playoff-payouts/

EntertainmentStrategyGuy.com (2019). *Pac-12 and College Sports*. https://entertainmentstrategyguy.com/category/analysis/pac-12-and-college-sports/

ESPN. (2021, March 18). *NFL announces TV deals with ESPN/ABC, NBC, CBS, Fox, Amazon*. www.espn.com/nfl/story/_/id/31088098/nfl-announces-tv-deals-espn-abc-nbc-cbs-fox-amazon

Hinnen, K. (2012, November 21). *ESPN reaches 12-year deal to air college football playoffs*. www.cbssports.com/college-football/news/espn-reaches-12-year-deal-to-air-college-football-playoffs/

Oz, M. (2018, November 15). *MLB, Fox strike new $5.1B TV deal that proves baseball isn't close to dying*. https://sports.yahoo.com/mlb-fox-strike-new-5-1b-tv-deal-proves-baseball-isnt-close-dying-183048053.html

Pearson, R. (2018). *The biggest TV rights deals in sports*. Pledge Sports. www.pledgesports.org/2018/01/biggest-tv-rights-deals-in-sport/

INDEX

A

A's Cast, 170

ACC Network, 24–25

Accessories, 155

Advertising, 130, 365–366

       sports media, 17–19

Affiliate revenues, 18–19

Alcohol sales, revenue from, 127

Allegiant Stadium, 287, 289

All-skills camps, 125

All-sports conference, 40

All-Star Game, 163

Amateur athletics, 368

Amateurism principle, 39, 40

Amazon Prime, 363

Ambition Ranking, 211

American Athletic Union (AAU), 256

American Basketball Association (ABA),
    249–250

American Football League (AFL), 278

American Ninja Warrior, 70

American professional leagues, 366. *See also*
    specific entries

Anti-Olympic alliances, 345–346

Apex Sports & Events complex, 70

Apparel, revenue from, 127

Appreciation, 98–102

Asian Football Confederation (AFC), 197

AT&T, 22, 283, 287

Athletic and sports fields, construction and
    installation of, 72–74

Athletic conferences, 42

Athletics arms race, 53

Atlanta Falcons, 283–284

Atlanta Olympic Games, 344

Attendance at sporting events, 365

Autonomous 5 conferences. *See* Power 5
    conferences

B

Baltimore Ravens, 288–289

BAMTech, 172, 323

Bank of America Stadium, 288

Barcelona Olympic Games, 343

Basketball Association of America (BAA), 239,
    241–242

"Basketball centric" schools, 44

Beekman, Bill, 61–63

Betting, legalized, 28–29
Bettman, Gary, 311–312
Bidding for Olympic Games, 347
Big East Conference, 3
Big Ten Channel, 23
Big Ten Network (BTN), 23
Billie Jean King National Tennis Center, 85–87
BITKRAFT Esports Ventures, 139, 147
Blended net local revenue, 165
Blue, Kevin, 61–63
Boland diagram, 102–105
Boston Celtics, 255
Bread Not Circuses (BNC), 345
Broadcast rights
    for live sports, 358–360
    National Football League, 290
        contracts, 294–296

C

Cable business models, 358–360
Cages, revenue and, 121–123
Calgary Flames, 317
California Community College Athletic Association (CCCAA), 41
Camps, revenue from, 125–126
Canadian Amateur Athletic Association (CAAA), 228
Canadian Women's Hockey League (CWHL), 227–230
Capital assets, 97–98
Capital budgets, 97–98
Capital project, 96
Carolina Hurricanes, 315
Central Ontario Women's Hockey League (COWHL), 227
Central revenues, 163
Cheney Stadium, 231

China, 366–367
Churn rate, 72, 77
Cincinnati Bengals, 283–284
Civil Rights Act, 220
Club seats, 104
Club World Cup, 197
ClubExpress, 82
Coach's Eye, 83
CoachCam, 83
Coaching fees, revenue from, 129–130
Coaching staff, salary of, 173–174
Collective Bargaining Agreement (CBA), 168, 177
    impact of pandemic, 3–4
    National Women's Soccer League, 223
College conference channels, 23–25
College Football Playoff (CFP), 43–44
    impact of revenue growth, 49
College sports, 37–40
    advantages of, 38–39
    case study, 61–63
    cost to start collegiate esports team, 147
    esports, 145–146
    financial forecasting in Division I athletics, 53
    governance structures, 40–42
    media contracts and other revenue partnerships, 53
    media revenues, explosion in, 25
    NCAA, 48–49
        Divisions II and III, finances in, 49–50
        facility costs, 51–52
        NAIA, NJCAA revenue distribution, 50
    other expense categories in, 55–56
    post–COVID-19 era, 56–60
    revenue distribution, 42

conference, 44–46

NCAA, 43–44

other institutional revenue sources, 46–48

salary structures, 54–55

tax status and liabilities, 54

tier one, two, and three revenues matter in, 26–27

Comcast, 283, 291–292

Comcast Sports Network (CSN), 15

Communication technology, 14

Community approach, 344

Community impact, of Fédération Internationale de Football Association, 199

Community watchdog, 345–346

Competitive advantage, 78

Competitive equity, 203–204

Competitive esports, 136, 140. *See also* Esports

Competitors, 117–118

Compound annual growth rate (CAGR), 75

Conduit borrower, 108

Conduit issuer, 107–108

Confederation of African Football (CAF), 197

Conferences, 40

revenue distribution, 44–46

Construction

Major League Baseball, 166–167

National Football League, 285–289

National Hockey League, 315–317

subsidies

National Pro Fastpitch, 232

National Women's Hockey League, 233

National Women's Soccer League, 233–234

Contracts, type of, 324–325

Contractual obligations, types of, 103–105

Contractually obligated income (COI), 93, 102

Conventional sports, 139, 155

Copyright Arbitration Royalty Panel, 163

Cord-adders, 364

"Cord-cutting/cord-shaving" consumers, 19, 290

Cord-nevers, 364

Cord-shavers, 364

Cord-shifters, 364

Core competency, 78–79

Coronavirus. *See* COVID-19 pandemic

Cosmetics, 155

Cost efficiencies, optimizing, 82–83

Cost per thousand (CPM), 18

COVID-19 pandemic

advertising and, 19

college sports and, 48, 56–60

customer behavior, 371

economic recovery, 370

esports, 135–136

as remedy for sports fans, 154

expenses of executing media rights deal, 20

impact on mega sport recreation complexes, 84

Major League Baseball's growth potential and, 183

National Basketball Association, 254

salaries, NCAA, 55

sports finance and, 2–4

Cowles Cup, 227

Customer behavior, coronavirus and, 371

Customizability of memberships, 77

D

Dallas Cowboys, 283–285f

David Beckham rule, 209

DAZN, 171, 364

Debt, 168–169

Debt Service Coverage Ratio (DSCR), 105–106

Defined gross revenue, 163

Digital distribution and disruption, 363–365
Digital racing, 154
Disney, 283
Division I Men's Basketball Tournament, 2, 44, 48
Division Series, 181
Double sponsorship, 130
Dow Jones Industrial Average, 100

E

Earnings before interest, taxes, depreciation, and amortization (EBITDA), 168
EBITDA Multiplier, 169
eChess, 146, 152–153
Economic recovery, coronavirus and, 370
Electronic Gaming Federation, 144
Electronic sports. *See* Esports
Electronic Sports League, 144
English Premier League (EPL), 203
    media payments in, 204
Entry-level contracts, 324–325
Equal Pay Act, 220
ESPN, 15, 170, 183, 246, 259, 363
ESPN+, 364
ESPN Wide World of Sports at Disney World, 71
Esports, 155
    audiences for, 137
    conventional sports vs., 142
    as coronavirus remedy for sports fans, 154
    cost to start collegiate team, 147
    definitions of, 138–139
    economic engine of microtransactions, 149
    endorsements and sponsorships for, 152
    evolution of, 135–137
    future of, 152–153
    by game type, style of play, title, and company, 141

gender equity and inclusion in, 141–142
global viewership estimates for, 136
history of, 137–138
labor market, 151–152
live events, 149–151
main platforms and gaming infrastructure, 139–141
prize pools and superstars, 151–152
soccer, 143
structures, organizations, and leagues
    college sports, 145–146
    gaming organizations, 144–145
    professional gaming video games, 142–144
ticket pricing, 151
understanding revenues, 147–148
Esports Earnings website, 151
Esports Observer, 144
European Football Association (UEFA), 197, 366
Event cancellation insurance, 3
Expenses
    in college sports, 55–56
    Fédération Internationale de Football Association, 199
    Olympic Games, 342

F

Facility costs, 51–52
Facility maintenance costs, 56
Facility revenue
    Major League Baseball, 166–167
    National Football League, 285–289
    National Hockey League, 315–317
    National Pro Fastpitch, 232
    National Women's Hockey League, 233
    National Women's Soccer League, 233–234
Fanatics, 169
FanDuel, 321–322

Fan-owned football club model, 202

FASTs, 364

Fédération Internationale de Basketball (FIBA), 333

Fédération Internationale de Football Association (FIFA), 195

finances of

community impact, 199

expenses, 199

finances of, 197–201

participants, 201

revenues, 197–198

women's World Cup, 200–201

history and structure of, 196–197

income statements, 198

stated mission of, 196

FedEx Field, 288

Financial forecasting

in Division I athletics, 53

of Major League Baseball, 167–168

National Football League, 289–292

National Hockey League, 317–318

Financing youth sports enterprise

case study, 131

gold standard athletics, 115–117

marketplace and competitors, 117–118

revenue streams

alcohol and vending machine sales, 127

apparel, 127

batting cages, new facility, 122–123

batting cages, old facility, 121–122

camps, 125–126

coaching fees, 129–130

fitness, 126

front desk workers, 129

memberships, 124

online video analysis, 129

parties, 127

private lessons, 124, 128–129

special programming, 129

sponsorship opportunities, 130

staff income, 128

team practices, 126

travel teams, 124–125

start-up costs, 118–121

Firm resources, 72–74

Fitness training, revenue from, 126

5G technology, growth of, 16

Fixed cost, 39–40

Flow-on tourism, 75

Football Confederation in North and Central America and the Caribbean (CONCACAF), 197

"Football for Schools" educational program, 199

Football Forward Programme, 199

Footprint, defined, 26

Forbes, 163, 314

Force majeure, 3–4

Formula 1, 154

Fox Sports Networks, 22, 154, 170–171, 183, 283

Front desk workers, revenue from, 129

G

Game Pass, 296

Gaming, 155. *See also* Video games

Gaming organizations, esports, 144–145

Gate receipt revenues

Major League Baseball, 181

National Basketball Association, 246

National Hockey League, 320

Gender equity in esports, 141–142

Gender-pay gap, in Women's National Basketball Association, 260

General obligation bonds, 108

Geofencing, 18
Giants Stadium, 98–101
Global Esports Market Report, 136, 139
Gold standard athletics, 115–117
Golf Channel, 15
Golf tournament, 130
Government subsidies, of NBA and WNBA, 265
Grand Park Sports Campus, 78–79
Grand slam sponsorship, 130
Grant of Media Rights, 20
Green Bay Packers, 279–282, 284–285
Group of 5 conferences, 42, 47
Growth potential, 83–84
Guarantee game, 47–48
GymMaster, 82
Gyms, Health, and Fitness Clubs industry, 71–72

H

Half- to full-day camps, 125
Hard Rock Stadium, 288
Havlicek, John, 248–249
High School Esports League (HSEL), 144
Hivebrite, 83
Hockey Related Revenue (HRR), 326, 327
Homerun sponsorship, 130
Homophobia, Women's National Basketball Association and, 257, 262
Hosting Olympic Games
        benefits of, 342–344
        drawbacks of, 346–347
Houston Astrodome, 103
Hudl, 83
Hulu, 363–364
Human resources for mega recreational sport complexes, 80

I

IAAF World Athletics Championships, 344
iFormula esports, 135
IMG Academy, 70, 71, 78
Impact of the Olympics on Community Coalition (IOCC), 346
iNASCAR esports, 135, 154
Inclusion in esports, 141–142
Independent professional football leagues
        league competitive equity, 203–204
        public ownership, 202–203
Indoor sports facilities, 74–75
Industry Growth Fund, 316
Infrastructure, 96
In-game currency, 149, 155
In-game microtransactions, 149
Initial capital investment for mega recreational sport complexes, 79–80
Institutional Performance Program (IPP), 53, 58
Insurance costs, 55–56
Insurance, impact of pandemic, 3
Interactive World Cup, 197
Intercollegiate athletics. *See* College sports
Interest rates, 96–97
International eGames Committee (IEGC), 144
International Esports Federation (IESF), 144
International federations (IF), 333
International football (soccer), 195. *See also* Professional soccer
International Olympic Committee (IOC), 332
        organizational structure, 332–334
Internet access, 16
Isobel Cup, 230

J

Job description, 7–11
Jock tax, 293
JOGO Smart Football Training, 83

K

Khoros, 83
Knight Commission on Intercollegiate Athletics, 56–60

L

Labor market, esports, 151–152
Ladies Professional Basketball Association, 256
Lake Placid Winter Games, 347
Larry Bird Exemption, 250
League Championship Series, 181
League competitive equity, 203–204
LeagueApps, 82
Legalized betting, 28–29
Liabilities
    college sports, 54
    Major League Baseball, 168–169
    National Football League, 292–293
    National Hockey League, 318–320
Liberty Basketball Association, 256
Licensing revenue
    Olympic Games, 341
    National Football League, 294–296
Lincoln Financial Field, 288
Linear TV, 155
Little Caesars Arena, 316
Live esports events, 149–151
    ticket pricing, 151
Live sports streaming, 28
Local area network (LAN), 155
Local revenues, 163–164
London Summer Games, 344
Los Angeles Clippers, 255
Luxury boxes, 103–104
Luxury tax, 177, 252–253

M

Madison Square Garden (MSG), 103–104, 317

Major League Baseball
    case study, 184–186
    collective bargaining agreement, 168, 177
    facility revenue, subsidies, and construction, 166–167
    final assessment of growth potential, 183
    financial forecasting, 167–168
    history of, 159–160
    league structure, 161
        ownership buy-in amount, 161–163
    media revenues
        individual teams, 170
        from league office, 170–172
    National Football League with, 295
    postseason financial structures, 181–182
    revenue distribution
        individual teams, 163
        from league office, 163–166
    revenue sources and partnerships, 169
    salary structures
        coaching staff, 173–174
        players, 174–176
        salary caps, 177–181
    tax status and liabilities, 168–169
Major League Baseball Advanced Media (ML-BAM), 160, 163, 171–172, 183
Major League Baseball Players Association (MLBPA), 160, 161, 183
Major League Baseball Properties Inc., 163
Major League Soccer (MLS), 203, 205–212, 221–224, 262–263
    financial impact of pandemic, 4
    relationships between United States Soccer Federation, and NWSL, 221–224
Manchester United, 202–203
March Madness. *See* Division I Men's Basketball Tournament
Marketplace, 117–118

Market research, 117
Maryland Stadium Authority, 288–289
McDavid, Connor, 324
Media consumption, 28–29
Media network, building
    data, 22
    second screening, 21–22
    technology, 21
Media revenue
    college sports, 53
    explosion in college sports, 25
    Major League Baseball
        individual teams, 170
        from league office, 170–172
    National Basketball Association, 246
    National Football League, 296–297
    National Hockey League, 322–324
    Summer Olympics, 336–339
    Winter Olympics, 337–339
Media rights deal, expenses of executing,
    20–21
Mega recreational sport complexes
    ancillary considerations
        growth potential, 83–84
        impact of technology, 82–83
        public funding and subsidies,
          availability of, 81–82
        revenues and cost efficiencies,
          82–83
    business model considerations
        competencies and revenue
          strategy, 77–78
        determining core, 77
        importance of memberships to
          revenue strategy, 76–77
        relevant costs, 79–80
    case study, 85–87
    COVID-19, impact on, 84
    history of, 68–71
    industry structure
        athletic and sports fields,
          construction and installation
          of, 72–74
        Gyms, Health, and Fitness
          Clubs, 71–72
        indoor sports facilities,
          management of, 74–75
        sport tourism, 75–76
    United States Tennis Association Billie Jean
        King National Tennis Center, 85–87
Memberships
    importance of, 76–77
    youth sports enterprise, 124
Men's World Cup, 197–199, 201
Mercedes-Benz Stadium, 293
MetLife Stadium, 287, 288
MGM Resorts, 321
Microtransactions, economic engine of, 149,
    155
Million Dollar Free Throw, 48
MindBody, 82
Mini camps, 125
Minnesota Stadium, 51–52
MLB Advanced Media, 323
MLB At Bat, 171
MLB Network, 15, 163
MLB.TV, 171
Modern league credit structures, 106–107
Montreal Summer Games, 346
Motorsports, 135, 154
Multiday camps, 125–126
Multnomah stadium, 231
Municipal bonds, 107–108
Municipal financing options, 107–108
Munson, Eric, 115–131
Munson, Shanda, 115–131
myDartfish, 83

N

Naming rights, 103
    partnership, 53
National Association for Intercollegiate
    Athletics (NAIA), 41
    revenue distribution, 50
National Association of Collegiate Esports
    (NACE), 144, 146
National Basketball Association (NBA), 239–241
    financial impact of pandemic, 2, 3
    government subsidies of, 265
    history of, 241–245
    income and payroll in, 247–248
    league growth potential, 255
    league organization, 245
    league revenues, 245–247
    league salaries, 247–254
National Collegiate Athletic Association
    (NCAA), 14
    Amateurism principle, 40
    athletic budget revenue for public
        institutions, 45–46
    controlling all revenue from college
        sports, 43
    Division I
        characteristics of, 41
        issues and recommendations
            for, 57–60
        membership in, 42
        Men's Basketball Tournament,
            44
    Division II
        characteristics of, 41
        finances in, 49–50
    Division III
        characteristics of, 41
        finances in, 49–50
    facility costs, 51–52
    financial impact of pandemic, 2

NAIA, NJCAA revenue distribution, 50
    receiving money from College Football
        Playoff, 43–44
    revenue distribution, 43
National Football League (NFL), 13–14
    case study, 303–305
    facility revenue, subsidies, and
        construction, 285–289
    final assessment of growth potential,
        301–302
    financial forecasting, 289–292
    financial impact of pandemic, 3
    history of, 278–279
    media revenues, 296–297
    Network, 296
    ownership buy-in amount, 280–282
    postseason financial structures, 300–301
    revenue distribution, 282–285
    revenue sources and partnerships,
        294–296
    salary caps, 299–300
    salary structures, 297–299
    structure, 279–280
    tax status and liabilities, 292–293
    valuations, 283–285
    Ventures, 296
National governing bodies (NGBs), 334
National Hockey Association (NHA), 309
National Hockey League (NHL), 172, 309–312
    case study, 329–330
    facility revenue, subsidies, and
        construction, 315–317
    final assessment of growth potential, 328
    financial forecasting, 317–318
    financial impact of pandemic, 2
    media revenues, 322–324
    ownership buy-in amount, 313–314
    postseason financial structures, 327–328
    revenue distribution, 314

revenue sources and partnerships, 320–322

salary cap, 326

salary structures, 324–326

structure

  eastern conference, 312–313

  western conference, 313

tax status and liabilities, 318–320

National Junior College Athletics Association (NJCAA), 41

  revenue distribution, 50

National League Constitution, 161

National Olympic Committee (NOC), 333–334

National Pro Fastpitch (NPF), 224–227

  stadium dilemmas, 230

National soccer programs, 196

National Strength and Conditioning Association (NSCA), 80

National Women' Hockey League Players Association (NWHLPA), 229

National Women's Basketball Association, 256

National Women's Hockey League (NWHL), 227–230

  stadium dilemmas, 231

National Women's Soccer League (NWSL), 218–221

  relationships between Major League Soccer, United States Soccer Federation and, 221–224

  ownership, 222

  stadium dilemmas, 231

NBA2K, 135

NBC, 15–16

  sports networks, 22

Net transfer value, 165

Netflix, 363–364

New York Islanders, 316

New York Rangers, 315

NFL.com, 296

NFLPA, 285, 295

Nike, 169

Ninja Evans, 152

North American Soccer League (NASL), 91–92, 99, 206, 219

Northwest Athletic Conference (NWAC), 41

O

Oakland Athletics, 164, 170

OFC in Oceania, 197

Olympic broadcast partnerships, 336–337

Olympic Channel, 15

Olympic Games, 331–332

  benefits of hosting, 342–344

  bidding for, 347

  case study, 348–351

  drawbacks of hosting, 346–347

  expenses, 342

  organizational structure, 332–334

  public opposition to, 344–346

  revenues, 334–335

    corporate sponsorship and partnership revenue, 335–336

    licensing revenue, 341

    media revenue, 336–339

    ticket revenue, 340

  Summer Olympics

    licensing revenue, 341

    media revenue, 336–339

    ticket revenue, 340

  Winter Olympics

    licensing revenue, 341

    media revenue, 337–339

    ticket revenue, 340

Olympic Movement, 332

Olympic sponsorship, 335–336

One-way contract, 325

Online video analysis, revenue from, 129

Organizing committees of the Olympic games (OCOGs), 334

Orioles Park, 92

Oscar Robertson rule, 249–250

Ovechkin, Alex, 324

"Over the air" channel, 19

Overwatch League (OWL), 150

Ownership buy-in amount

    Major League Baseball, 161–163

    National Football League, 280–282

    National Hockey League, 313–314

    National Women's Soccer League, 222

Ownership of revenue

    National Pro Fastpitch, 232

    National Women's Hockey League, 233

    National Women's Soccer League,
        233–234

    Women's National Basketball
        Association, 266

P

Pac-10 Conference, 23–24

Pac-12 Conference, 23–24

Para Athletics World Championships, 344

Paralympics, 331–333

Parties, revenue from, 127

Partnership revenue, 335–336

    college sports, 53

    Major League Baseball, 169

    National Football League, 294–296

    National Hockey League, 320–322

Pay equity

    in Women's National Basketball
        Association, 267–269

    in Women's Professional Basketball,
        267–269

    women's sports and. *See* Women's
        sports and pay equity

Pay-per-view model, 27–28

Payroll cap. *See* Salary cap

People Ingeniously Subverting the Sydney
    Olympic Farce (PISSOF), 345

Personal seat licenses (PSLs), 103

Pitch f/x, 171

Plant, land, and equipment (PPLE) resources,
    73

Player Compensation Cost Redistribution
    System, 315

Players, salary of, 174–176

Postseason financial structures

    Major League Baseball, 181–182

    National Football League, 300–301

    National Hockey League, 327–328

Power 5 conferences, 24–25, 42, 47

Principal, 96

Private lessons, revenue from, 124, 128–129

Prize pools, esports, 151–152

Pro Bowl, 301

Professional athletes, 368–369

Professional certifications, development, and
    training costs, 56

Professional soccer, 195–196

    Fédération Internationale de Football
        Association

        community impact, 199

        expenses, 199

        finances of, 197–201

        history and structure of, 196–197

        participants, 201

        revenues, 197–198

        women's World Cup, 200–201

    financial impact of pandemic, 4

    independent professional football
        leagues

        league competitive equity,
            203–204

        public ownership, 202–203

    Major League Soccer, 205–212

Professional Women's Hockey Players Associa-
    tion (PWHPA), 229

Public funding, availability of, 81–82
Public opposition to Olympic Games, 344–346
Public ownership, 202–203
Public–private partnership (P3), 81, 367
Puck-and-player-tracking system, 321

Q

Qualifying Veteran Free Agent Exemption, 250

R

Racism, Women's National Basketball Association and, 257, 262
Radio broadcasts, use of, 14
Radio stations, advertising and, 17
Real Madrid, 202
Recession Games, 344
Red Sox, 179–180
Regional sports networks (RSNs), 22–23, 363
Reserve rule, 249
Retransmission consent agreements, 19
Revenue bond, 108
Revenue distribution
    college sports
        conference, 44–46
        National Collegiate Athletic Association, 43–44
        other institutional revenue sources, 46–48
    Major League Baseball
        individual teams, 163
        from league office, 163–166
    National Association for Intercollegiate Athletics, 50
    National Football League, 282–285
    National Hockey League, 314
    National Junior College Athletics Association, 50

NCAA Division I from postseason football and men's basketball, 45–46
Revenue sources
    esports, 147–148
    Fédération Internationale de Football Association, 197–198
    financing youth sports enterprise
        alcohol and vending machine sales, 127
        apparel, 127
        batting cages, new facility, 122–123
        batting cages, old facility, 121–122
        camps, 125–126
        coaching fees, 129–130
        fitness, 126
        front desk workers, 129
        memberships, 124
        online video analysis, 129
        parties, 127
        private lessons, 124
        private lessons, 128–129
        special programming, 129
        sponsorship opportunities, 130
        staff income, 128
        team practices, 126
        travel teams, 124–125
    forms for streaming events, 27–28
    Major League Baseball, 169
    maximizing, 82–83
    mega recreational sport complexes
        competencies and, 78–79
        importance of memberships, 76–77
    modern North American sports, 102–105
    National Basketball Association, 245–247
    National Football League, 294–296

National Hockey League, 320–322

National Women's Hockey League, 228–230

Olympic Games, 334–335

    corporate sponsorship and partnership revenue, 335–336

    licensing revenue, 341

    media revenue, 336–339

    ticket revenue, 340

sports media, 17–19

stadium financing, 98–102

streams, college sports, 38

Summer Olympics

    licensing revenue, 341

    media revenue, 336–339

    ticket revenue, 340

Tier one, two, and three revenues matter in college sports, 26–27

Winter Olympics

    licensing revenue, 341

    media revenue, 337–339

    ticket revenue, 340

Women's National Basketball Association, 258–259

Rich Stadium, 103

Rio Tinto stadium, 231

Robinson, Glenn, 251–252

Rogers Media, 322

Rule 4 Draft, 174, 179–180

S

Salary cap, 203, 246, 250

    Major League Baseball, 177–181

    National Football League, 299–300

    National Hockey League, 326

    National Women's Soccer League, 223–224

Salary structures

    college sports, 54–55

Major League Baseball

    coaching staff, 173–174

    players, 174–176

    salary caps, 177–181

National Basketball Association, 247–254

National Football League, 297–299

National Hockey League, 324–326

National Women's Hockey League, 228–230

Women's National Basketball Association, 260–262

Salt Lake City Winter Games, 343–344

Scholarships, 39–40

    esports, 146

    to play sports, 42

Scrap Yard Fast Pitch, 226

Seattle, 316–317

Series Event Model, 227

Sexism, Women's National Basketball Association and, 257, 262

Shoutcasting, 138

Silver, Adam, 262

Single sponsorship, 130

Single-sport conference, 40

Sirius XM, 170, 172, 322

Skills & Drills App, 83

Social media, 296

Socios, 202

SoFi Stadium, 92, 287

Software as a service (SaaS), 82–83

South American Football Confederation (CONMEBOL), 197

Southeastern Conference (SEC), 24

Special programming, revenue from, 129

Special Purpose Acquisition Companies (SPAC), 357

Spectrum, 22

Sponsorship opportunities, revenue from, 130

Sponsorship revenue, 365–366
    esports, 152
    Major League Baseball, 169
    National Football League, 294–296
    National Hockey League, 320
    National Women's Soccer League, 223
    Olympic Games, 335–336
    Women's National Basketball
        Association, 259
Spooky Nook Sports complex, 70
Sport tourism, 75–76
Sport tourist, defined, 75
Sports betting lounge, 289
Sports fields, construction and installation of,
    72–74
Sports finance, 1–7
    advertising and sponsorship, 365–366
    case study, 373–375
    coronavirus, 2–4
        economic recovery, 370
        customer behavior, 371
    demand, 357
        broadcast rights and
            "traditional" distribution,
            358–360
        subscribers TV network
            summary, 360–361
        TV network summary, 361–363
    digital distribution and disruption,
        363–365
    future trends in, 355–356
    international growth, 366–367
    live events, 365
    professional
        challenge for, 16
        job description, 7–11
    supply
        professional athletes, 368–369
        stadiums and public push
            back, 367

    youth and amateur athletics, 368
    women's sports, reinvention of, 373–375
Sports inventory space, new competitors enter-
    ing, 30
Sports media
    advertising, 17–19
    building media network
        data, 22
        second screening, 21–22
        technology, 21
    case study, 31–33
    college conference channels, 23–25
    emergence of legalized betting and
        media consumption, 28–29
    evolution and revolution, 13–17
    expenses of executing media rights
        deal, 20–21
    explosion in college sports media
        revenues, 25
    new competitors entering sports
        inventory space, 30
    regional sports networks, 22–23
    revenue basics, 17–19
    streaming, 27–28
    Tier one, two, and three revenues
        matter in college sports, 26–27
Sports tourism, 5
Sports United Marketing (SUM), 207
Stadium financing, 91–93
    appreciation, revenue, and history,
        98–102
    Boland box, 102–105
    capital assets and capital budgets, 97–98
    case study, 109–111
    debt service coverage ratios, 105–106
    interest rates, 96–97
    modern league credit structures, 106–107
    municipal financing options, 107–108
    public–private partnerships for
        building or renovating, 367

revenue streams in modern North
American sports, 102–105
technology breakthroughs, 105
Yankee Stadium, 93–95
Staff income, revenue from, 128
Stanley Cup, 310
Start-up costs, 118–121
Statcast technology, 171
Stewart, Breanna, 262
Stick and ball sports, 139
Streaming, 27–28, 155
esports, 148, 152
services, 26–27
Sub rate (subscribers) to conference channel, 26
Subscribers TV network summary, 360–361
Subscription model, 27–28
Subsidies
availability of, 81–82
Major League Baseball, 166–167
National Basketball Association of, 265
National Football League, 285–289
National Hockey League, 315–317
Women's National Basketball
Association, 265
Super Bowl, 14
Superstar labor market, 151–152
Supply, future of
professional athletes, 368–369
stadiums and public push back, 367
youth and amateur athletics, 368

T

Tampa Bay Lightning, 319–320
Targeted Team Player Compensation, 316
Taurasi, Diana, 261
Tax status
college sports, 54
Major League Baseball, 168–169
National Football League, 292–293

National Hockey League, 318–320
Team practices, revenue from, 126
Technology
esports and, 137
impact on mega recreational sport
complexes, 82–83
infrastructure and enhancement costs, 56
revolution in media business, 13–17
in stadium financing, 105
Telecommunications Act of 1996, 16, 22
Television revenue
advertising and, 17
National Basketball Association, 246
sports and, 14
Women's National Basketball
Association, 259, 263–264
Tennis Channel, 15
Texas Stadium, 103
The Olympic Partners (TOP) program, 334
Thursday Night games, 291–292
Ticket pricing, 151
Ticket revenue
college sports, 46
National Football League, 291
Olympic Games, 340
Ticketmaster, 171
Tier 1 events, 26–27
Tier 2 events, 26–27
Tier 3 events, 26–27
Tiered membership, 77
T-Mobile Arena, 316, 329
Toronto Maple Leafs, 318–319, 324, 327
TrackMan, 83
Traditional broadcast, 358–360
Traditional sports (Tsports), 137, 139, 155
Transfer percentage, 165
Travel baseball teams, revenue from, 124–125
Triathlon World Grand Final, 344
TriHabitat, 79

Triple sponsorship, 130
Turner Broadcasting, 170, 183, 246
Turner Sports, 170
TV network summary, 361–363
Twarynski, Carsen, 325
Twitch, 137, 148
Two-way contract, 325

U

U.S. Men's National Team (USMNT), 219–221
U.S. National Soccer Federation, 200–201
U.S. Soccer Federation (U.S. Soccer), 218–221
    relationships between Major League Soccer and NWSL, 221–224
      U.S. Women's National Team against, 220–221
U.S. Women's National Team (USWNT), 200, 218–221
      against U.S. Soccer Federation, 220–221
UC Irvine Esports Program, 142
United Soccer League, 219
United States College Athletics Association (USCAA), 41
United States Olympic & Paralympic Committee (USOPC), 334
United States Olympic Committee, 334
United States Soccer Federation (USSF), 221–224
United States Tennis Association (USTA), 85–87
University of California Irvine (UCI), 146

V

Vancouver Canucks, 315
Vancouver Winter Games, 347
Vanilla, 83
Variable costs, 39–40
Vending machine sales, revenue from, 127
ViacomCBS, 283, 291–292

Video games, 136, 138–139, 155
    in-game microtransactions, 149
    popular video game titles by sales, 155
    professional gaming, 142–144
    publishers, 142–144
Virtual MVPDs, 25, 364
Volt, 83

W

Walt Disney Company, 172
Wild Card games, 181
William Hill, 321–322
WNBA League Pass, 259
Women's American Basketball Association, 256
Women's Basketball Association, 256
Women's Basketball League, 256
Women's National Basketball Association (WNBA), 241
    analysis of pay equity in, 267–269
    case study, 266
    financial impact of pandemic, 3
    government subsidies of, 265
    history of, 256–258
    lack of pay in, 260–261
    lack of sports media coverage, 262–263
    league growth potential, 262–264
    league ownership, 266
    league revenues, 258–259
    league salaries, 260–262
    regular and super maximum salaries in, 261
    reinvention of, 373–375
Women's Pro Fastpitch (WPF), 224
Women's Pro Softball League (WPSL), 224
Women's Professional Basketball, 267–269
Women's sports and pay equity
    case study, 236
      Major League Soccer, United States Soccer Federation, and NWSL, 221–224

National Pro Fastpitch, 224–227
National Women's Hockey League, 227–230
National Women's Soccer League, 218–221
stadium dilemmas
    NPF softball, 230
    NWHL hockey, 231
    NWSL soccer, 231–234
structures and finances of three different leagues, 217–218
U.S. Women's National Team, 218–221
Women's World Cup, 197–201, 219
World Anti-Doping Agency (WADA), 342
World Cup, 196–197. *See also* Fédération Internationale de Football Association
    gender disparity in prize money, 201

men's, 197–199, 201
participants of, 201
women's, 197–201, 219
World Esports Association (WESA), 144–145
World Hockey Association (WHA), 311
World Series, 181

Y

Yankee Stadium, 93–95
Youth athletics, 368
Youth World Cup, 197
YouTube, 148

Z

Zepp Play, 83